Dan Levenson's Master Collection *of* Old-Time Tunes

Over 300 tunes in standard notation for all instruments

Dan Levenson

All tunes are traditional except:

"Meadow Prancer" by Ryck Kaiser
"Nixon's Farewell" by Curt Bouterse
"Old Savannah" by Beverly Smith
"Snake River Reel" by Peter Lippincott

All used by permission of the composer.

WWW.MELBAY.COM

Table of Contents

About this book 6
Recordings 6
Tune name 6
The Version 6
Source 7
Order of the parts 7
Crooked Tunes 7
My Bowing 7
Chords 7
Repeats 7
Time Signature(s) 8
Waltzes 8
Tunings 8
Special notations used 8
In Conclusion 8

The Tunes

Ain't Gonna Get No Supper Here Tonight 9
Altamont 9
Angelina Baker (aka Angeline the Baker) 9
Antelope Gap 10
Arkansas Traveler 10
Avalon Quickstep 10
And the Cat Came Back 11
Barlow Knife (John Salyer) 11
Barlow Knife (Song) 11
Banjo Tramp 12
Been to the East, Been to the West 12
Big Eyed Rabbit 13
Big John McNeil 13
Big Scioto 13
Bill Cheatam 14
Billy in the Low Ground 14
Black Eyed Suzianna (aka Susiana) 14
Black Cat in a Briar Patch 15
Black Hills Waltz 15
Black Jack Grove 15
Blackbird Says to the Crow 16
Boatman 16
Bob Tailed Mule 16
Booth Shot Lincoln 17
Bowl-a-Rama 17
Breaking Up Christmas 17
Briar Picker Brown 18
Broken Down Gambler 18
Buck Mountain 18
Buffalo Gals (KY version in G) 19
Buffalo Gals (Common version in G) 19
Buffalo Gals (in A) 19
Buckin' Dun 20
Bull at the Wagon 20
Camp Chase 21
Camp Meeting on the 4th of July 21
Candy Girl 21
Chase the Squirrel 22
Chattanooga 22
Cincinnati Hornpipe 22
Cherokee Shuffle (in A) 23
Cherokee Shuffle (in D) 23
Chinese Breakdown 24
Climbing the Golden Stairs 24
Chinquapin Hunting (in A) 25
Chinquapin Hunting (in D – Stamper) 25
Coast Is Clear 25
Cluck Old Hen 26
Colored Aristocracy 26
Cookhouse Joe 26
Crow Little Rooster 26
Crook Brothers Breakdown 27
Crow Creek 27
Cuffy 27
Cuckoo's Nest in D 28
Cuckoo's Nest 2 in A (aka Richmond) 28
Dance All Night with a Bottle in My Hand 28
Devil Eat the Groundhog 29
Dinah 29
Doctor, Doctor 29
Dogs in the Dishes 30
Double File 30
Dry and Dusty 30
Drunken Hiccups 31
Ducks on the Mill Pond 31
Dubuque 32
Duck River 32
Ducks in the Pond 32
Duke of Kent's Waltz 33
Mr. Fishar's Hornpipe (aka Fisher's Hornpipe) 33
Durang's Hornpipe 34
Dusty Miller 34
Ebenezer 34

Fly Around My Pretty Little Miss (in D aka Western Country) 35
Fly Around My Pretty Little Miss (in G from The Tar Heel Rattlers) 35
Flying Clouds (aka Flying Cloud Cotillion) 35
Elzic's Farewell 36
Five Miles From Town 36
Flying Indian 37
Folding Down the Sheets 37
Forked Deer 37
Fortune 38
Fun's All Over 38
Gaston 38
George Booker 39
Georgia Railroad 39
Gilsaw 39
Get Off Your Money 40
Give the Fiddler a Dram 40
Girl I Left Behind 41
Glory Medley 41
Goodbye Girls, I'm Going to Boston 41
Going Up Town 42
Goodbye My Little Darling 42
Grey Cat on a Tennessee Farm 42
Grand Picnic 43
Grasshopper Sitting on a Sweet Potato Vine 43
Greasy Coat (Hammons) 43
Greasy String (Tommy Jarrell) 44
Greasy String (Melvin Wine) 44
Great Big Taters in a Sandy Land 44
Green Willis (aka The Raw Recruit) 45
Grey Eagle 45
Grub Springs 45
Hangman's Reel 46
Happy Hollow 46
Half Past Four 47
Hell and Scissors 47
Henry Reed's Breakdown 47
Hey Little Girl Do What You Want 48
High Yellow 48
Hollow Poplar 48
Home With the Girls in the Morning 49
Hooker's Hornpipe 49
Hop Light Ladies (aka Miss McLeod's Reel) 49
Hunt the Buffalo 50
I Don't Love Nobody 50
Icy Mountain 50
I'm Going to Get My Mustache Blacked 51
Indian Ate the Woodchuck 51
Jackie Wilson 51
Indian Corn (aka Ol' Woodard's Tune) 52
I've Got No Honey Babe Now 52
Jaybird 52
Jaybird Died of the Whooping Cough 53
Jeff City 53
Jeff Sturgeon 53
Jenny on the Railroad 54
Jimmy in the Swamp 54
Jimmy Shank 54
John Brown's Dream 55
John Brown's March 55
John Henry 55
John Lover's Gone 56
John Sharp's Reel 56
John Stenson's #2 56
Johnny Cope 57
Johnny Don't Get Drunk 57
Johnson Boys 57
Johnson Gals 58
Jonah in the Windstorm 58
Juliann Johnson 58
Jump in the Well My Pretty Little Miss 59
Jump Jim Crow 59
Kash Kersey 59
Just From the Fountain 60
Katy Hill 60
Kansas City Reel 61
Lady of the Lake 1 61
Lady of the Lake 2 61
Ladies on the Steamboat 62
Leather Britches 62
Liberty 62
Little Burnt Potato 63
Little Betty Brown 63
Little Billy Wilson 64
Little Dutch Girl 64
Little Girl with Her Hair Down Behind 65
Little Sadie 65
Log Chain 65
Logan County Blues 66
Love Somebody 66
Lonesome Train 66

Lost Indian (Ed Haley) 67
Maggots in the Sheep Hide 67
Magpie 68
Martha Campbell 68
Meadow Prancer (Ryck Kaiser) 68
Merry Blacksmith 69
McMichen's Reel (aka Hog Trough Reel) 69
Mike in the Wilderness 69
Mississippi Sawyer 70
Mole in the Ground 70
Monkey on a Dogcart 70
Money Musk 71
Money Musk (Wooliver's) 71
Moses Hoe the Corn 72
Muddy Roads 72
Natchez Under the Hill 72
Needlecase (aka Latch Key) 73
New Five Cents 73
New Money 73
Nixon's Farewell (Curtis Bouterse) 74
North Carolina Breakdown 74
Oh My Little Darling 74
Oklahoma Rooster 75
Old Belle Cow (2 part) 75
Old Belle Cow (3 part) 75
Old Bunch of Keys 76
Old Horse and Buggy 76
Old Joe Clark 76
Old Melinda 77
Old Molly Hare 77
Old Mother Flannigan 77
Old Savannah (Beverly Smith) 78
Old Yellow Dog Come Trotting Through the Meeting House 78
Ora Lee 78
Opera Reel (aka The Celebrated Opera Reel) 79
Orvetta Waltz 79
Over the Waterfall 80
Pikes Peak 80
Polly Put the Kettle On 80
Pig Ankle Rag 81
Policeman 81
Possum in the Well 82
Possum on a Rail 82
Porter's Reel 83
Quince Dillon's High D 83
Ragtime Annie 84
Railroad Through the Rocky Mountains (aka Marmaduke's Hornpipe) 84
Rainy Day 85
(The) Rattlesnake 85
Rattlesnake Bit the Baby 85
Red Bird 86
Red Fox Waltz 86
Red Haired Boy (aka Little Begger Man) 87
Richmond Cotillion 87
Rickett's Hornpipe 87
Rock That Cradle Lucy 88
Rock the Cradle Joe (1) 88
Rock the Cradle Joe (2) 88
Roaring River 89
Rochester Schottische 89
Rocky Mountain Goat 89
Rocky Mountain Hornpipe 90
Rocky Pallet 90
Rocky Road to Jordan 91
Rolling River 91
Roscoe 91
Run Down Boot 92
Run Rabbit Run 92
Rye Straw (aka Joke on the Puppy) 92
Saddle Up the Gray 93
Sailing Over England 93
Saint Anne's Reel 93
Sally Anne Johnson 94
Sal's Got Mud Between Her Toes 94
Salty River Reel 95
Sandy Boys 95
Sandy River Belle 95
Sarah Armstrong (collected as Old Reel) 96
Saturday Night Breakdown 96
Seneca Square Dance 96
Shepherd's Walk 97
Shoes and Stockings 97
Shoo Fly 97
Shortening Bread (Doc Roberts') 98
Shove That Pig's Foot a Little Further Into the Fire 98
Shuckin' the Brush 99
Shuffle About 99
Silly Bill 99
Sleepy Eyed Joe 100
Sleepy Eyed John 100

About this book: There are more than a few books of this type in the world today, and SO many tunes that no one book could cover all of them. The way we play them is also a fluid thing, so unless you take the time to figure out how x player played x tune x number of times, no one book will give you everything you want to know. This is a book of over 300 of my favorite old-time fiddle tunes as I have come to play them over the years. To the best of my knowledge, all but four of them are traditional and have a long history as a part of the old-time repertoire as it is played today.

In order to keep this volume manageable, I have kept it to just the tunes. Each tune has a history and a story. My son Josh felt you would want to hear my stories about the tunes and how they have come to me so I have put those online for you. Some of the stories are pretty detailed; others may only be a line or two. You can see my notes on the tunes, which can include information on the techniques I utilize, as well as read my stories at my website: **Clawdan.com/aboutthetunes**

Along with my online reference, there are several websites that have more complete historic and tune information that would be good to check out. Two great ones that provide very good information are:

Slippery-Hill: https://www.slippery-hill.com
Traditional Tune Archive: https://tunearch.org/wiki/TTA

Here are some details to help guide you through this book:

Tune name: I have listed the tune names as I know them. AKAs (alternate names) are plenty, so you may know a tune by a different name. The one here is the one used by me and/or my source.

The Version: I won't make any bones about it, these are not "dead accurate" transcriptions of any one source. I have strived, in fact often agonized, about these versions, and while a "source" may be quoted, please don't expect my version to be an exact copy or transcription of anyone else's. I have learned them from source musicians, recordings, jam sessions and those who know more than me. I play these tunes as they have developed over the years. I have added my own twists and turns, too. They will continue to develop. That is how music is.

Many of my transcriptions are about what you would expect if you heard the tune before or played it in a local jam. Others are way older in style than what is currently played and reflect older sources. Still others show how I have morphed a tune to suit my taste or they just happened to come out that way. That was what most of the old timers did. Remember, sound recorders and amazing slow-downers didn't yet exist or were not available to average folks.

This book is for those who want to build their repertoire, get closer to a source, and play more than just the bare-bones version that you hear at many sessions, as well as advance their playing and knowledge of the tunes they play. You should plan on using the versions in this book as a jumping-off point or reminder to get the tune in your head. You don't have to play them "just as written". Also, these are not "baby" or skeletal versions of these tunes. I have not put in all of my (or anyone else's) bells and whistles but I have included enough ornamentation to give the tunes some life. You can add or subtract from these versions. Just don't strip them down so much that the tune itself is lost.

Source: When I learn a tune I want to go "to the source", the oldest one I can find. In the online notes for this book, I have noted the person or recording artist who was my primary source. If my source was not recorded, this is the name of the person the tune is attributed to.

Still, this does not mean I play or have transcribed it exactly as they did, only that it is or was a good go-to as a starting point to hear the tune in an earlier (purer) form.

Order of the parts: I usually write the parts in the order that my source plays them if I have a recording of the tune or as I have been told it was originally written. *Angelina Baker* is a great example of this. My A part is what Stephen Foster wrote as an A part. Often (as in that case) it is the verse melody followed by the chorus. Many popular jams have reversed those parts. Sometimes I have put the parts in the order that seems right to me, especially if there are many recordings that have it both ways. *Arkansas Traveler* and *Forked Deer* are good examples of that.

Crooked Tunes: Crooked tunes are those that do not come out even for today's dancers – particularly the contra dance crowd. These songs have extra beats, dropped beats, extra measures or missing ones – and there can be an even or odd number of any of those. There is a lot of speculation about how these tunes became that way or were written that way – including everything from "mistakes" in how someone played it to a fiddler changing it to personalize it for a contest or, as one fellow is heard on an old recording, "so he couldn't 'kitch' (catch) my tune!"

Many communities have codified how they play that part in their area, others not. I have written how I usually play it, but not always. These are not mistakes, just interpretations. Use your own, use your communities' or take 'em out. Up to you.

My Bowing: I had not originally planned to include my bowing, so I have not put in up-and-down bow markings. I am not a "down bow" fiddler, nor am I a "shuffle bow" or "saw stroke" fiddler. We could discuss that concept some day at a workshop, but for now I do find that my bowing can change on each pass of a tune. Several test players of some of my early transcriptions for this book mentioned that they would like to have a place to start. For that reason, I have put in slurs to indicate notes I am playing with one bow stroke. You can use them or ignore them. I learned a lot about my *own* bowing as I decided on my slurs. I settled on something I could play and repeat when playing the tune slowly. It was quite a project!

Chords: Always a source of contention! The chords here are how I hear them and play them in my circles and how I would ask a bandmate to play them to accompany me in a show. You may hear different ones. Some are considered modern interpretations such as the F♯m that many of us play in *Booth Shot Lincoln*. (Yes, there were minor chords played in the past.) Some are implied by a particular fiddler's double-stop (fiddle chord) which defines two of the notes in the chord the fiddler wants to hear. In short, sometimes the chord choice is clear, other times not so. Your community and fiddler will usually guide you. Chords in parenthesis ( ) are optional or alternate chords.

Repeats: Most repeat signs are self-explanatory and a repeat at the end of a phrase (:| |) refers the player back to the forward repeat before it (| |:). However, at the end of a tune you may see several ending measures.

"1" – repeat the phrase from the last forward repeat.

"2" – use this one as you head into the next part *instead* of the "1" repeat.

"Tune repeat" – use this one instead of any other to go back to the beginning of the tune if you are going to play the tune again. This would be "Da capo al fine" in standard music notation.

"Final" – use this ending instead of "1" or "Tune repeat", your last time through to end the tune. Sometimes there are combinations as in *Little Dutch Girl* where all phrases end the same to go back into the first part, head into the second part or repeat the tune.

Time Signature(s): I have chosen to use the "Cut" or 2/2 time signature since that way you don't have to look at a flurry of 16th notes (as in 2/4) and the metronome setting will be more accurate in relation to the speed most of us play the tunes.

Also, when there are crooked measures (more or fewer beats in a measure) I have tried to accurately mark the time signature in the score, though I may have missed one or two.

Waltzes: Waltzes are a bit rough to correctly write out because, while they may write out as fixed value notes (i.e., eighth, quarter and half notes), you don't really "play" them as fixed values. You have to "swing" it. Listening to other folks play this waltz will better express the "swing" concept without getting too technical in the writing. Put some sweetness and swing into it when you play it. In reality, this goes for most tunes and meters, though it is particularly important for waltzes. "It don't mean a thing if it ain't got that 'swing'." Remember, most of these are dance tunes, so dance a bit with the timing.

Tunings: I have written these transcriptions to reflect standard notes on the staff. That means you should be able to play all of the tunes here in standard fiddle tuning (GDAE low to high) and any instrument can play these tunes from the music written here.

Many old-time fiddlers used (and use) alternate tunings for different keys. Tunes in the key of G are usually played in what we today consider standard tuning, GDAE low to high. D is often also played out of standard tuning but often the G-string is tuned up to A resulting in a D tuning of ADAE. There is another D tuning used for specific tunes of DDAD often called "dee-dad" or "dead man" tuning, which is the native tuning of tunes such as *Midnight on the Water*, *Bonaparte's Retreat, Dry and Dusty, Washington's March* and several others that appear in this volume. Tunes in the key of A are often played out of "A cross" which is AEAE (low to high). To get there you tune your G-string up to A and your D string up to E. I almost always use this tuning for my A tunes. But, again, there is another A tuning often called "Calico" which is AEAC# low to high. Tune like you would for A-cross but then drop your E string down to C♯. *Jack of Diamonds* (aka *Drunken' Hiccups*) and Benny Thomasson's three-part *Old Belle Cow* take advantage of this tuning to allow you to pluck some of the strings with your left hand ("left hand pizzicato") to get the notes with the effect they wanted.

Special Notation: "SL" under the notes would be a slide. This is often accompanied by a diagonal line between the notes. LP is "Left hand pizzicato" where you pluck the notes with your left hand. Often this technique is accompanied by an alternate tuning such as in the three-part *Old Belle Cow* or *Jack of Diamonds* where the plucked notes include an open C# as the high string.

In Conclusion: I will close by saying that the tunes in this book could comprise an entire repertoire for many players, and while they are not the total of the tunes I know and play, they can either give you a lifetime of work, play, and joy or a foundation upon which to build for a, well, lifetime of work, play, and joy! SO go forward and work, play and enjoy old-time fiddle tunes and the history that ties the thread to the past. Old Time is key to me. Play them as-is, add or subtract your bits, circulate them in your community, but play them and always...

Play Nice,
Dan *Clawdan* Levenson - June 2022

Ain't Gonna Get No Supper Here Tonight

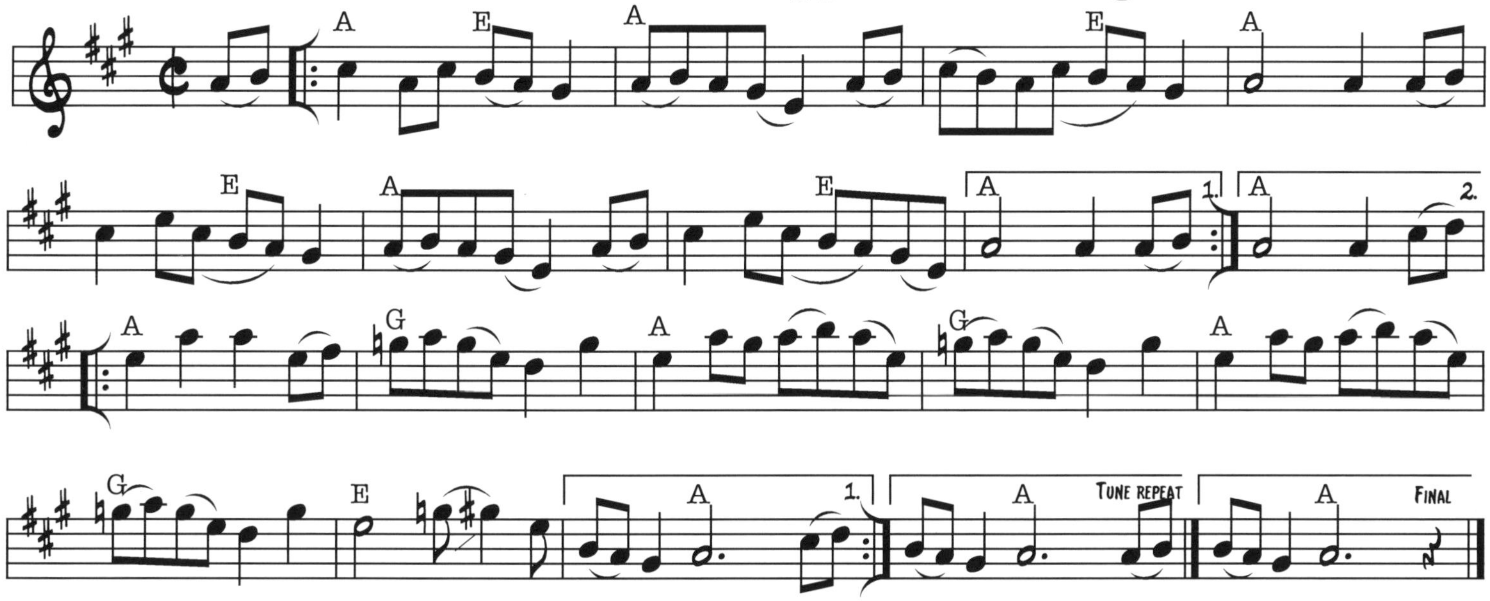

Altamont

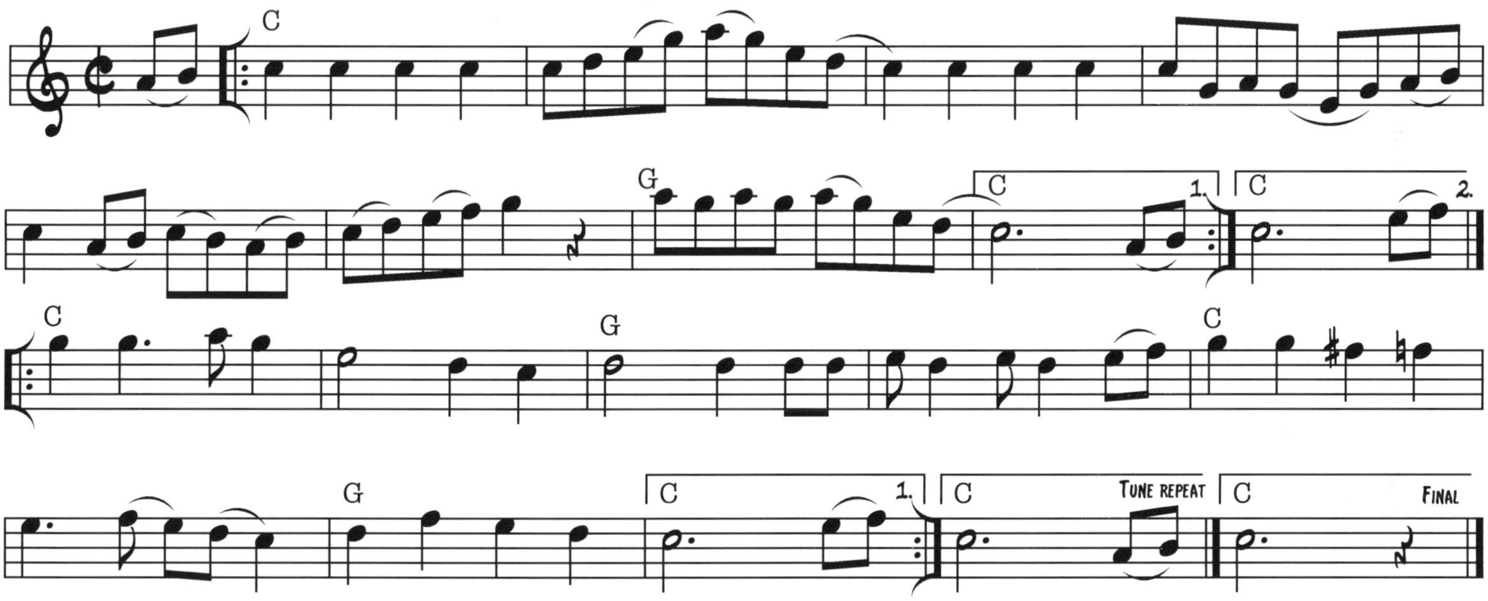

Angelina Baker (aka Angeline the Baker)

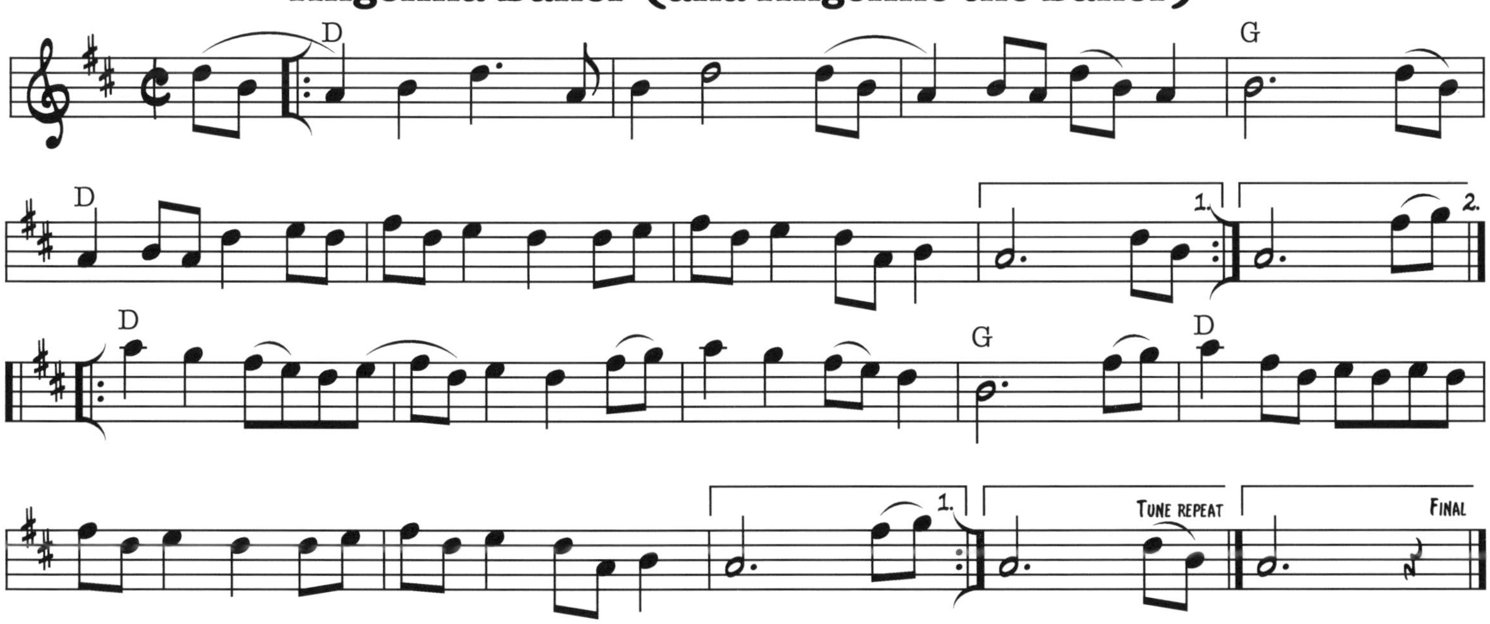

Antelope Gap

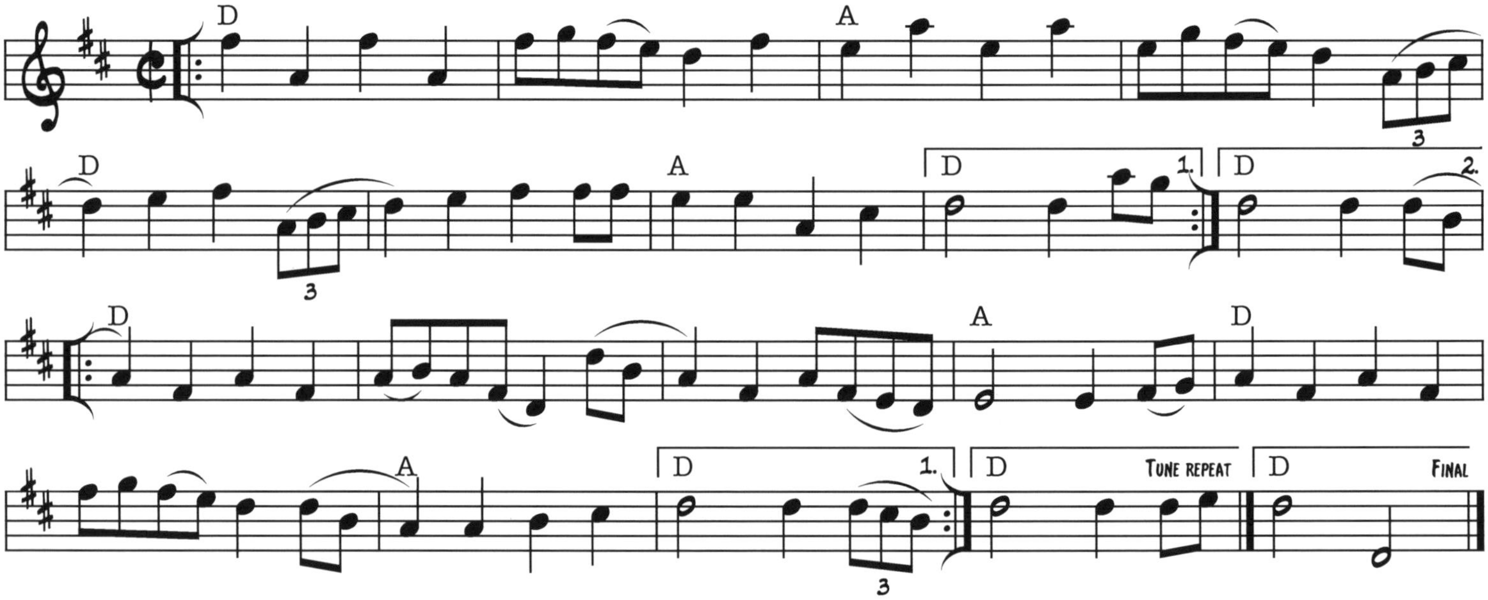

Arkansas Traveler

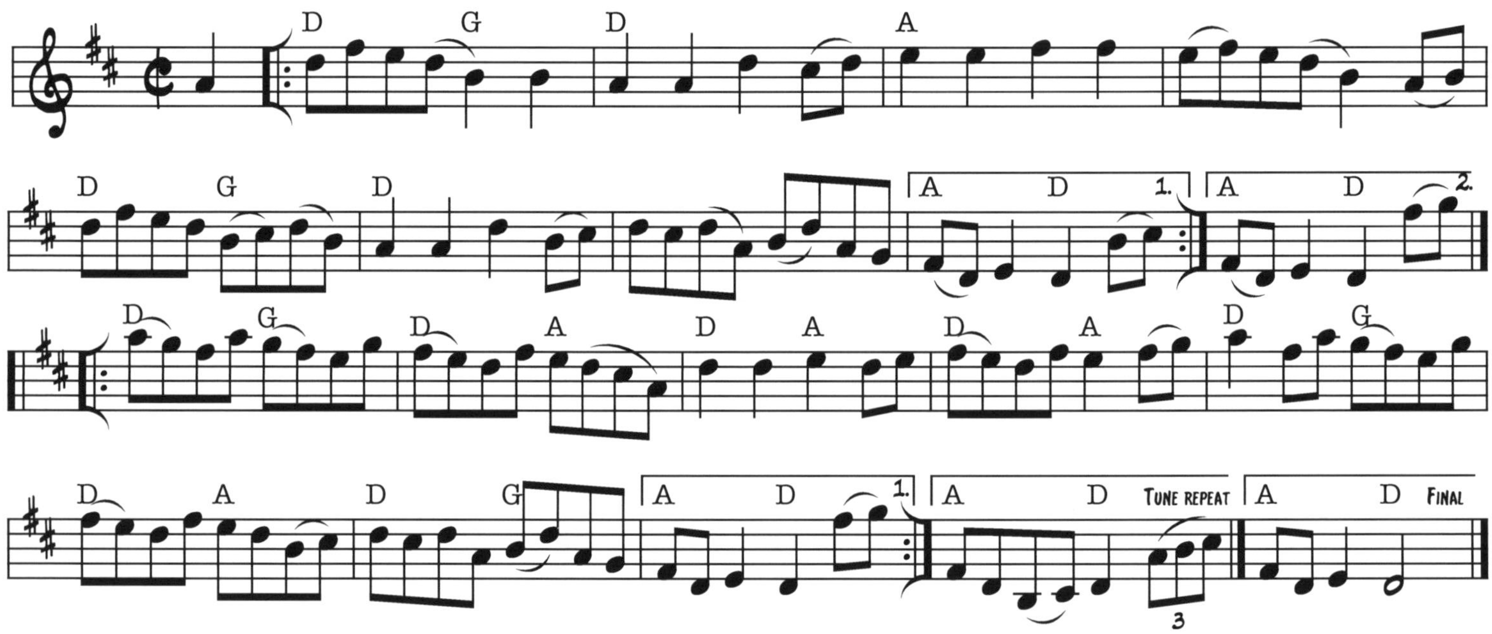

Avalon Quickstep

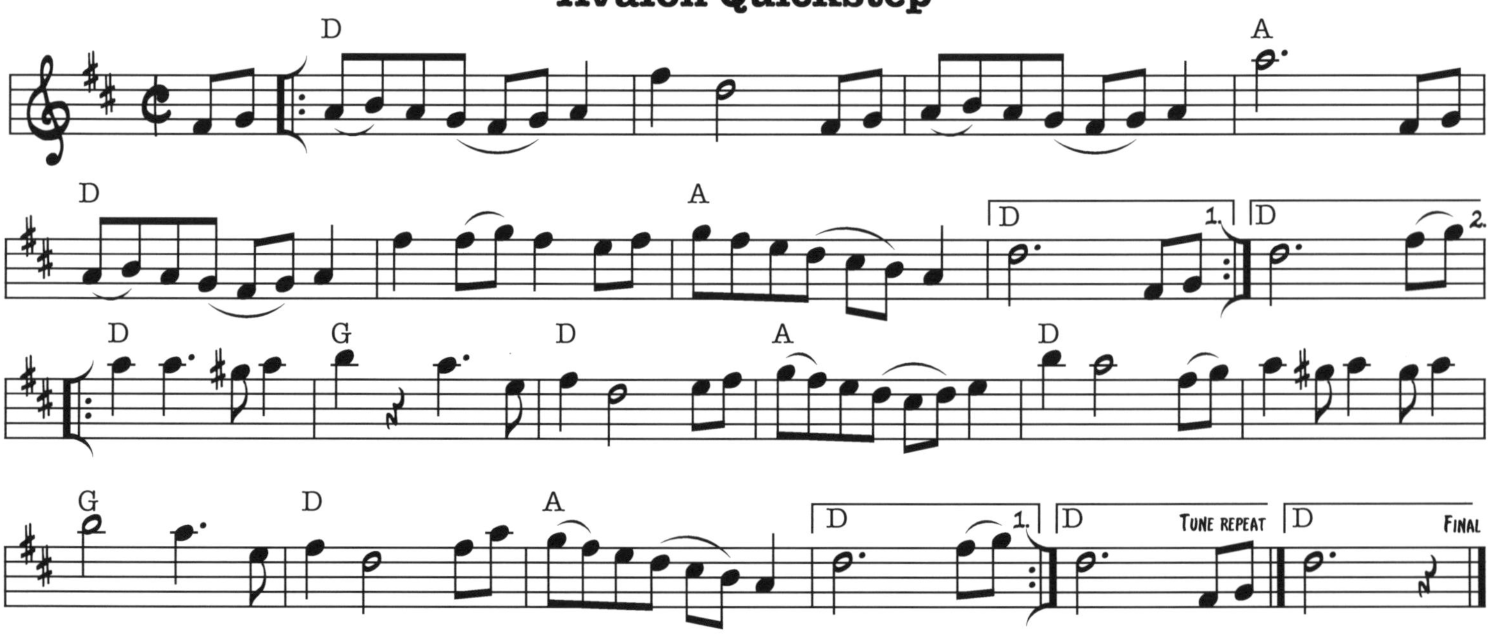

And the Cat Came Back

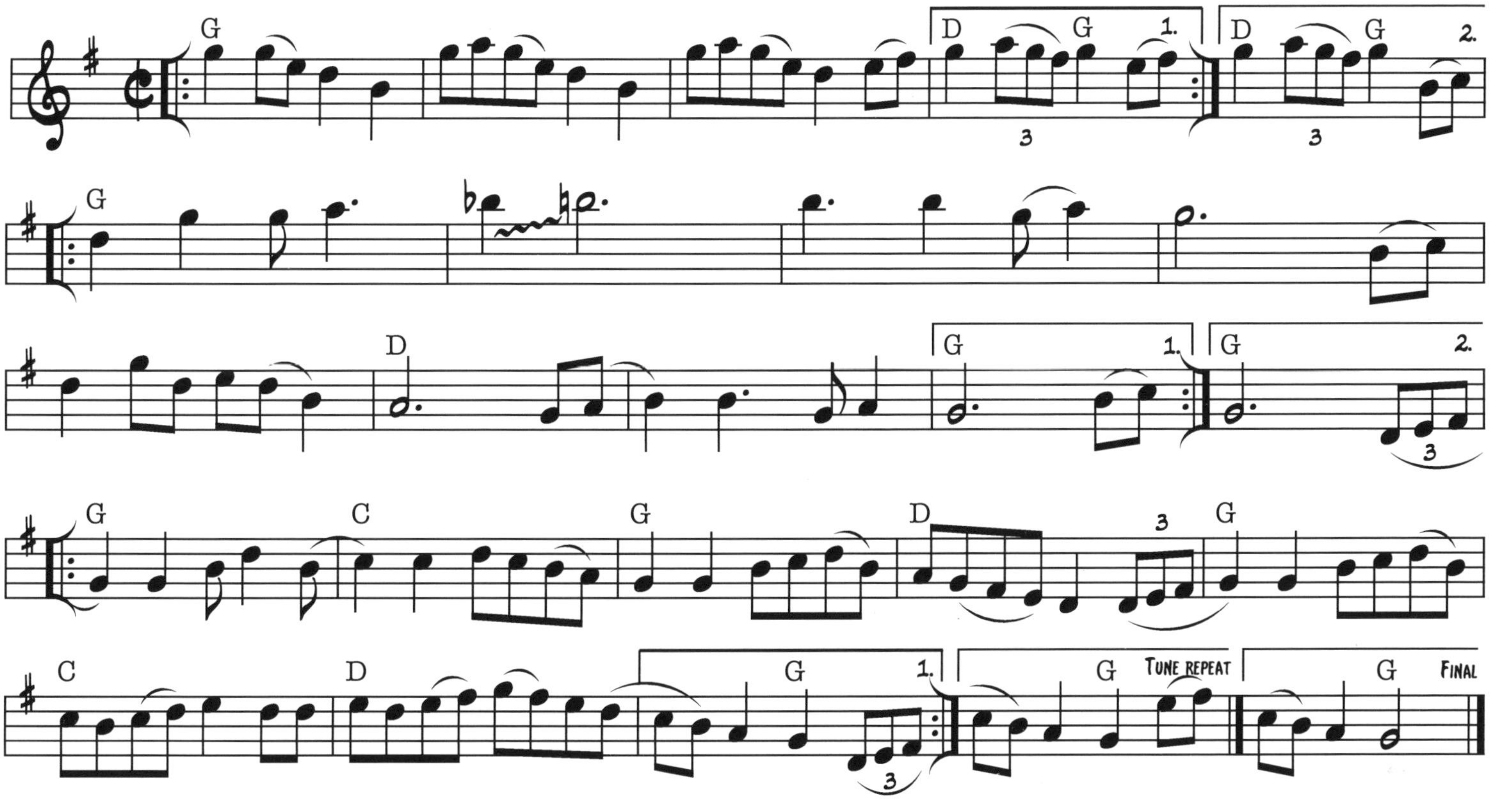

Barlow Knife (John Salyer)

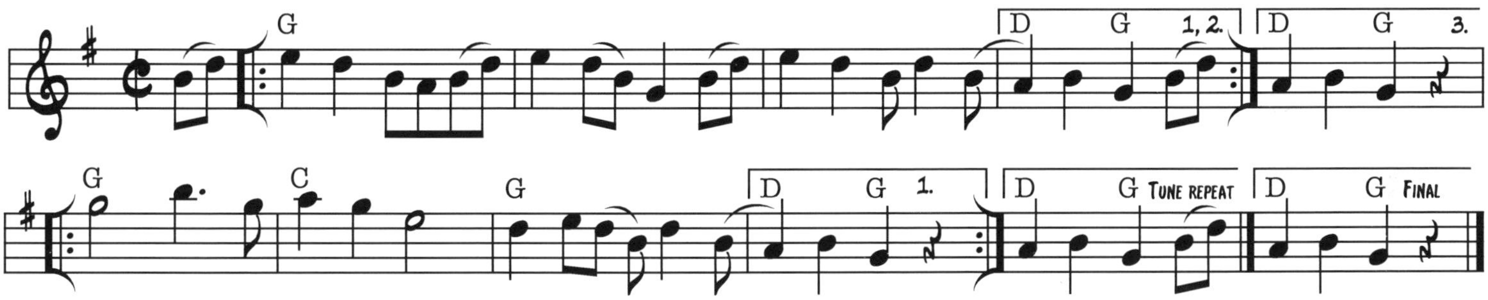

Barlow Knife (Song)

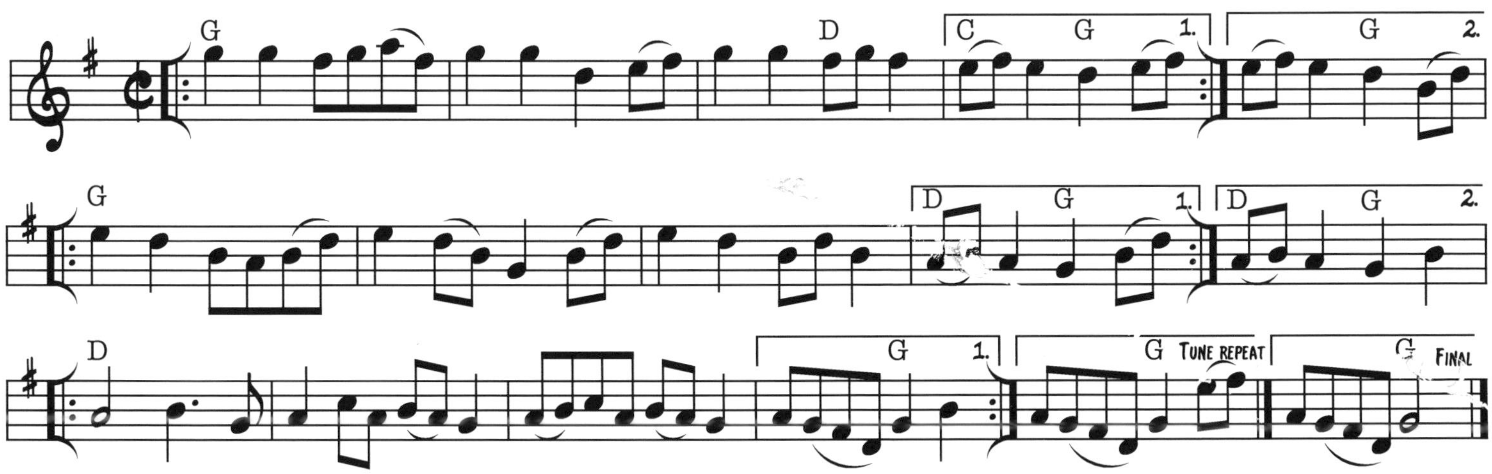

Banjo Tramp

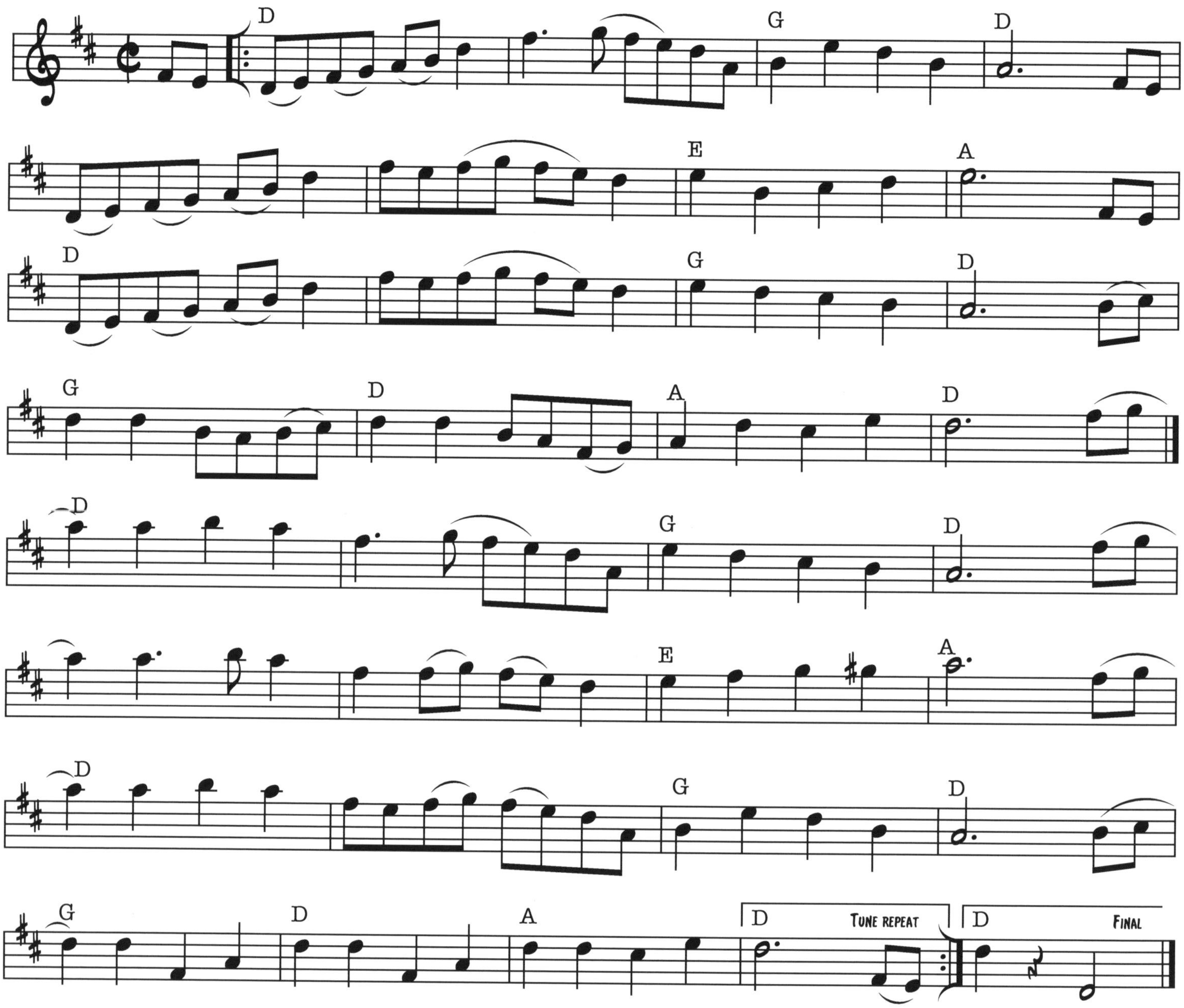

Been to the East, Been to the West

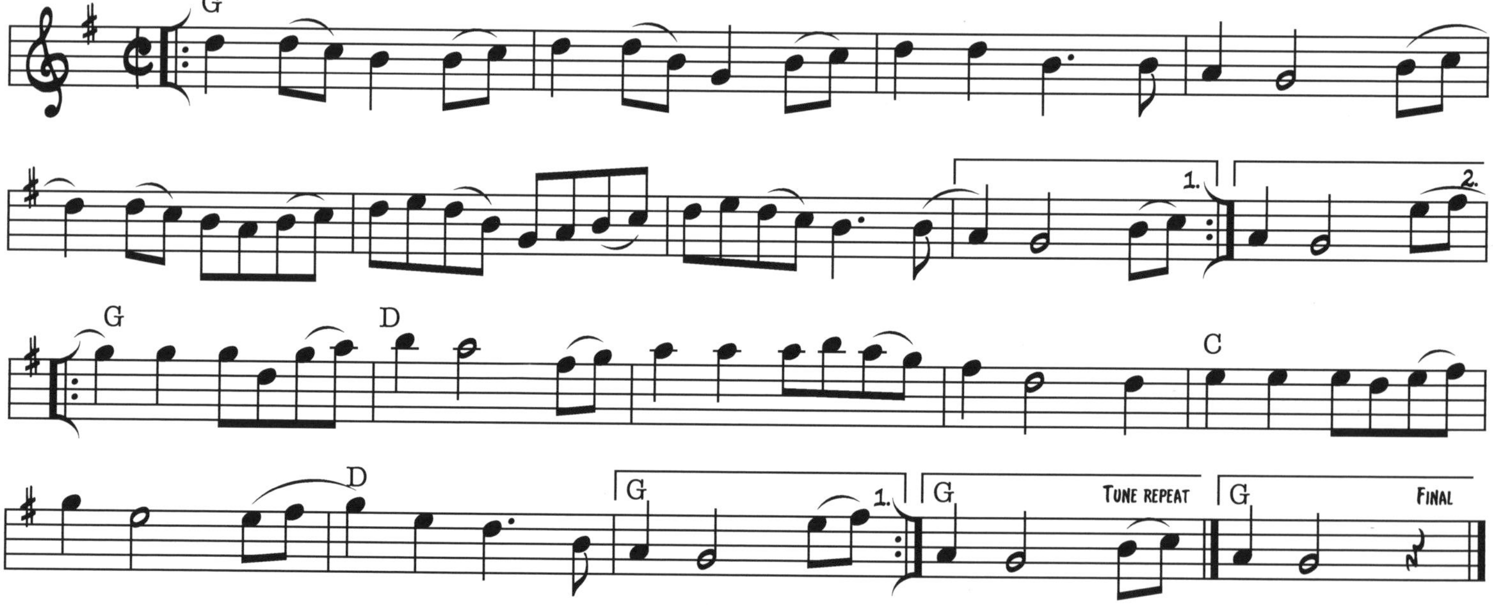

Big Eyed Rabbit

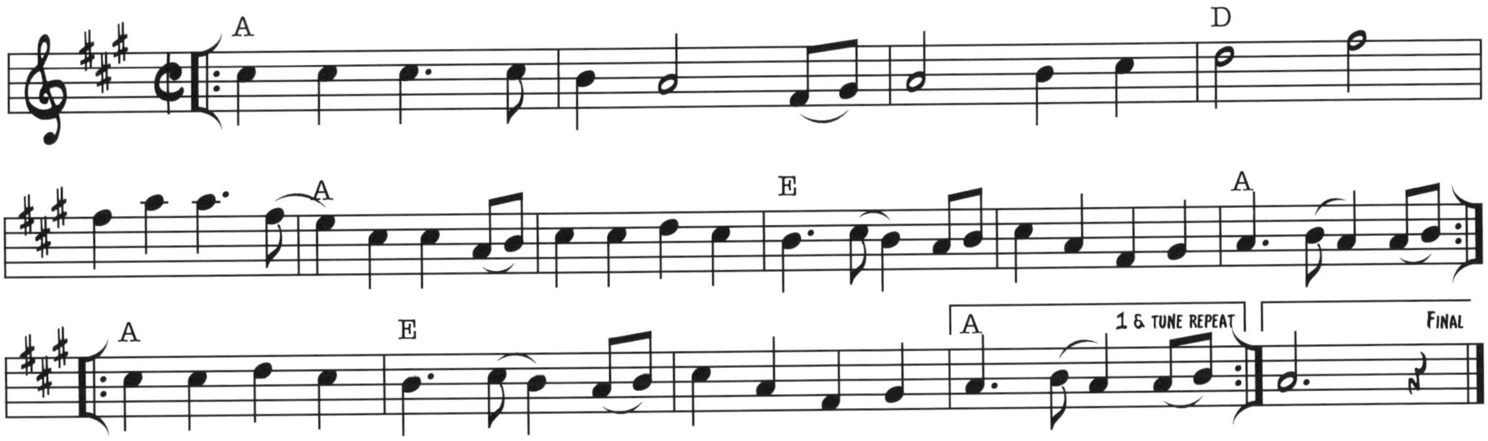

Big John McNeil

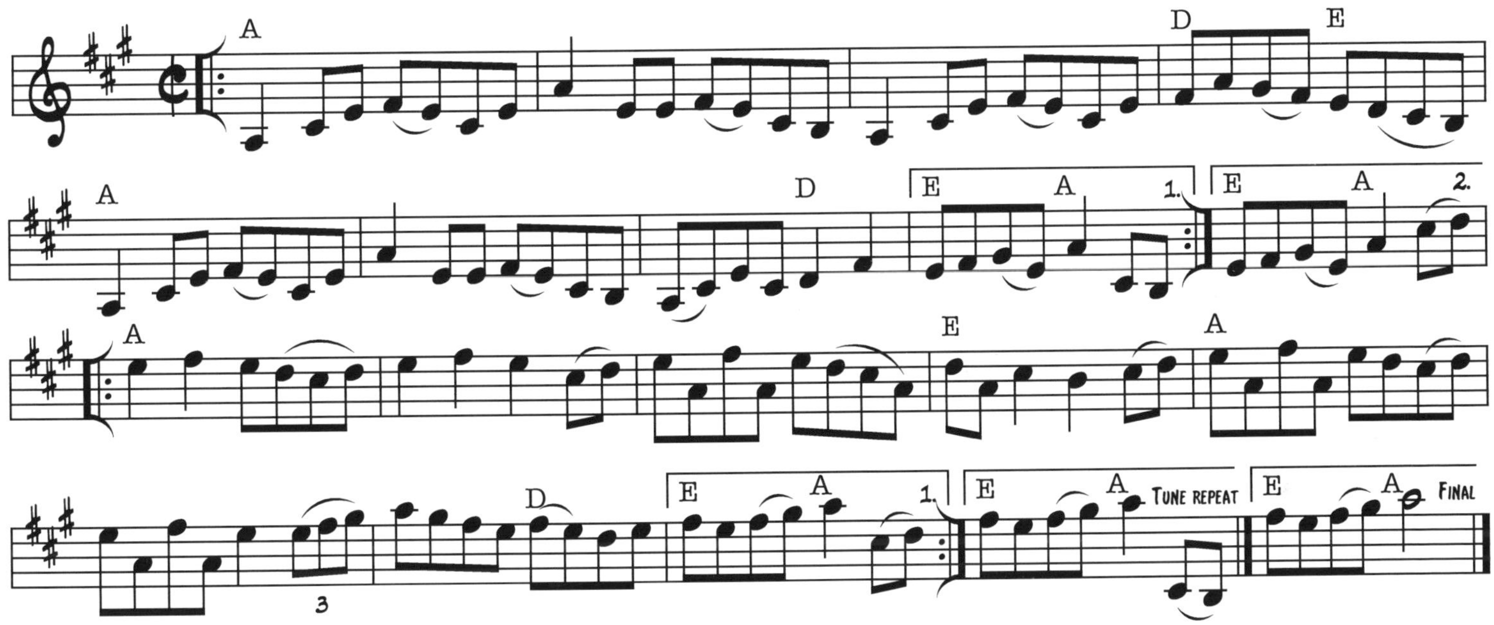

Big Scioto

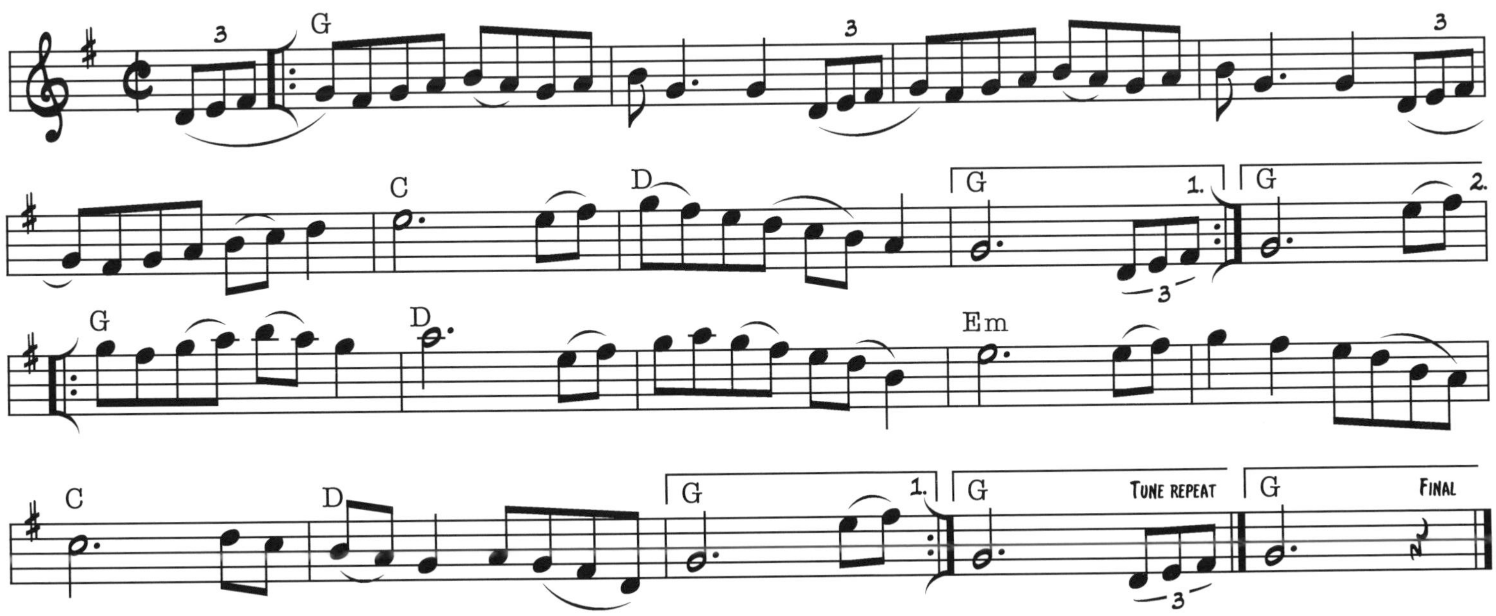

Bill Cheatam

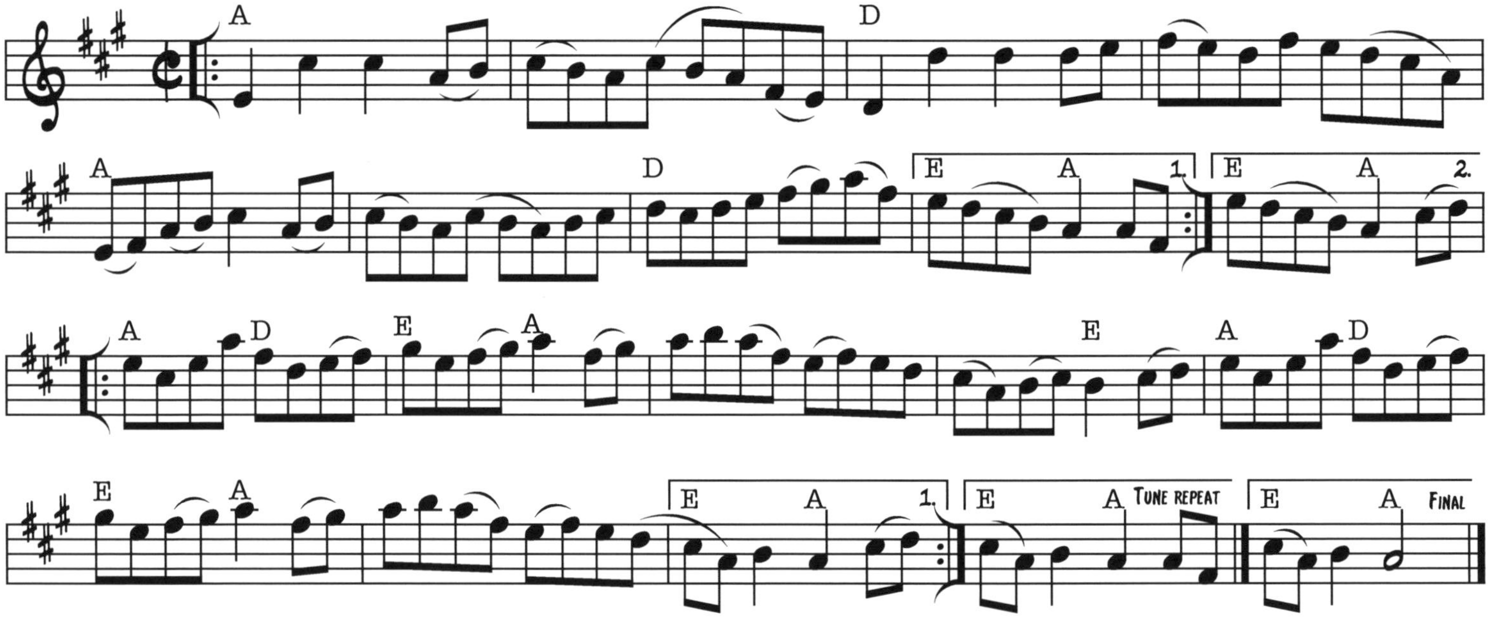

Billy in the Low Ground

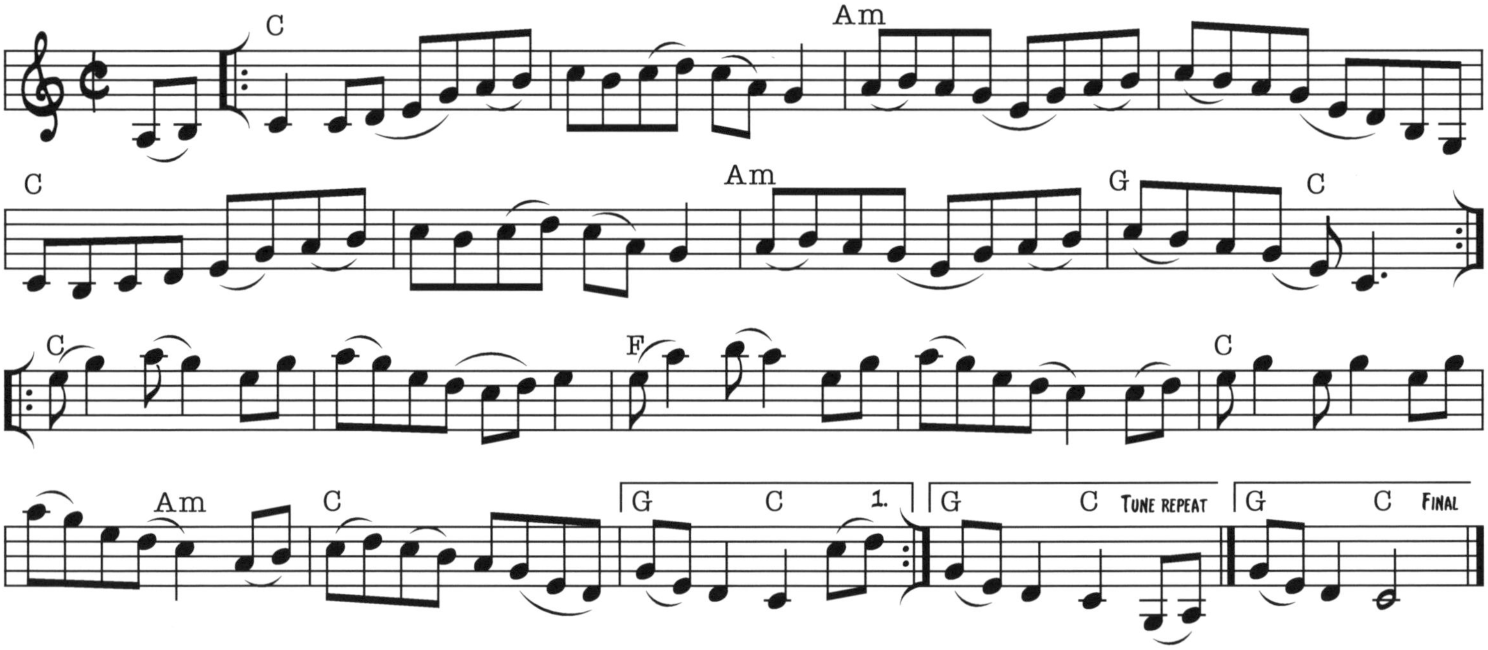

Black Eyed Suzianna (aka Susiana)

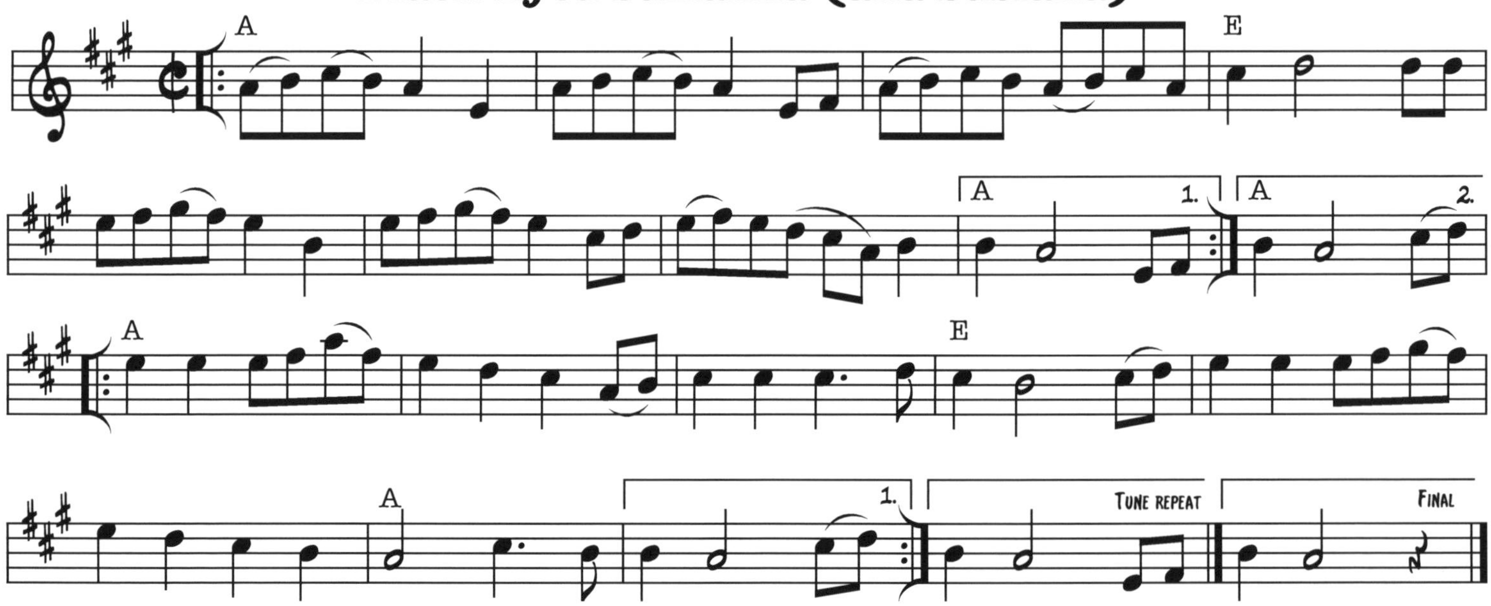

Black Cat in a Briar Patch

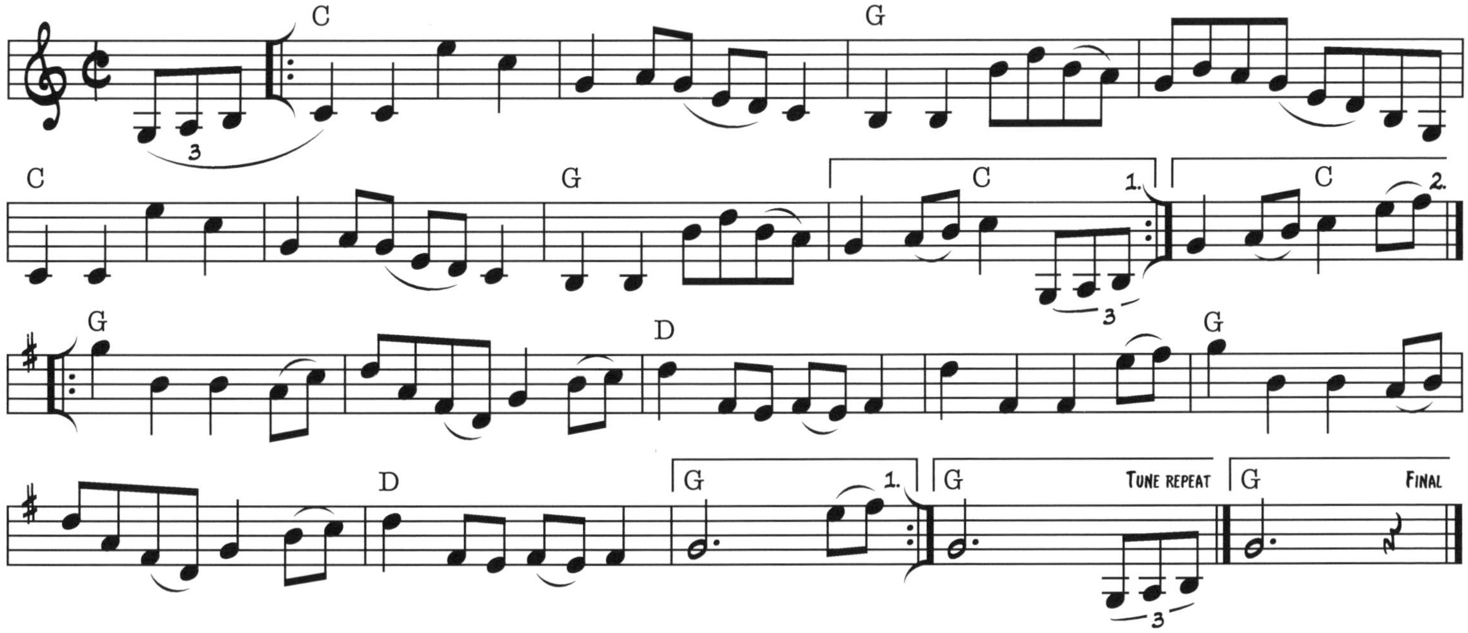

Black Hills Waltz

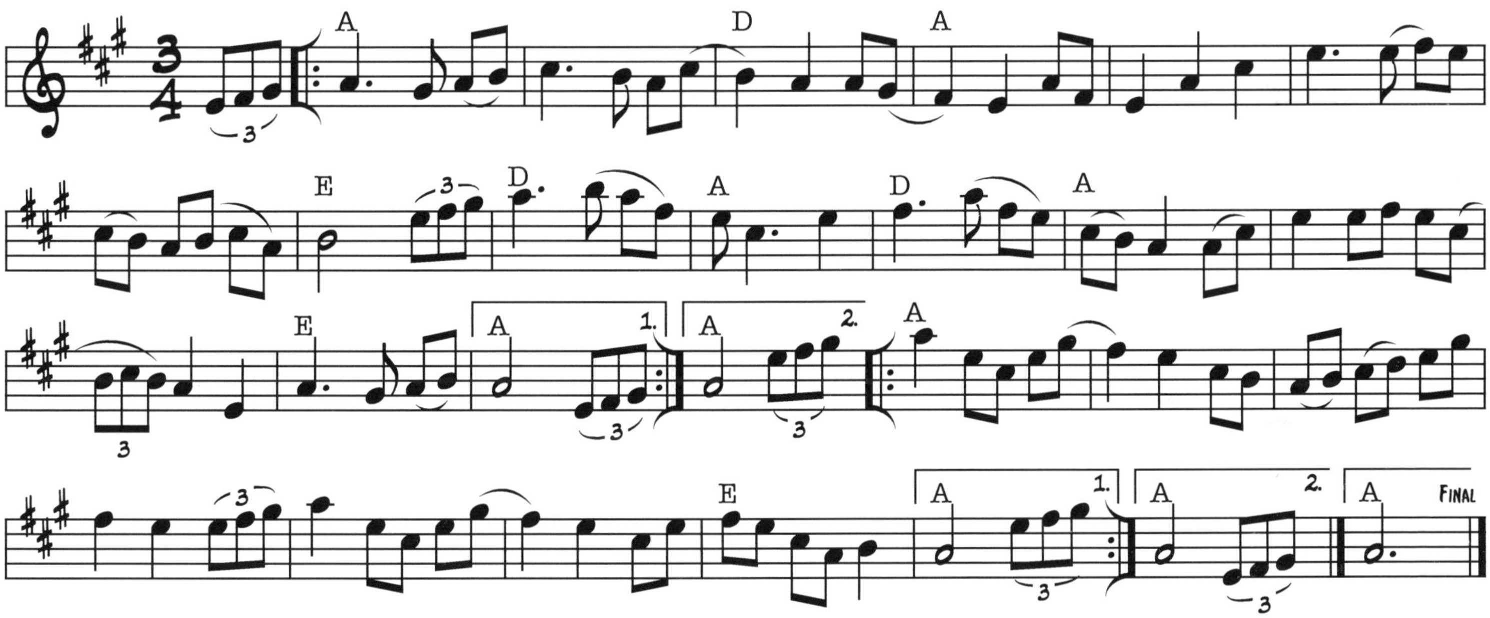

Black Jack Grove

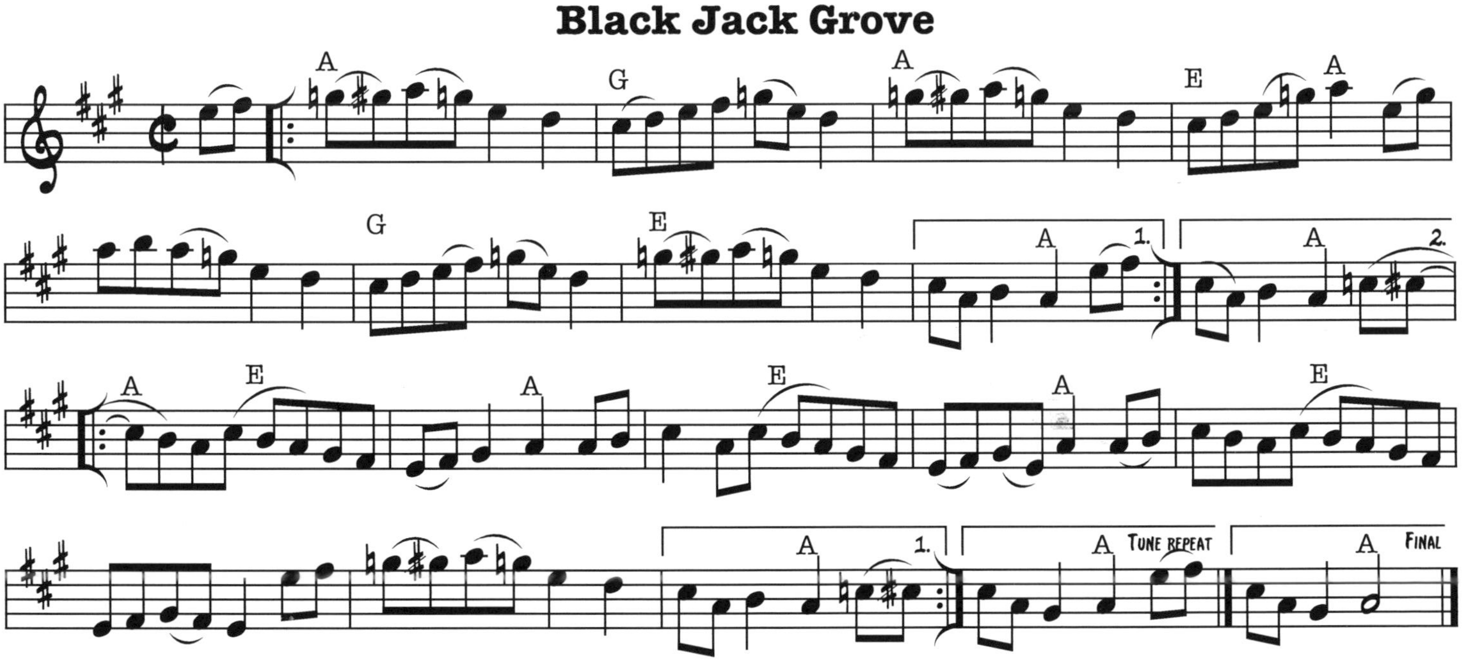

Blackbird Says to the Crow

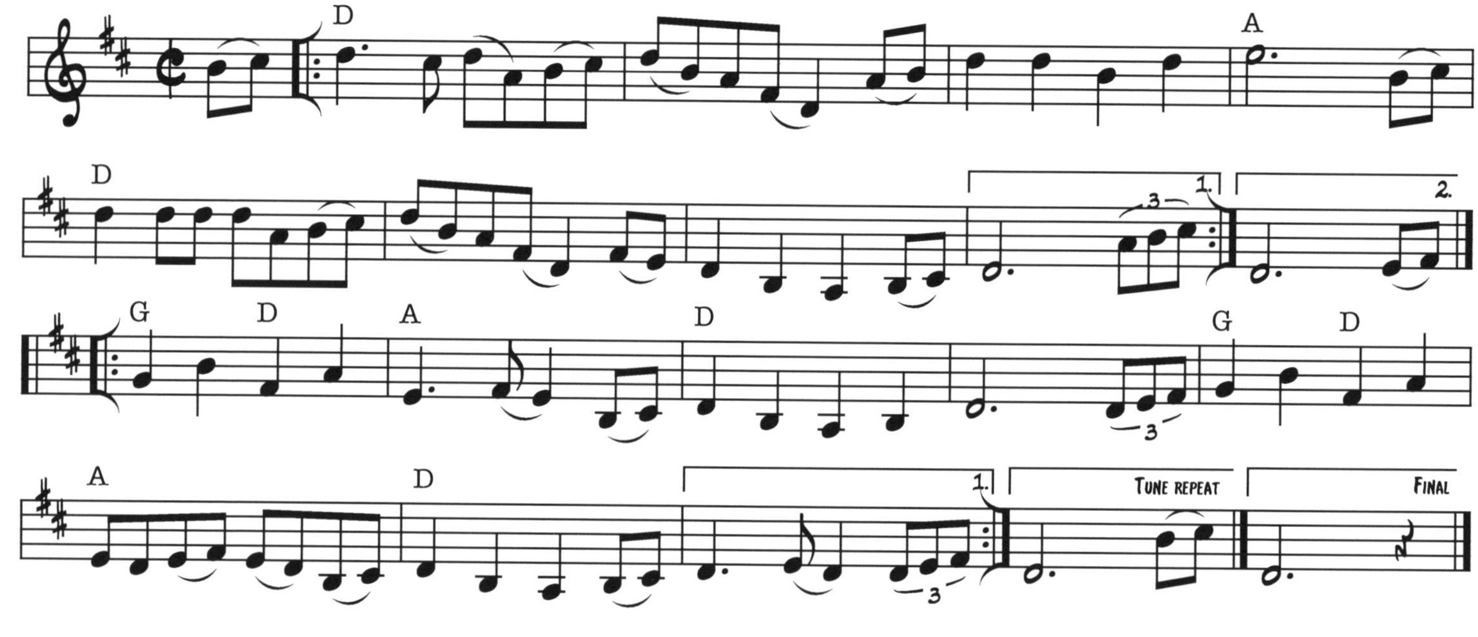

Boatman

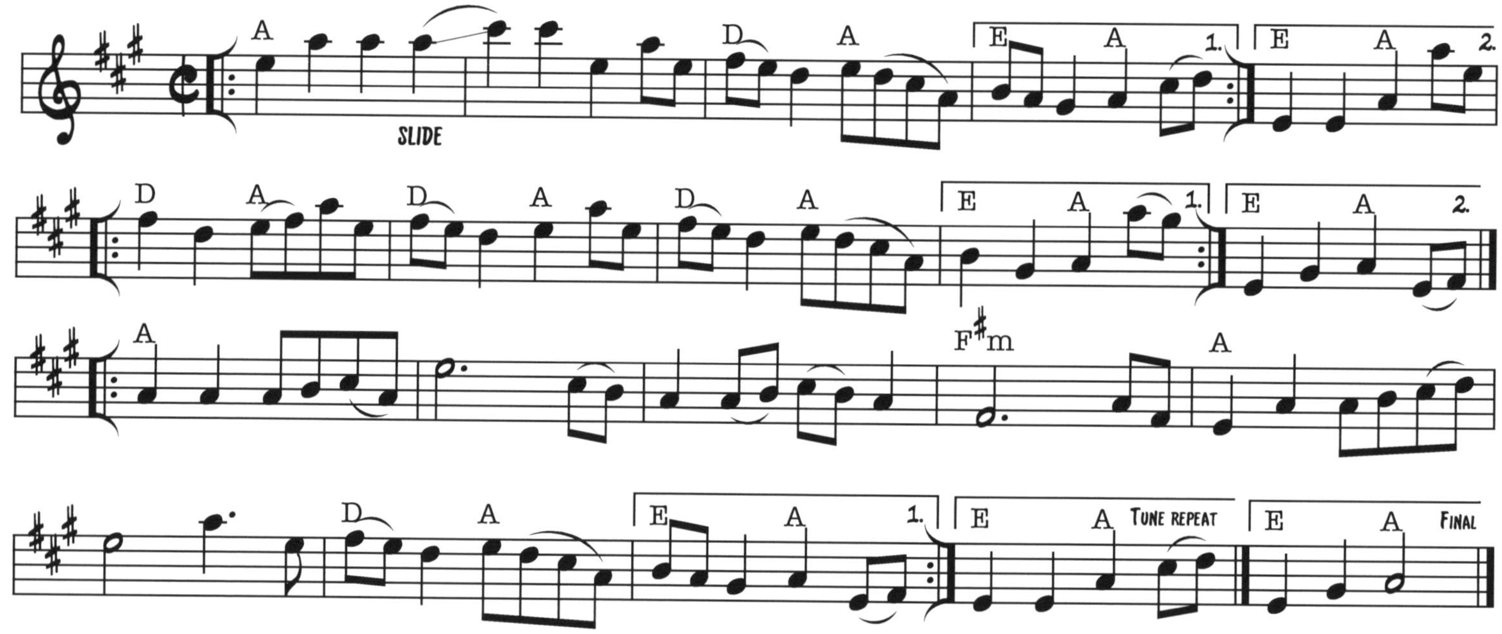

Bob Tailed Mule

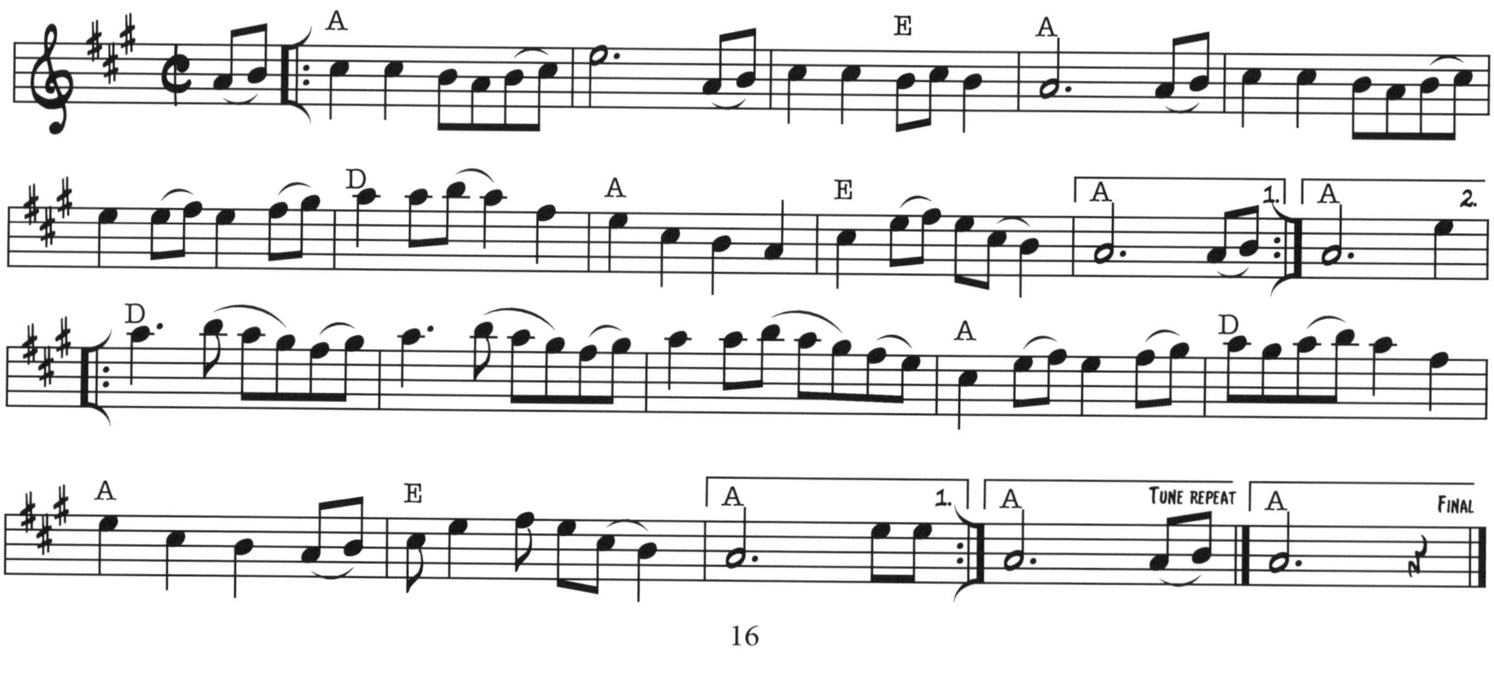

Booth Shot Lincoln

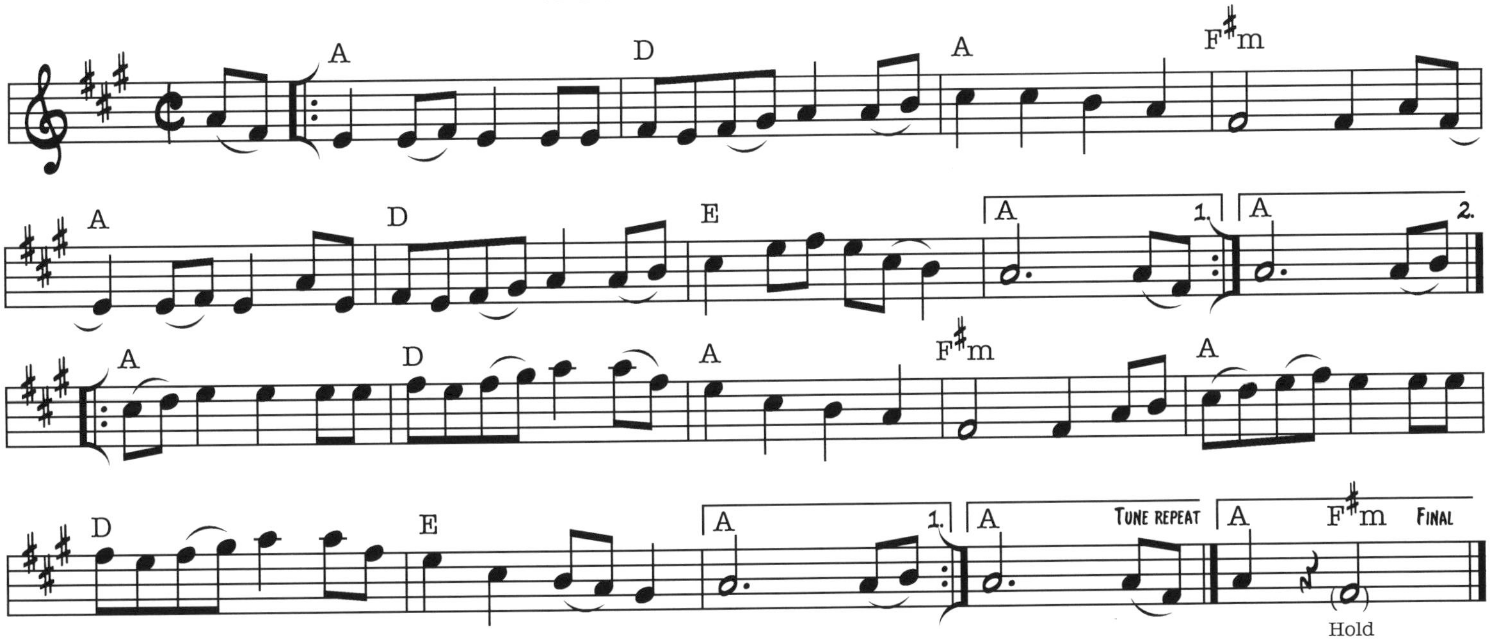

Bowl-a-Rama

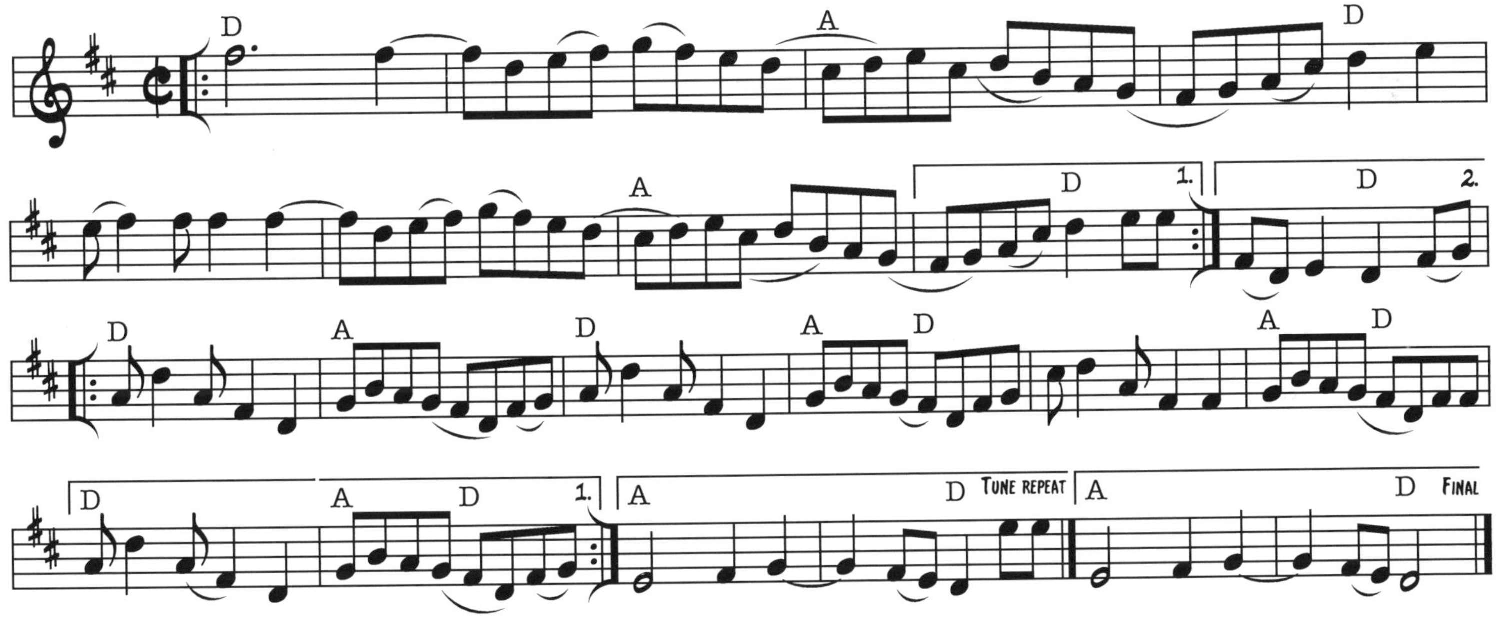

Breaking Up Christmas

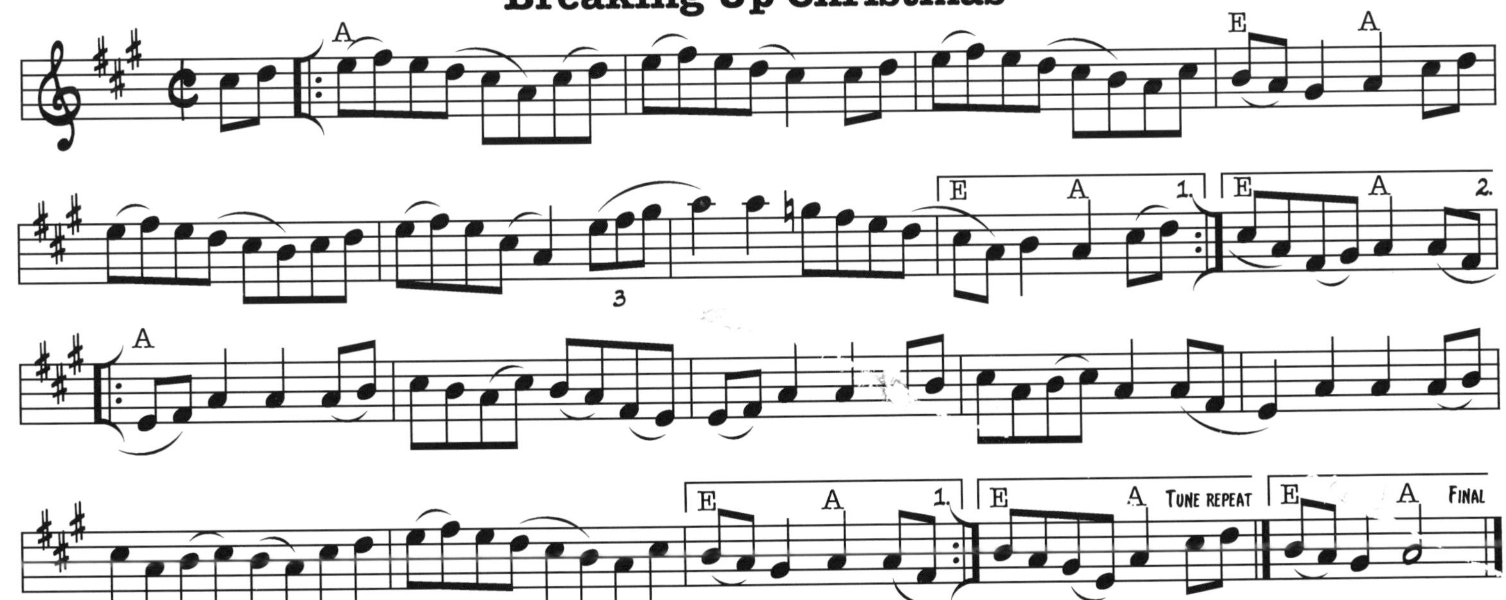

Briar Picker Brown

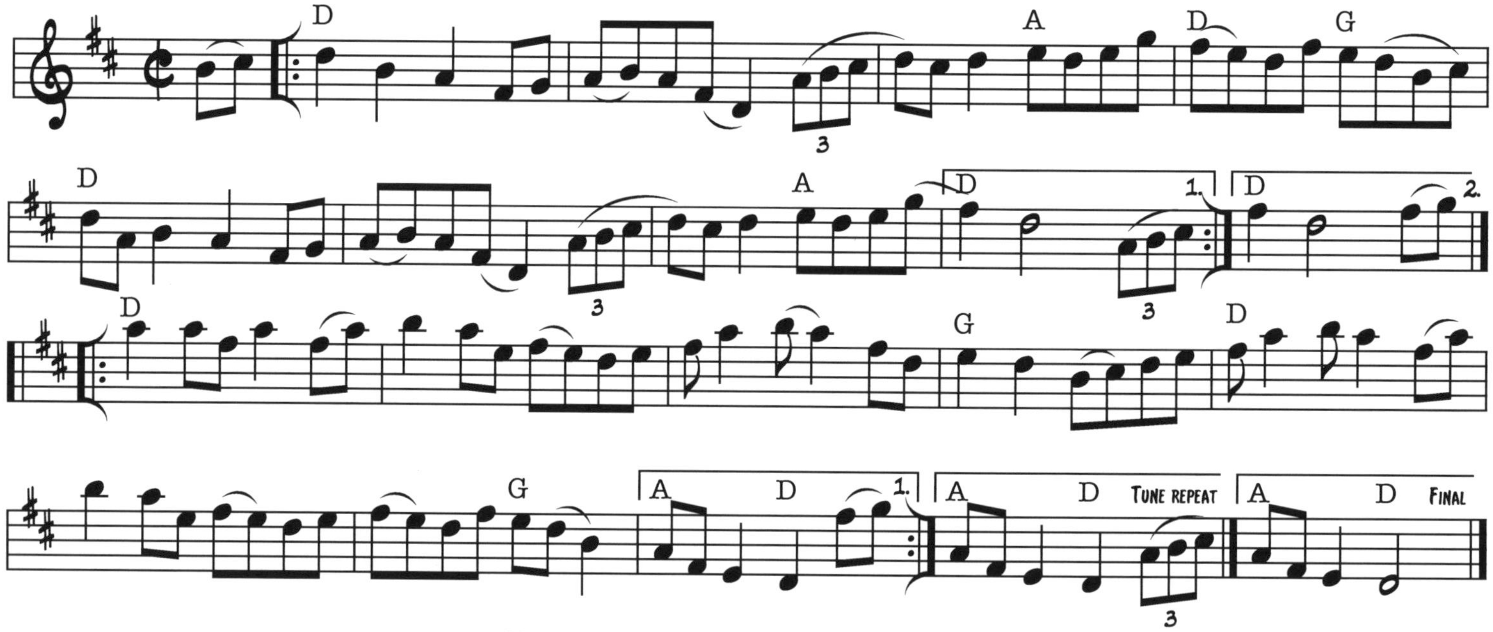

Broken Down Gambler

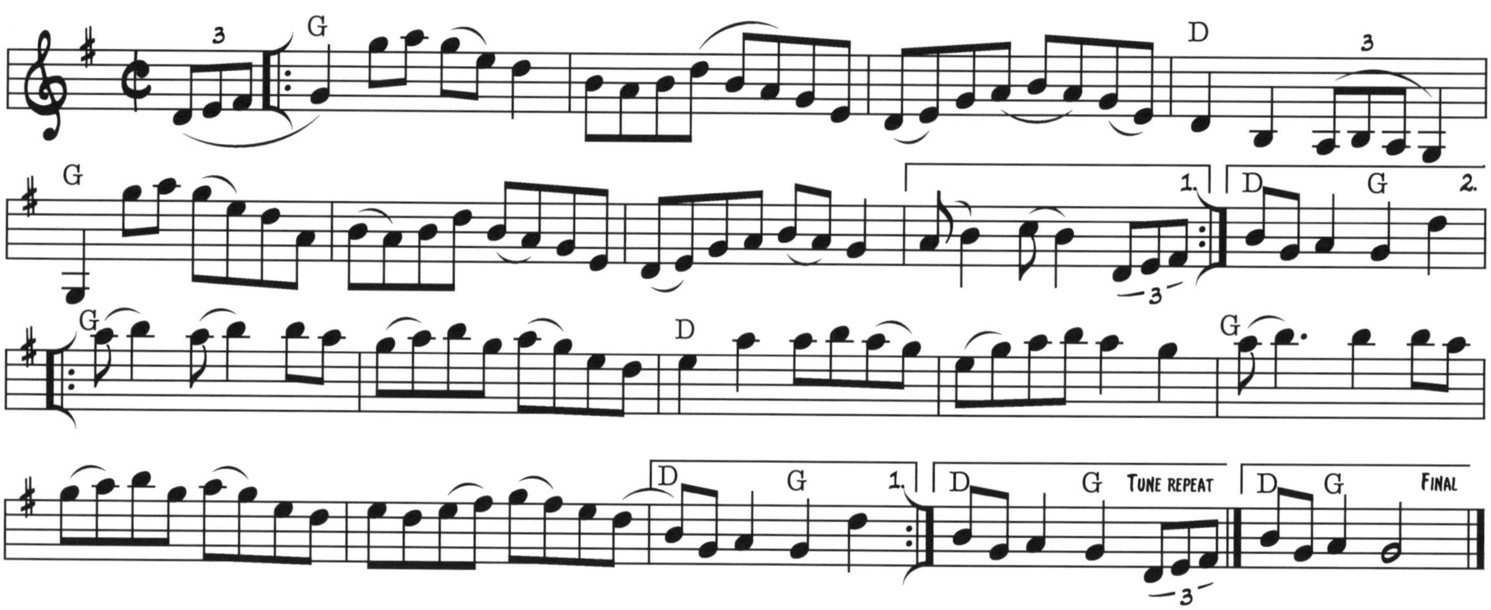

Buck Mountain

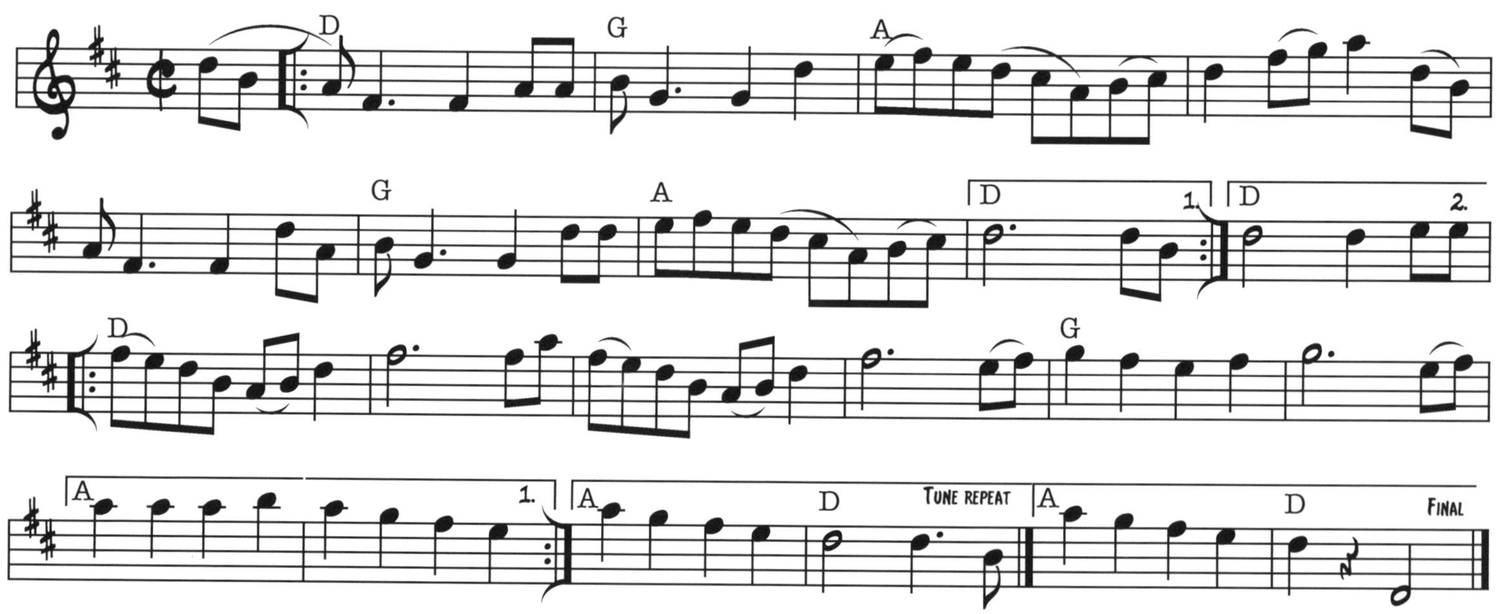

Buffalo Gals (KY version in G)

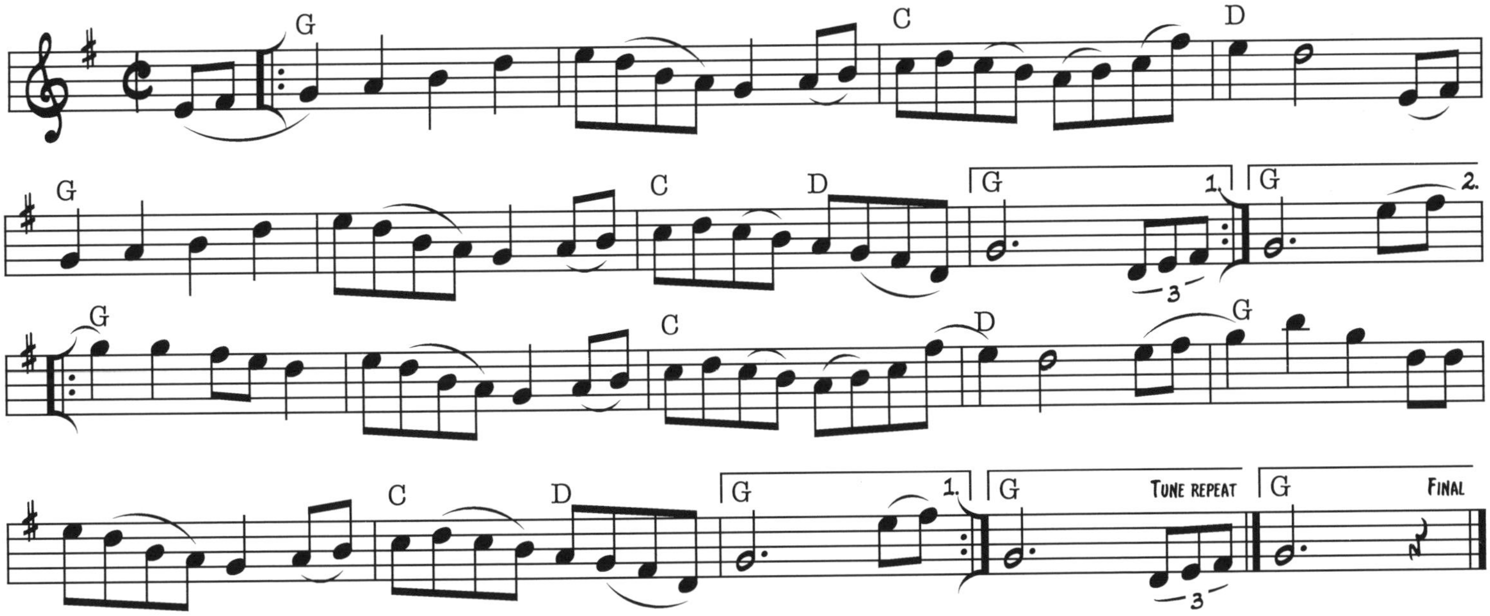

Buffalo Gals (Common version in G)

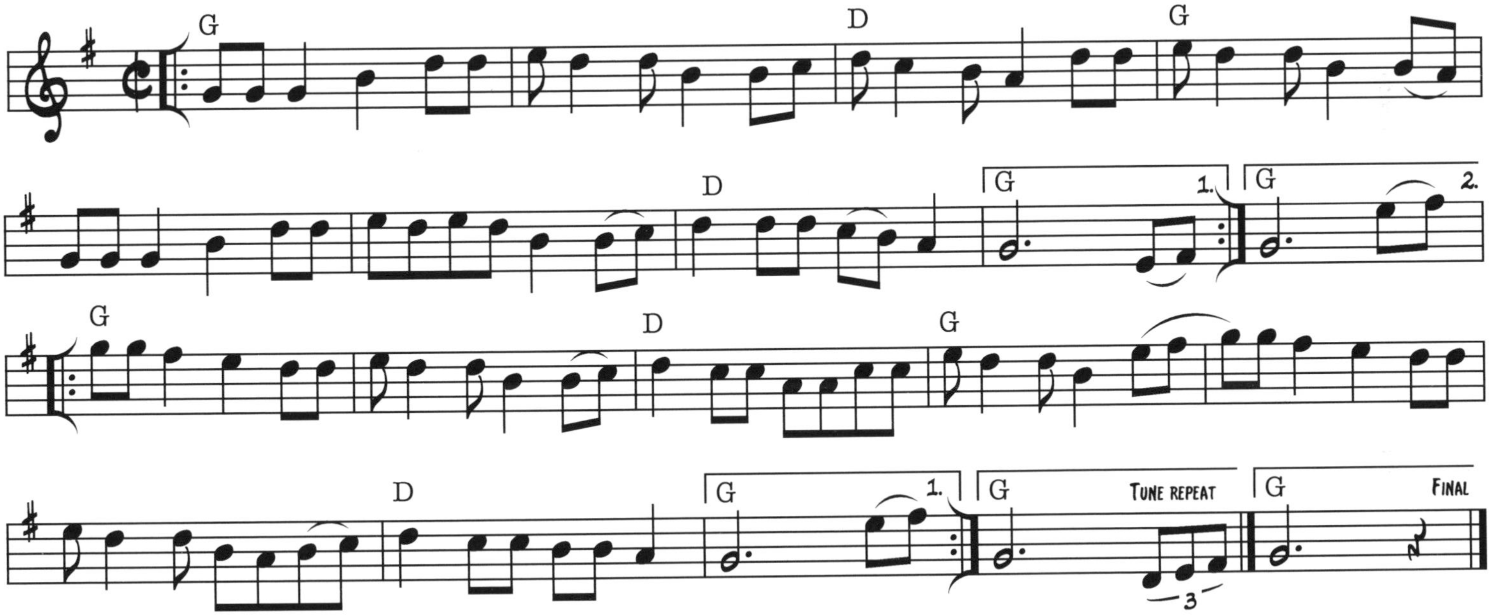

Buffalo Gals (in A)

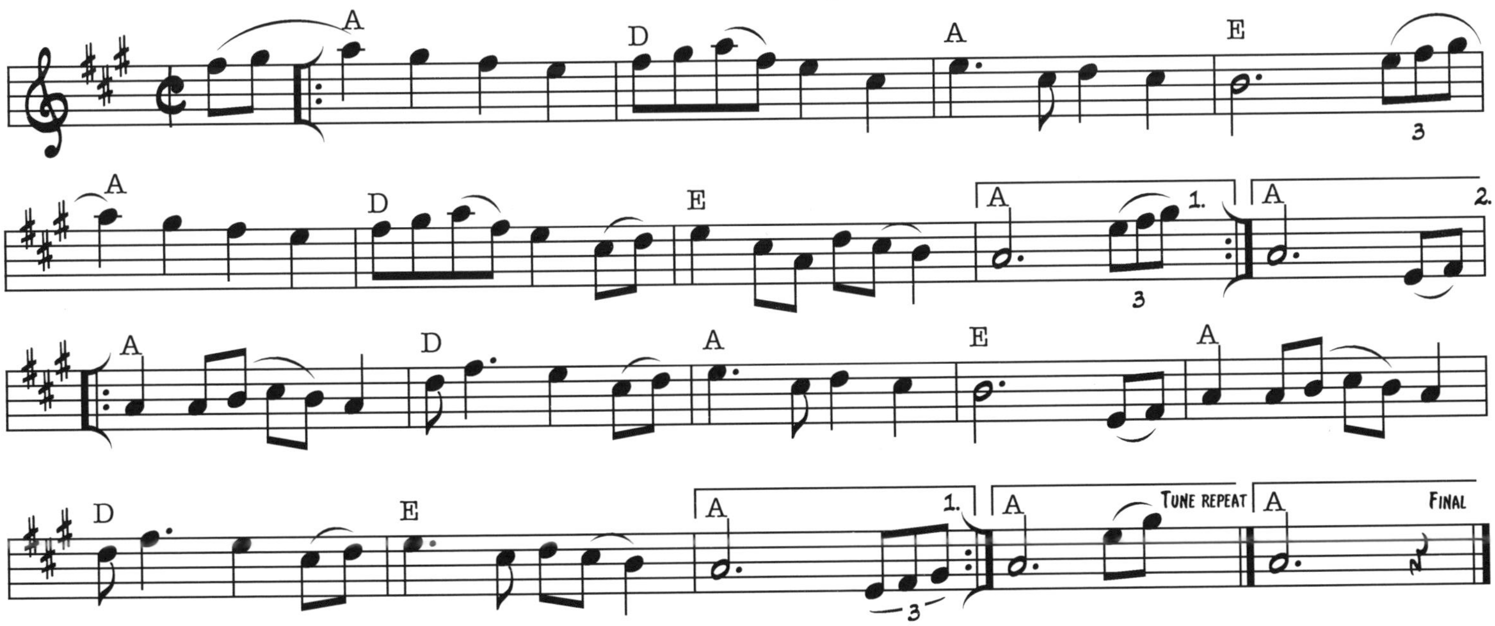

Buckin' Dun

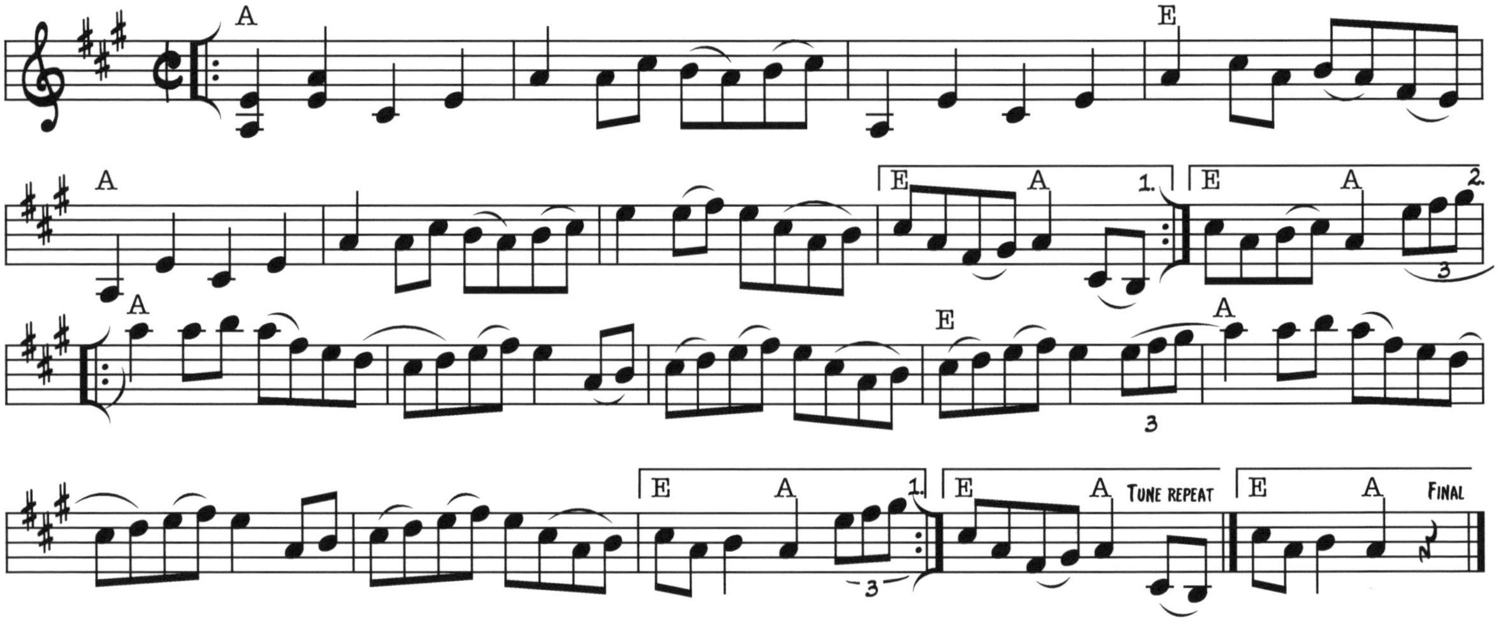

Bull at the Wagon

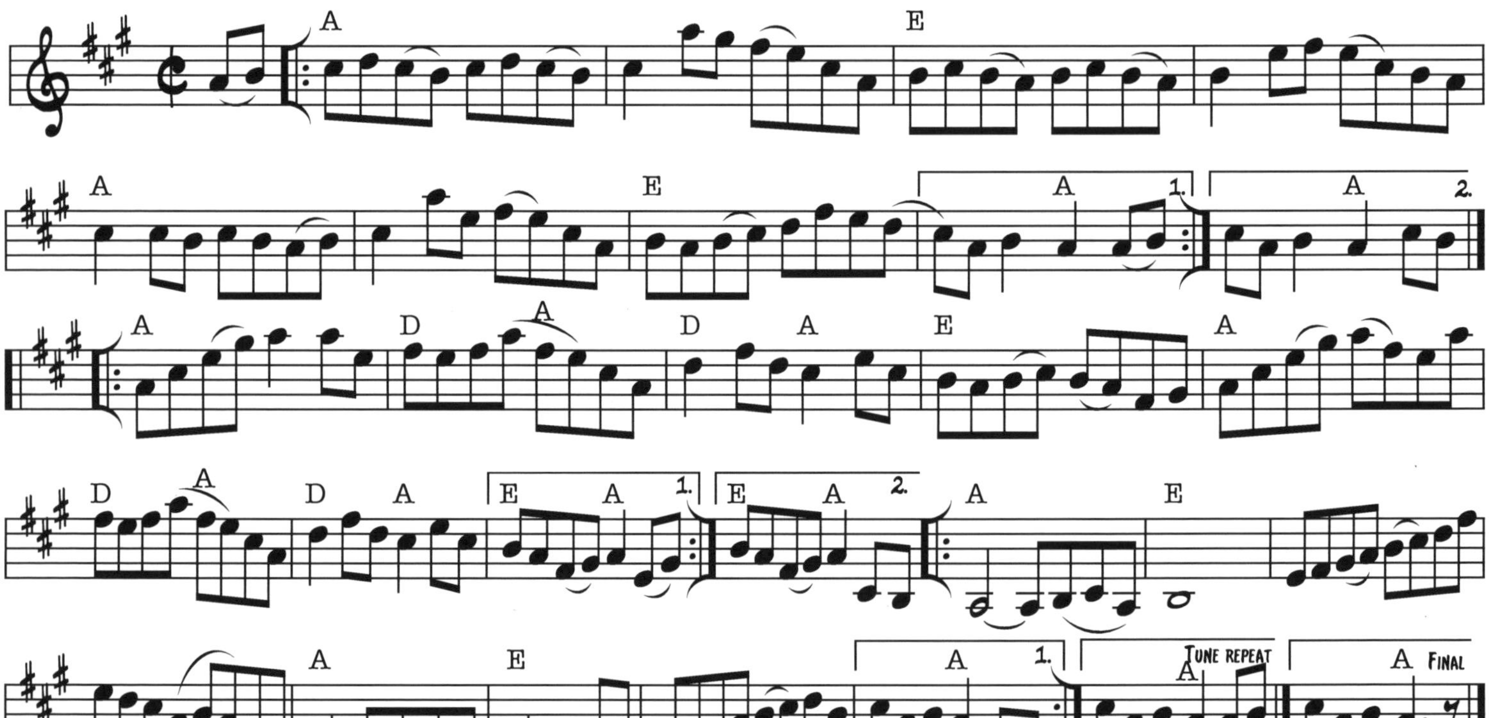

Camp Chase

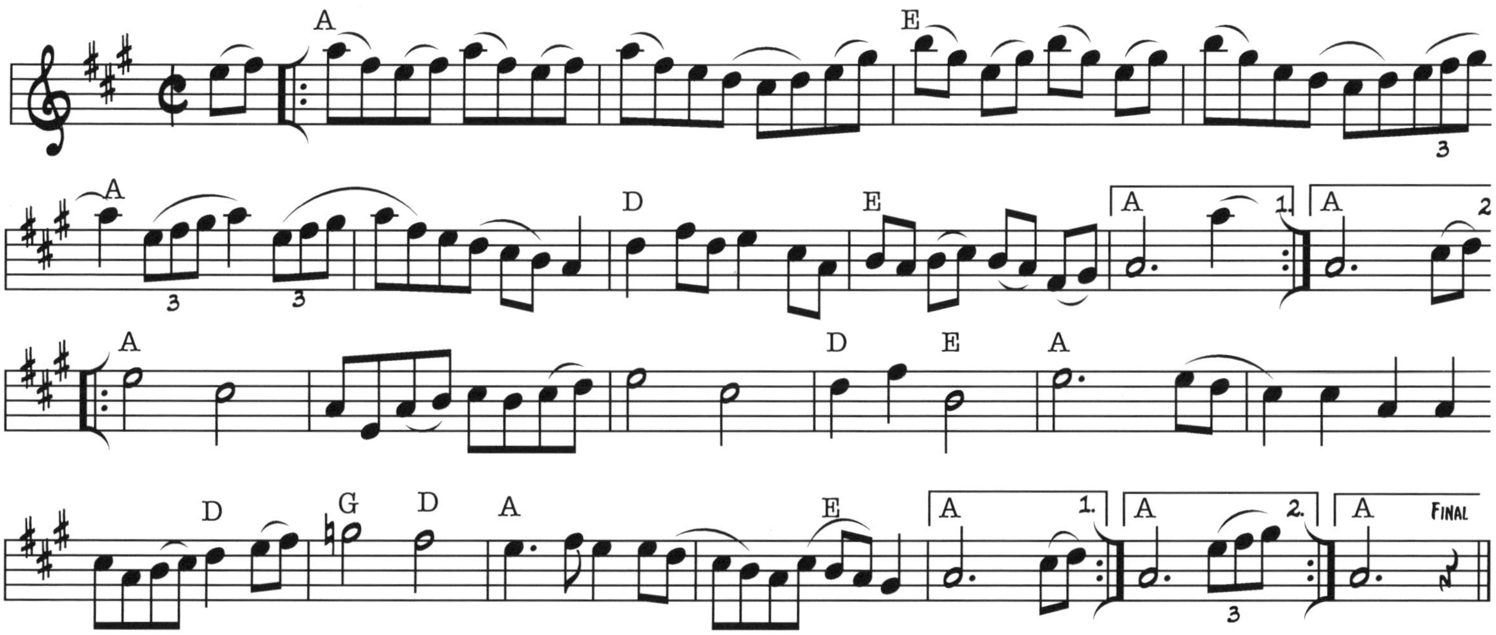

Camp Meeting on the 4th of July

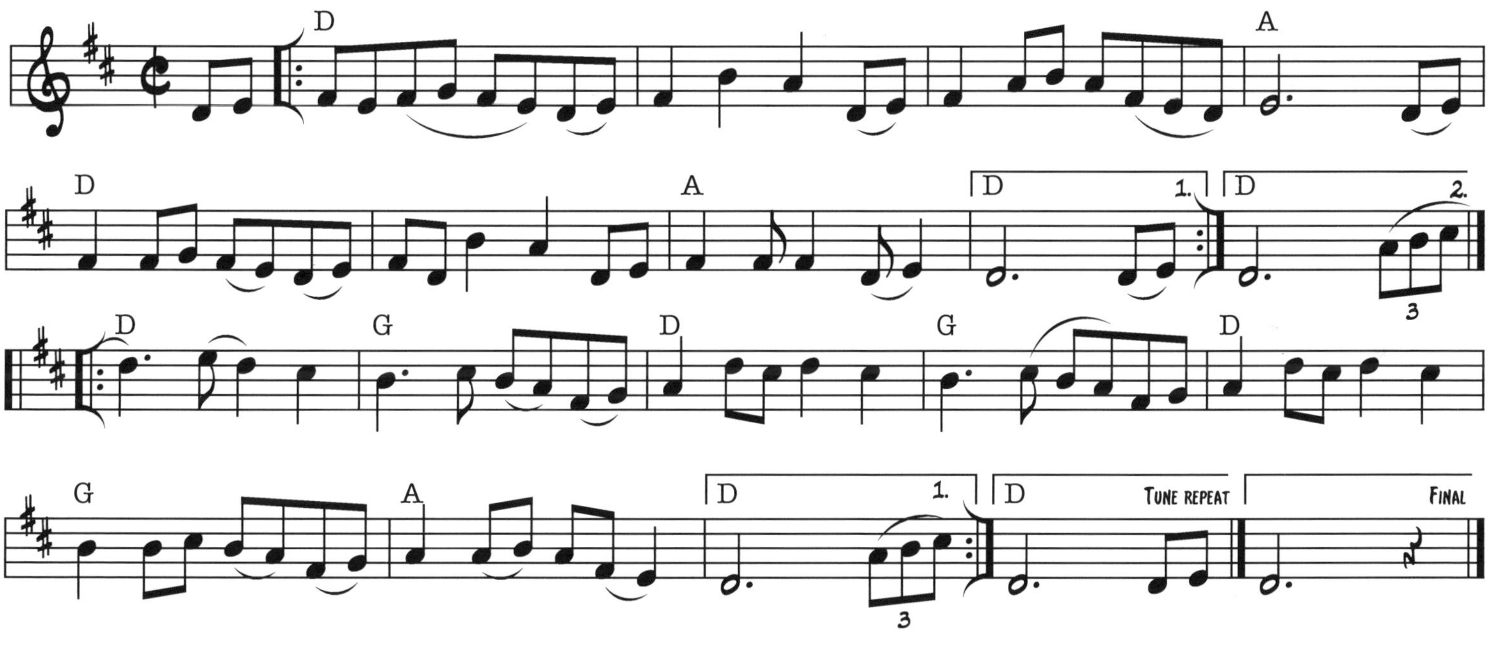

Candy Girl

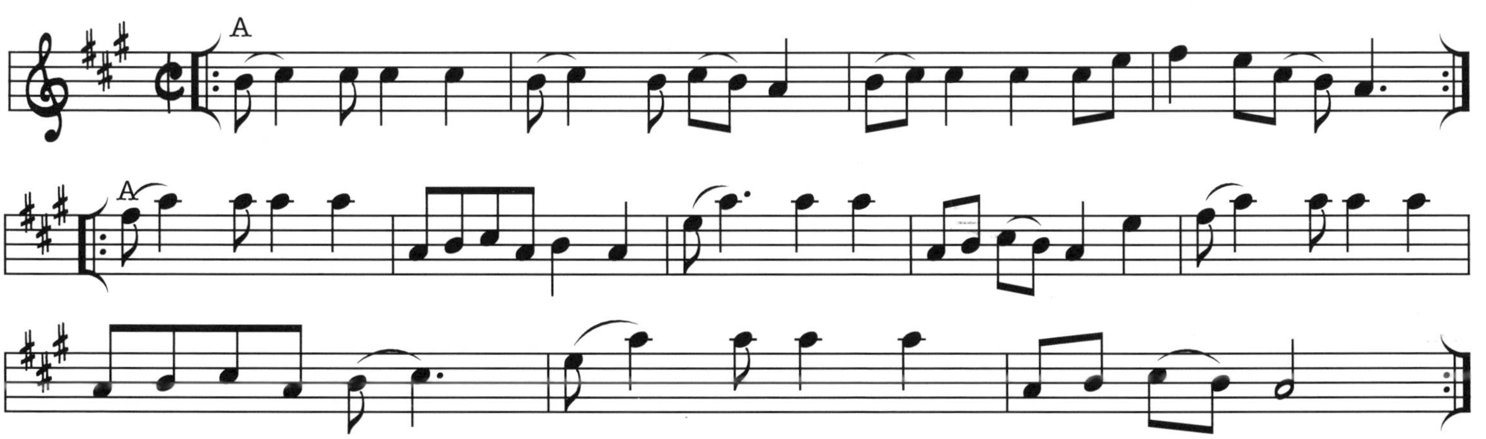

Chase the Squirrel

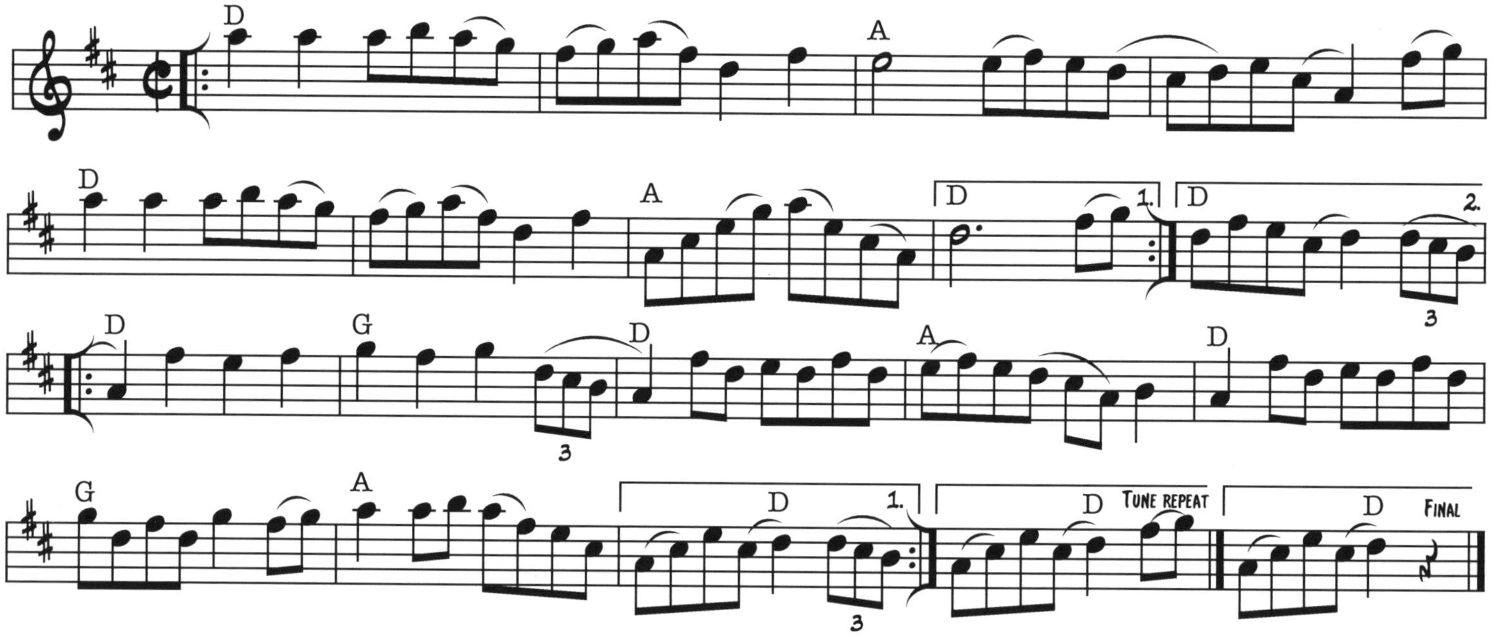

Chattanooga

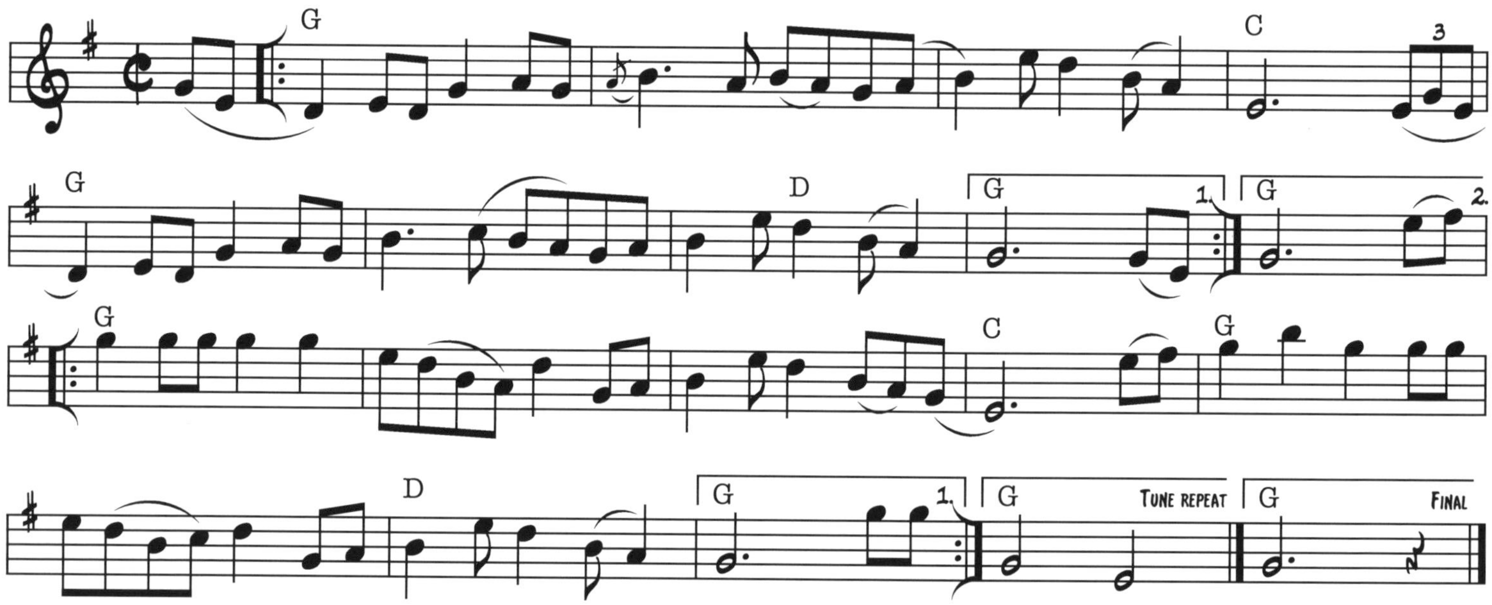

Cincinnati Hornpipe

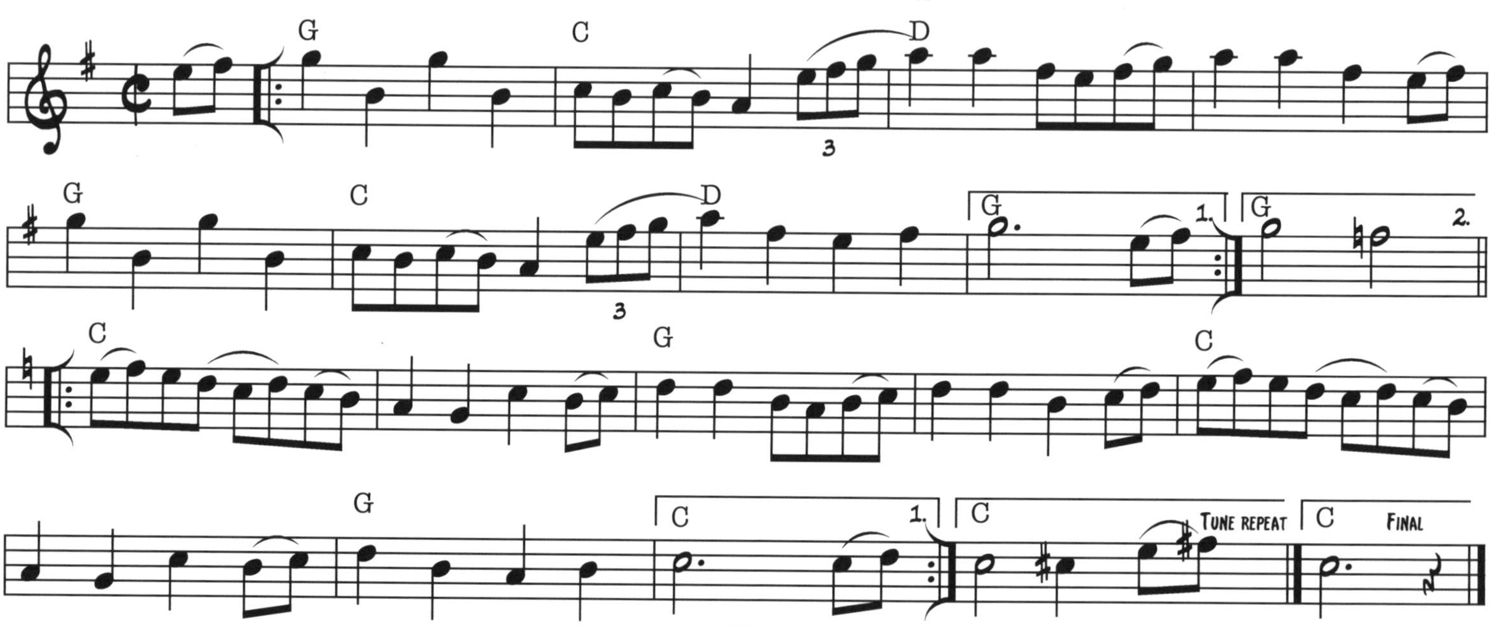

Cherokee Shuffle (in A)

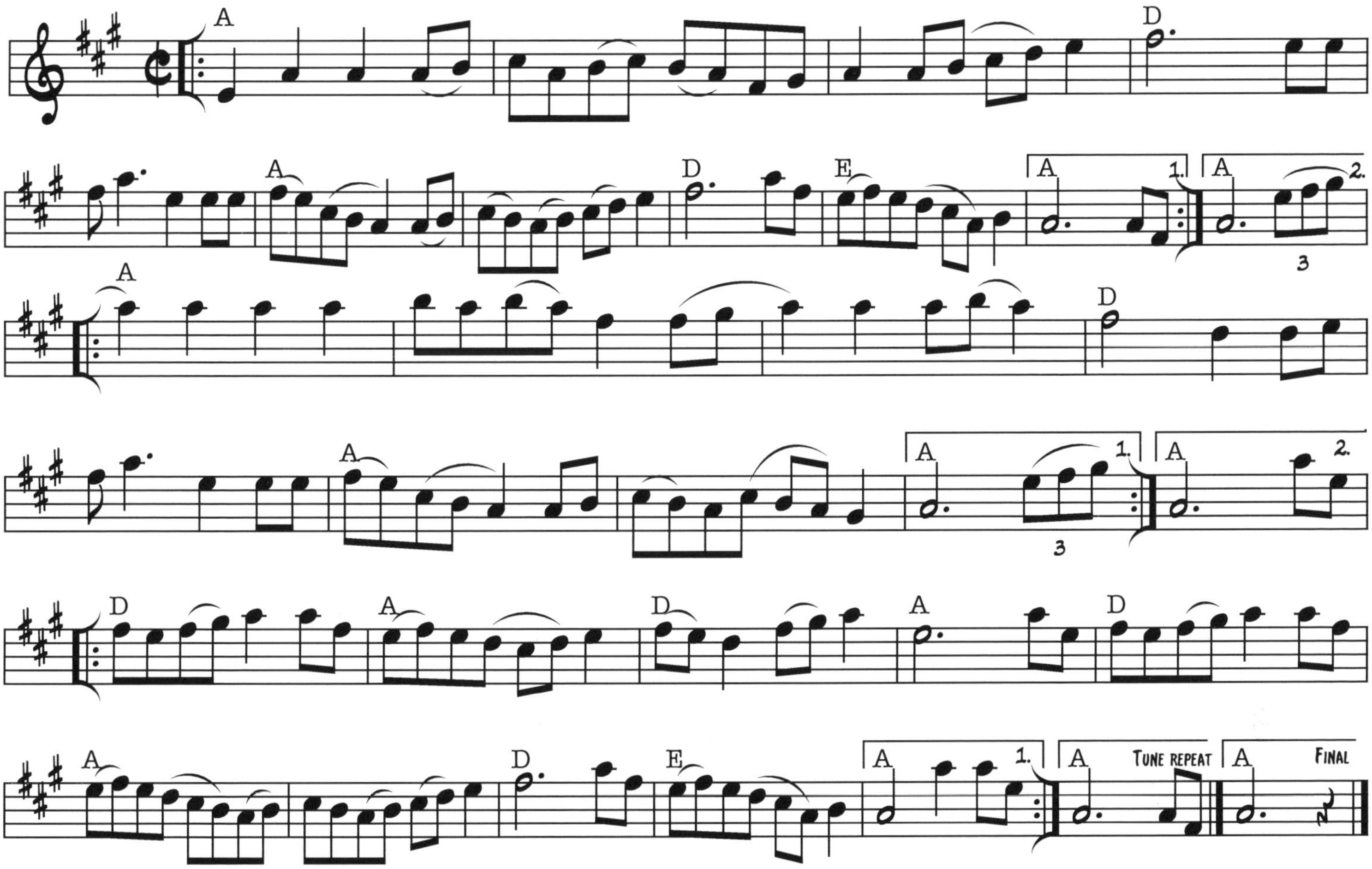

Cherokee Shuffle (in D)

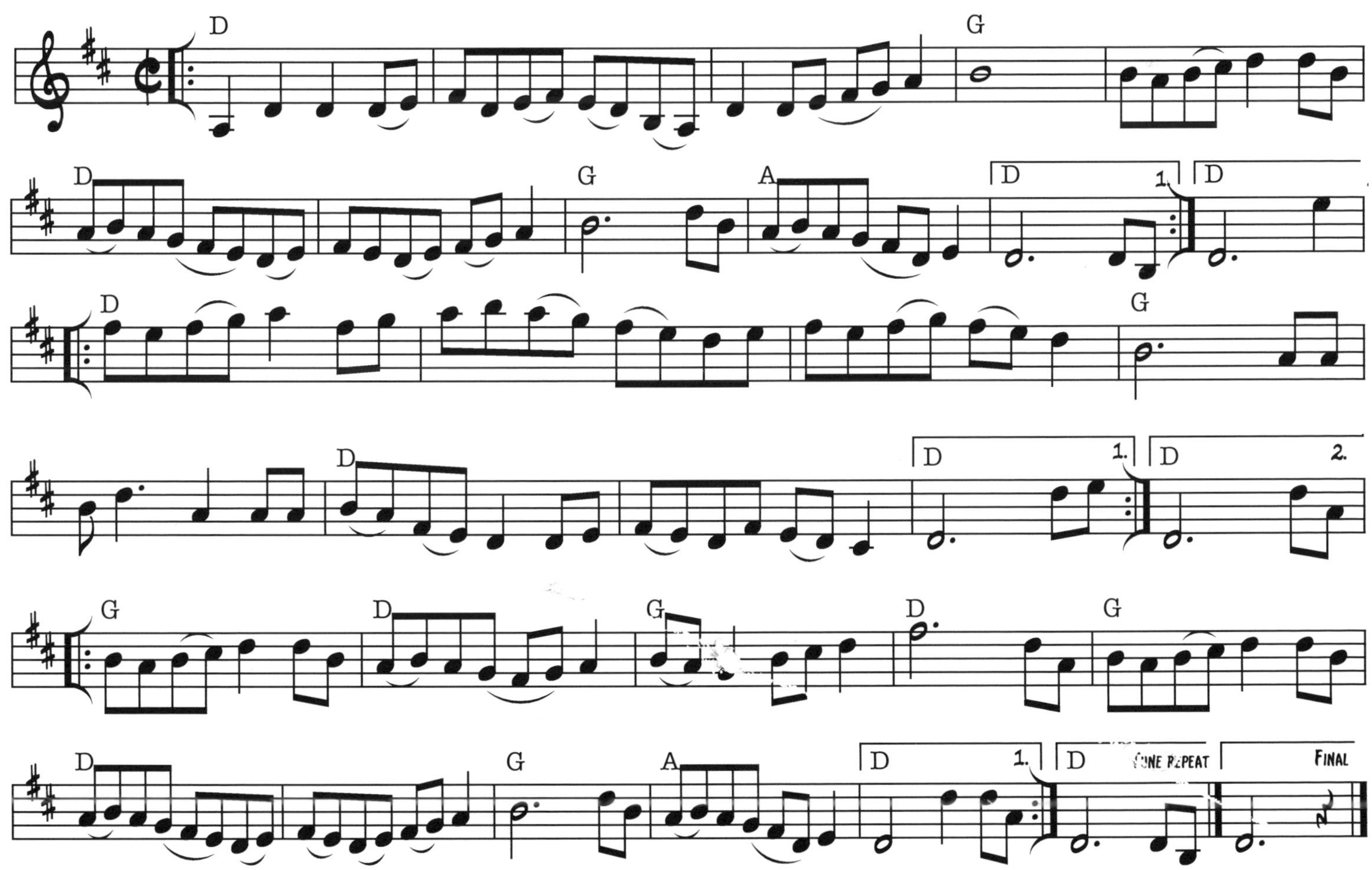

Chinese Breakdown

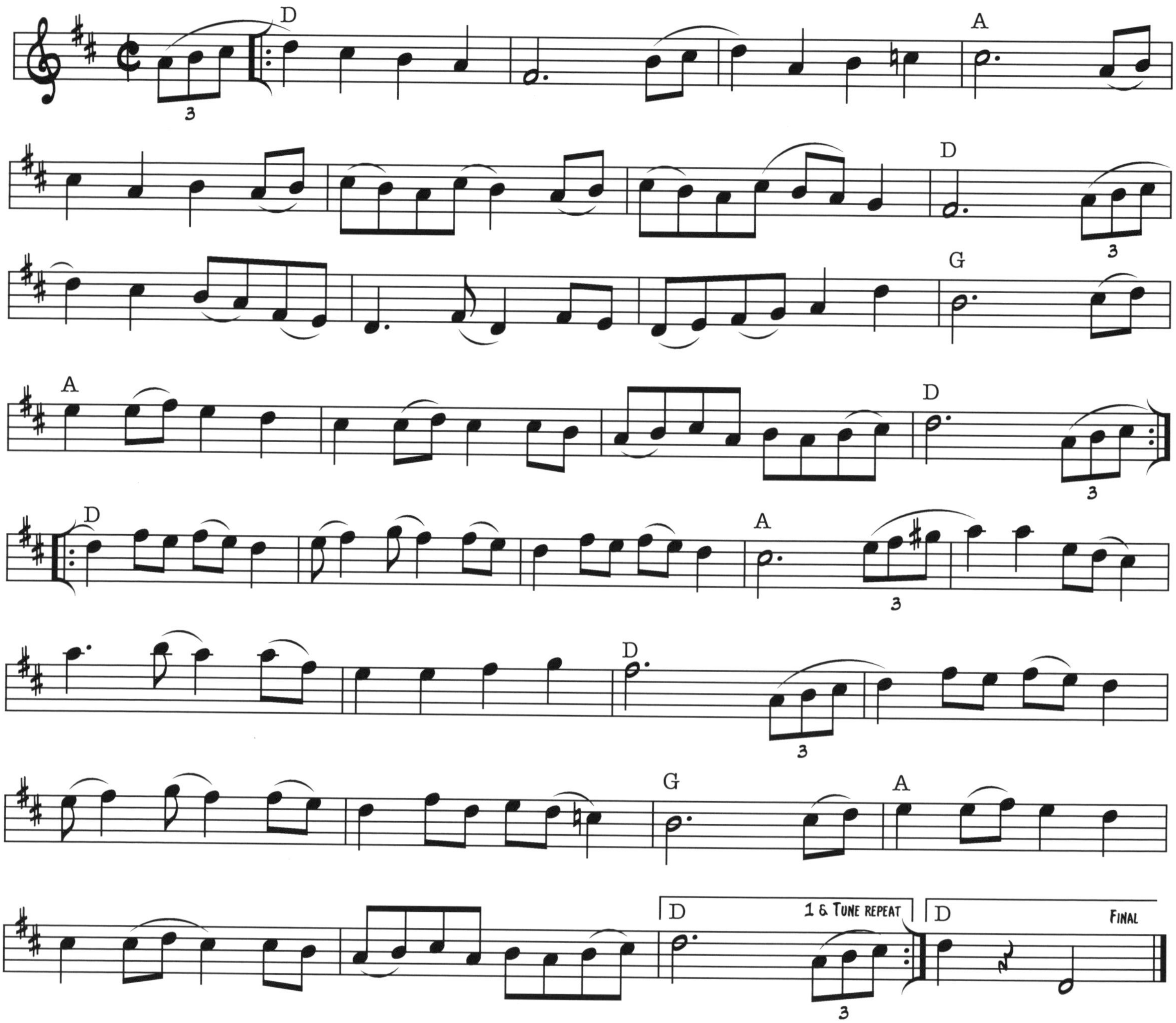

Climbing the Golden Stairs

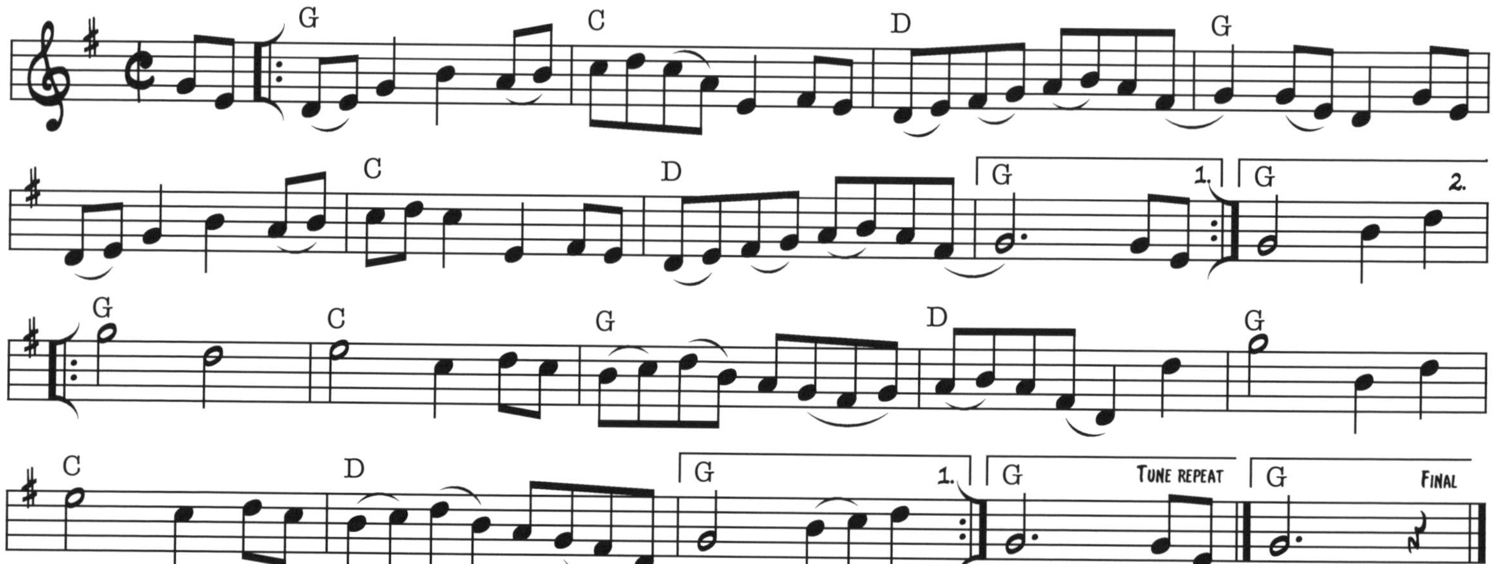

Chinquapin Hunting (in A)

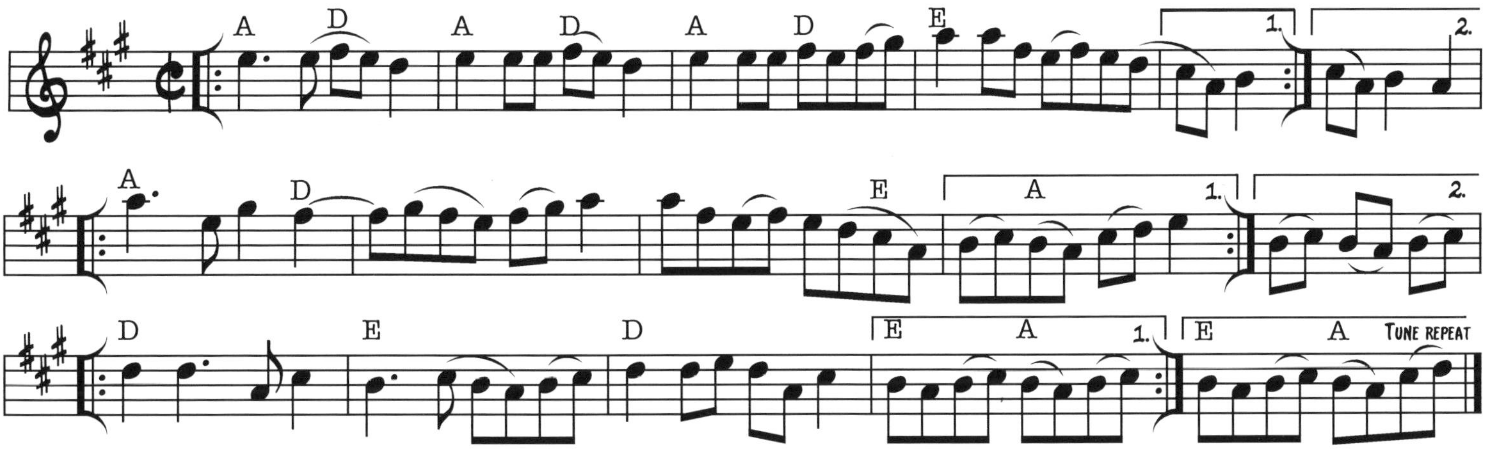

To end the tune, just use the FIRST ending of the last line then add a half note open A note afer the last measure.

Chinquapin Hunting (in D - Stamper)

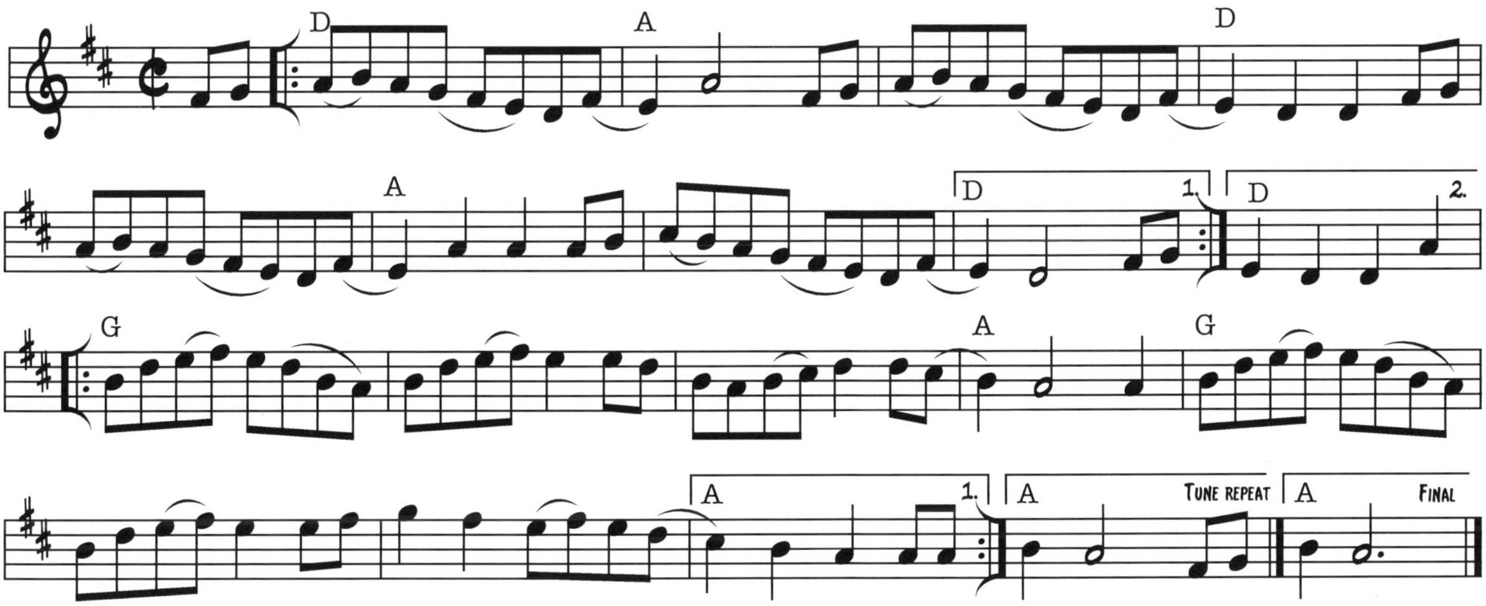

Coast Is Clear

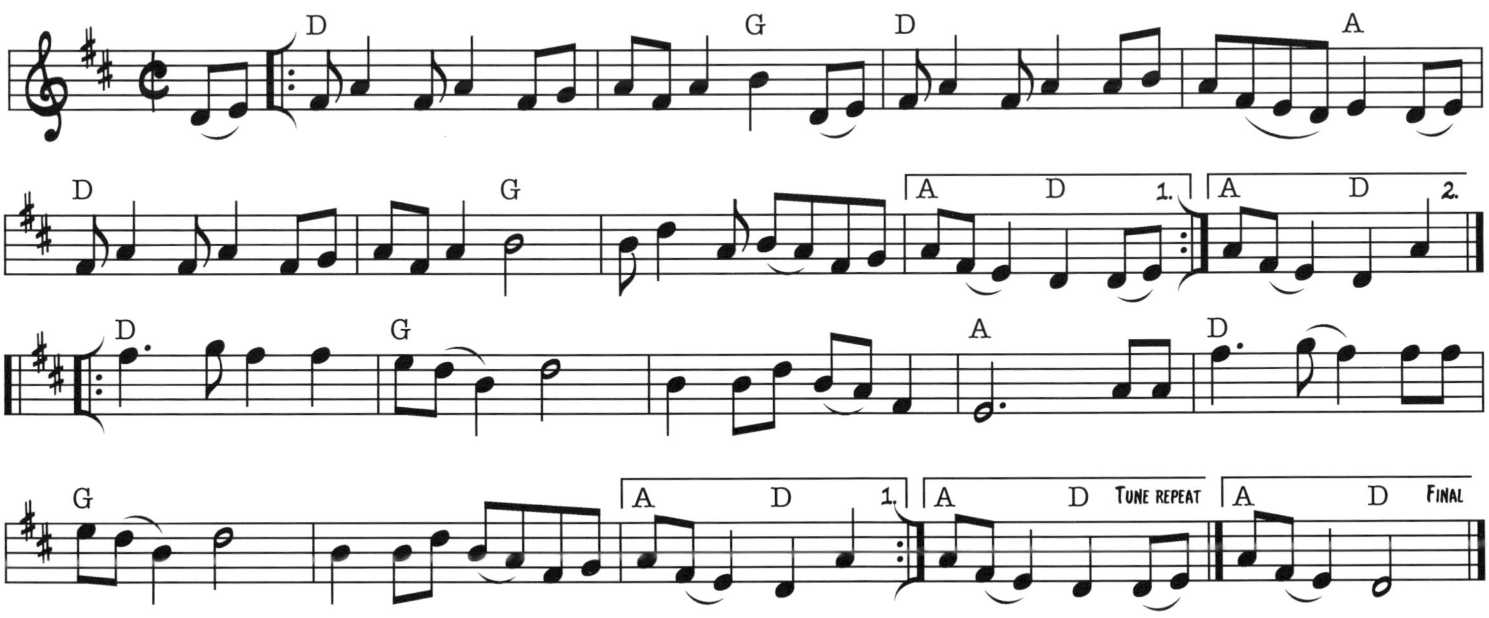

Cluck Old Hen

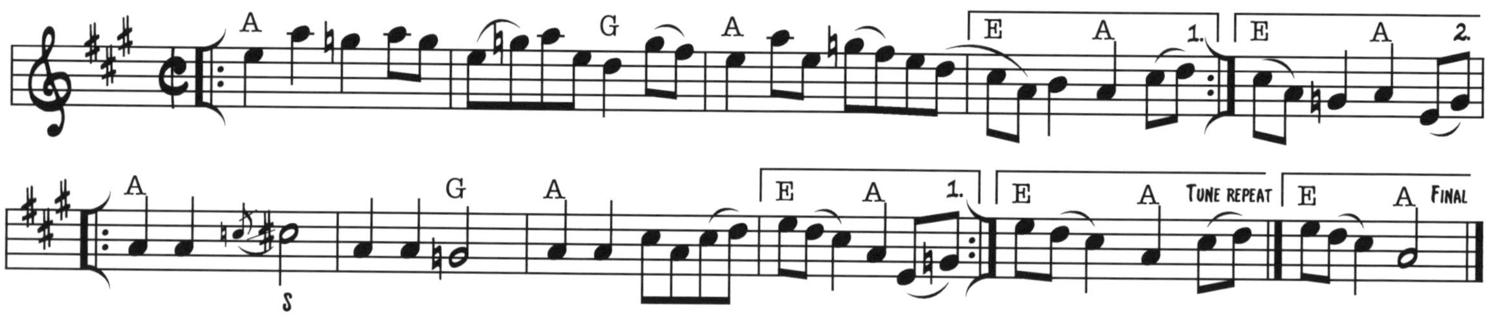

Colored Aristocracy

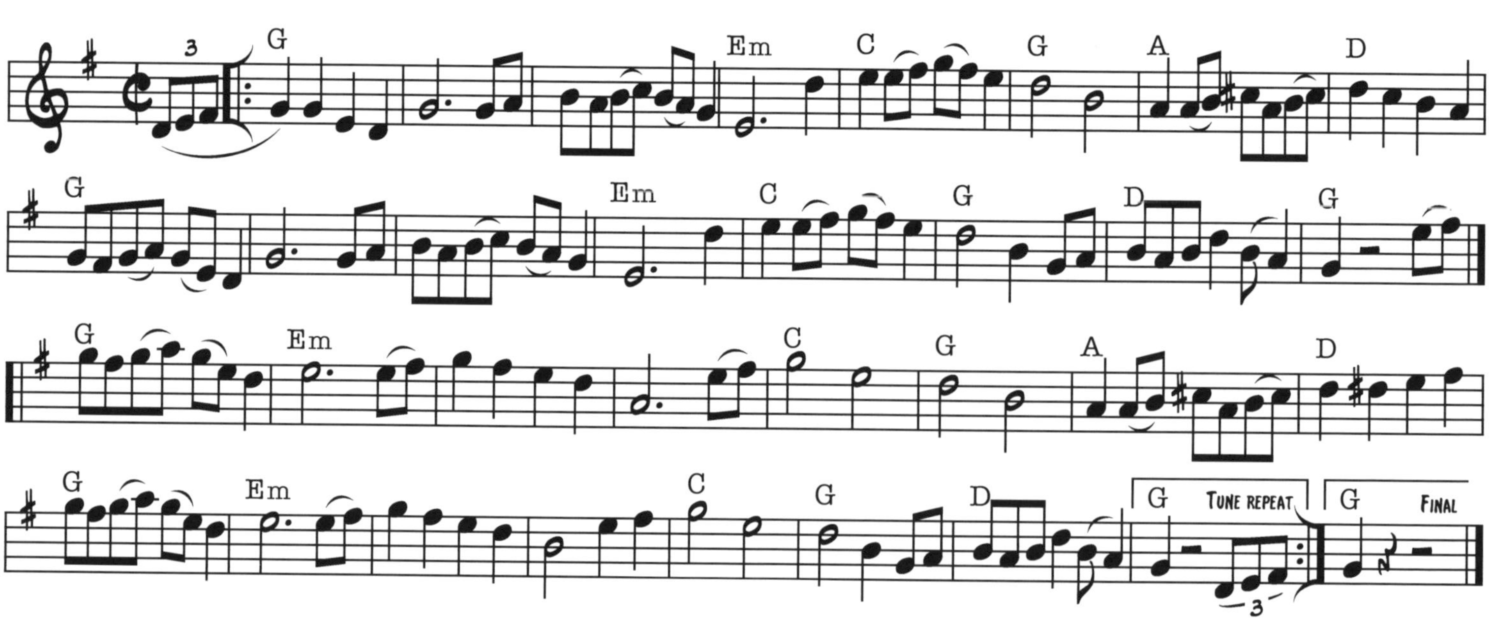

Cookhouse Joe

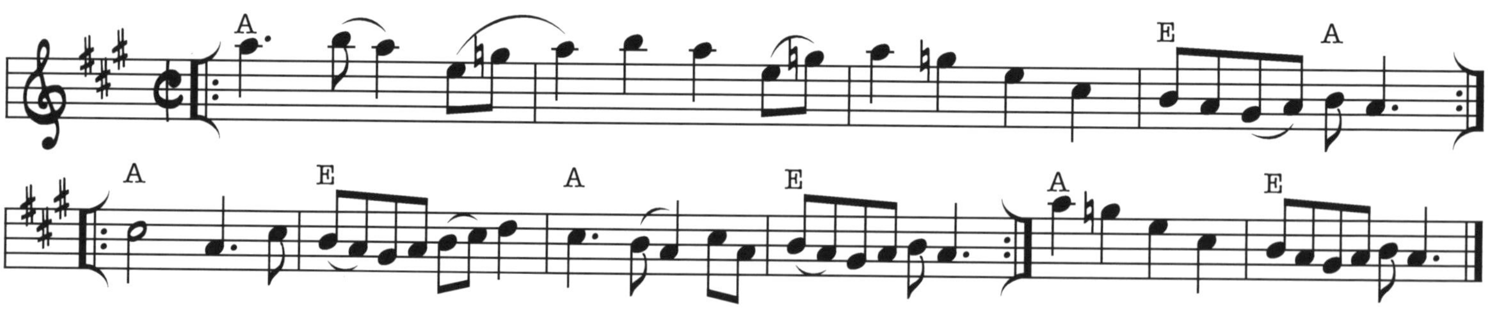

Crow Little Rooster

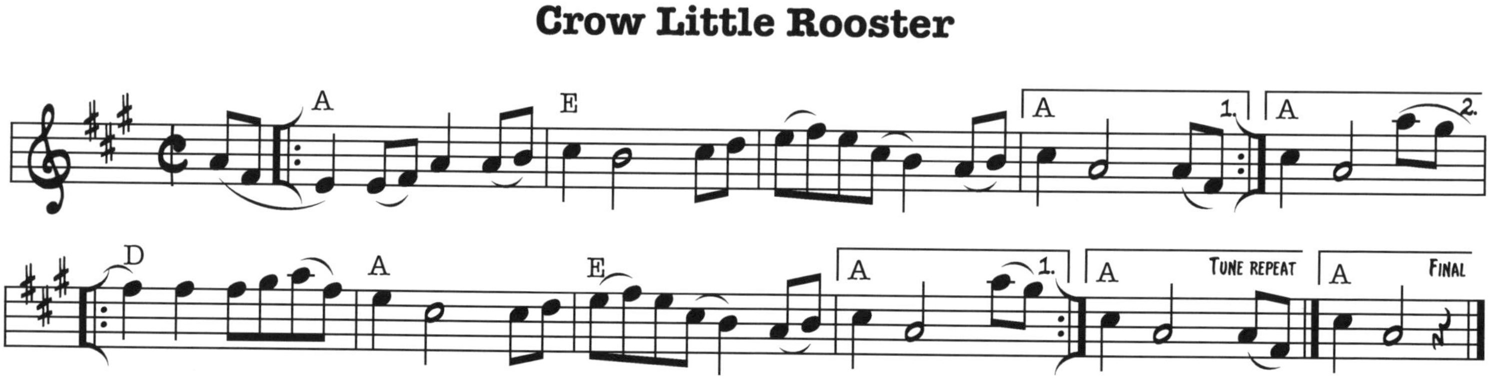

Crook Brothers Breakdown

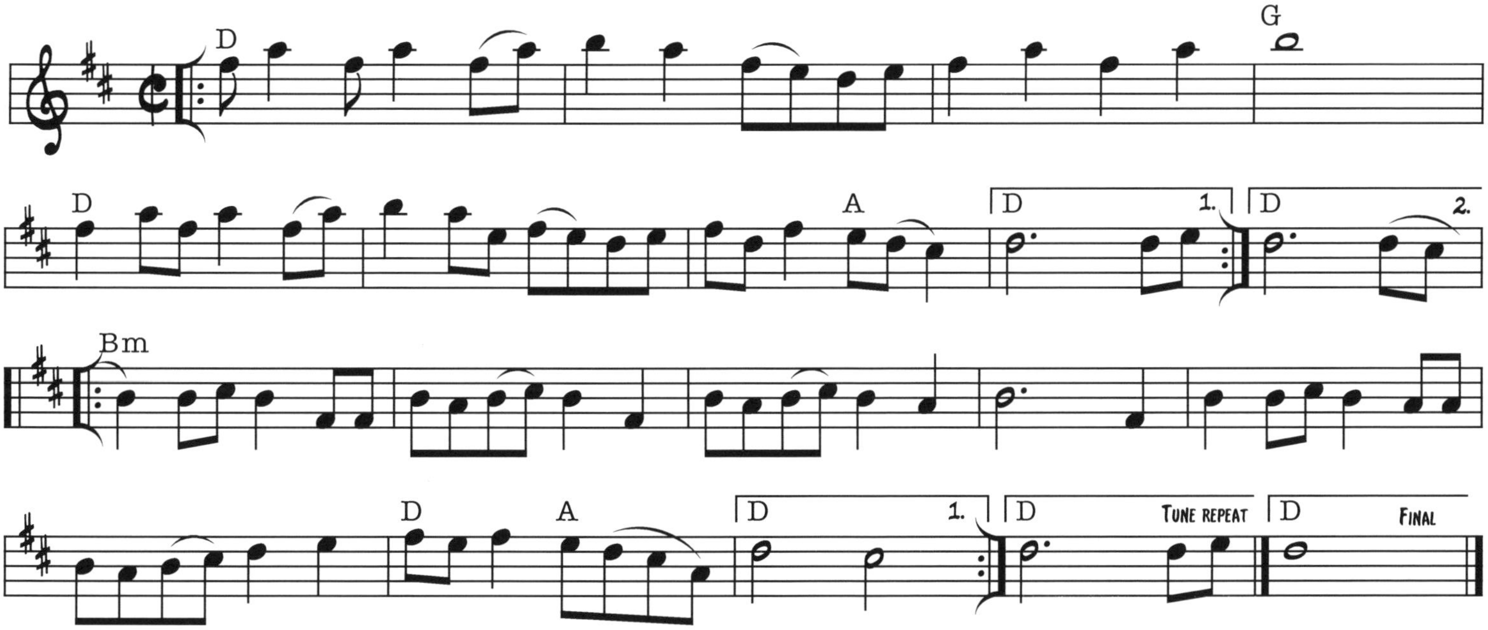

Crow Creek

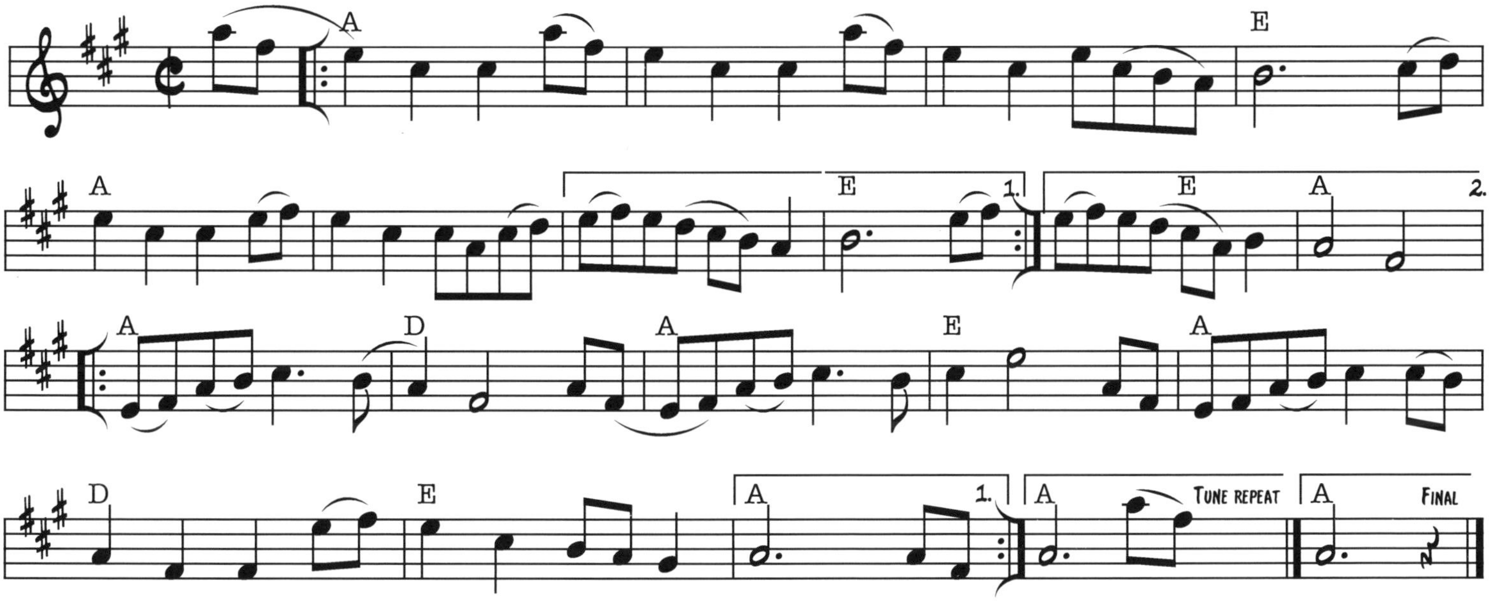

Cuffy

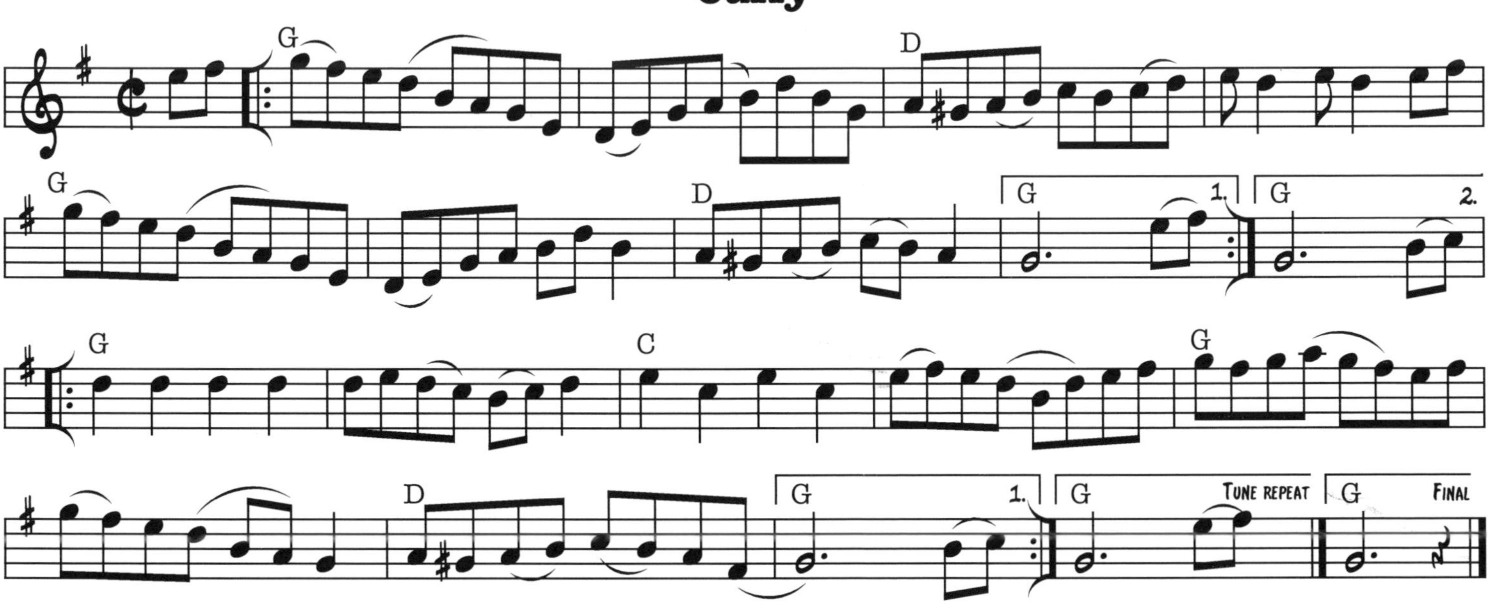

Cuckoo's Nest in D

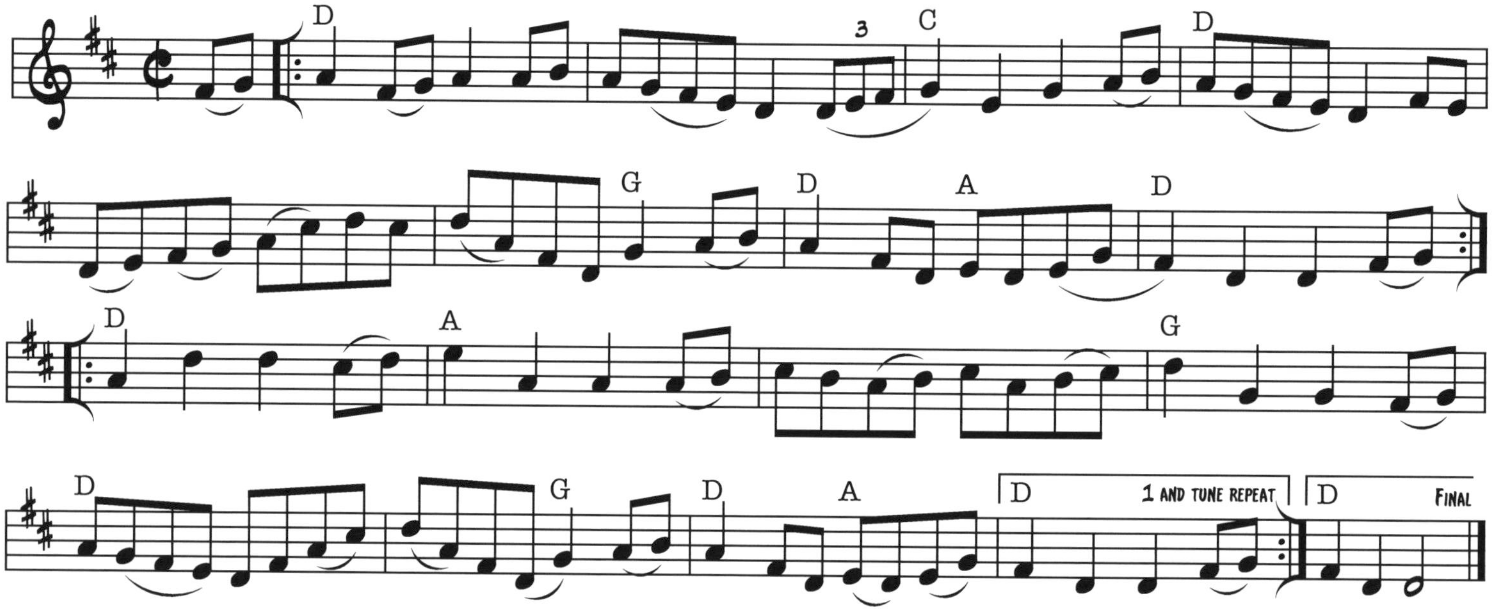

Cuckoo's Nest 2 in A (aka Richmond)

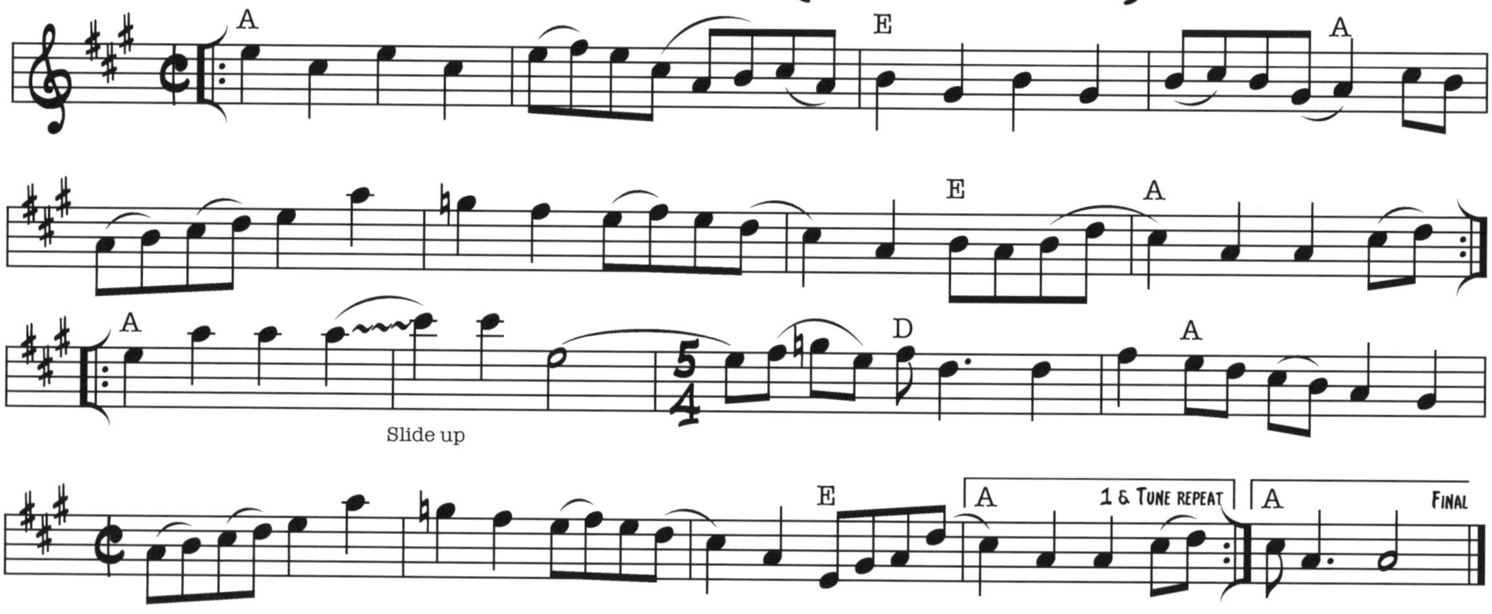

Dance All Night with a Bottle in My Hand

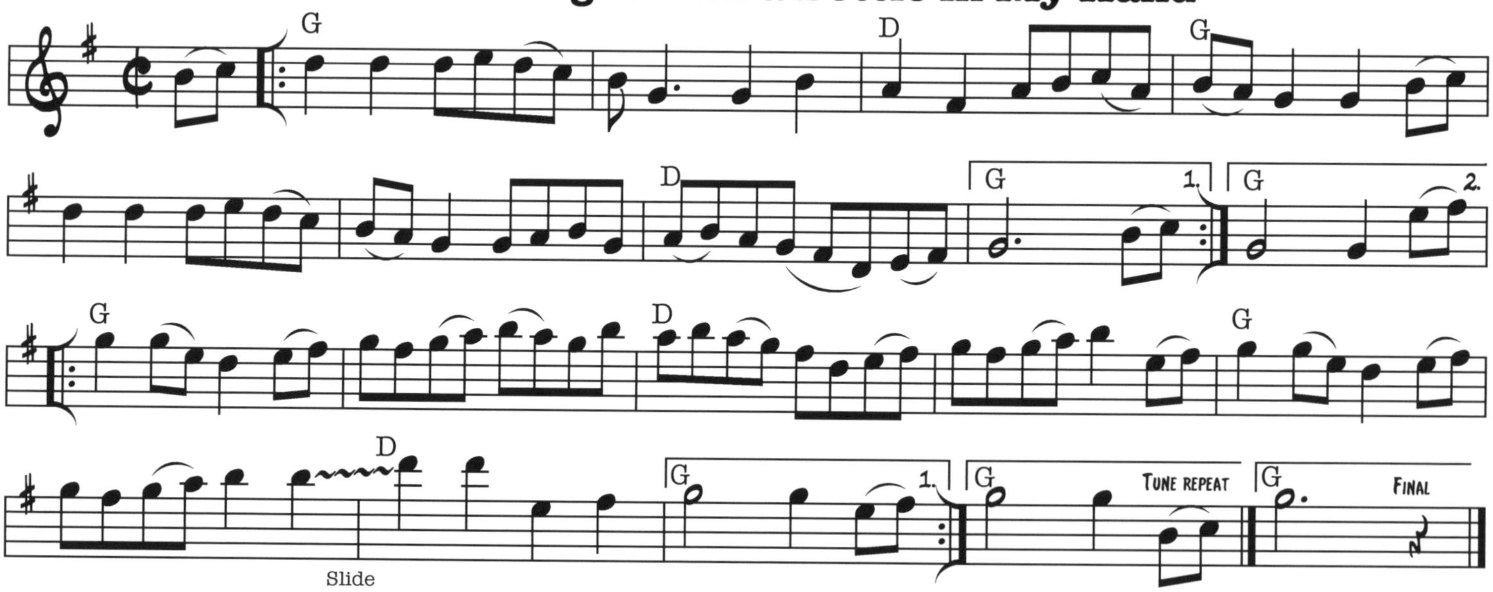

Devil Eat the Groundhog

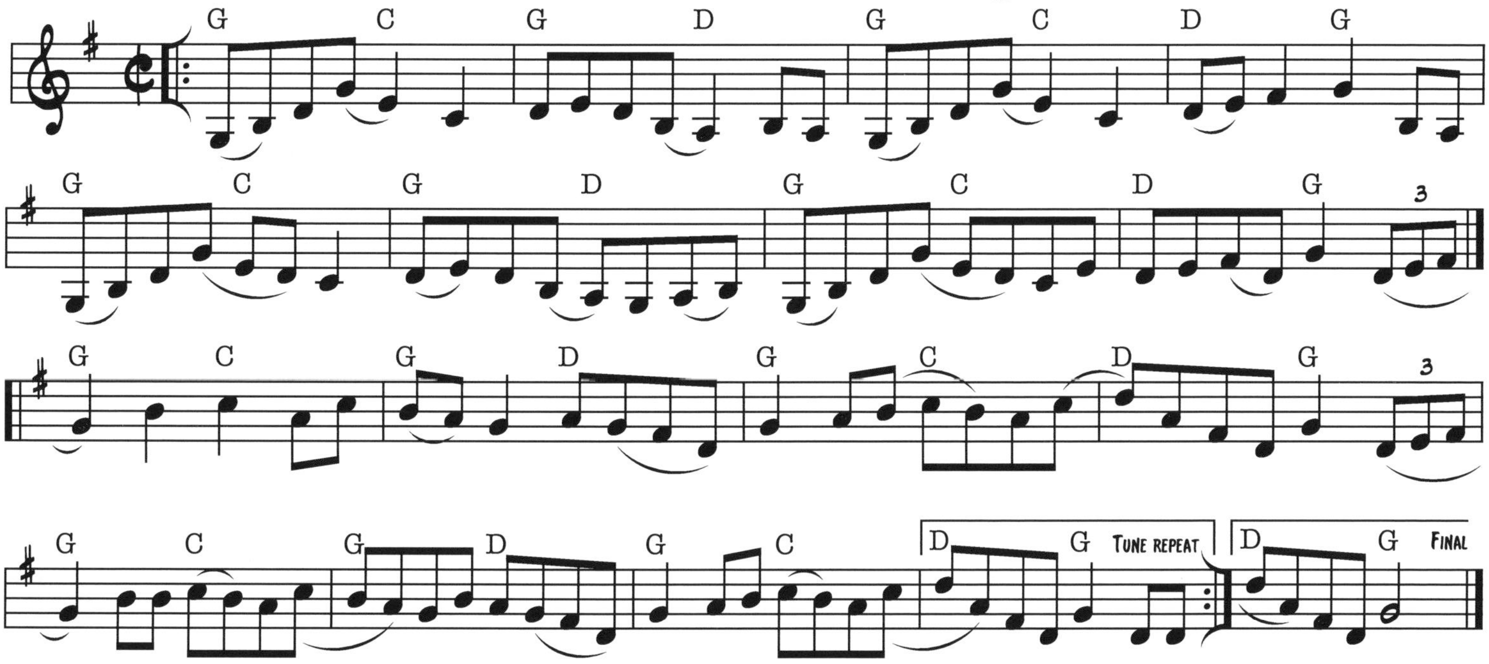

Dinah

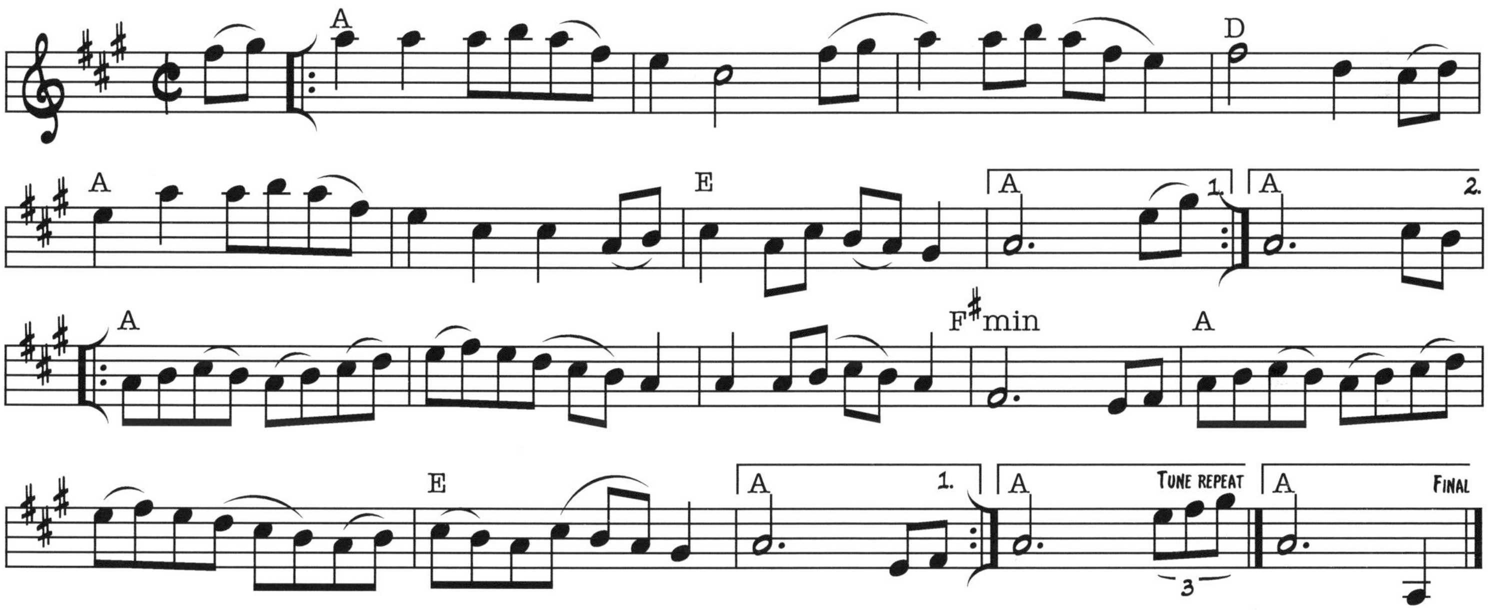

Doctor, Doctor

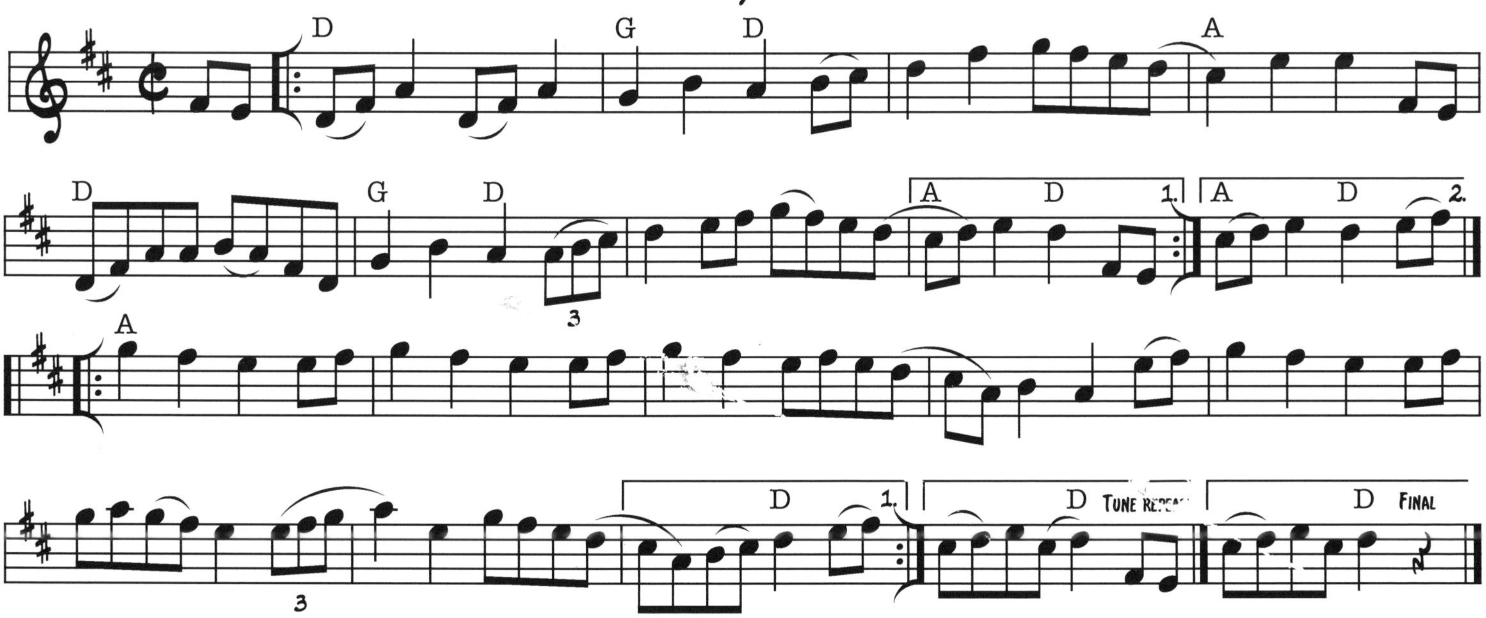

Dogs in the Dishes

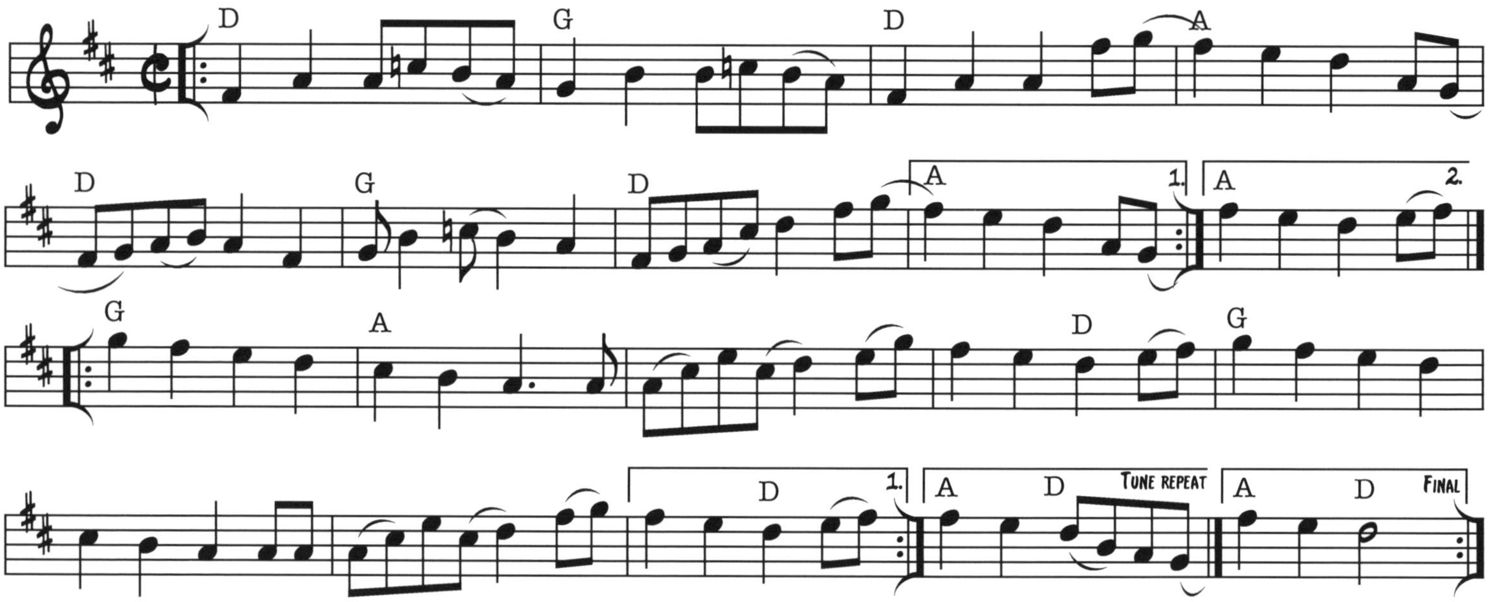

Double File

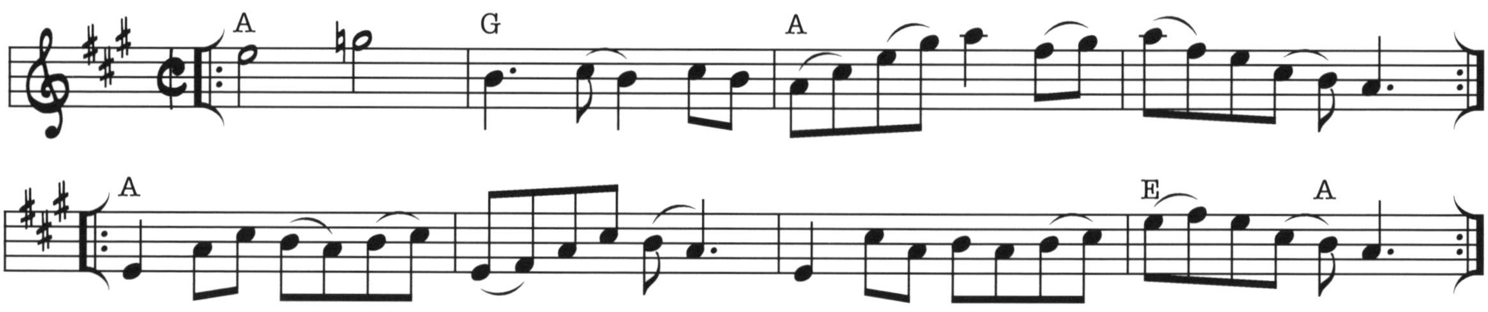

Dry and Dusty

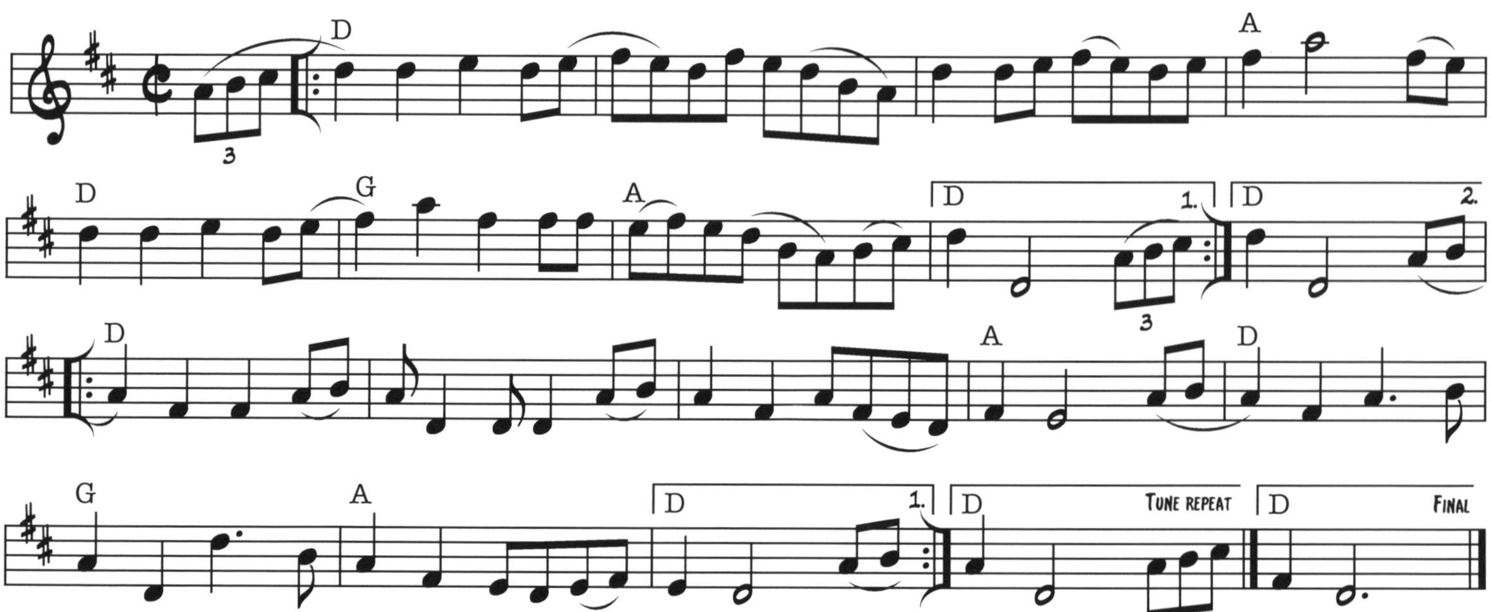

Drunken Hiccups

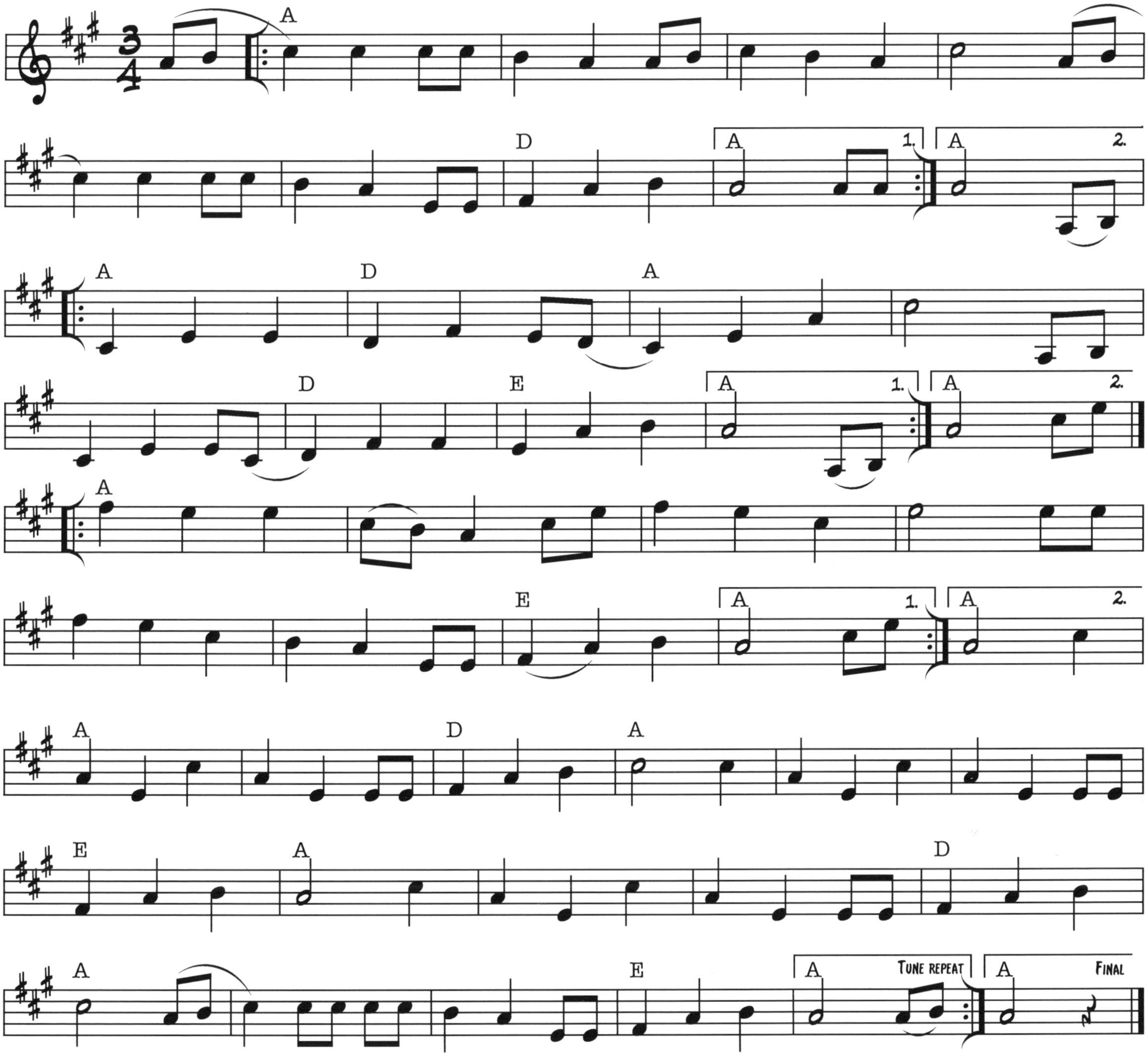

Ducks on the Mill Pond

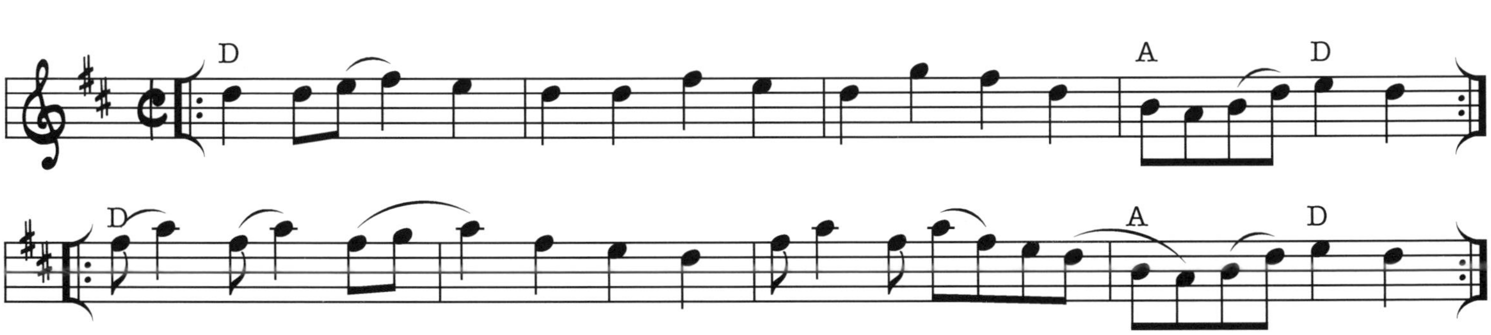

Dubuque

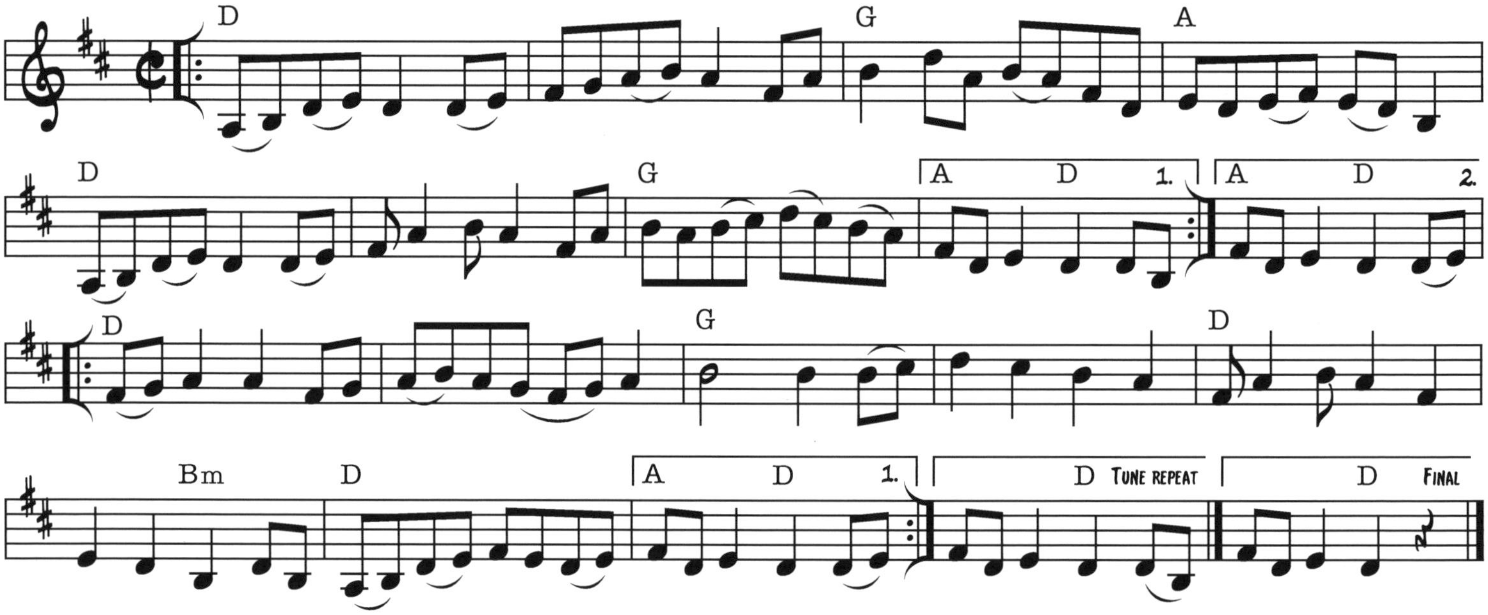

Duck River

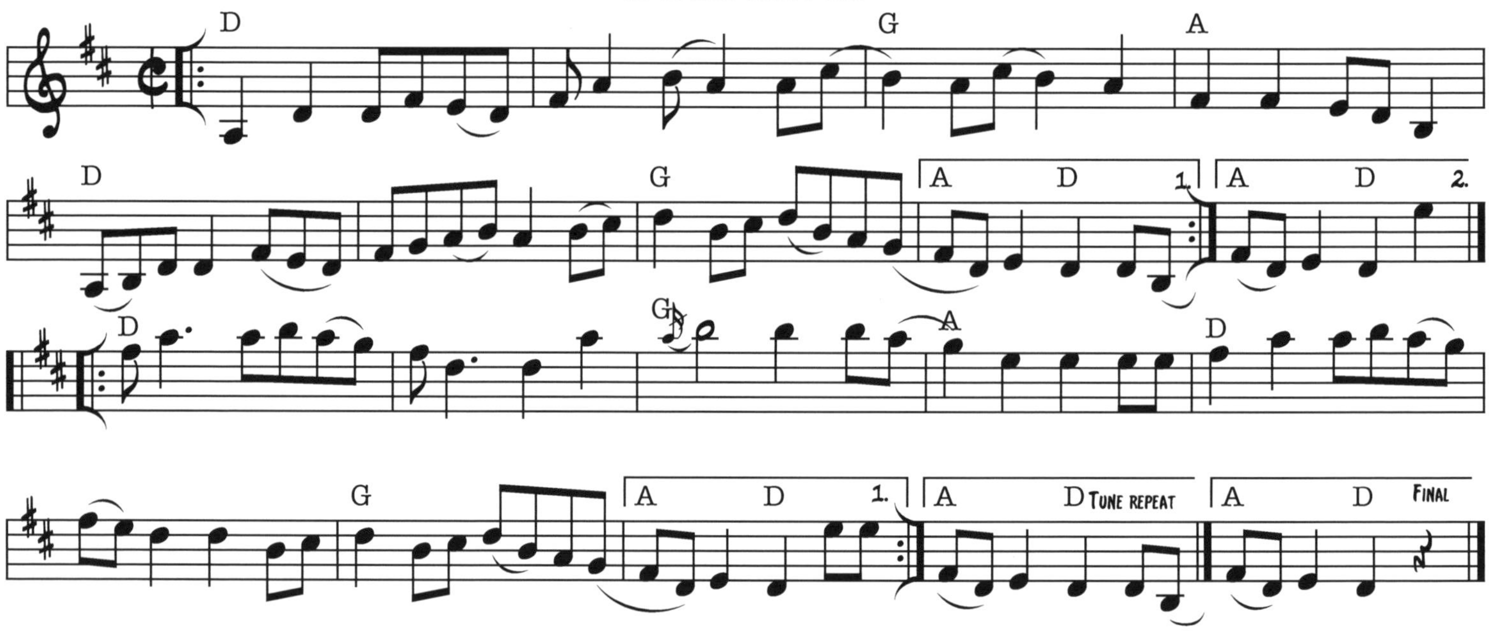

Ducks in the Pond

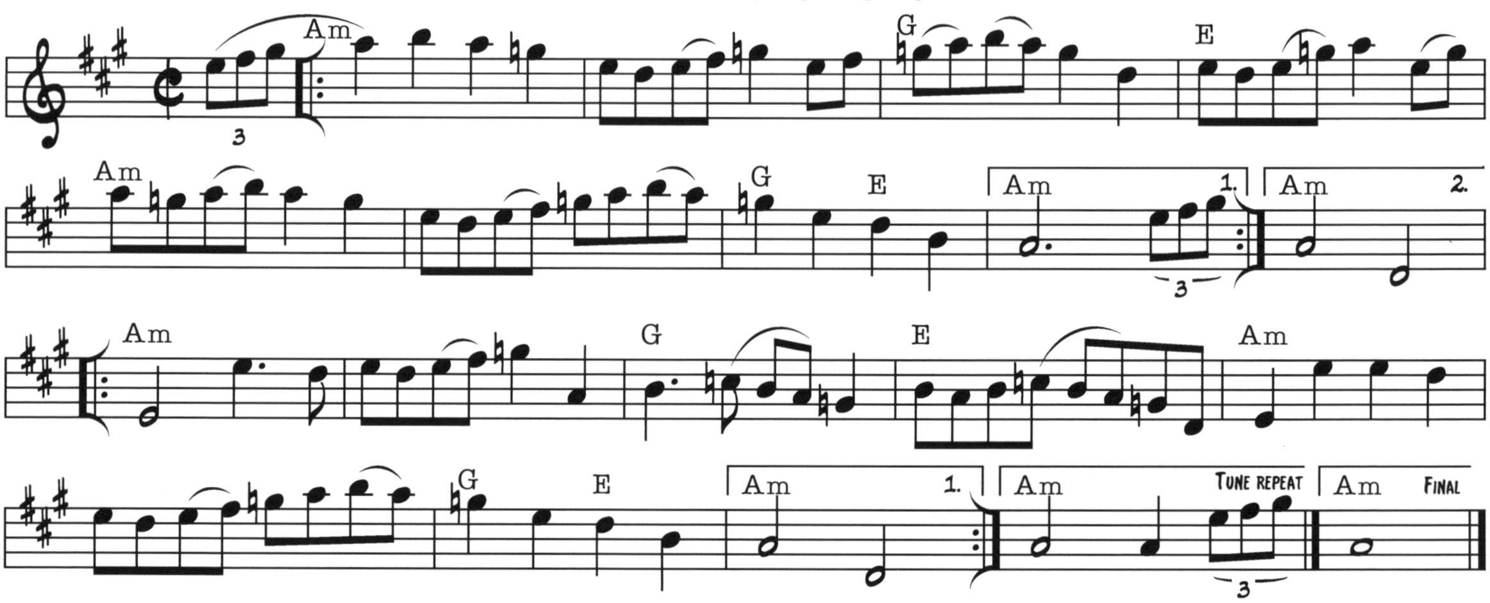

Duke of Kent's Waltz

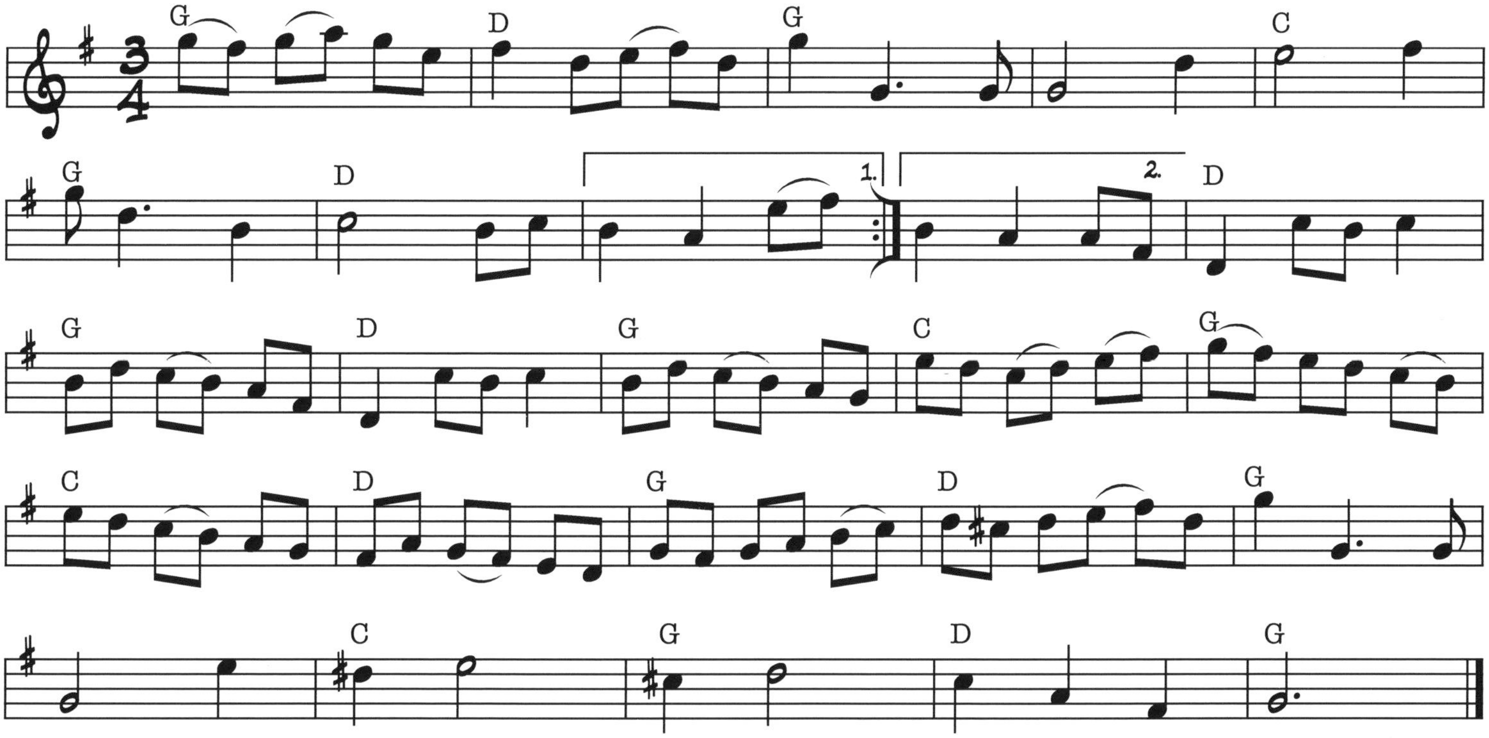

(Mr.) Fishar's Hornpipe (aka Fisher's Hornpipe)

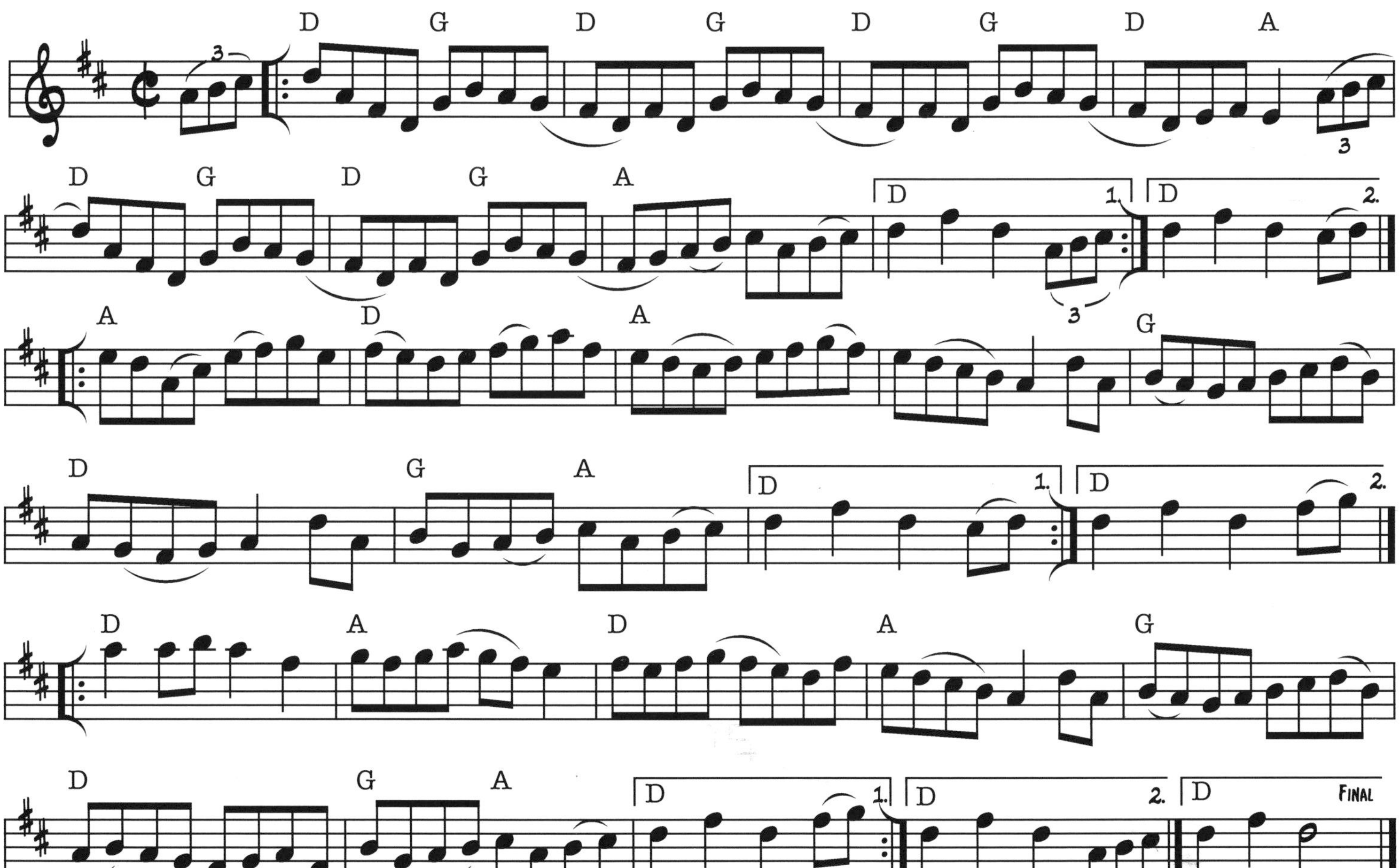

Durang's Hornpipe

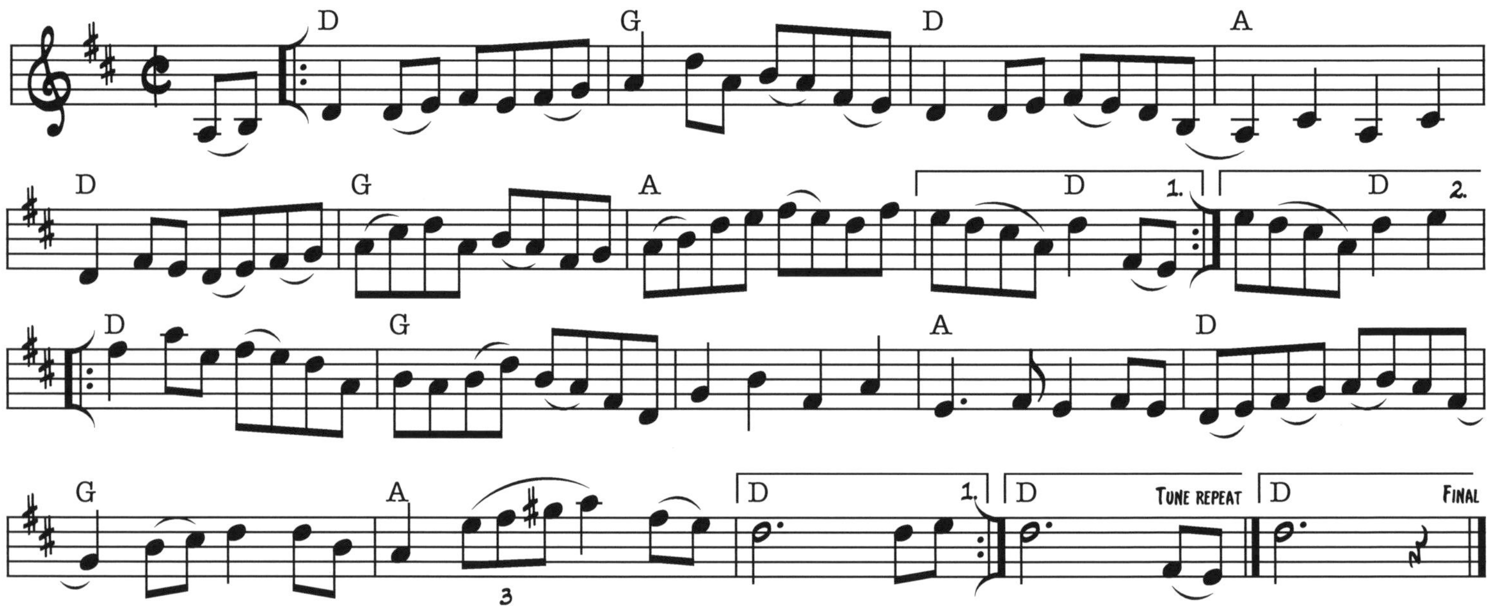

Dusty Miller

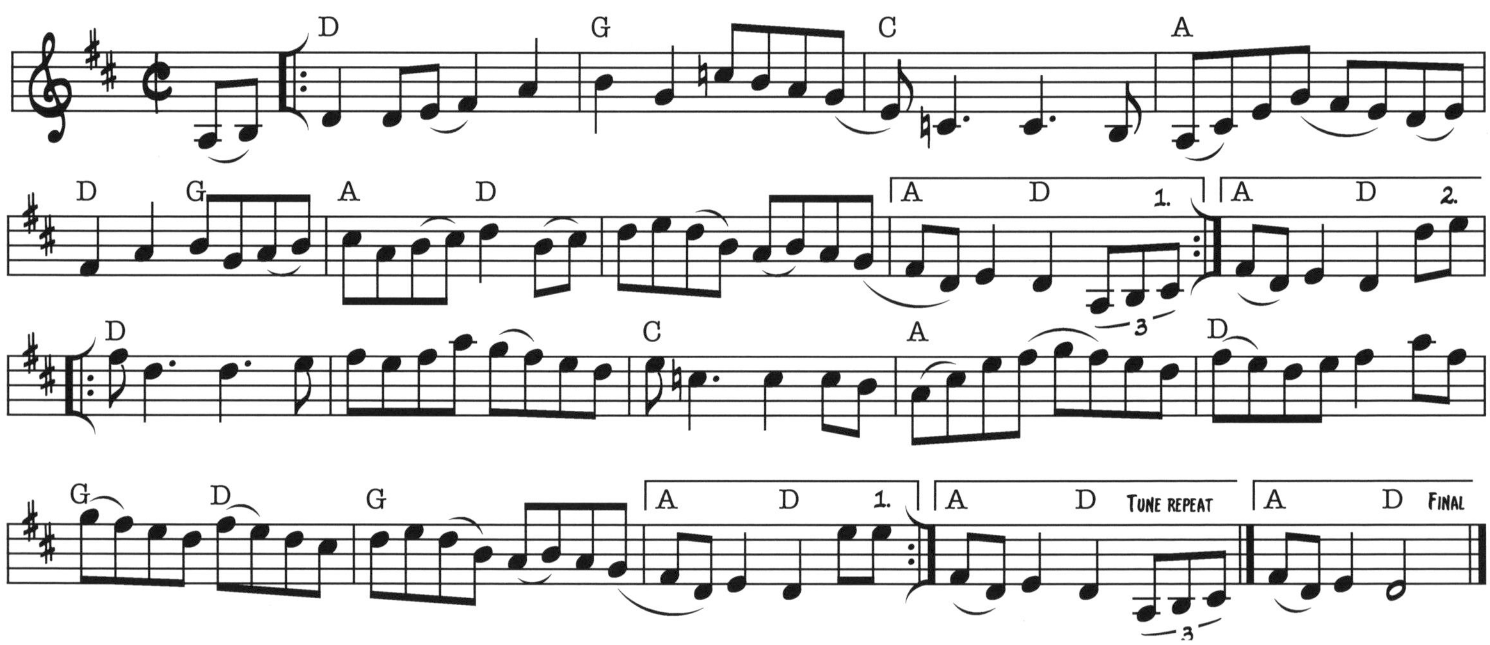

Ebenezer

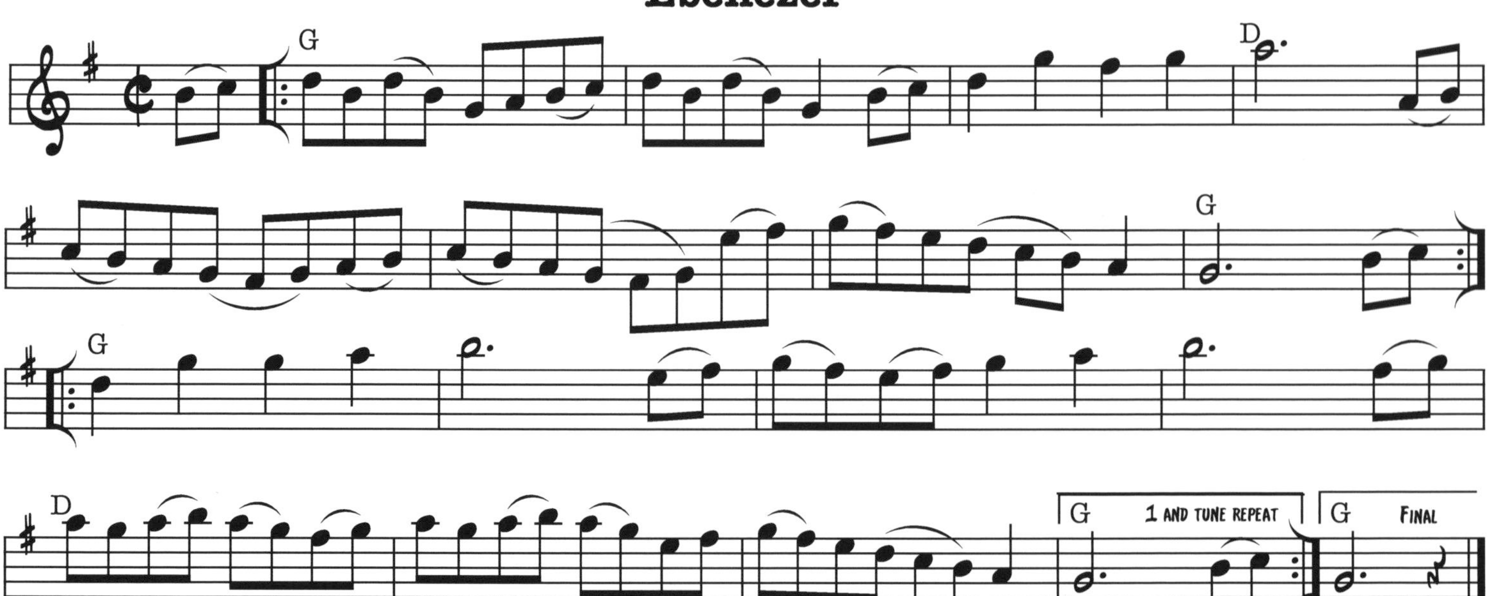

Fly Around My Pretty Little Miss (in D aka Western Country)

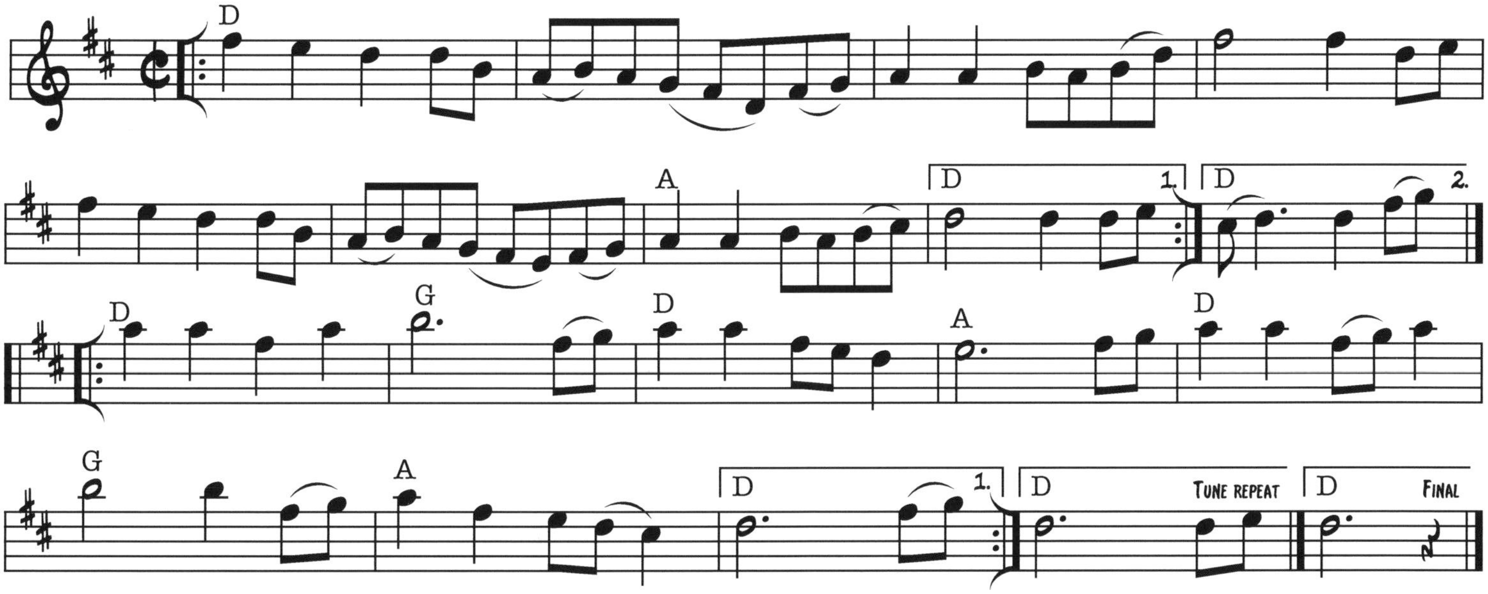

Fly Around My Pretty Little Miss (in G from The Tar Heel Rattlers)

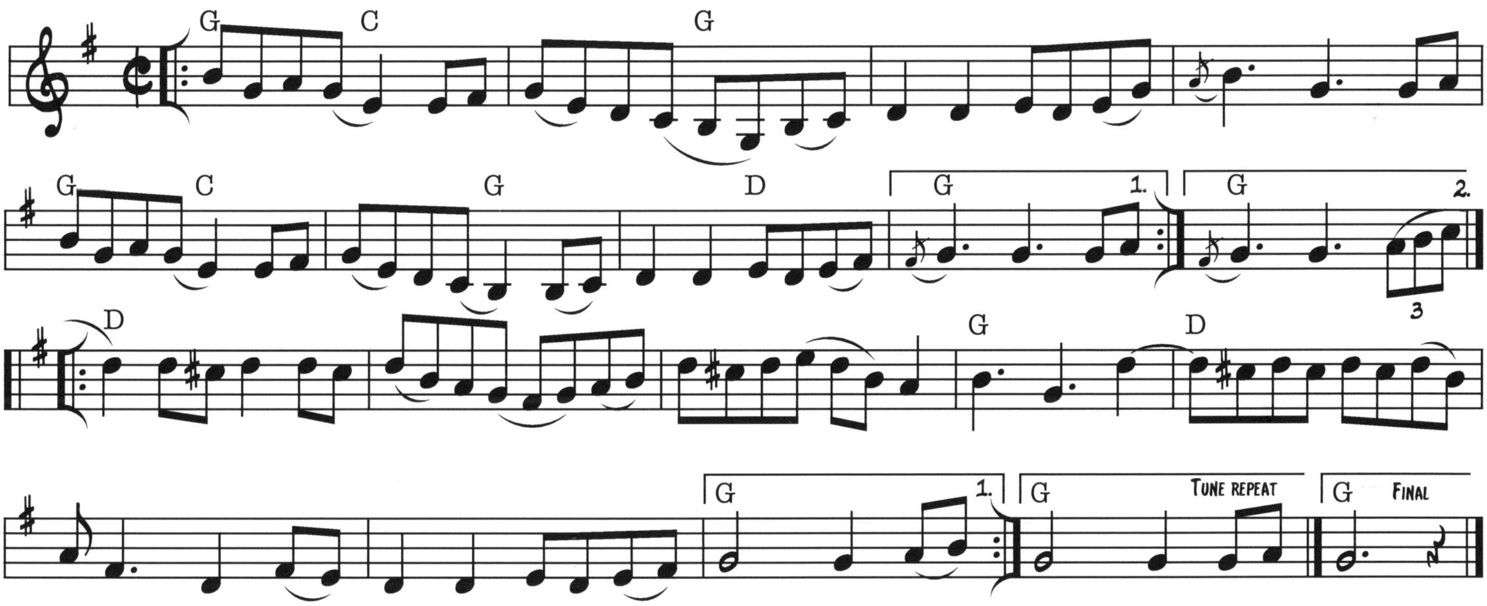

Flying Clouds (aka Flying Cloud Cotillion)

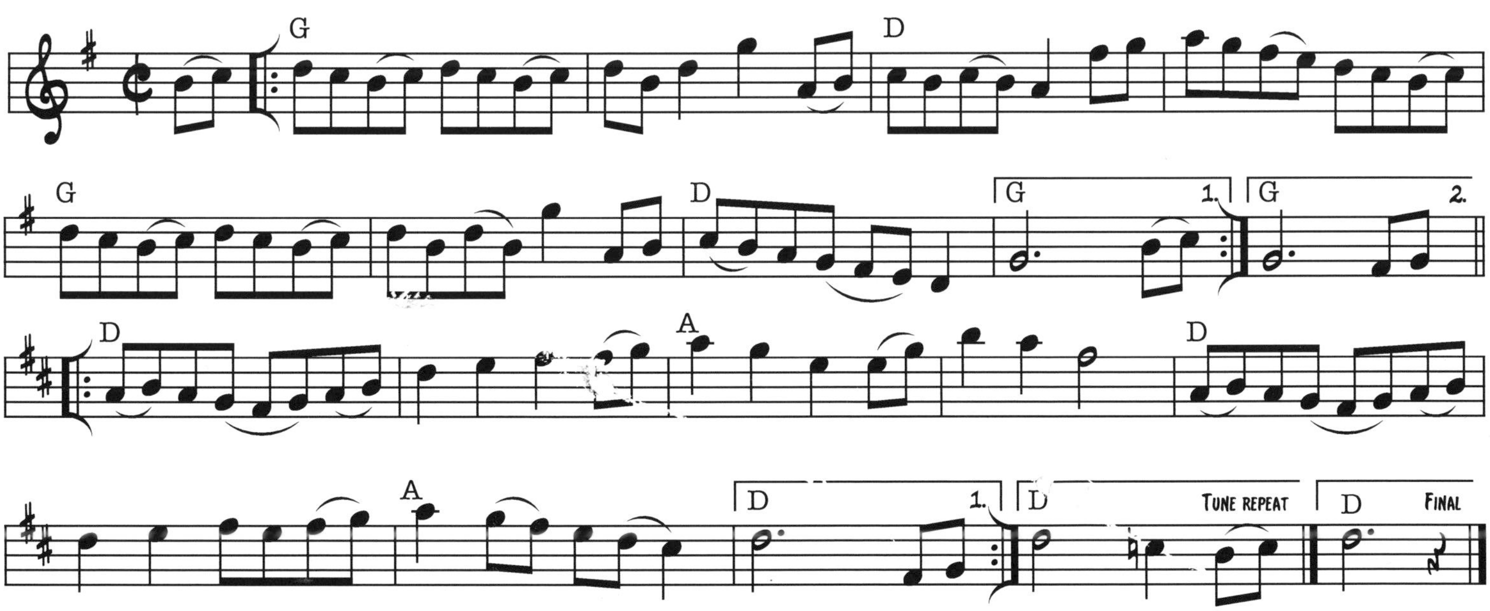

Elzic's Farewell

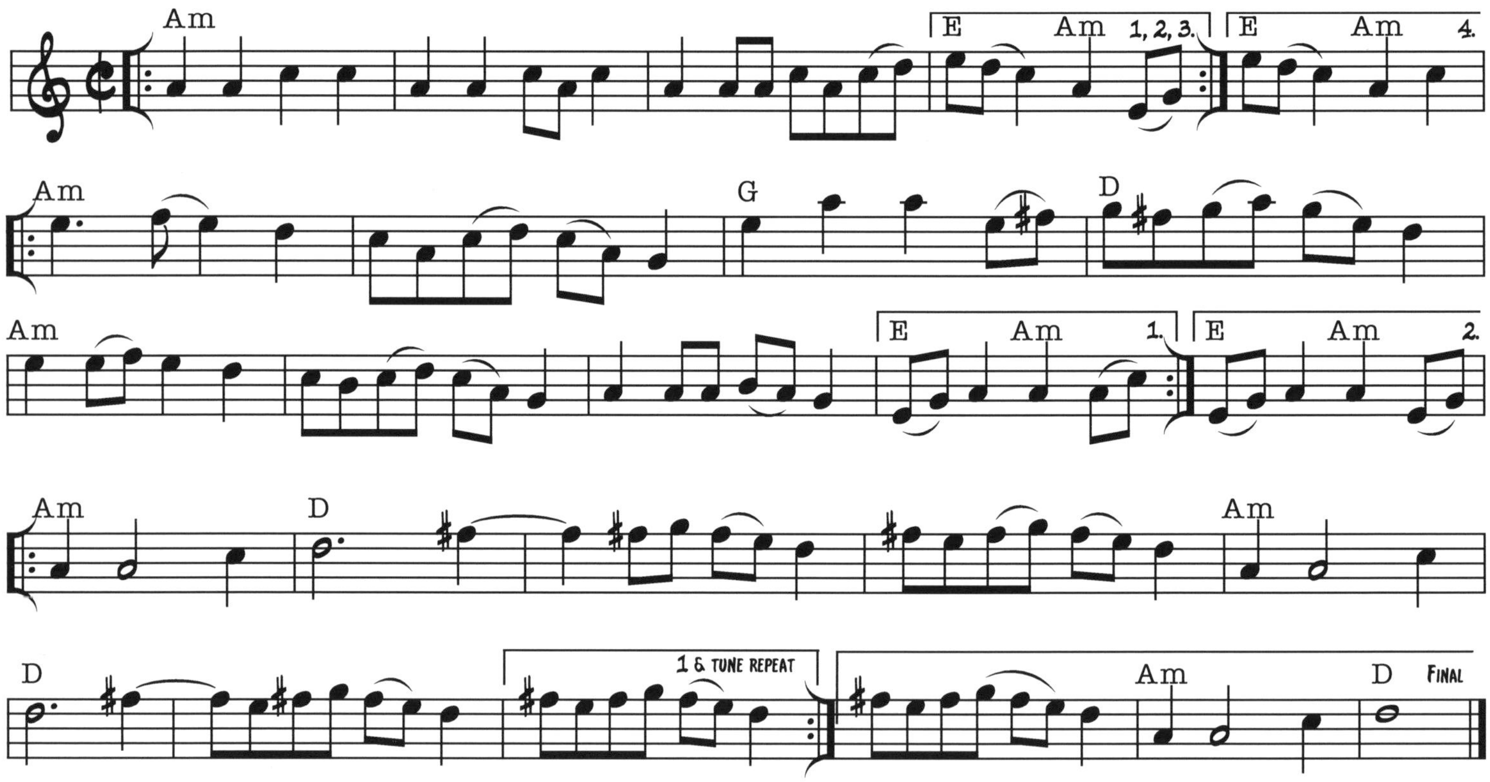

Five Miles From Town

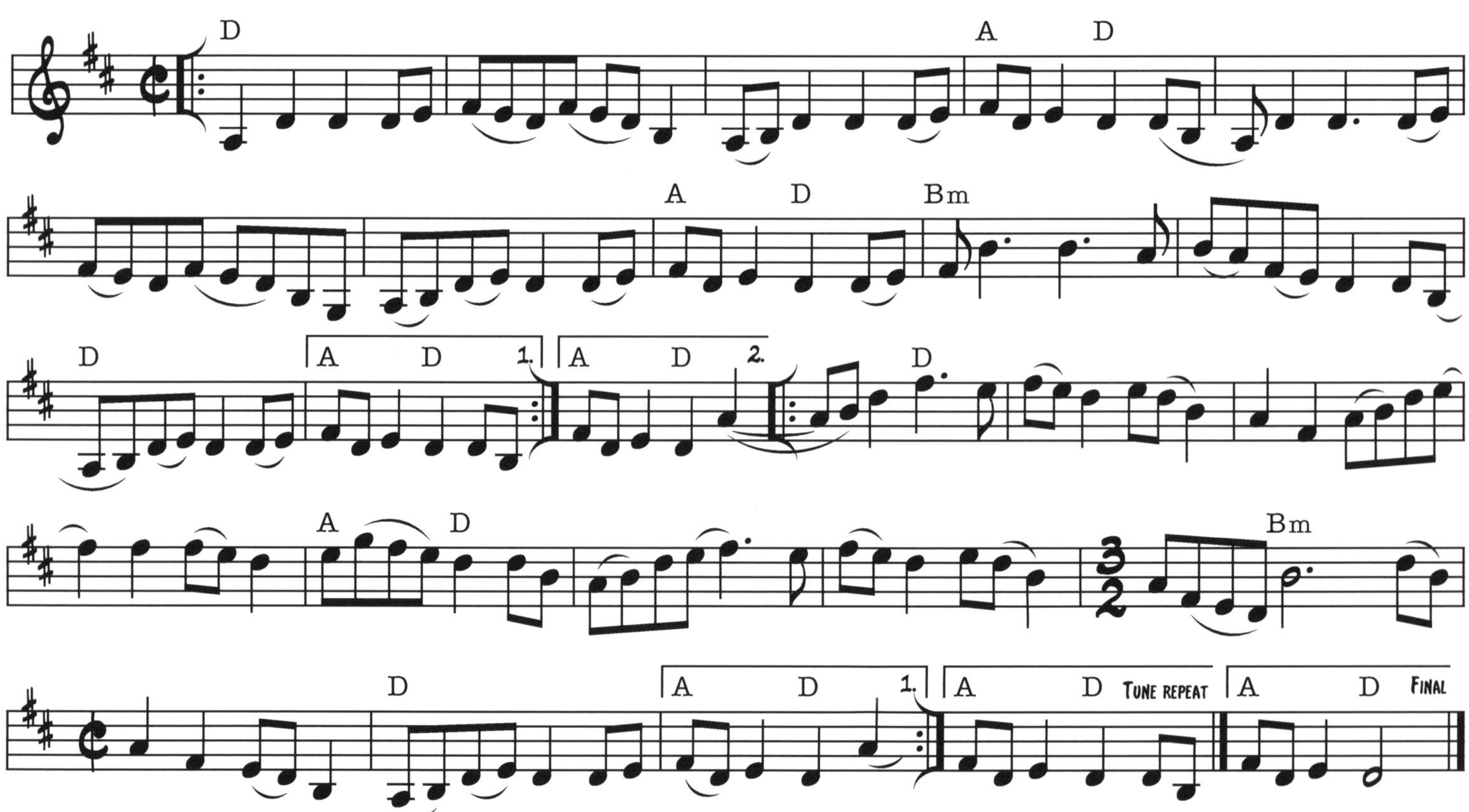

Flying Indian

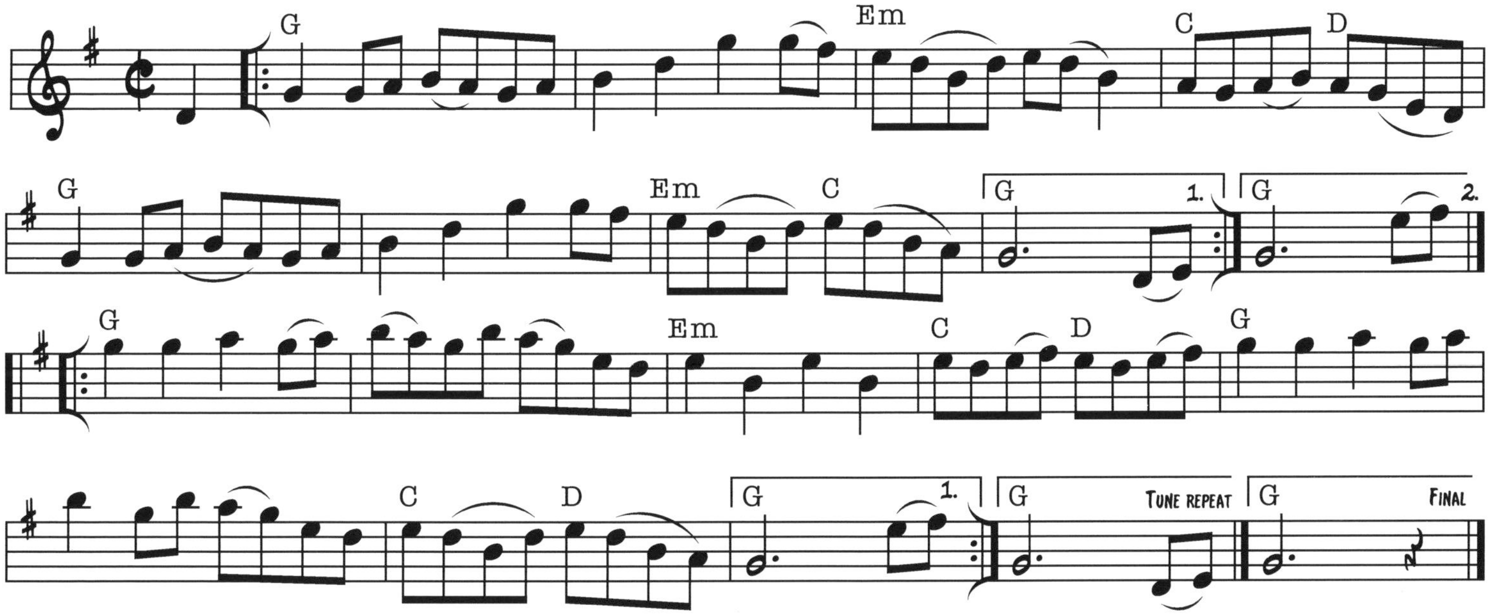

Folding Down the Sheets

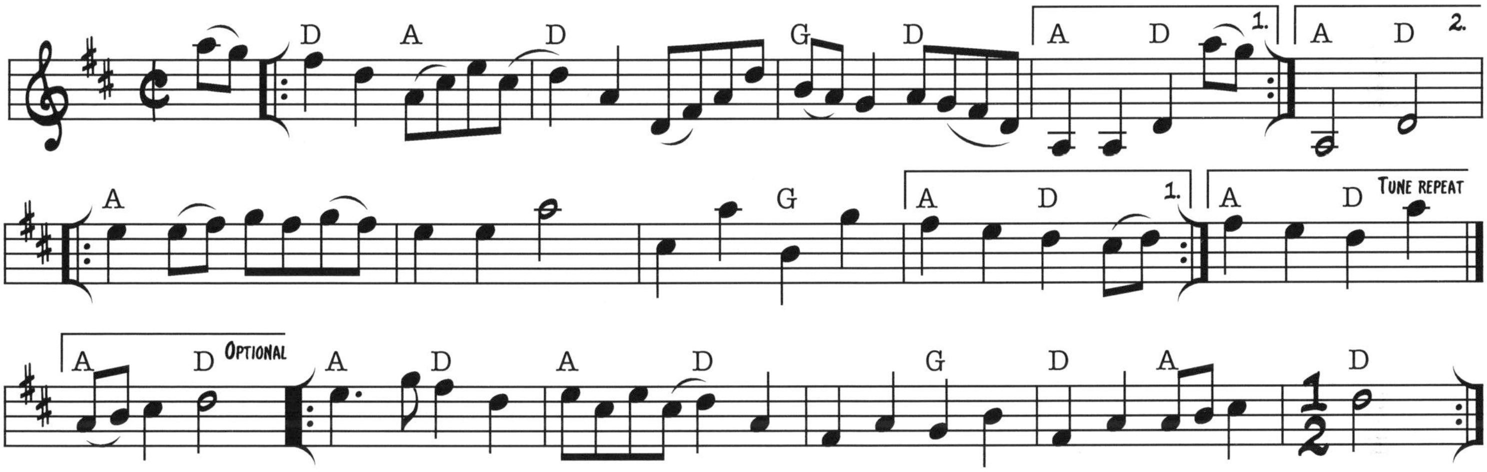

Henry Reed added the third part which he played as though it was an alternate A part. In that case you would play the parts in the following order: AABBCCBB - AABBCCBB

Forked Deer

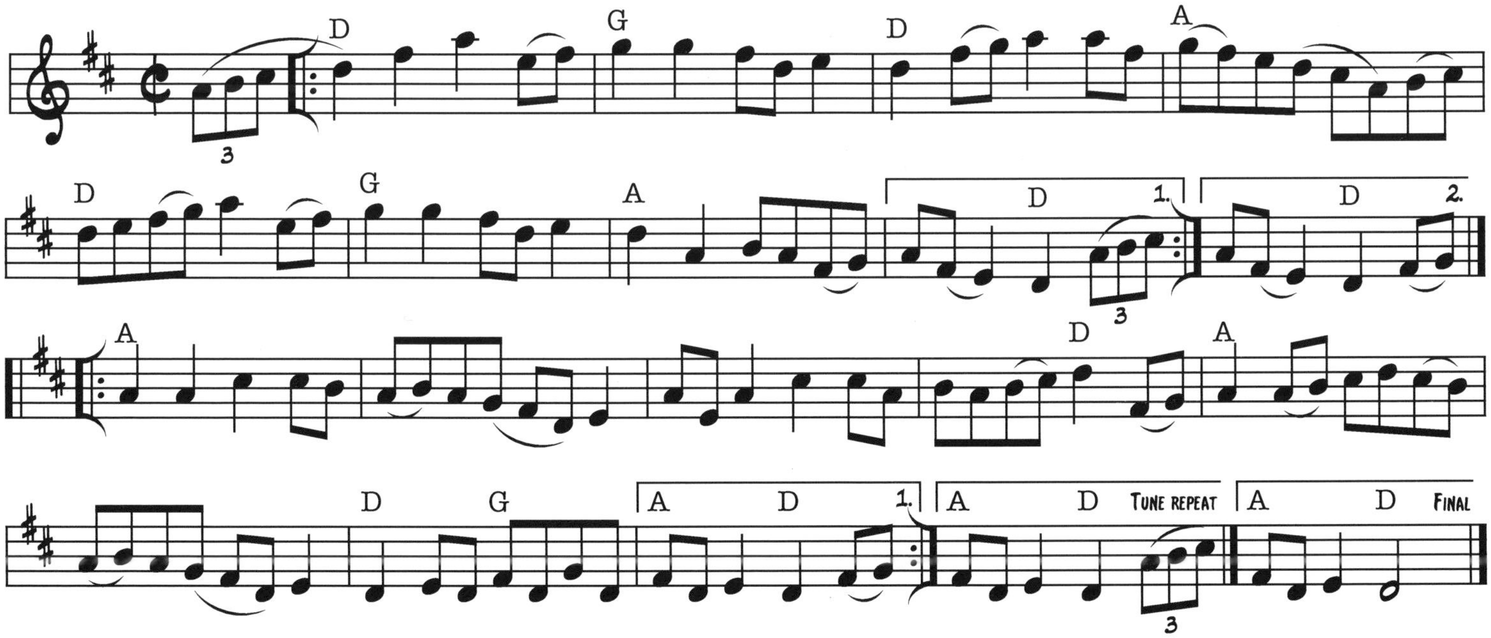

Fortune

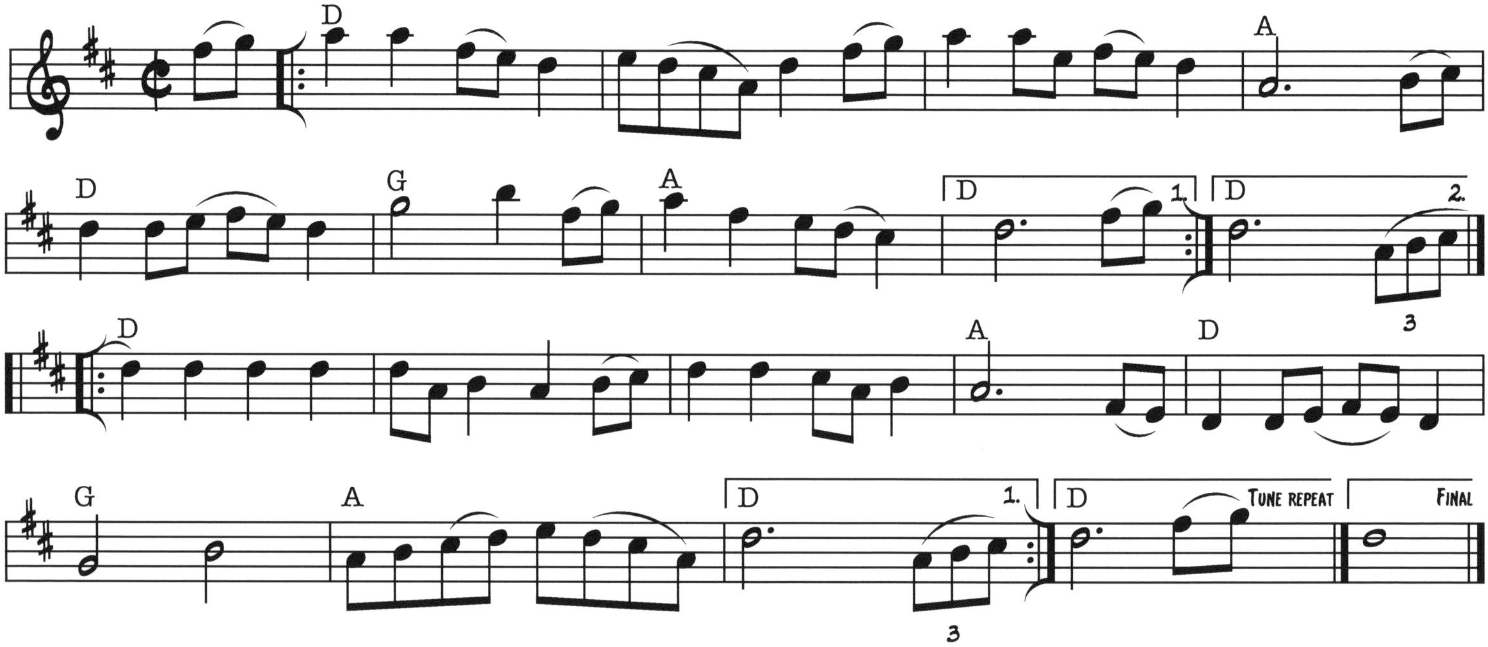

Fun's All Over

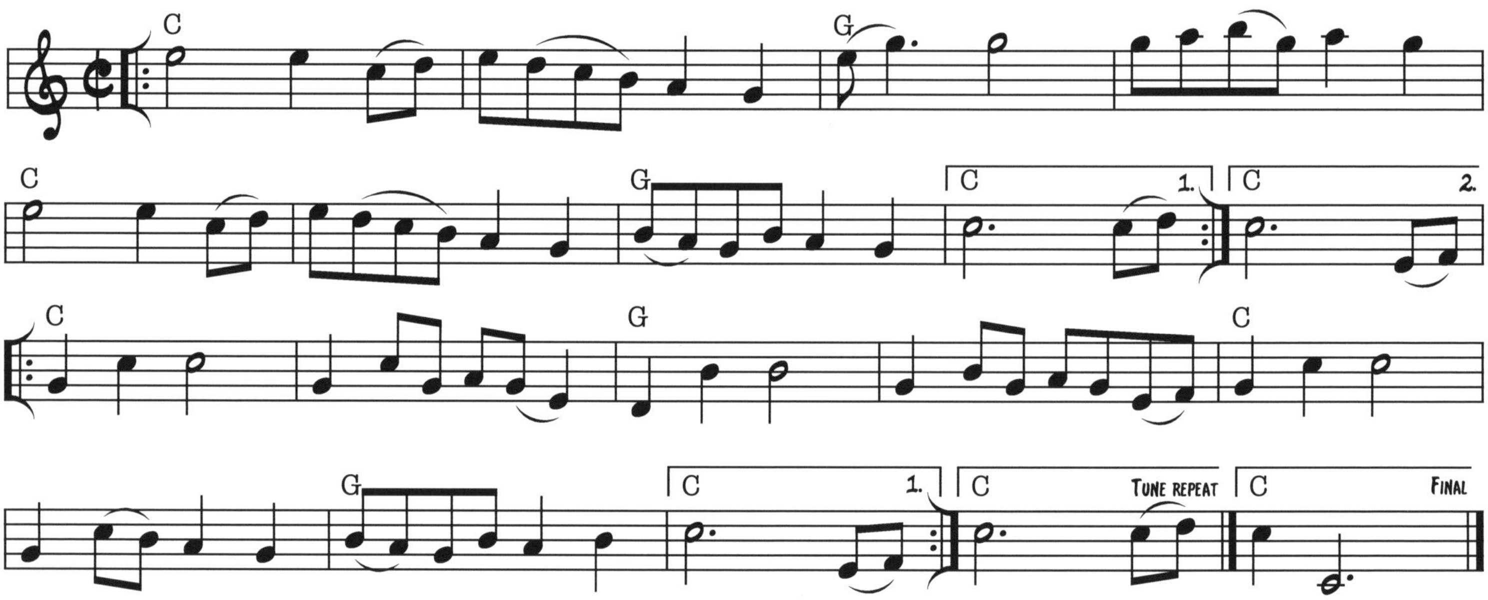

Gaston

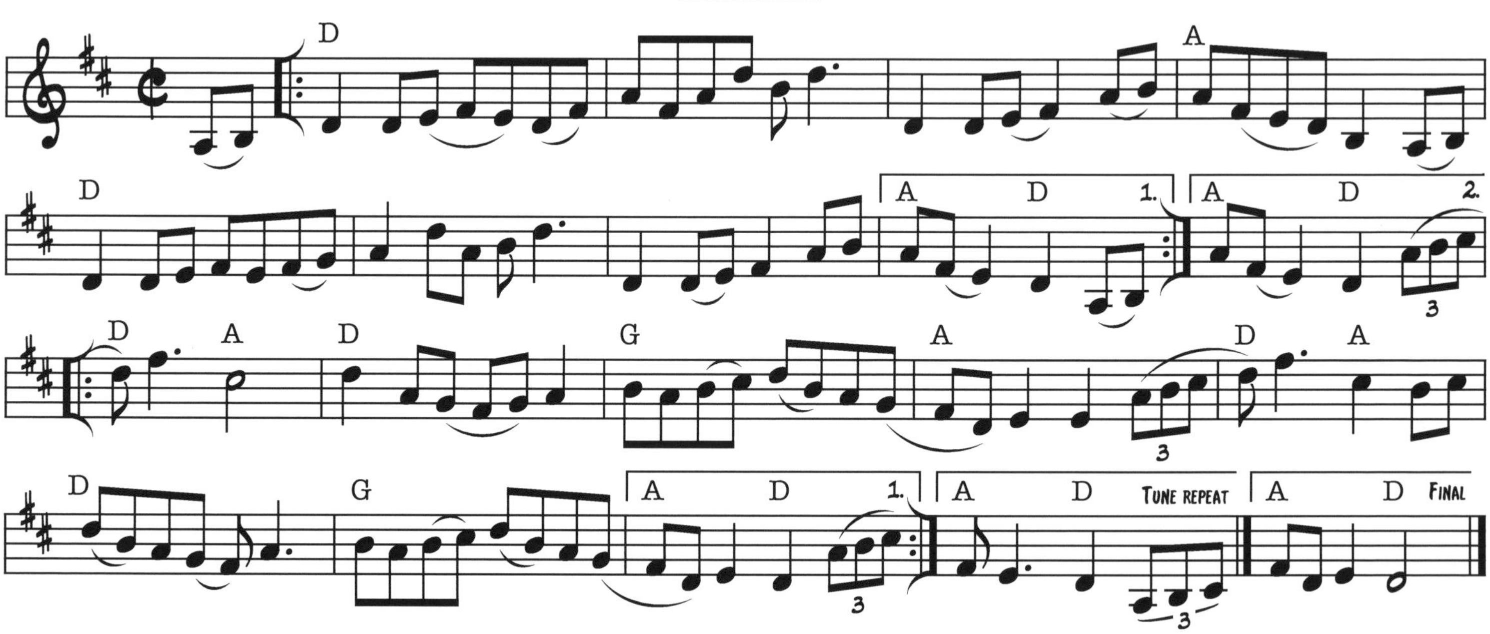

George Booker

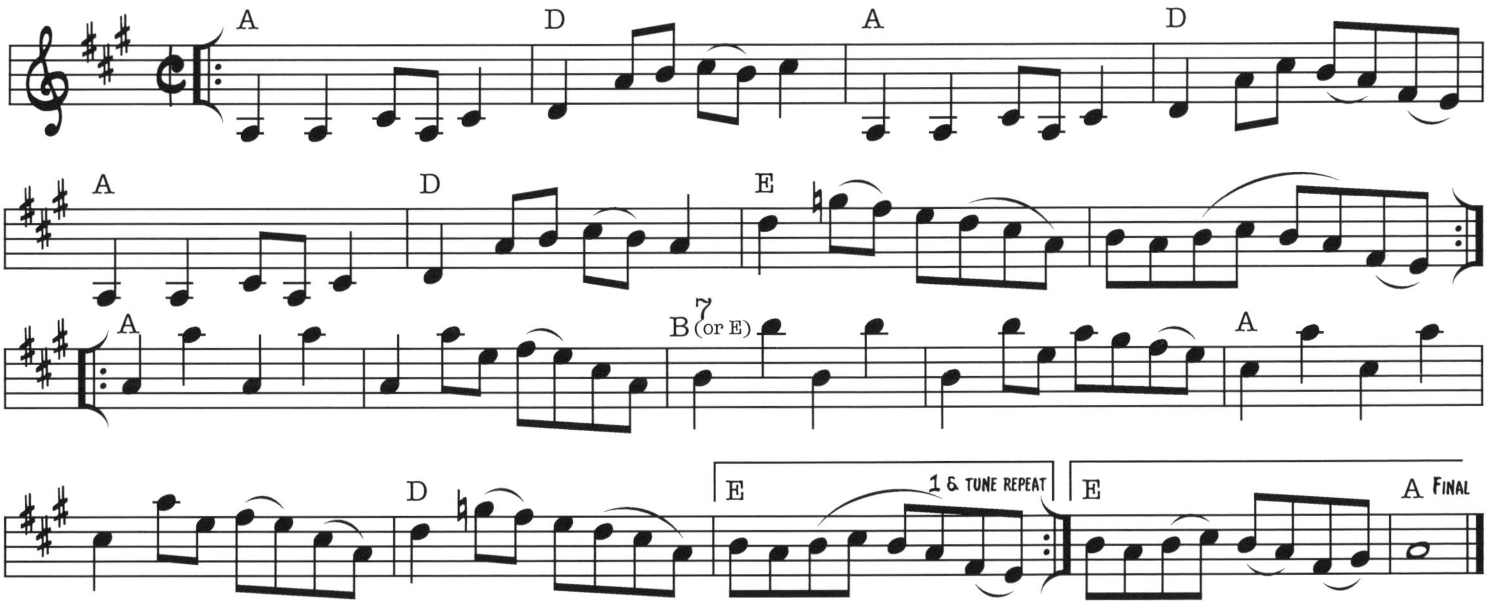

Georgia Railroad

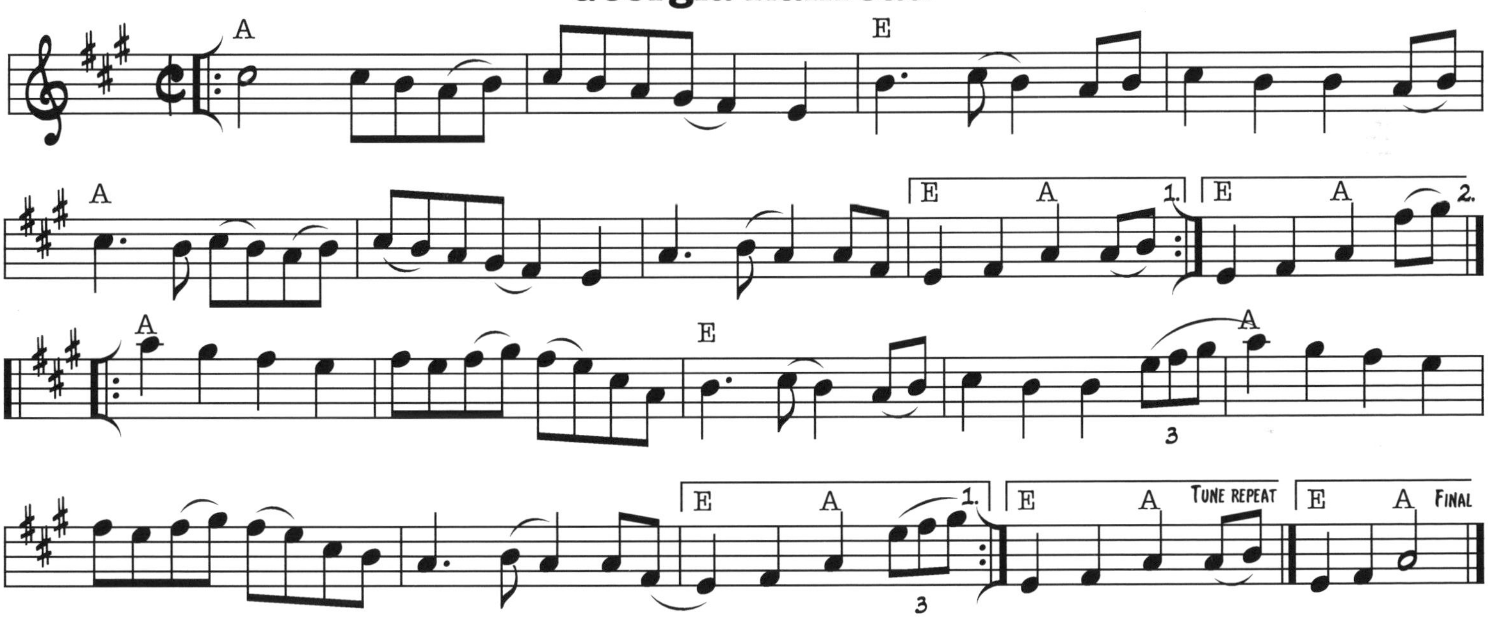

Gilsaw

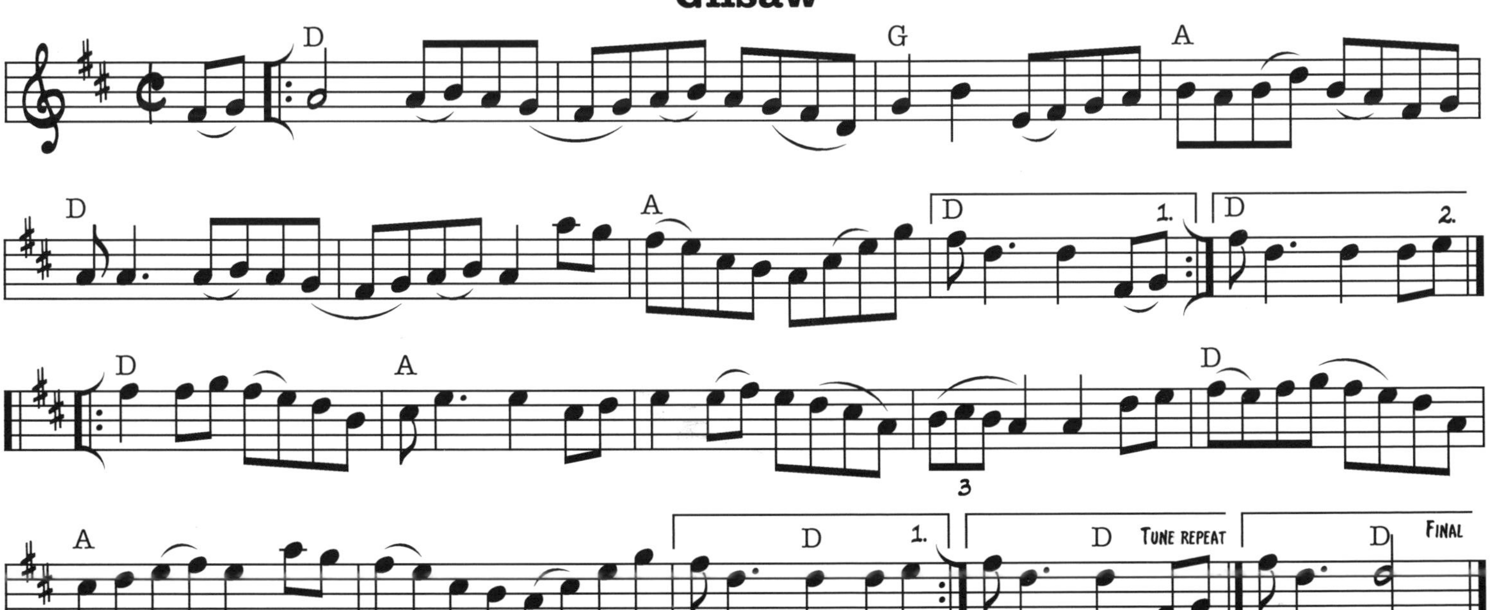

Get Off Your Money

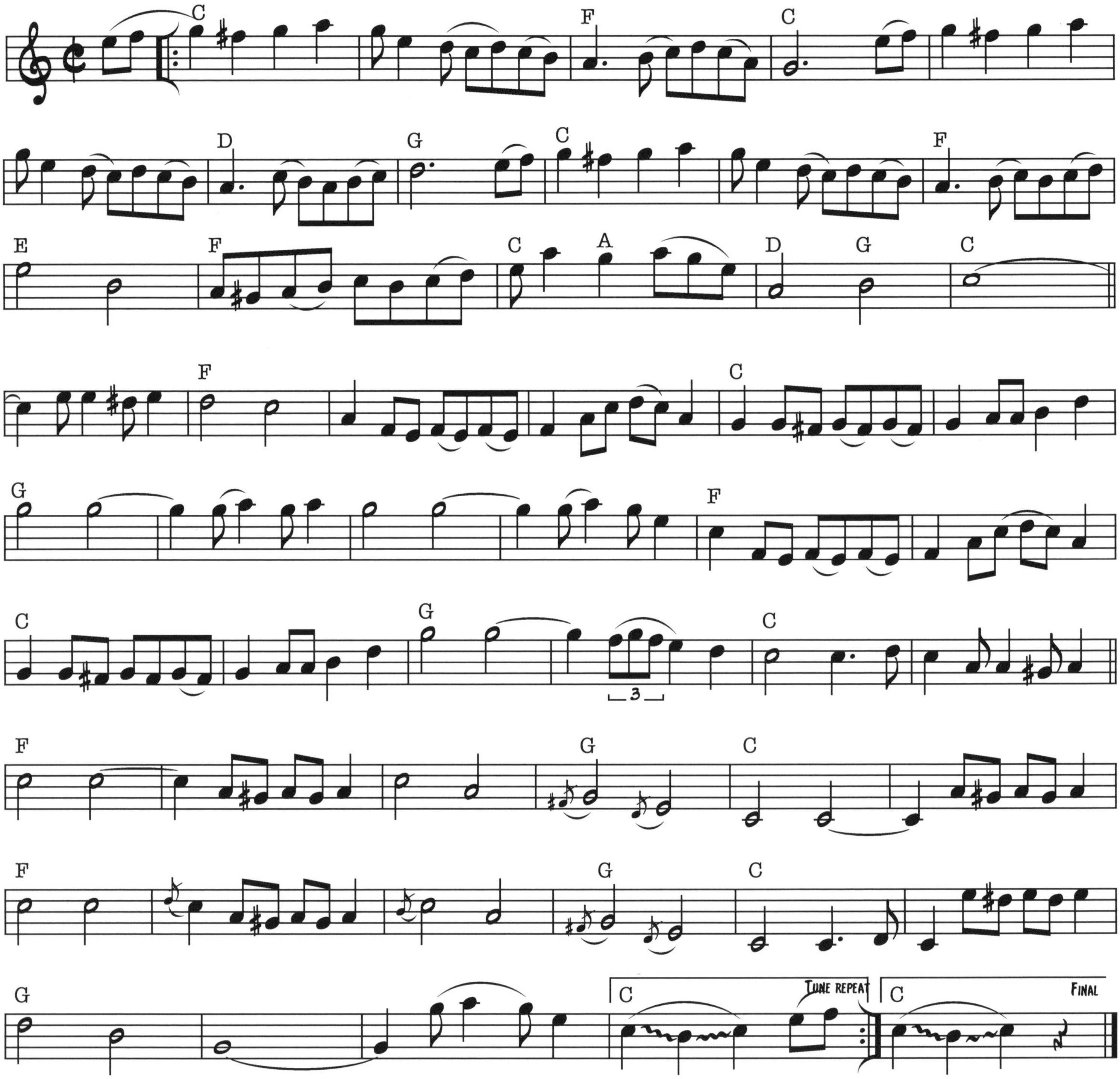

Give the Fiddler a Dram

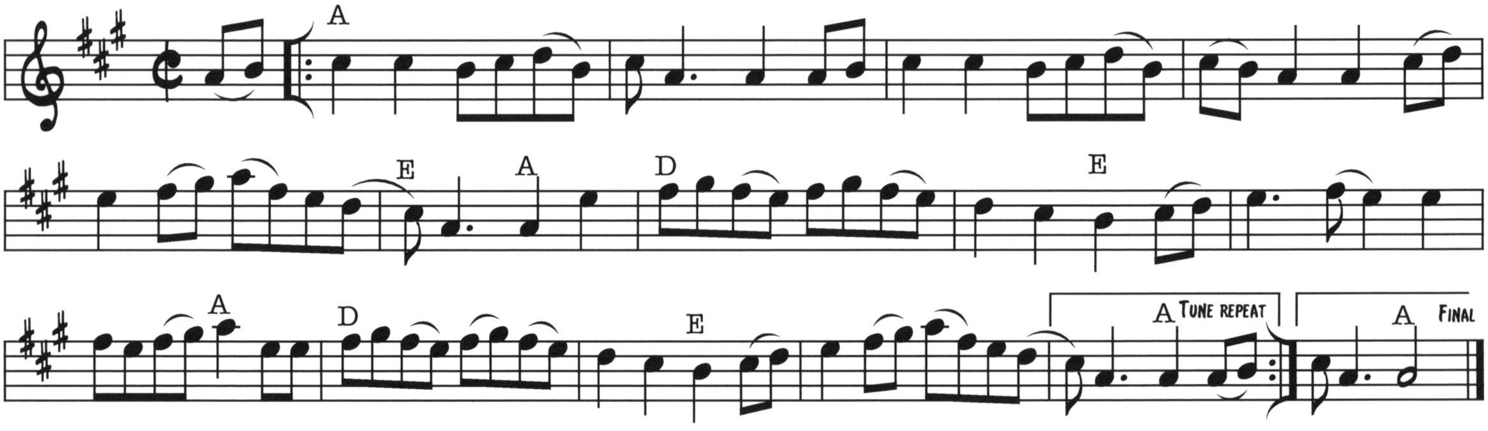

Girl I Left Behind

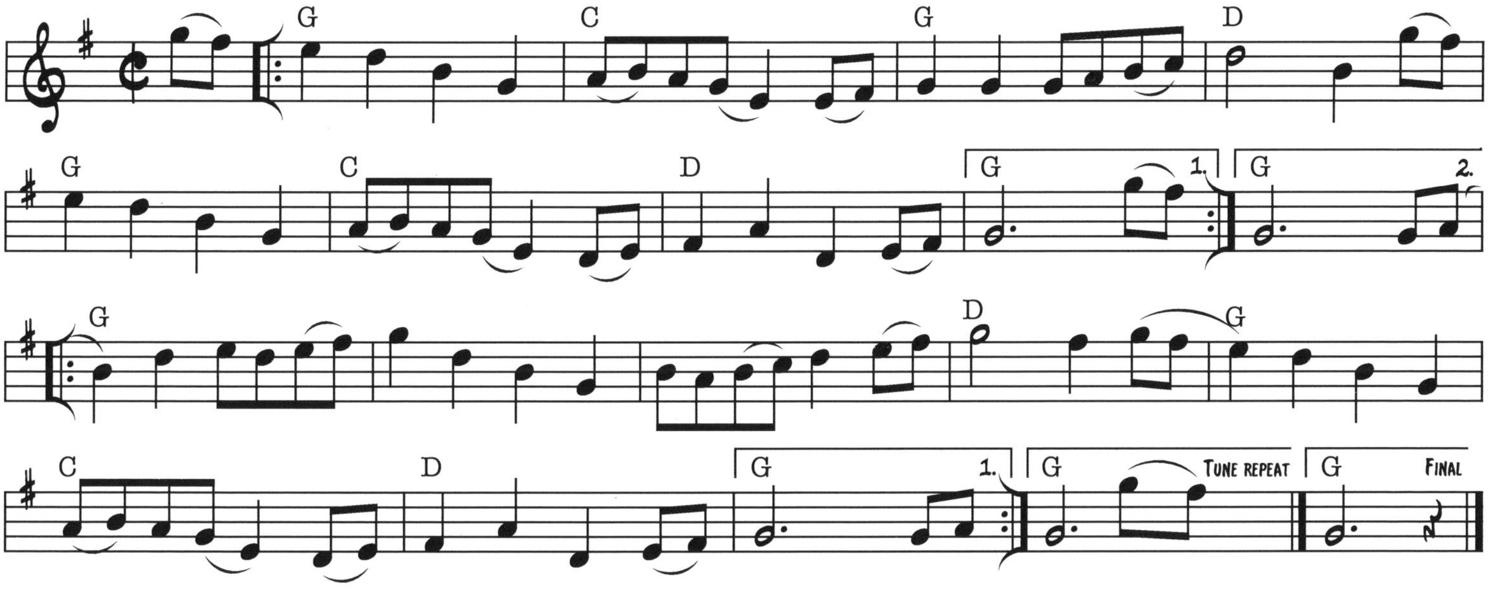

Glory Medley

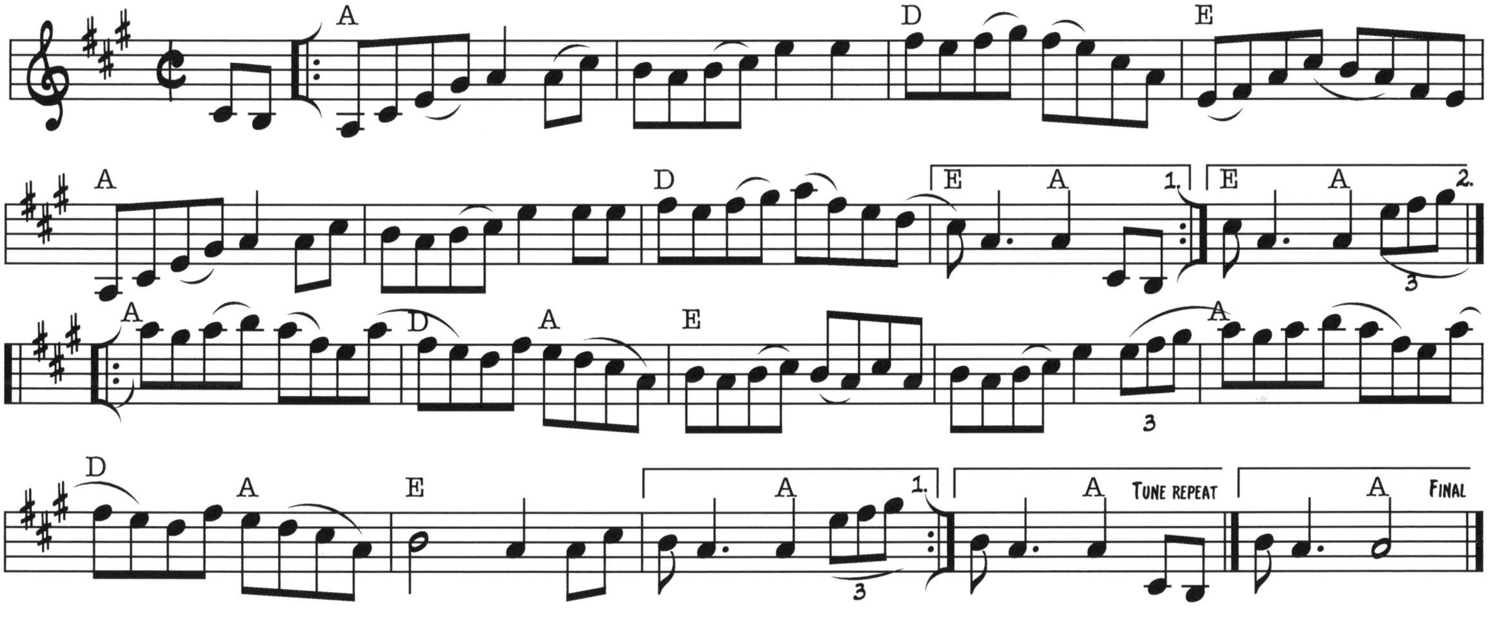

Goodbye Girls, I'm Going to Boston

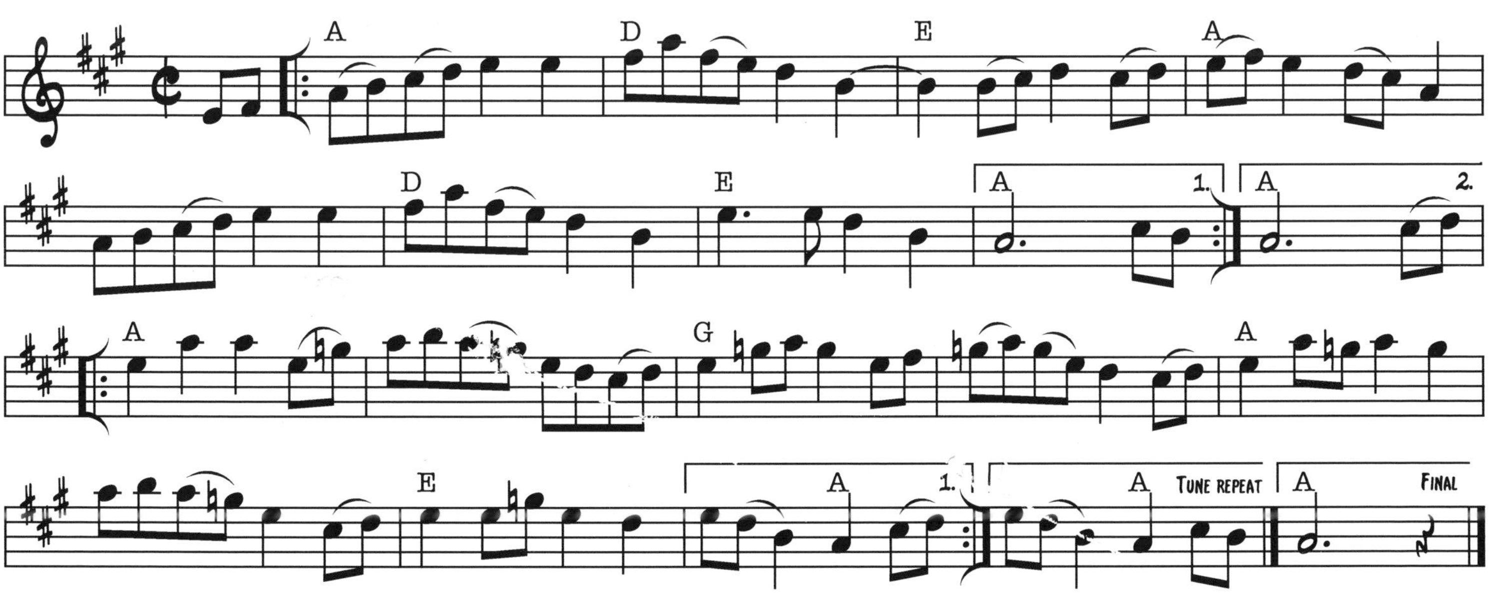

Going Up Town

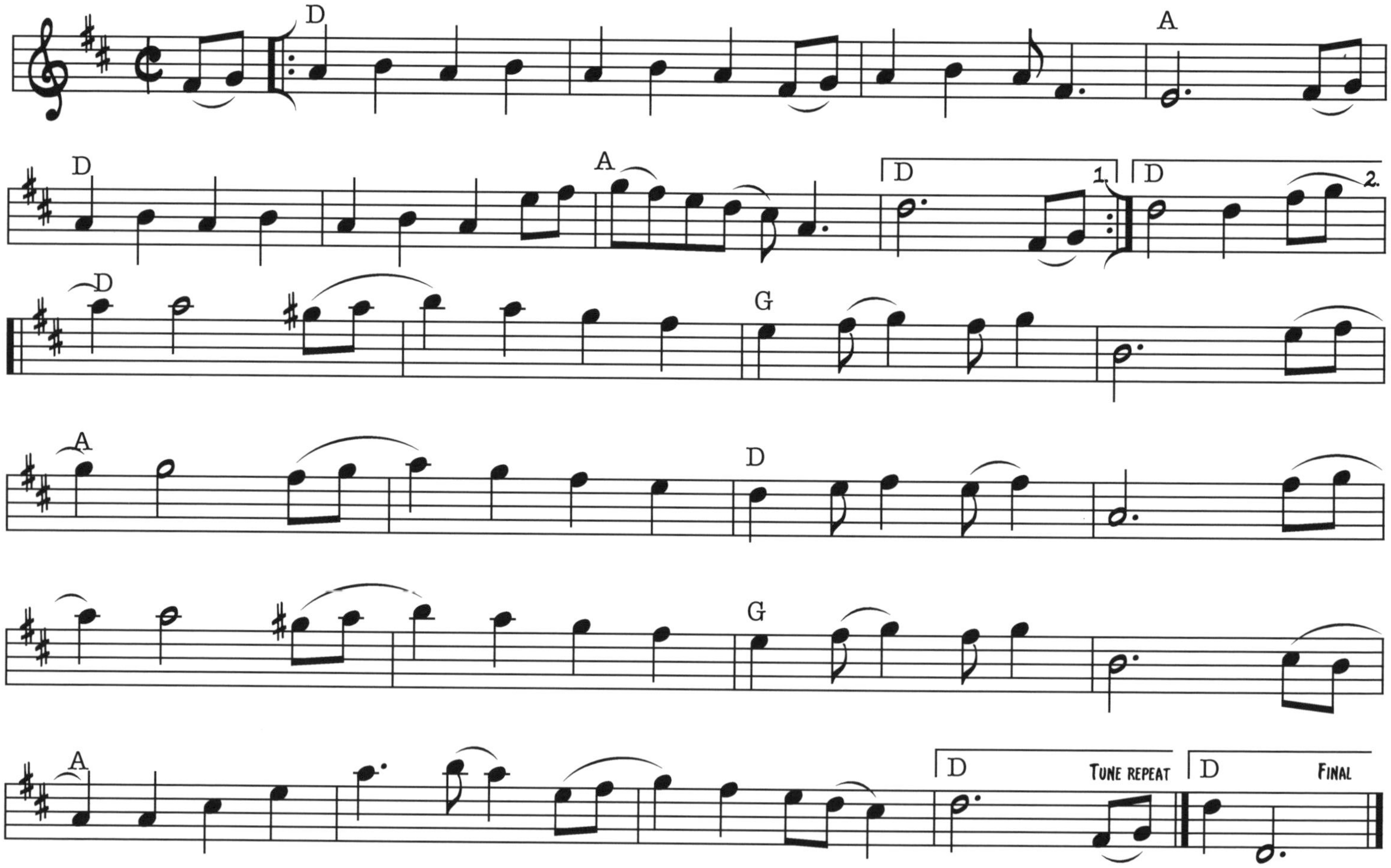

Goodbye My Little Darling

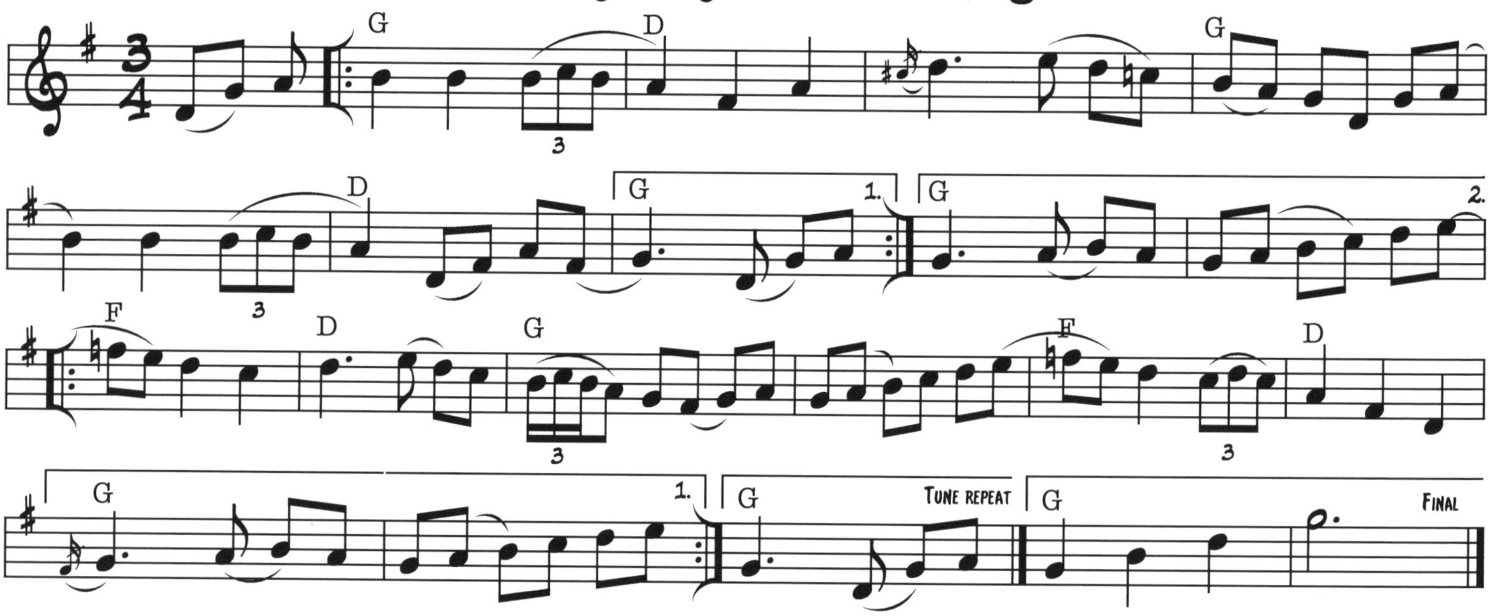

Grey Cat on a Tennessee Farm

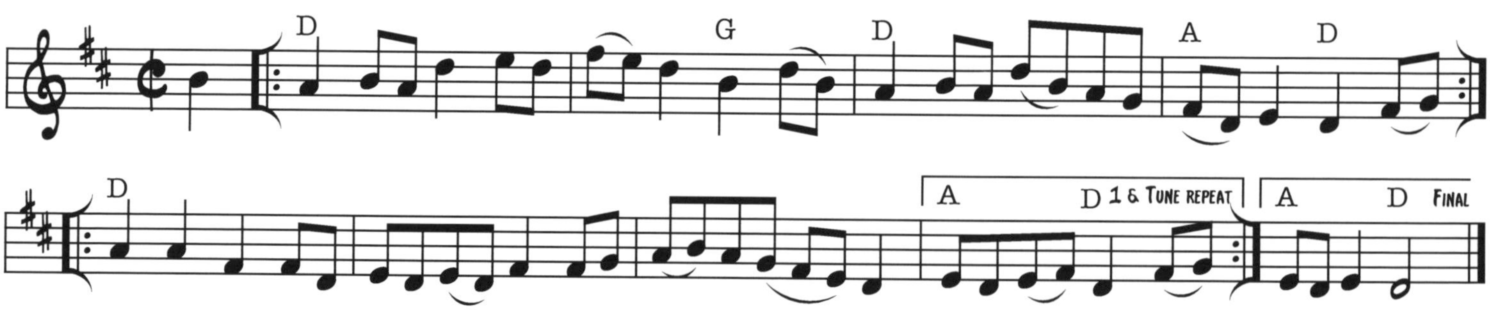

Grand Picnic

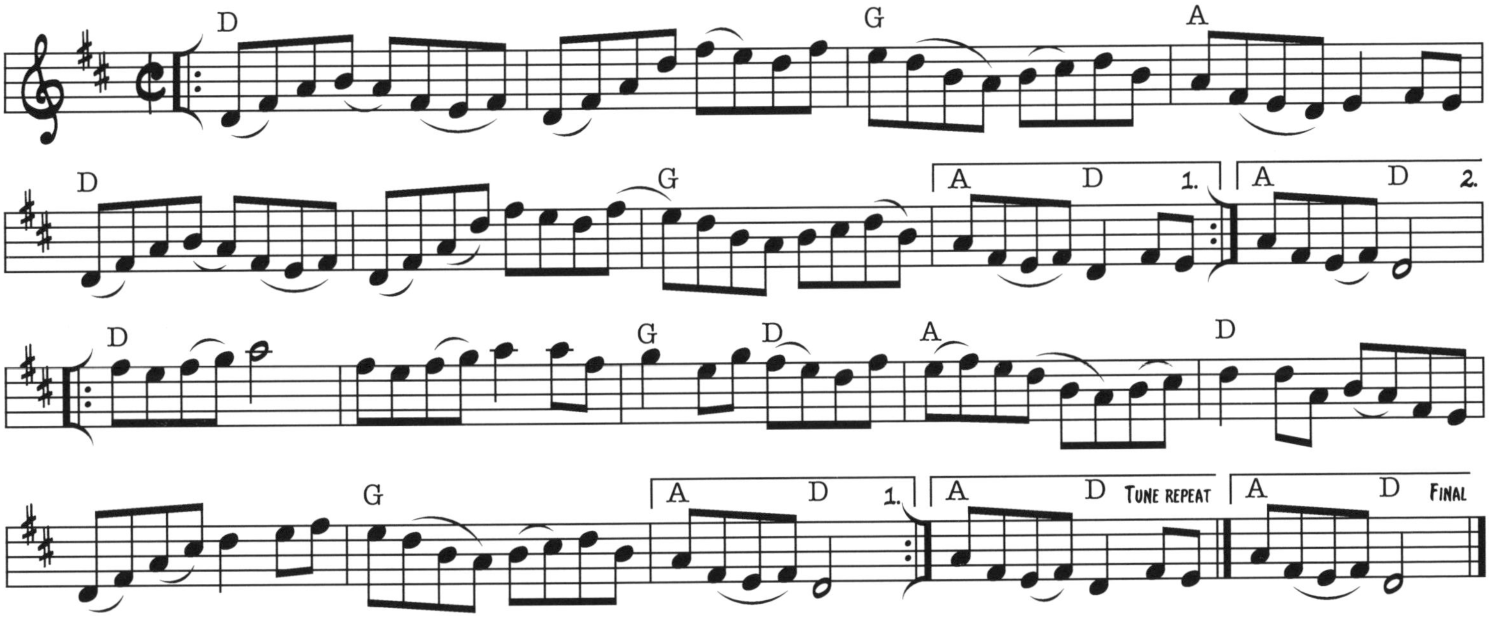

Grasshopper Sitting on a Sweet Potato Vine

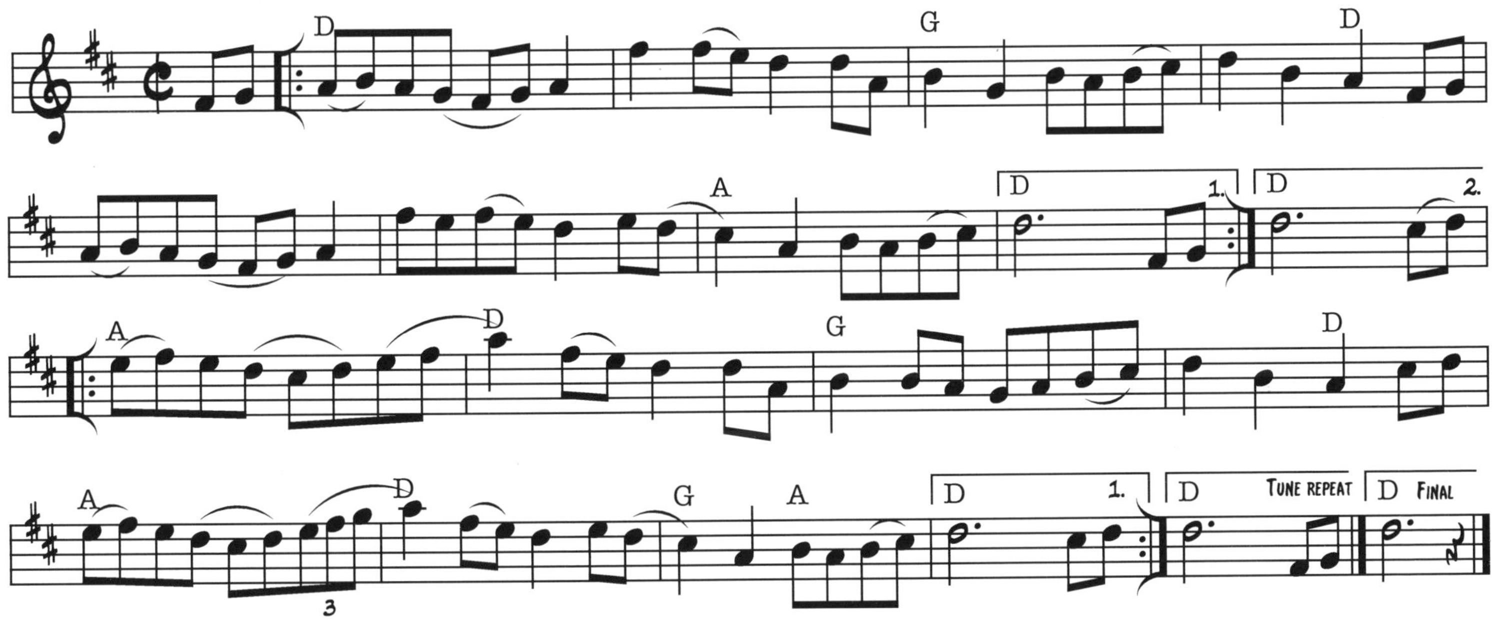

Greasy Coat (Hammons)

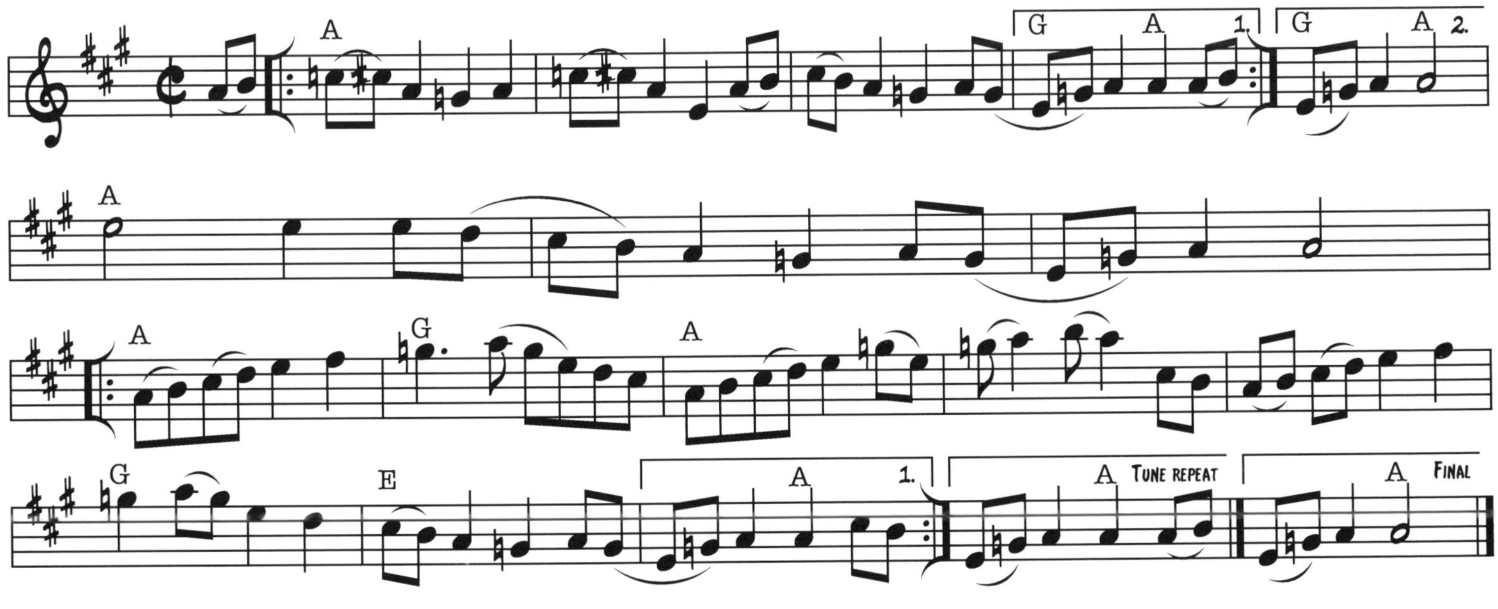

Greasy String (Tommy Jarrell)

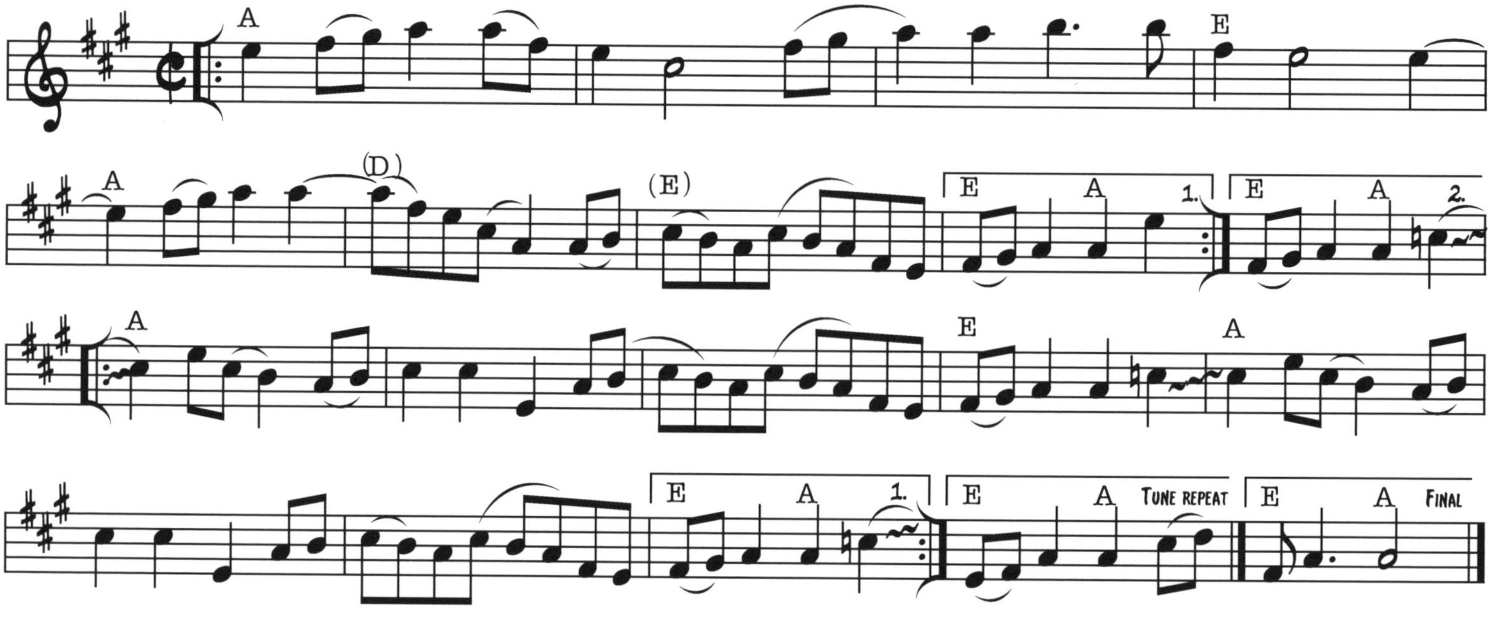

Greasy String (Melvin Wine)

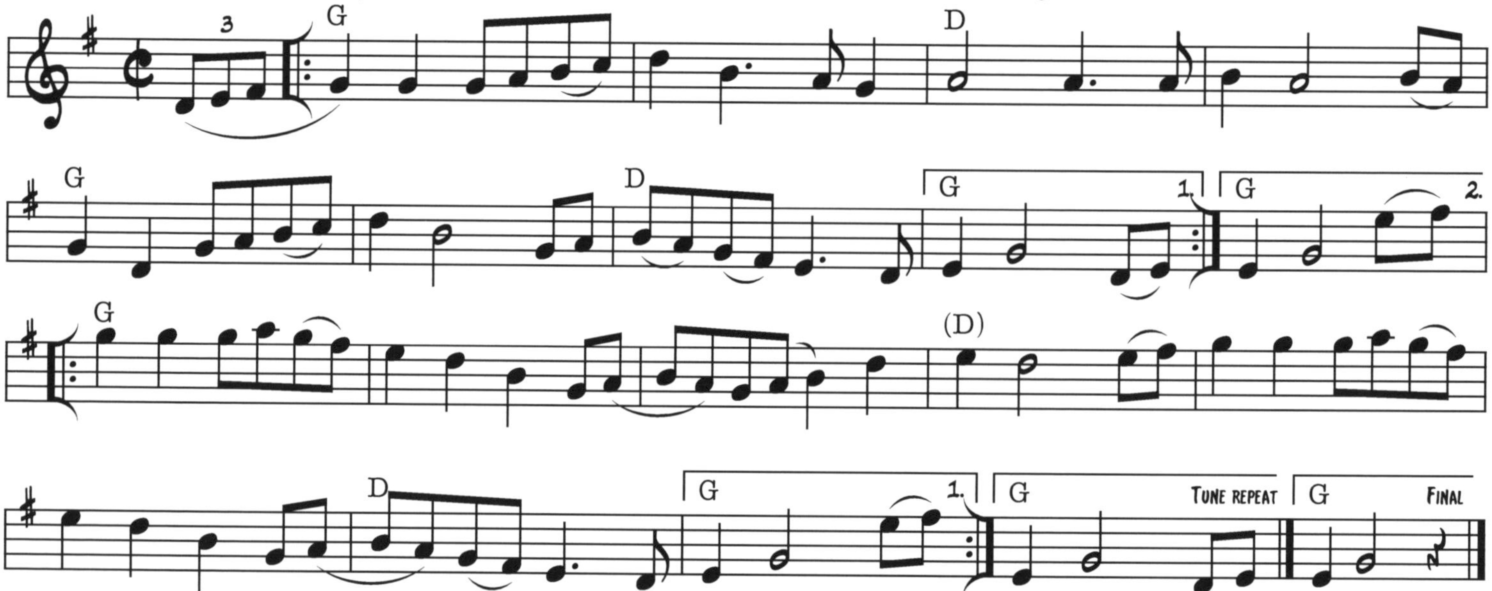

Great Big Taters in a Sandy Land

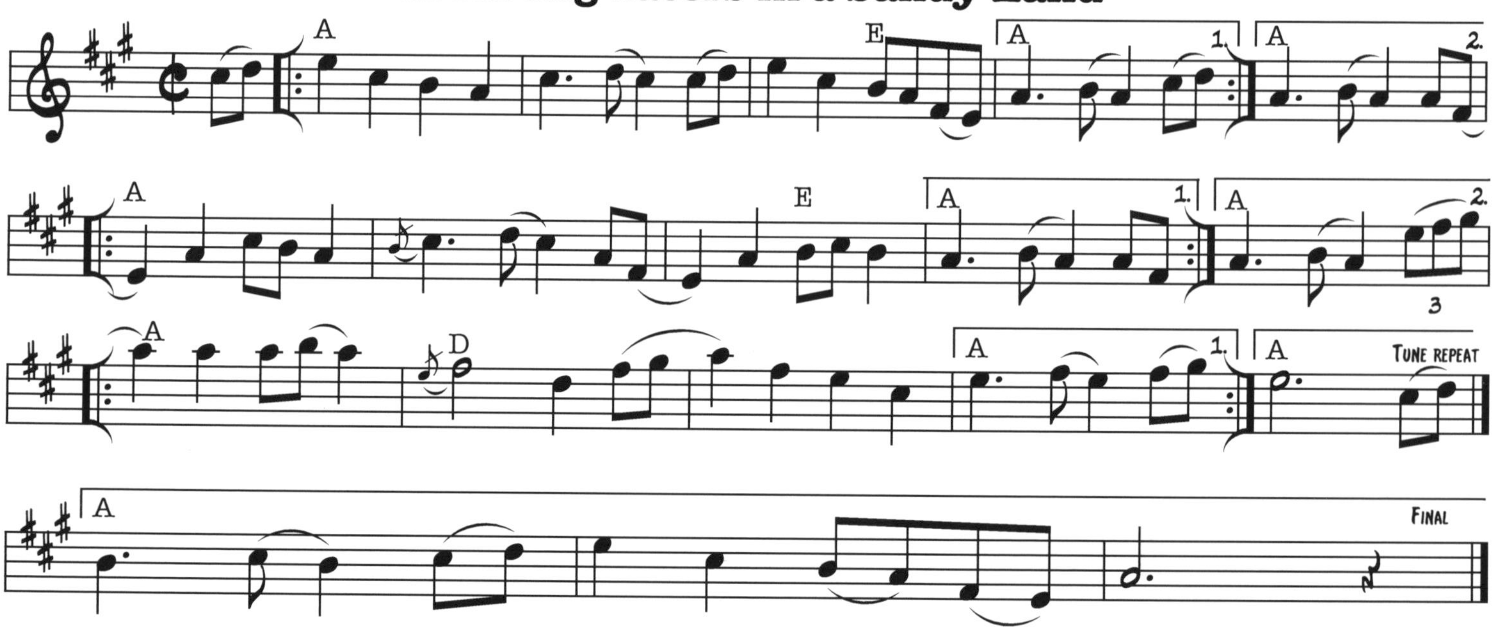

Green Willis (aka The Raw Recruit)

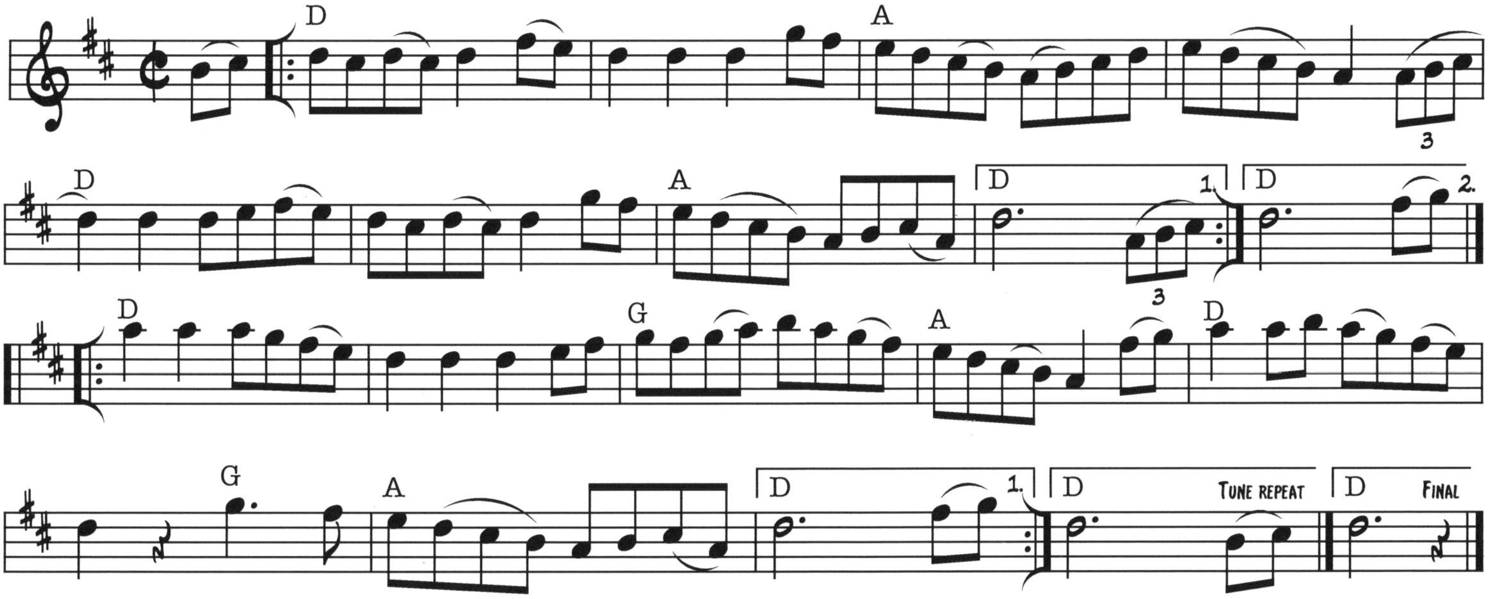

Grey Eagle

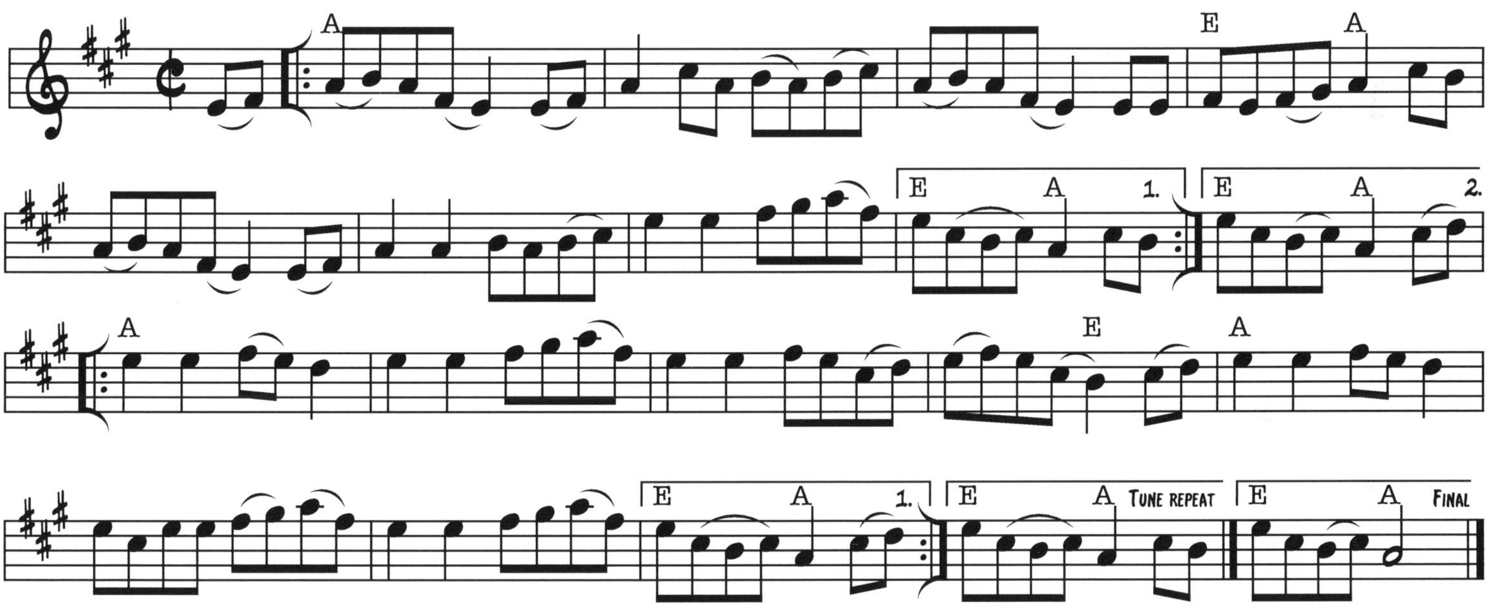

Grub Springs

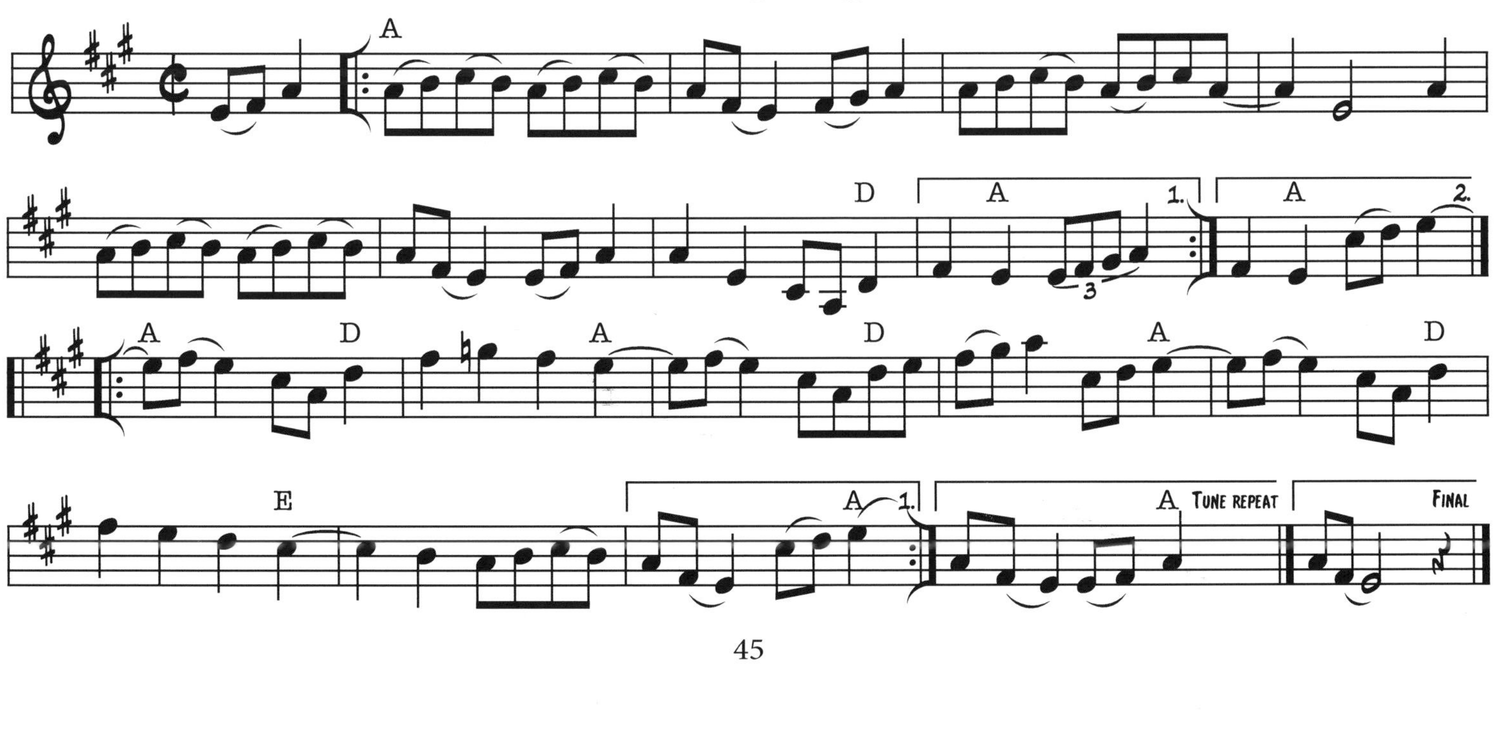

Hangman's Reel

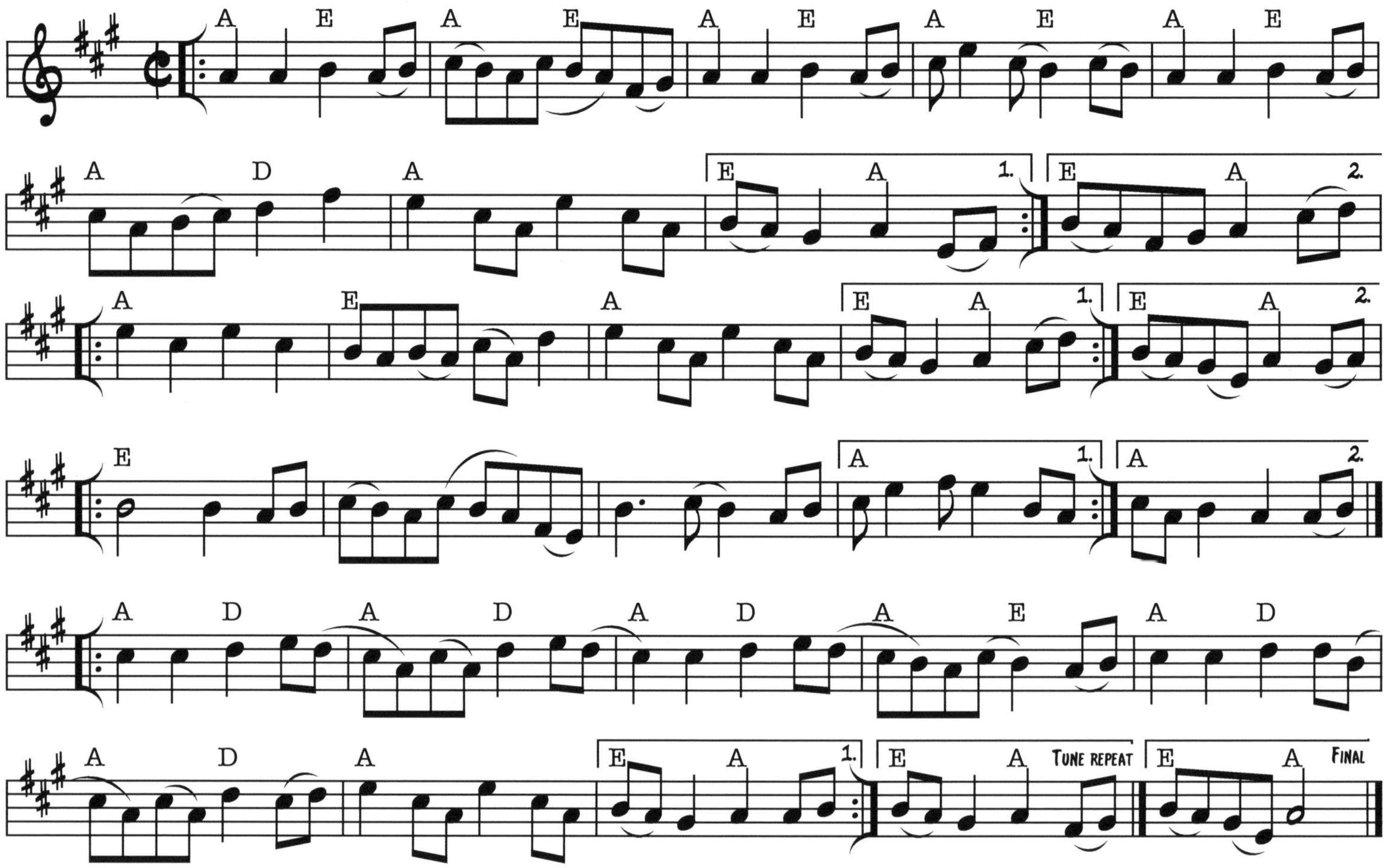

Happy Hollow

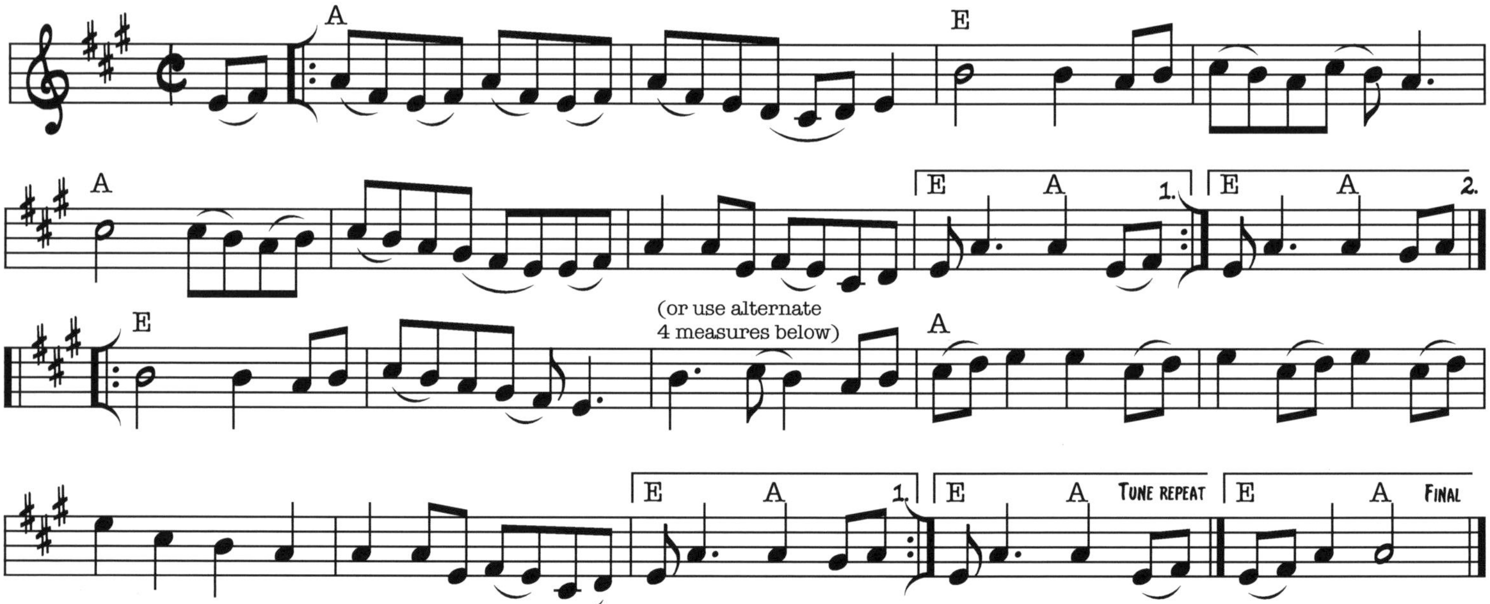

Alternate B part measures 3-6

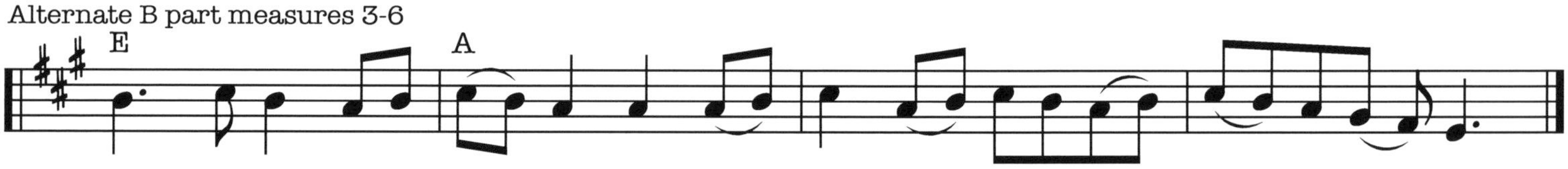

Half Past Four

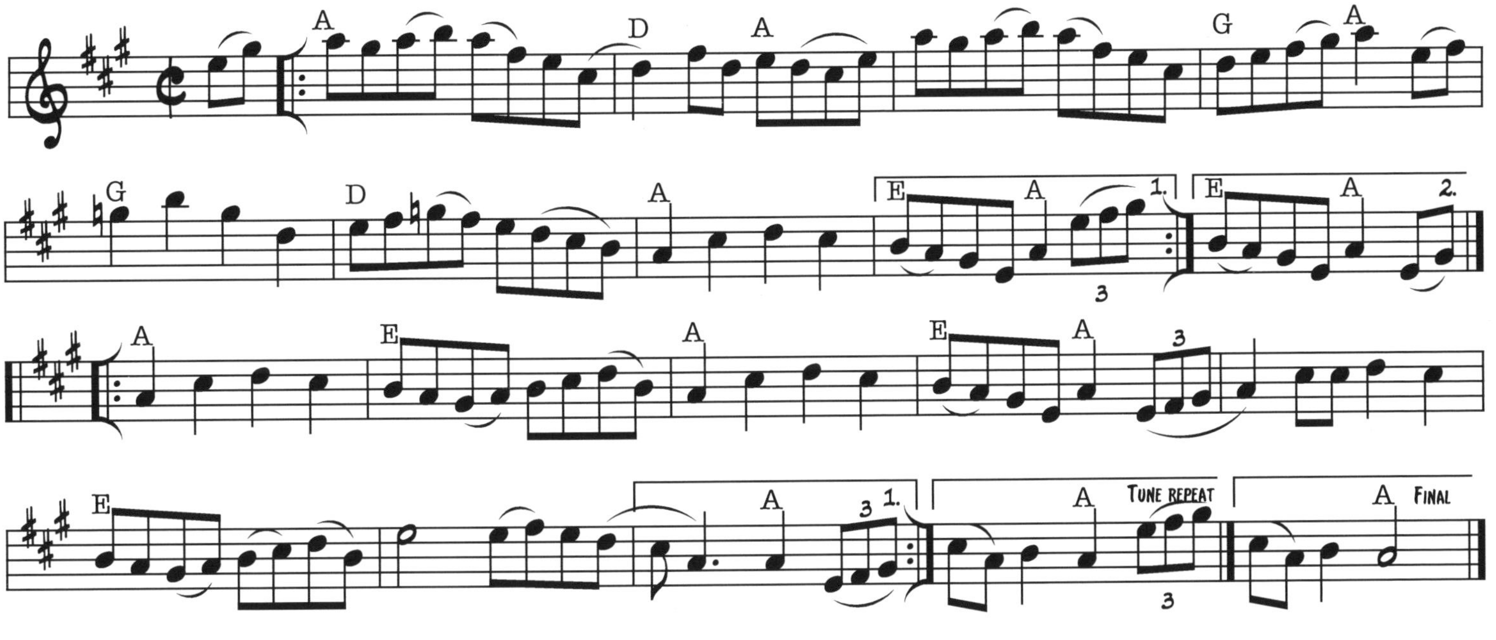

Hell and Scissors

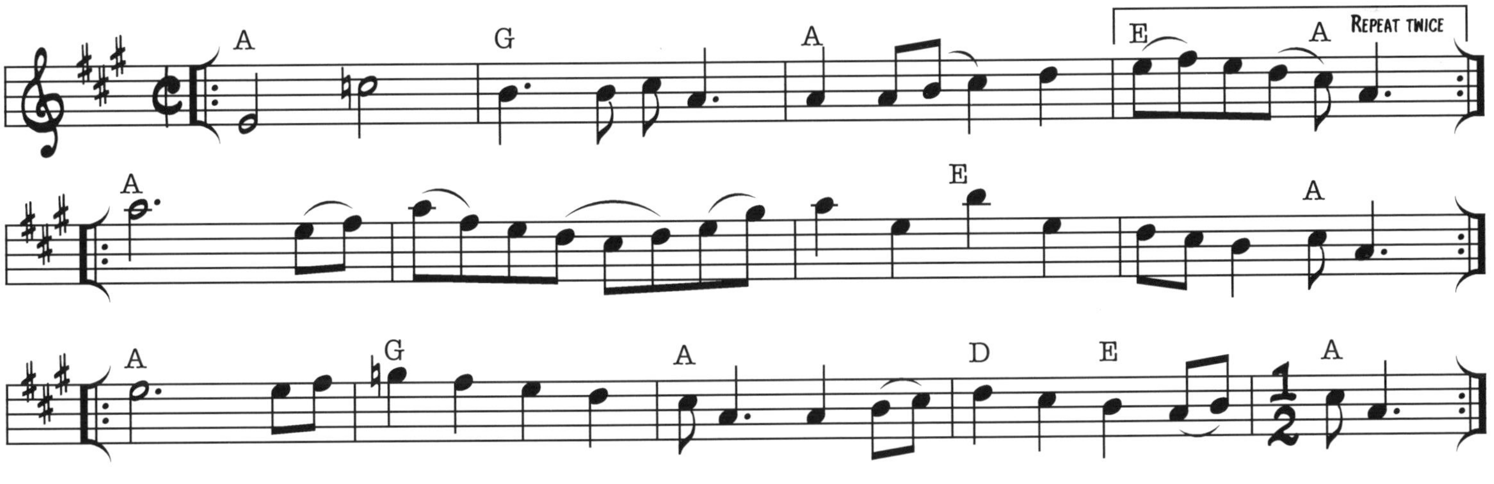

Henry Reed's Breakdown

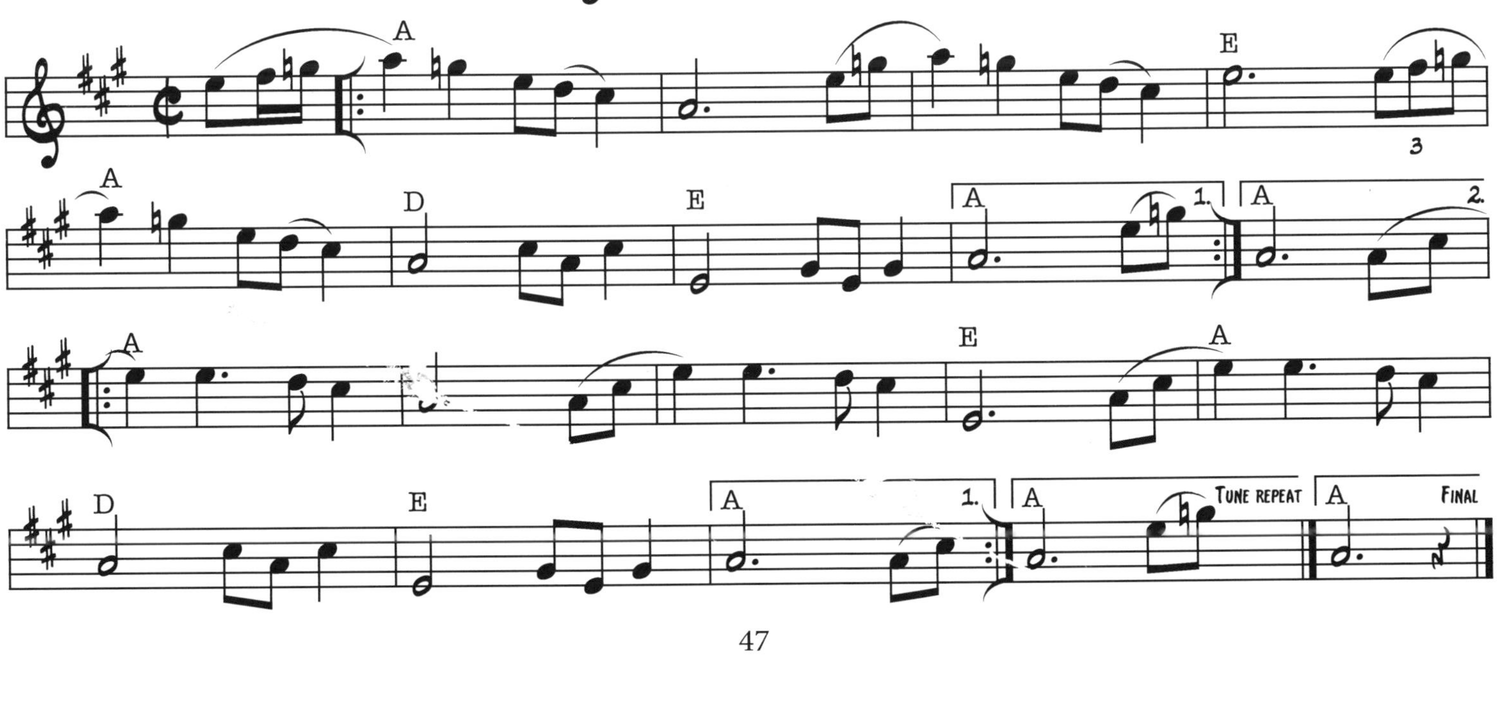

Hey Little Girl Do What You Want

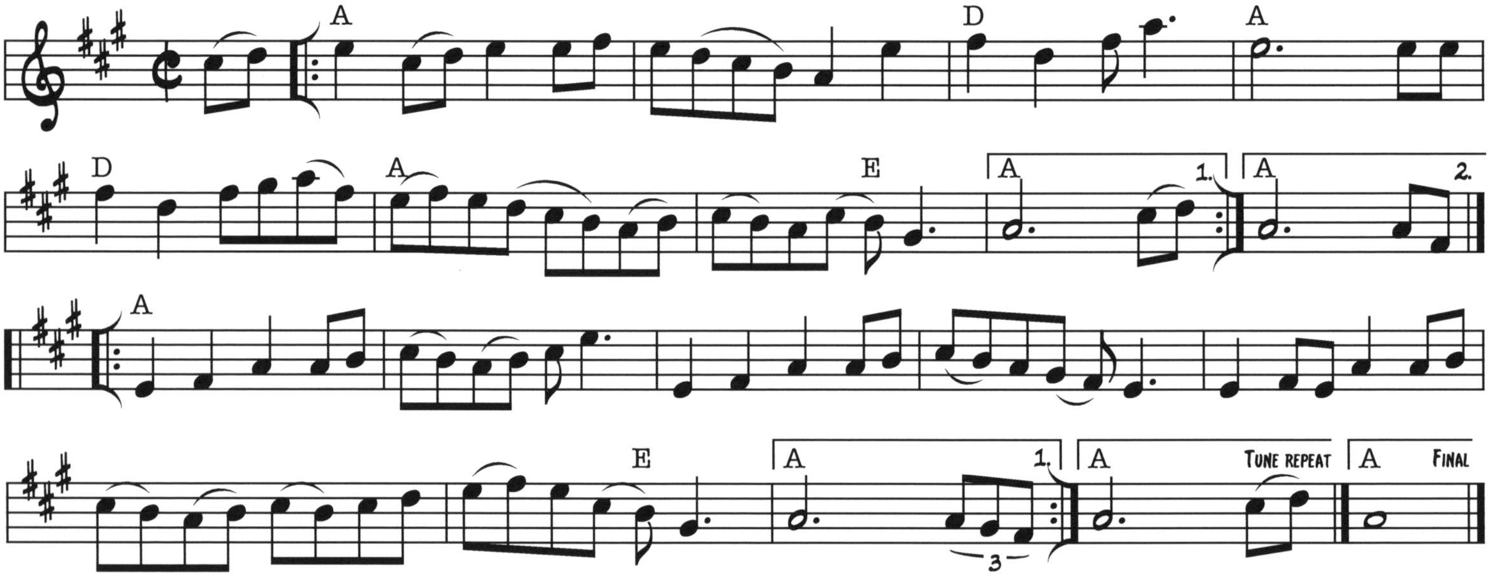

High Yellow

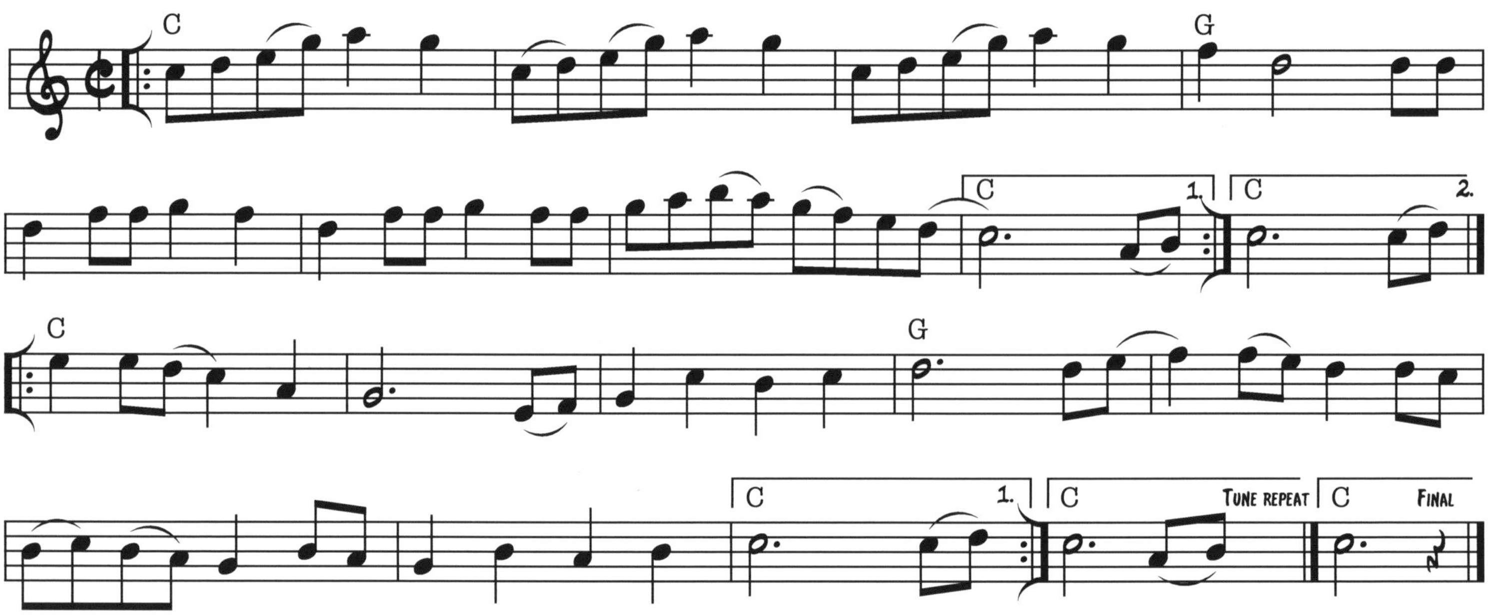

Hollow Poplar

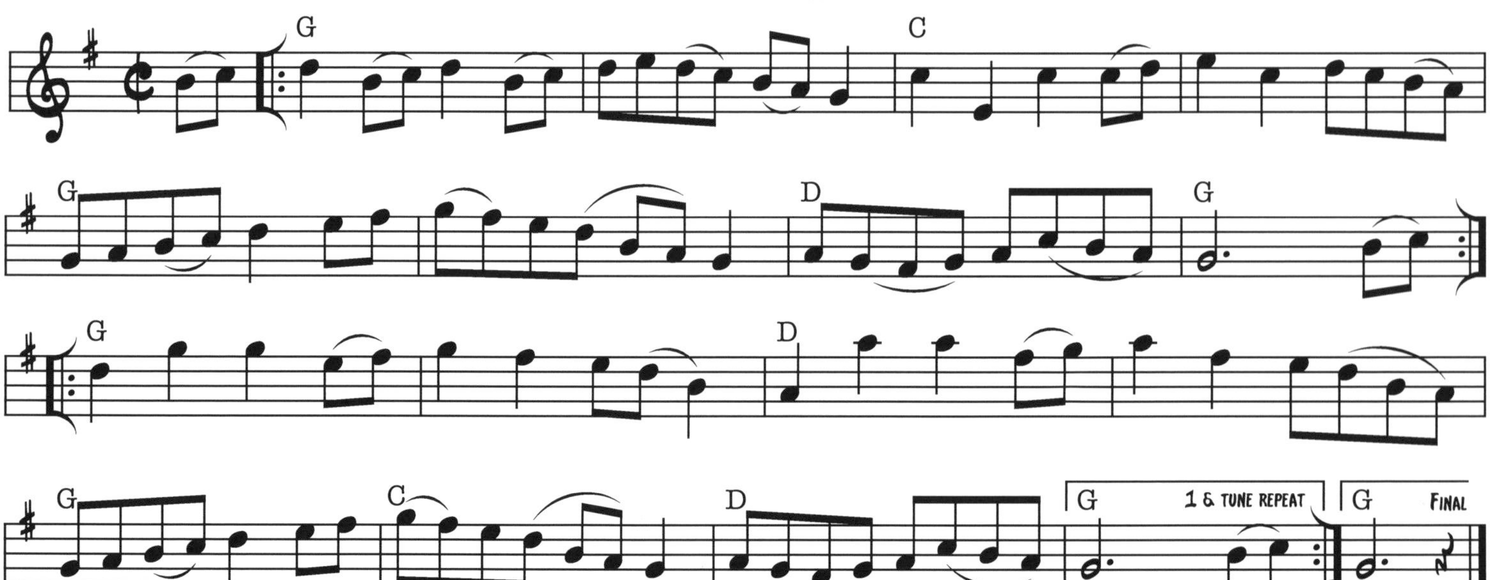

Home With the Girls in the Morning

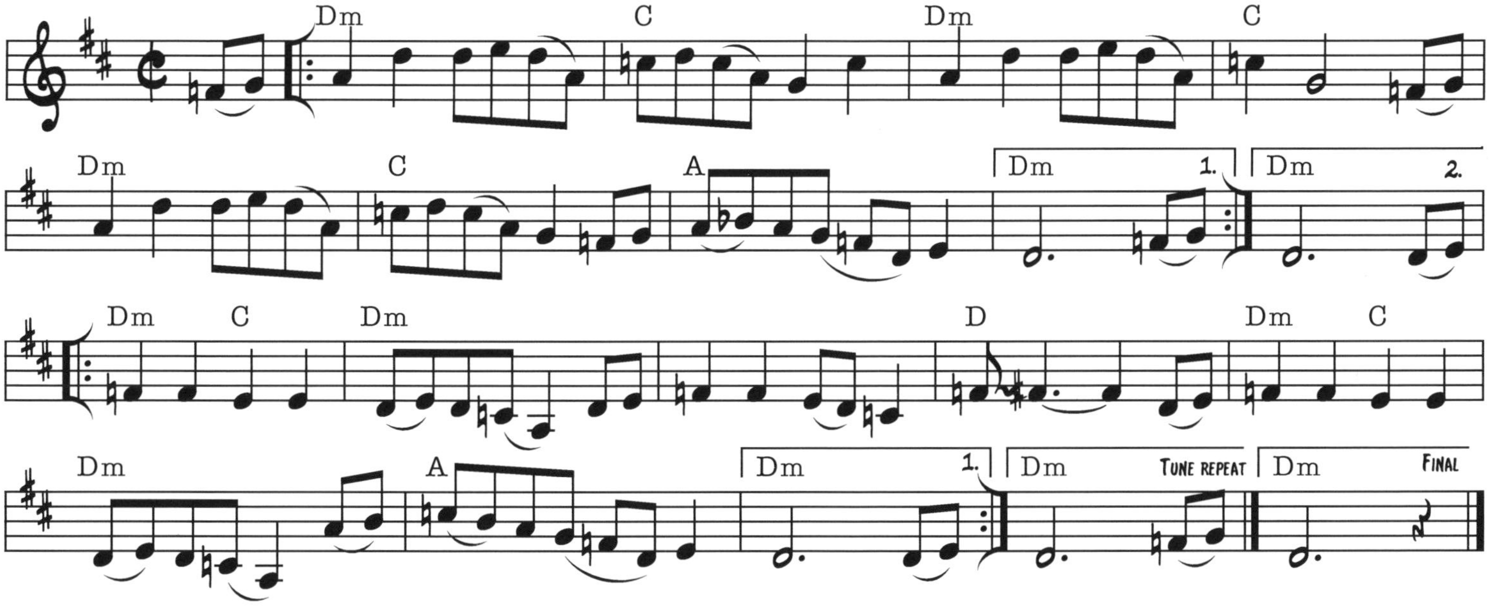

Hooker's Hornpipe

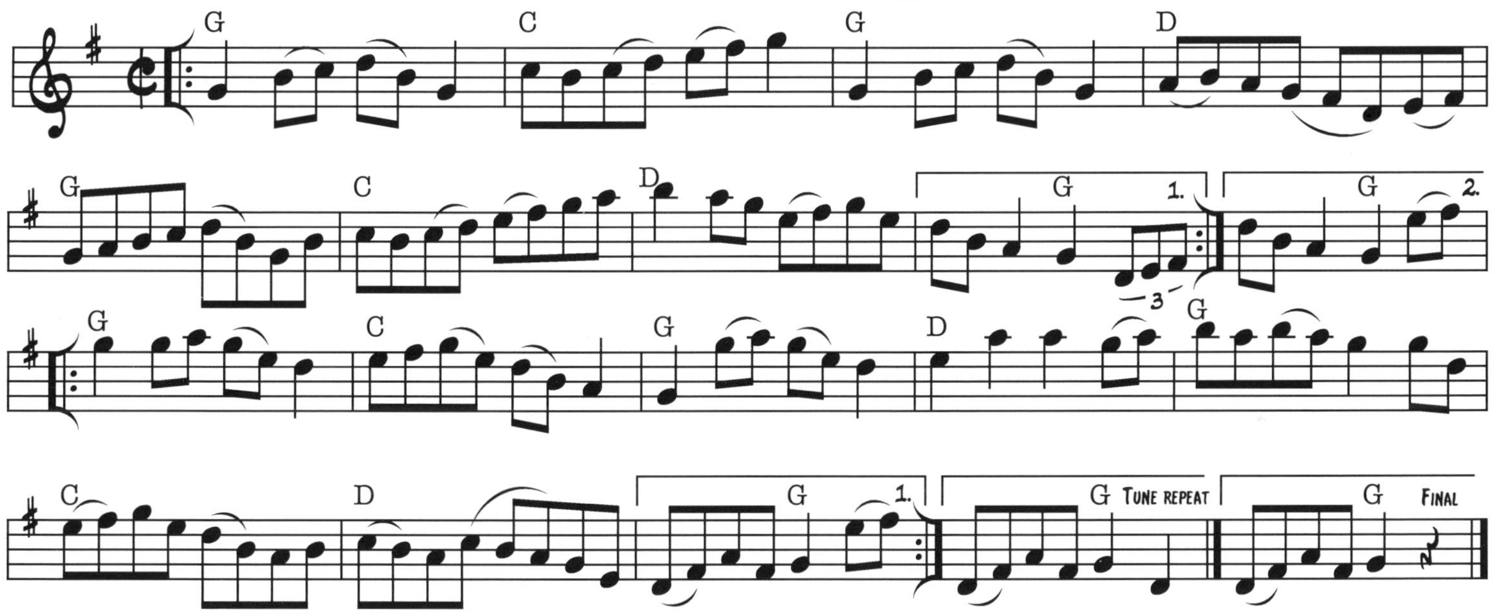

Hop Light Ladies (aka Miss McLeod's Reel)

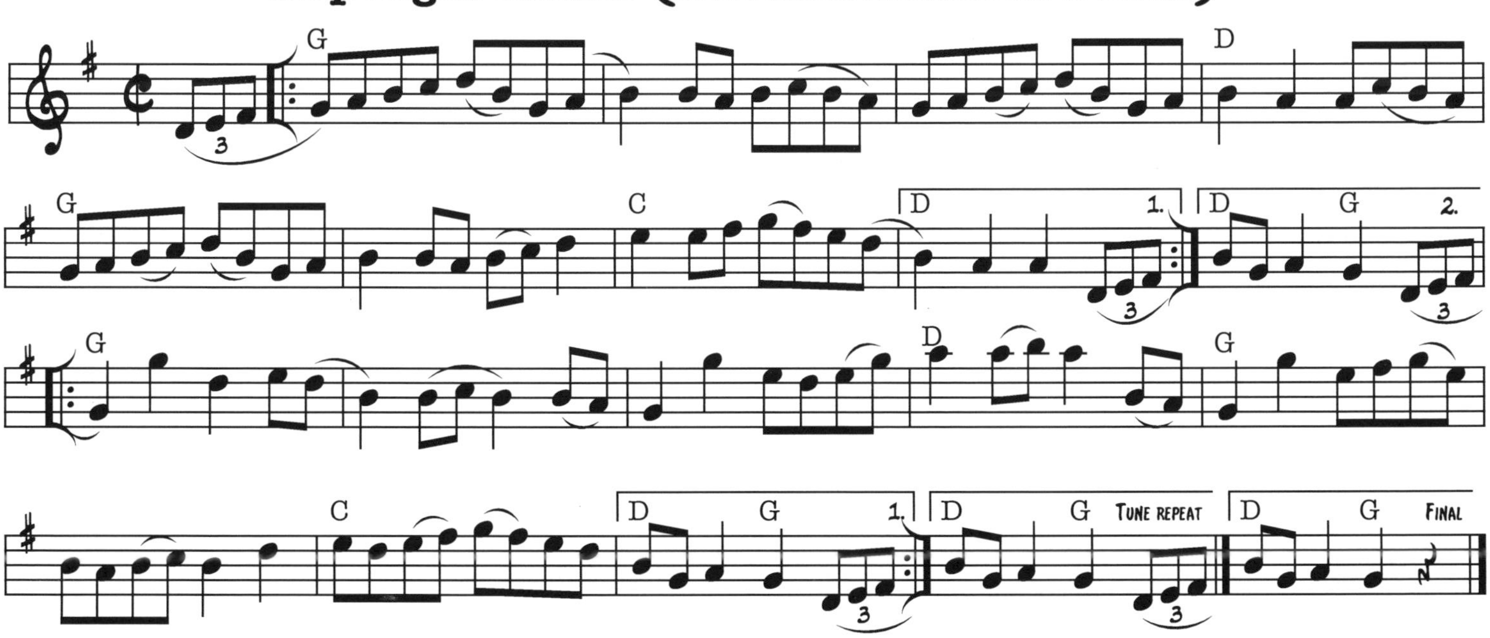

Hunt the Buffalo

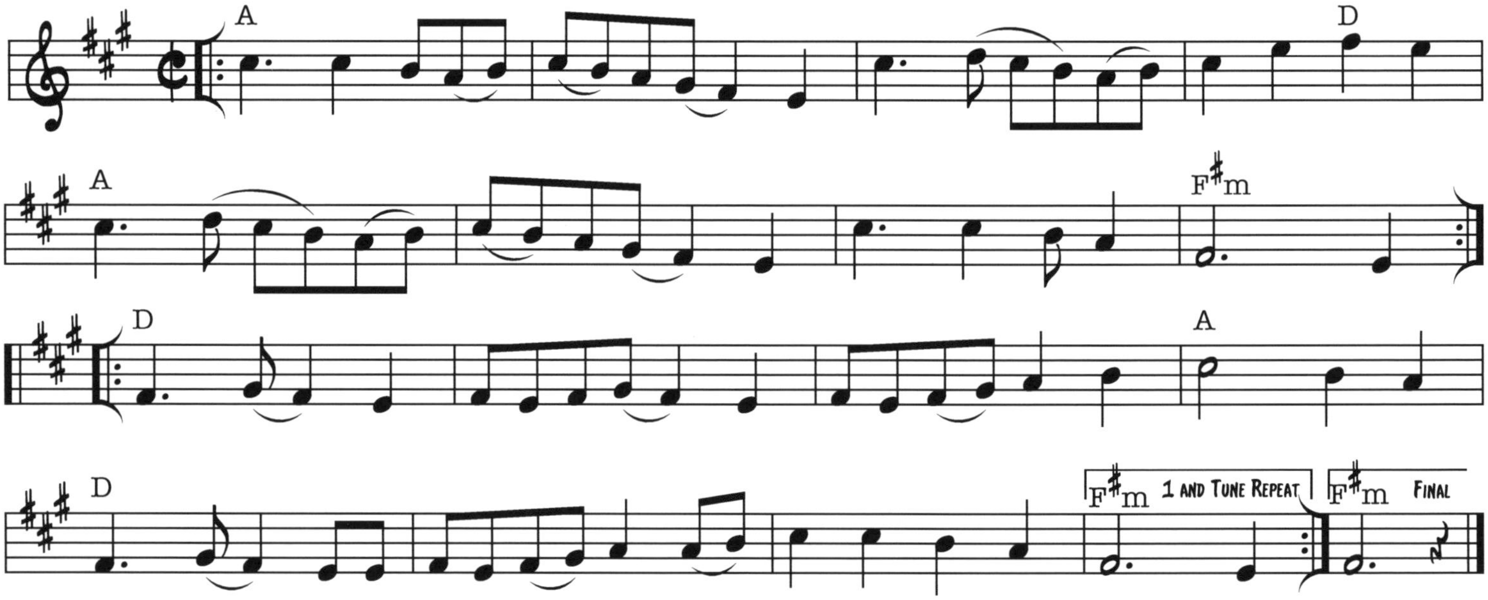

I Don't Love Nobody

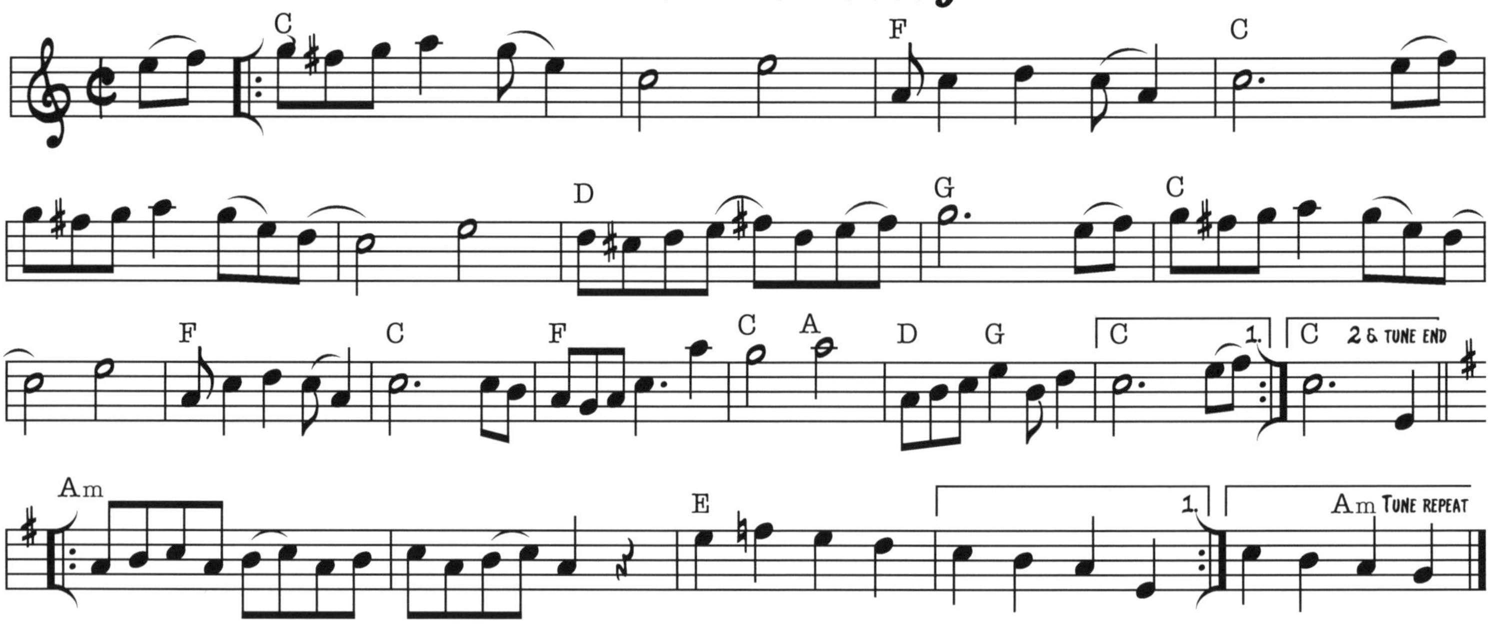

Icy Mountain

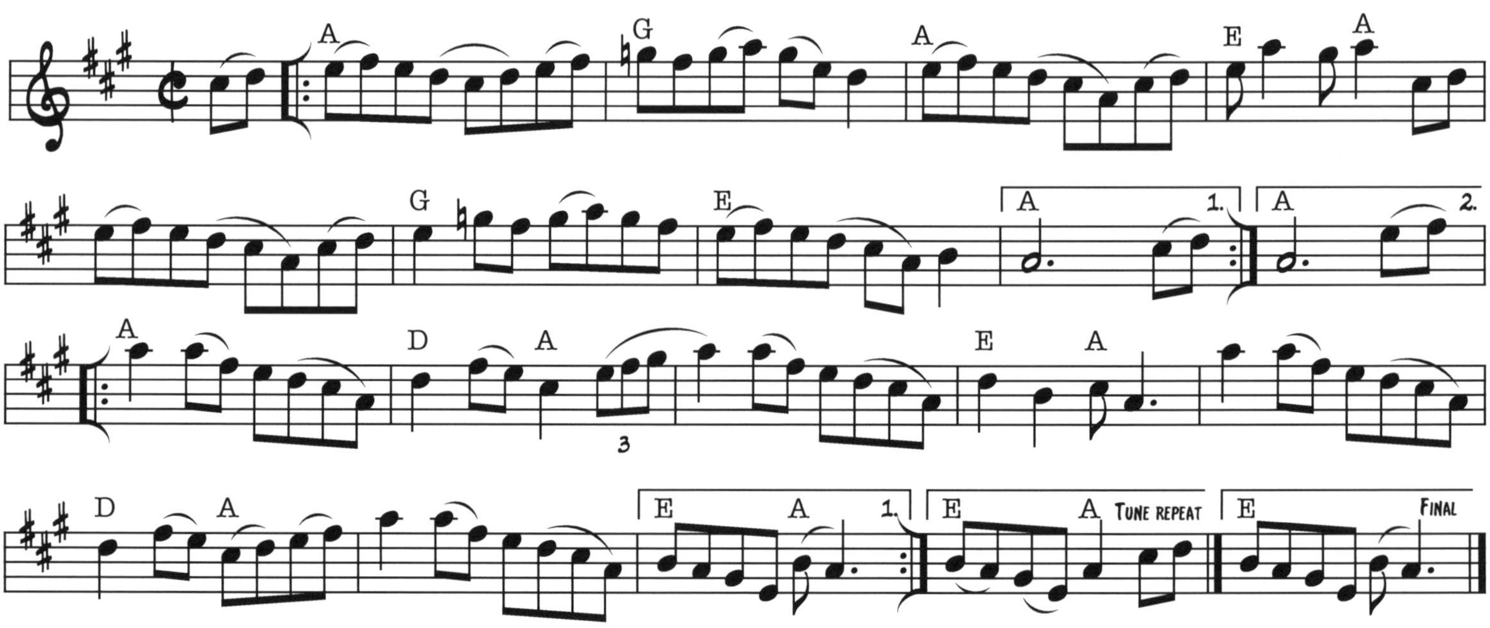

I'm Going to Get My Mustache Blacked

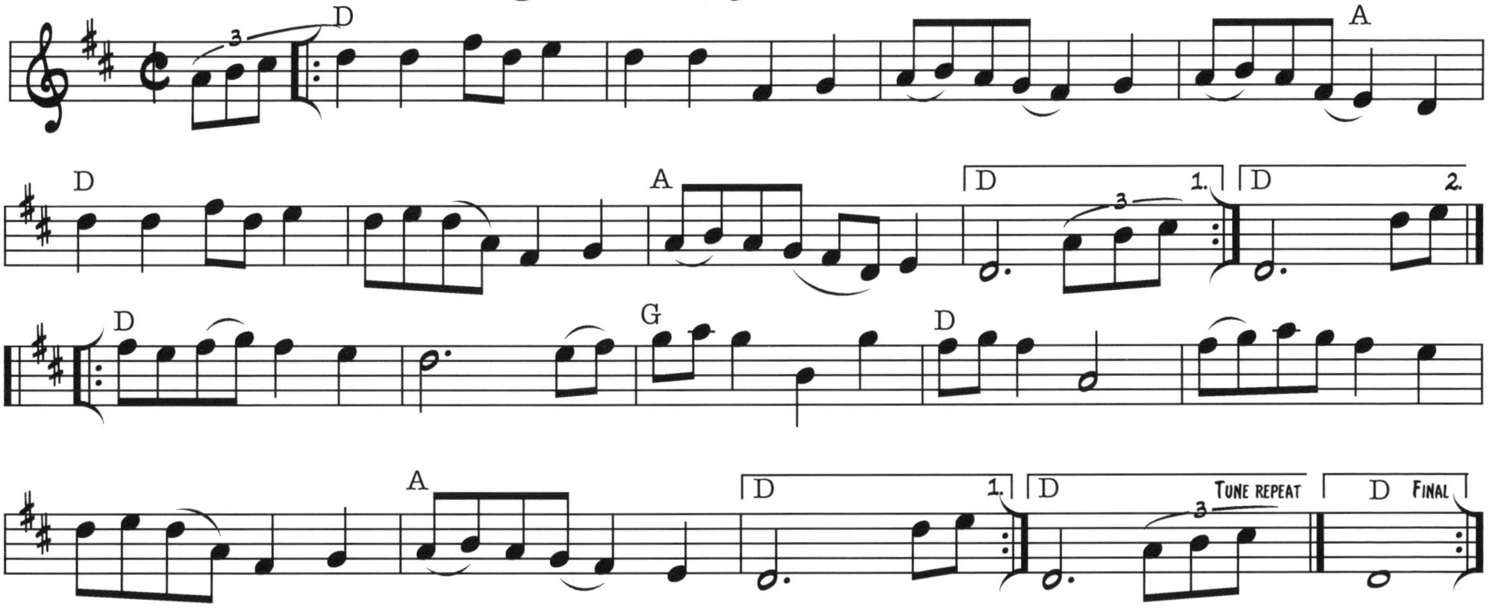

Indian Ate the Woodchuck

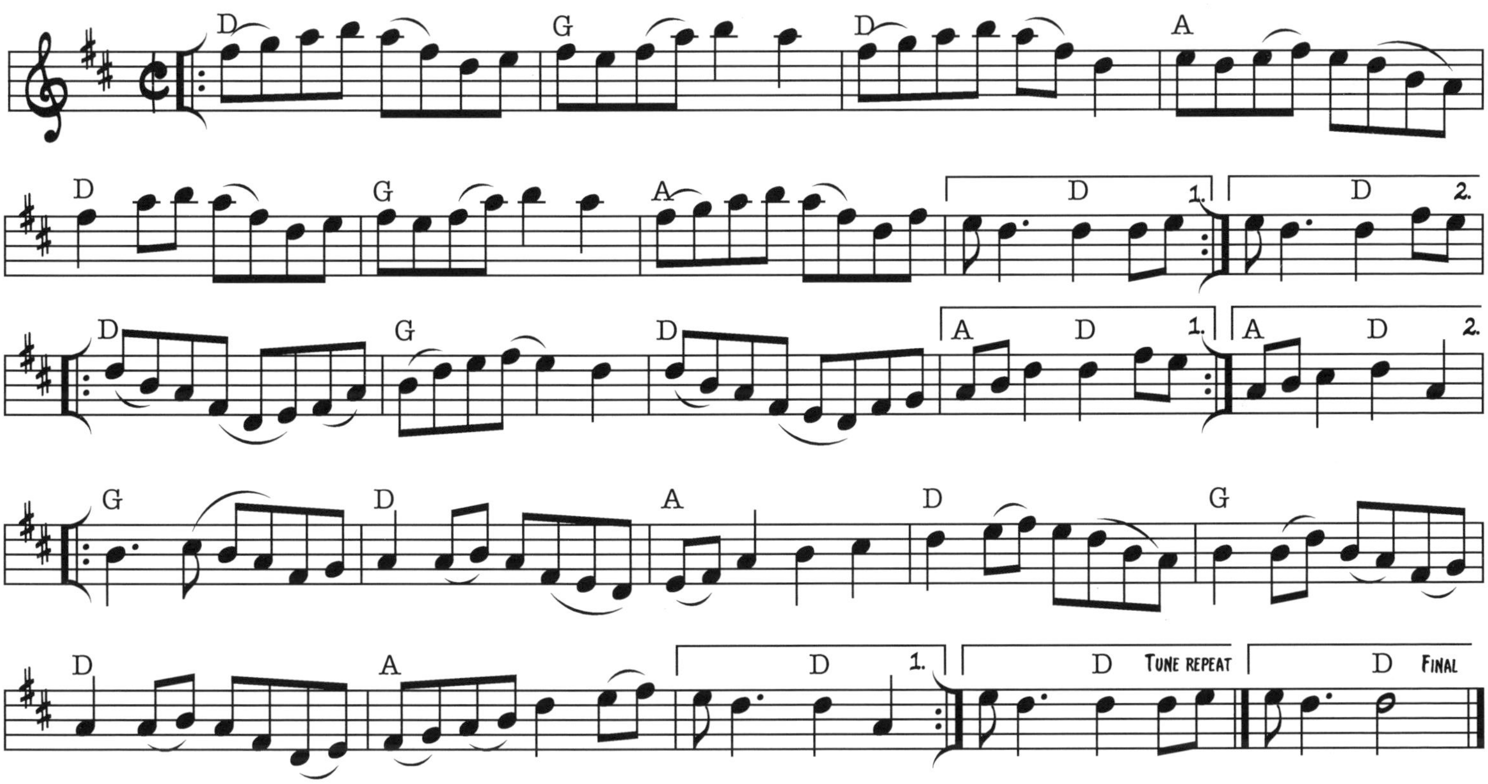

Jackie Wilson

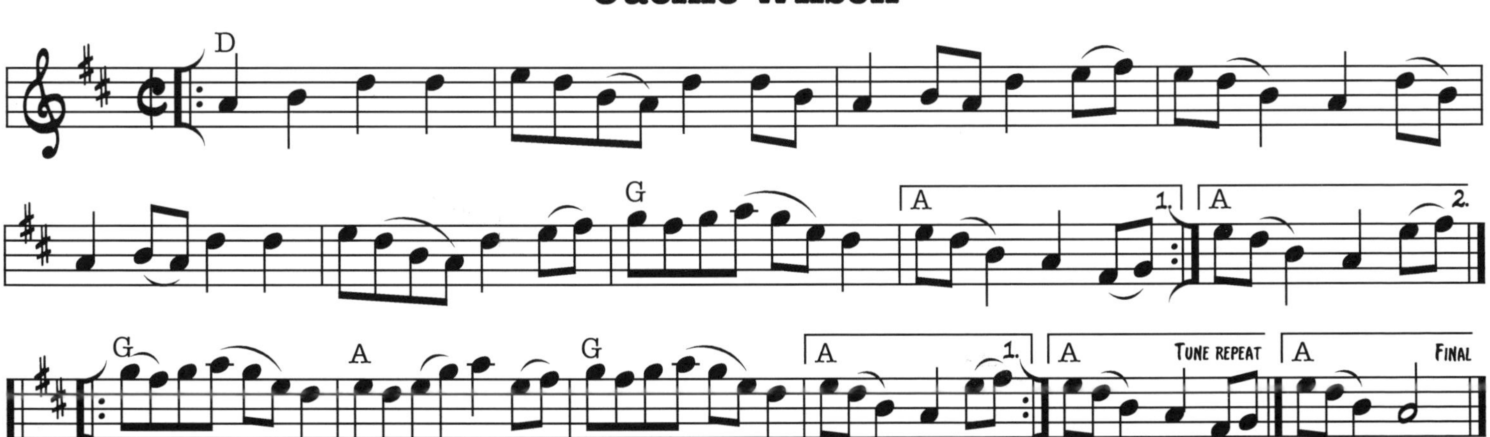

Indian Corn (aka Ol' Woodard's Tune)

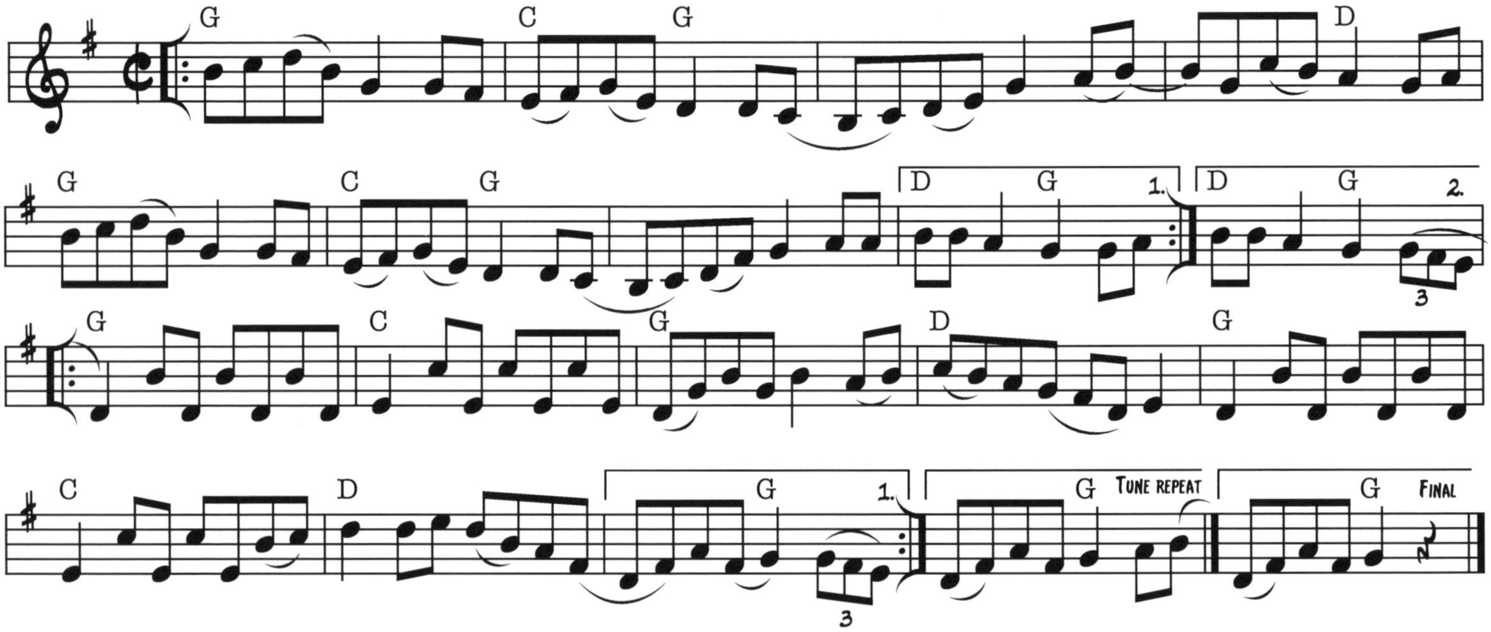

I've Got No Honey Babe Now

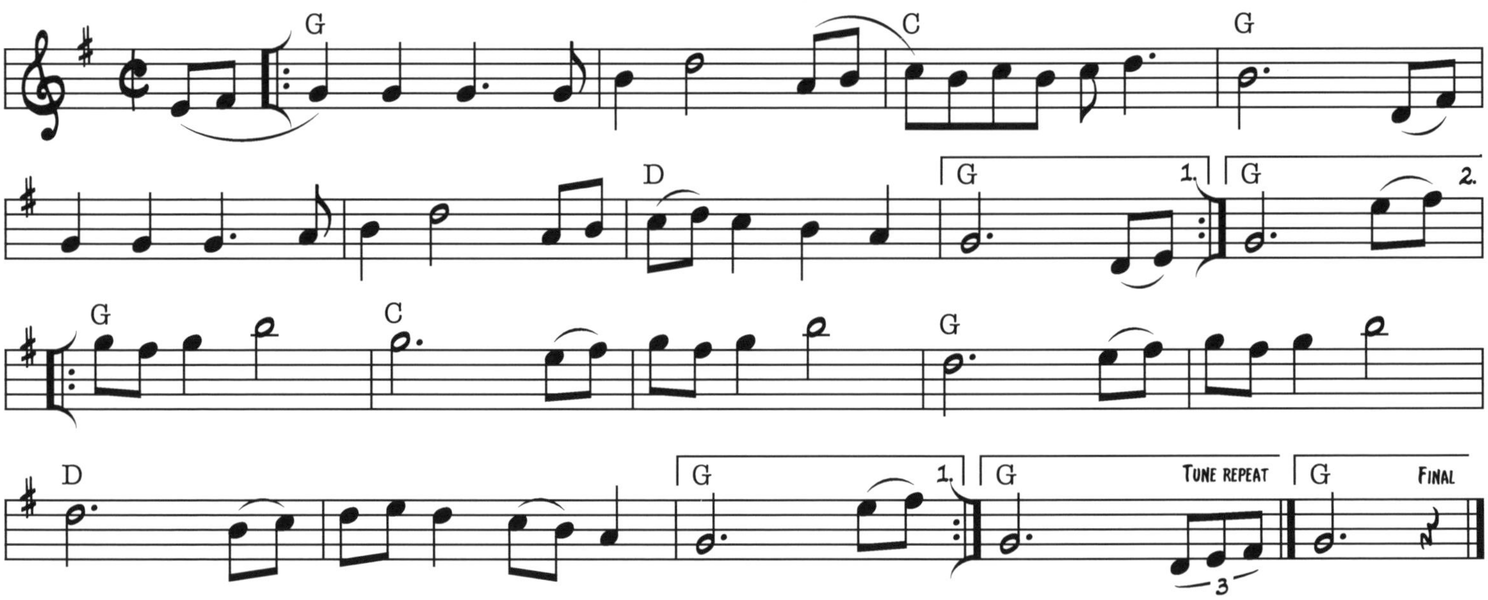

Jaybird

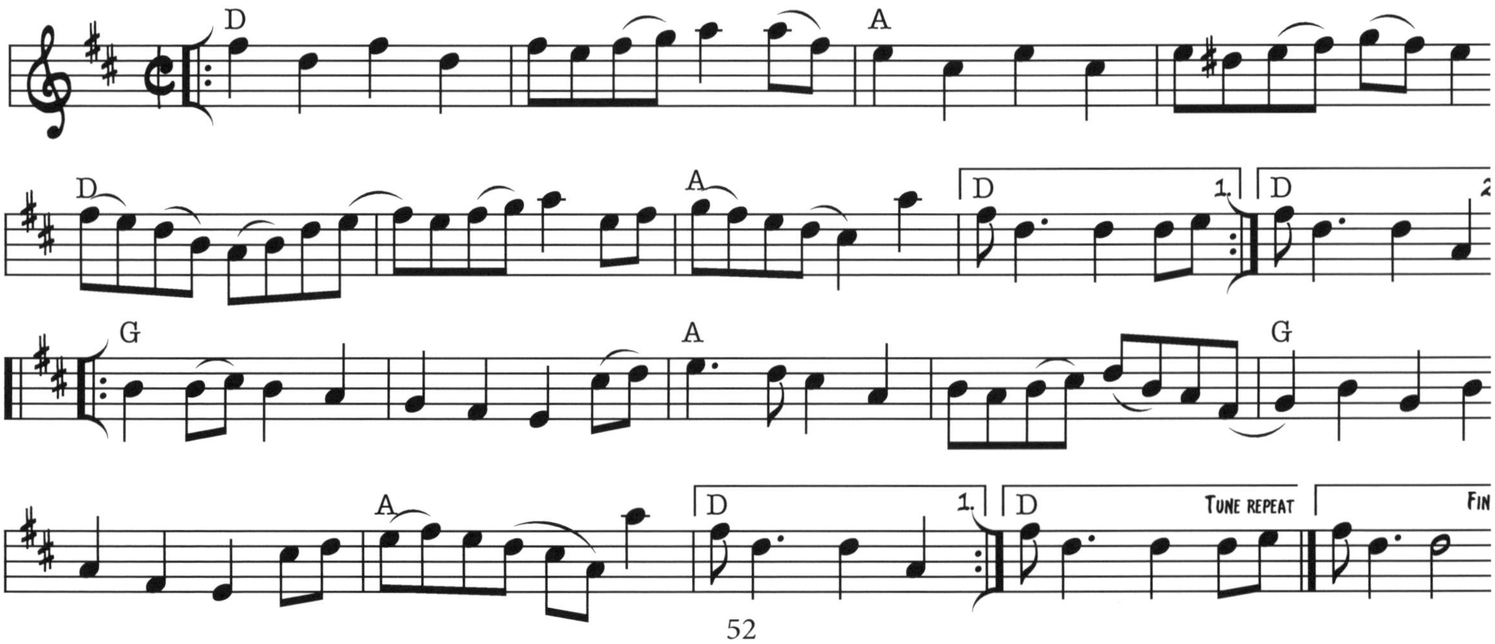

Jaybird Died of the Whooping Cough

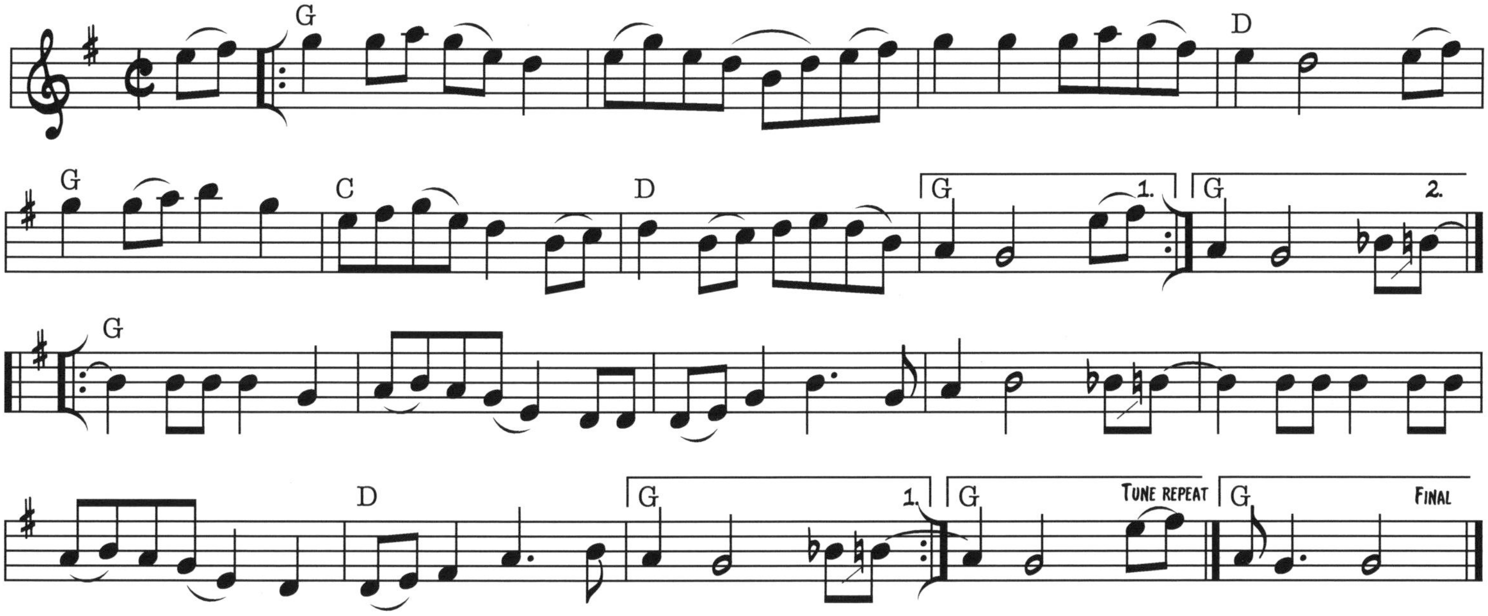

Jeff City

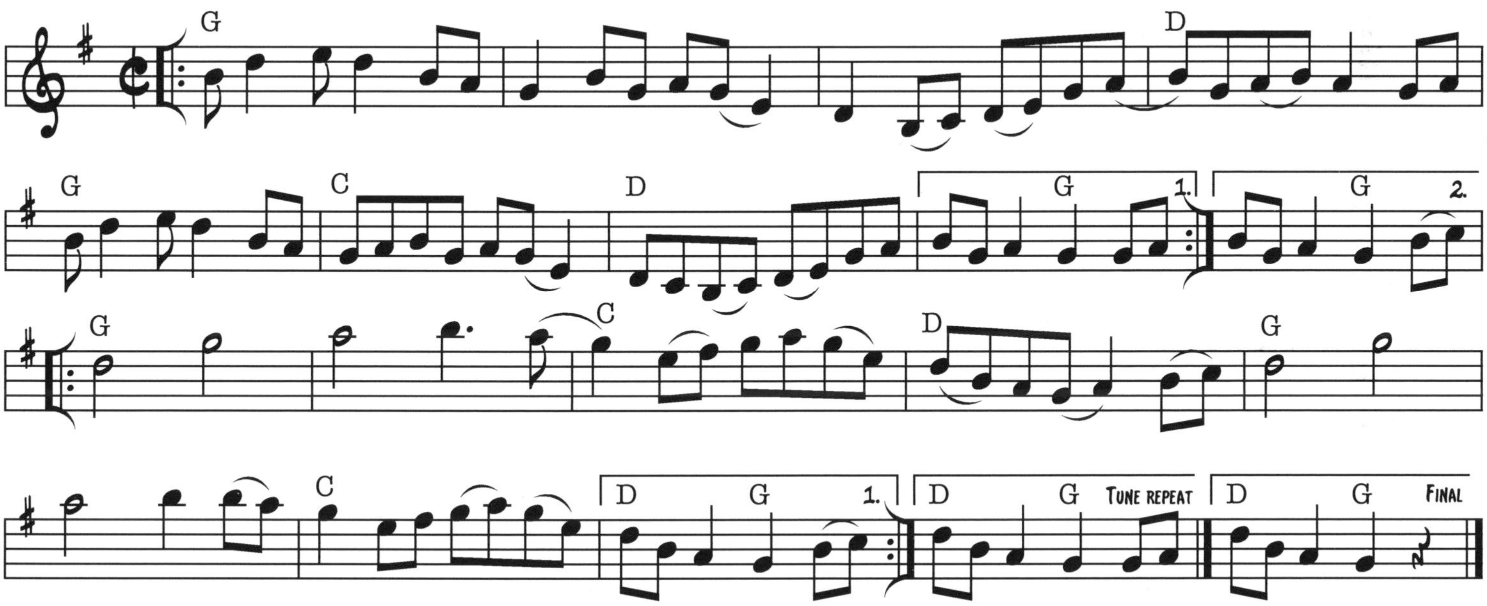

Jeff Sturgeon

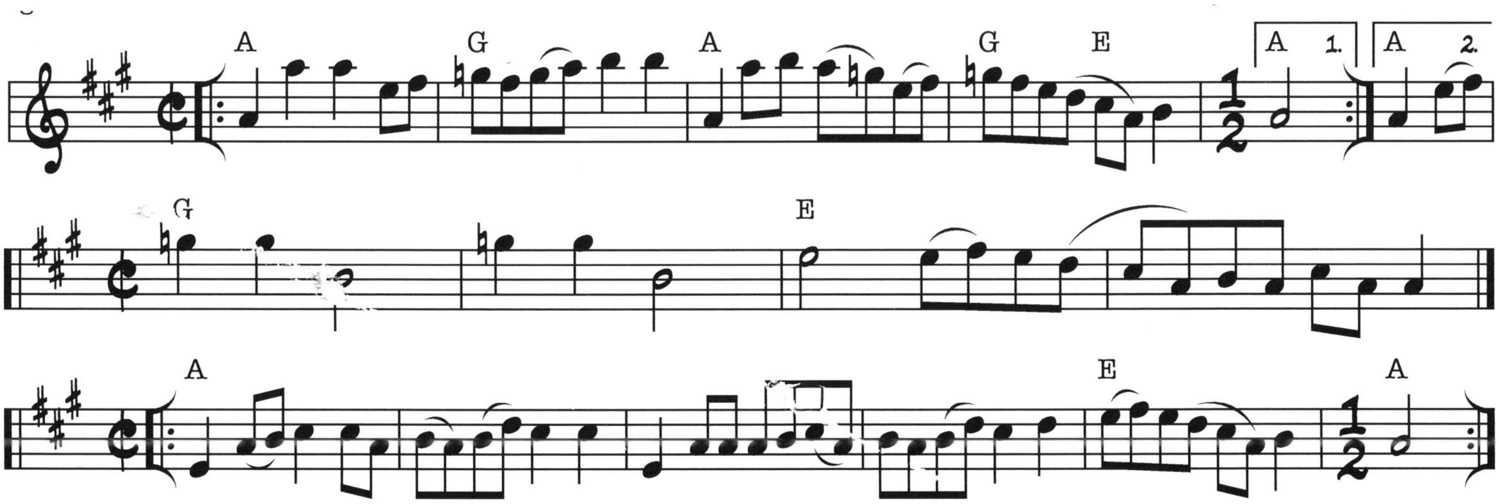

Jenny on the Railroad

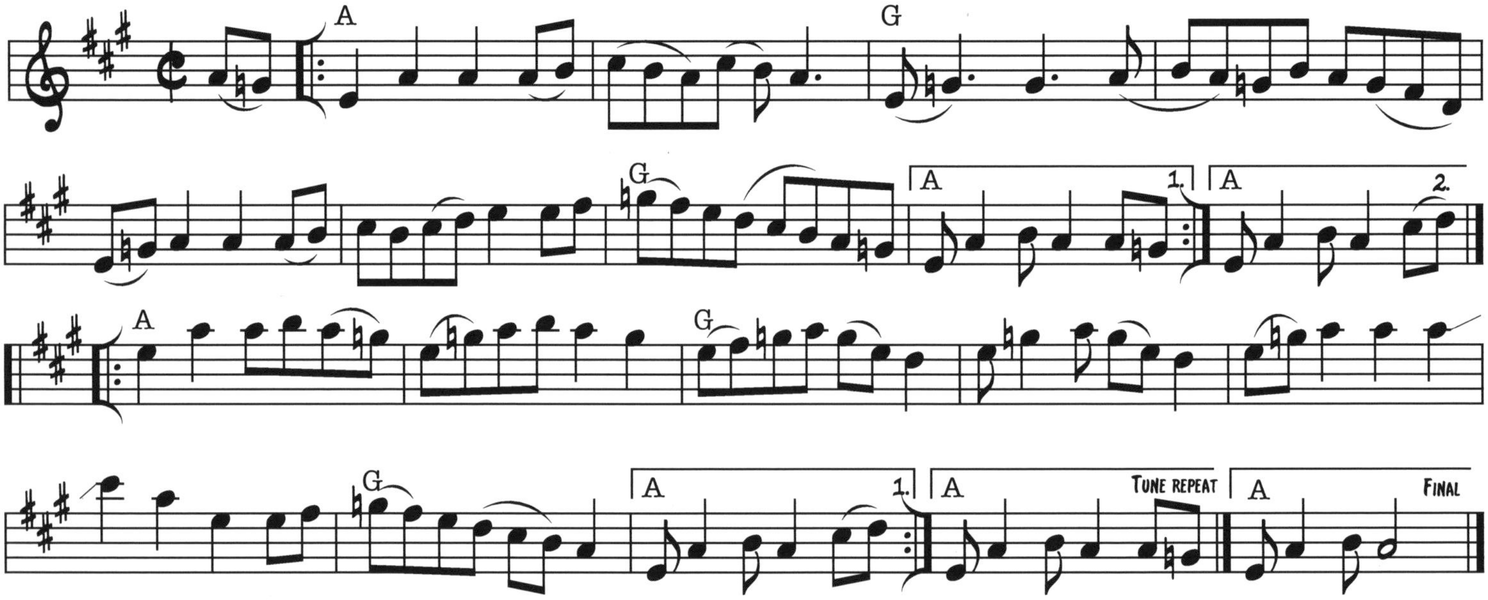

Jimmy in the Swamp

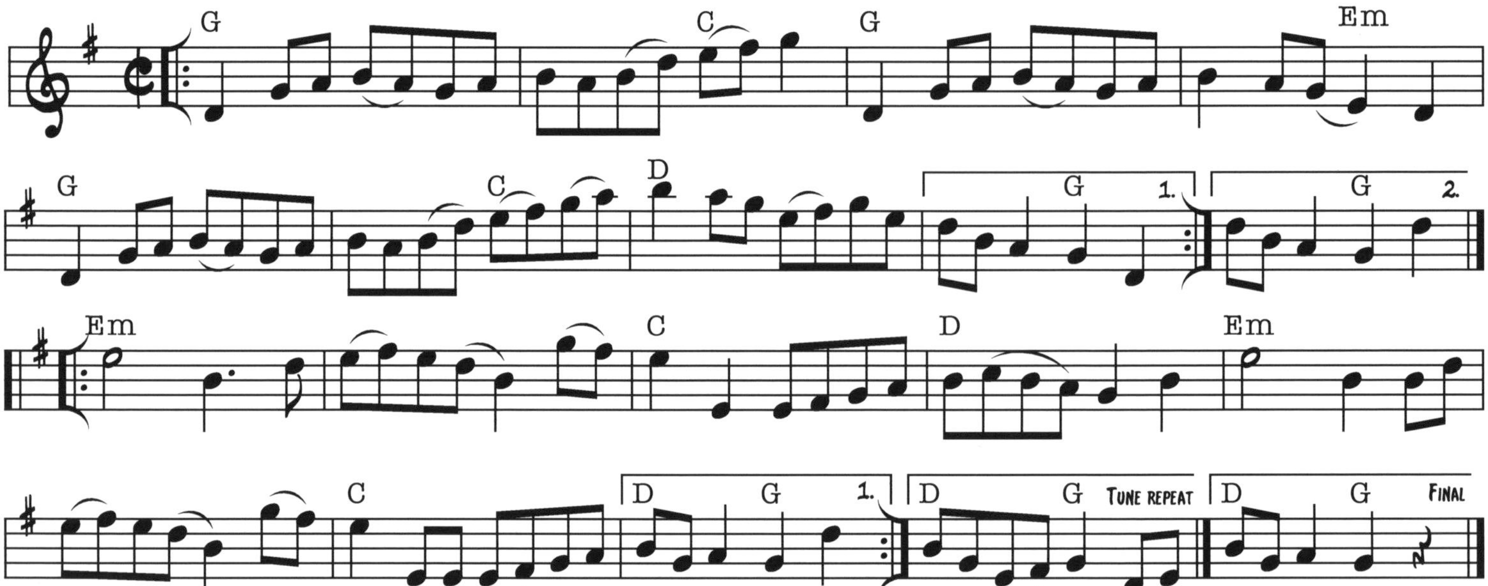

Jimmy Shank

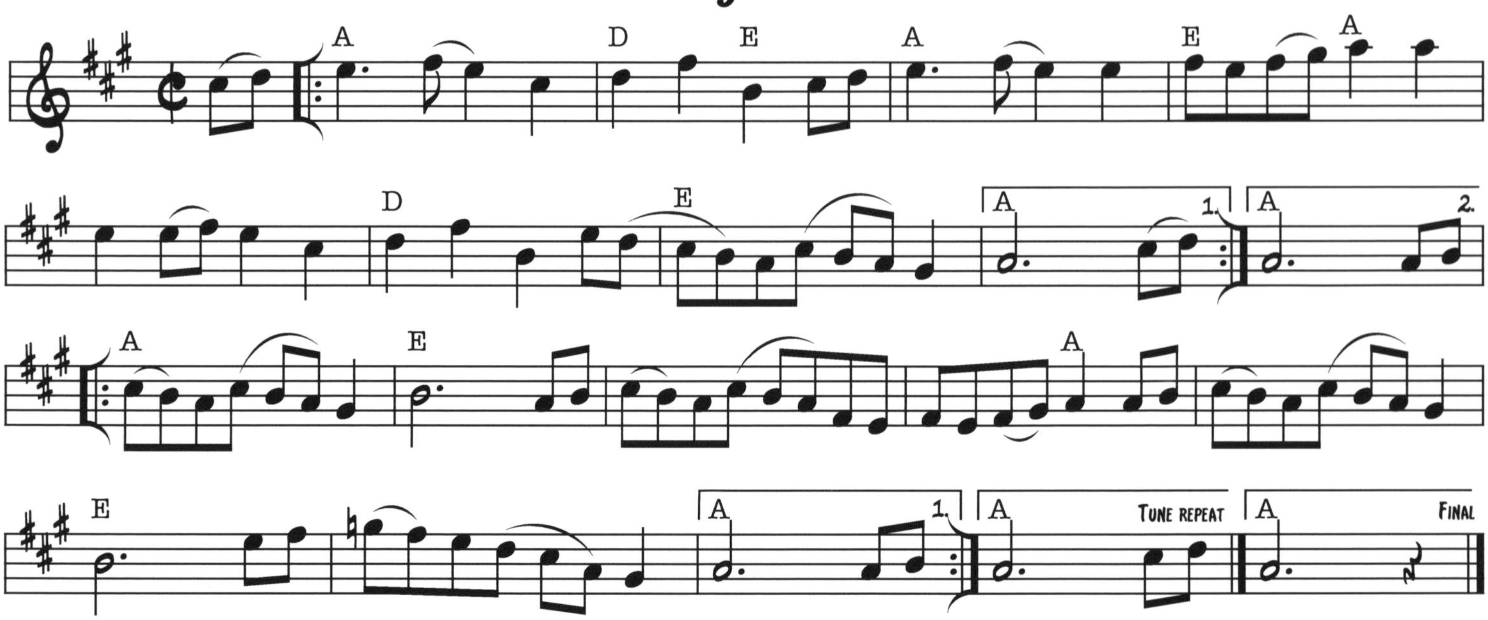

John Brown's Dream

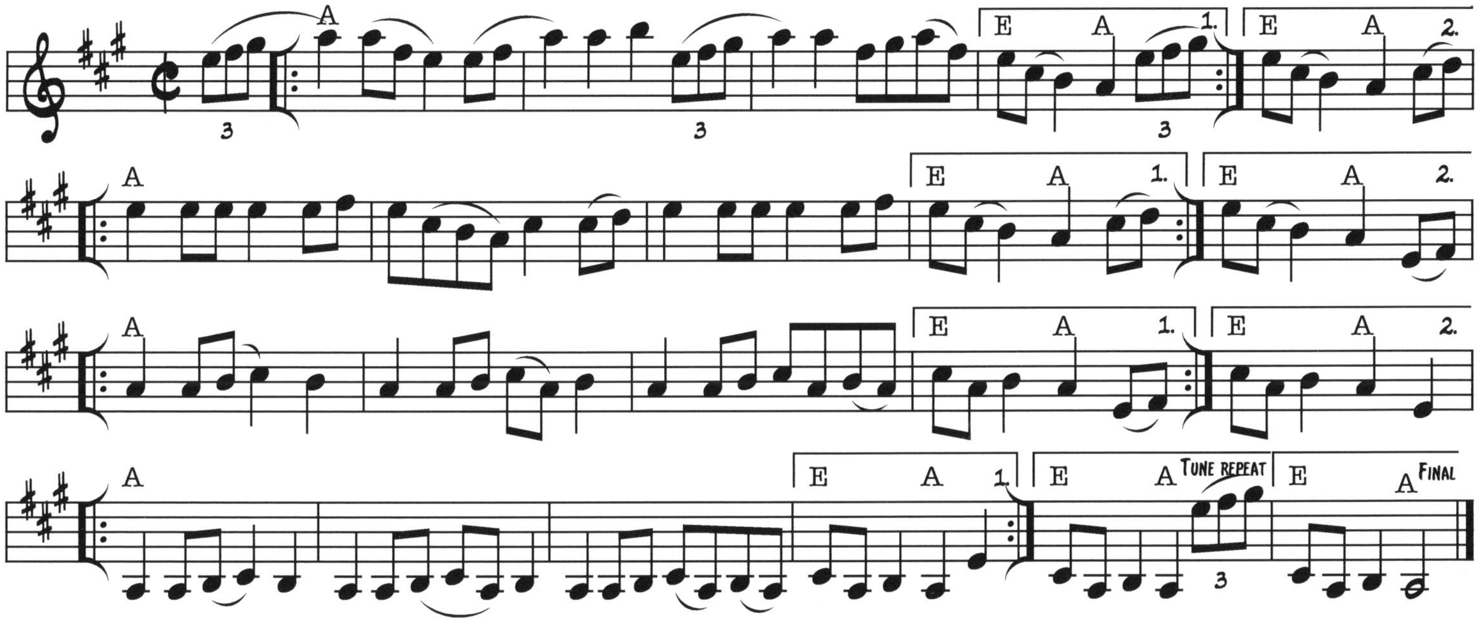

John Brown's March

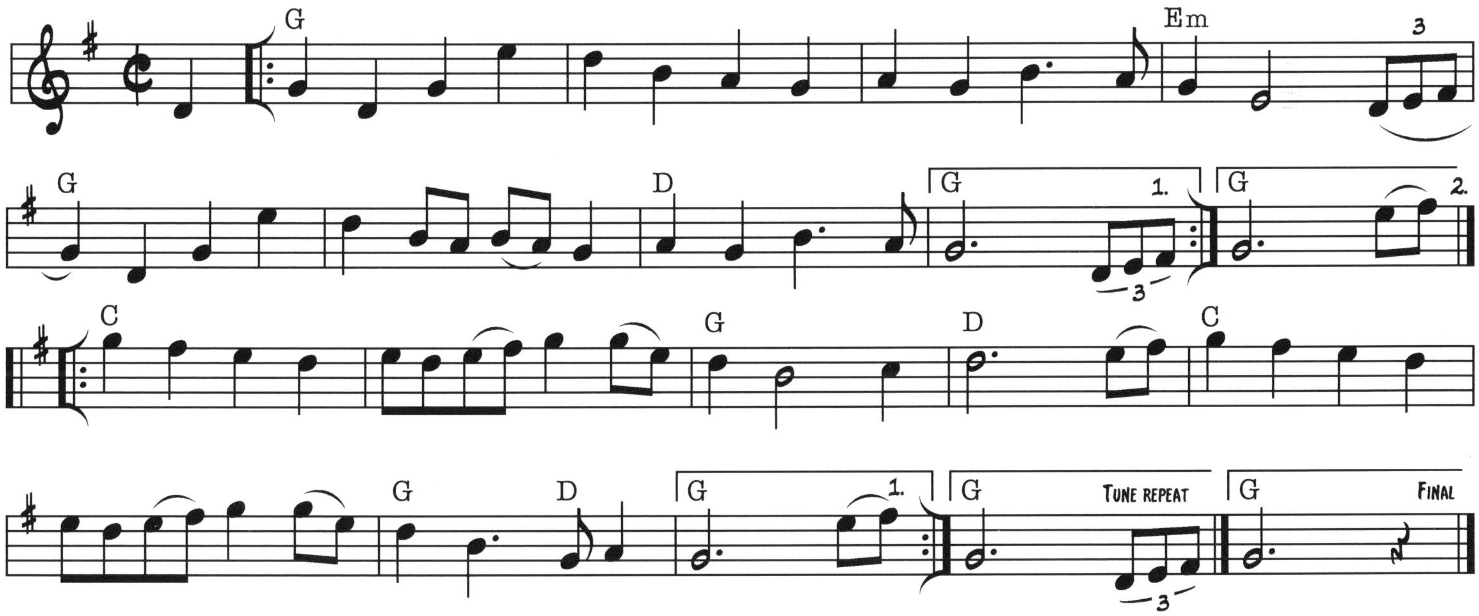

John Henry

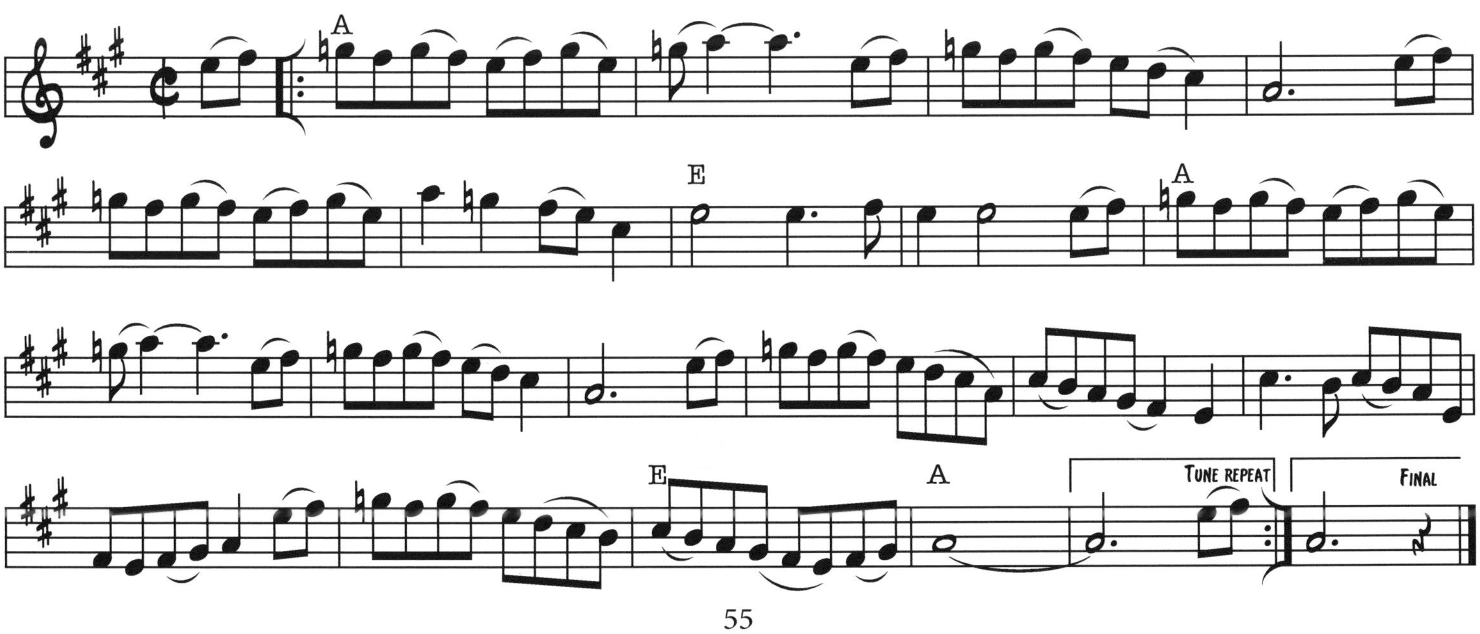

John Lover's Gone

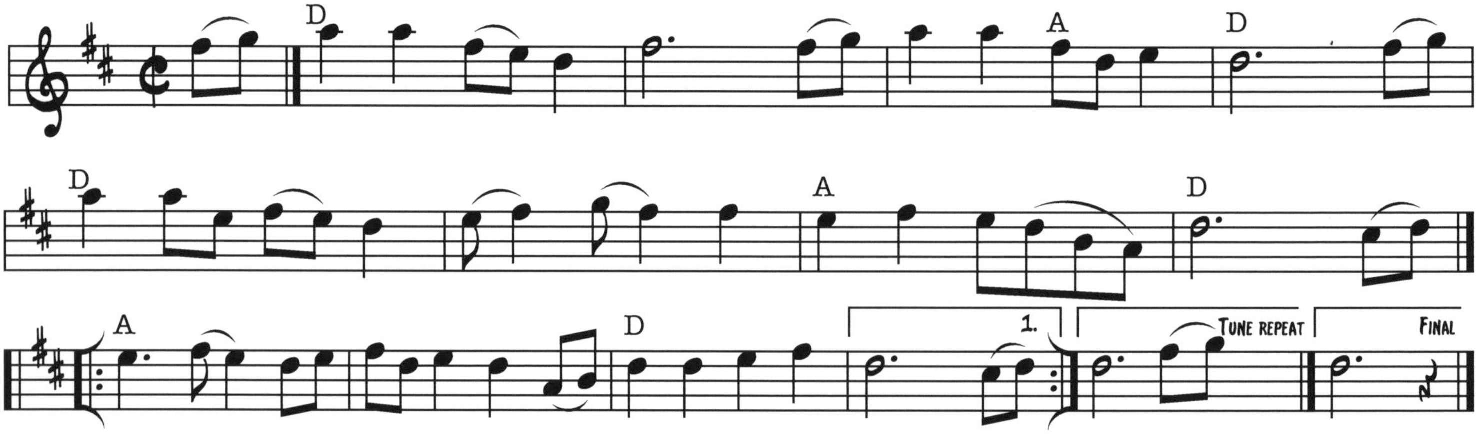

John Sharp's Reel

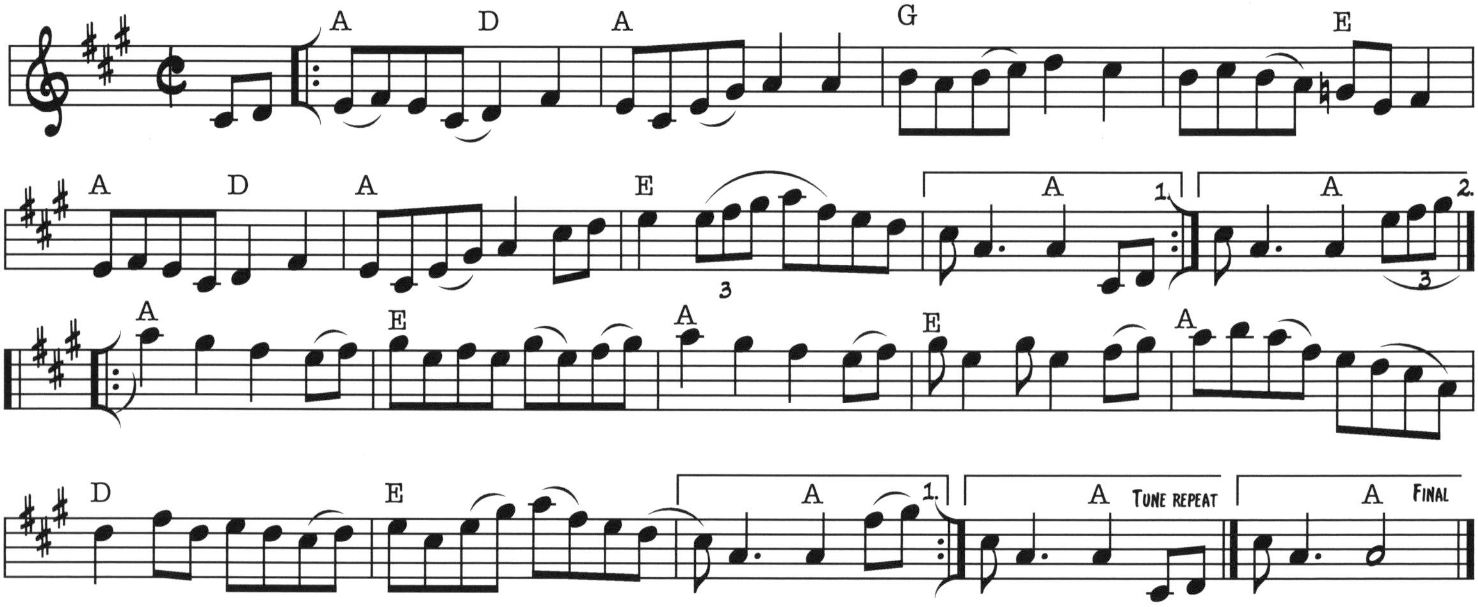

John Stenson's #2

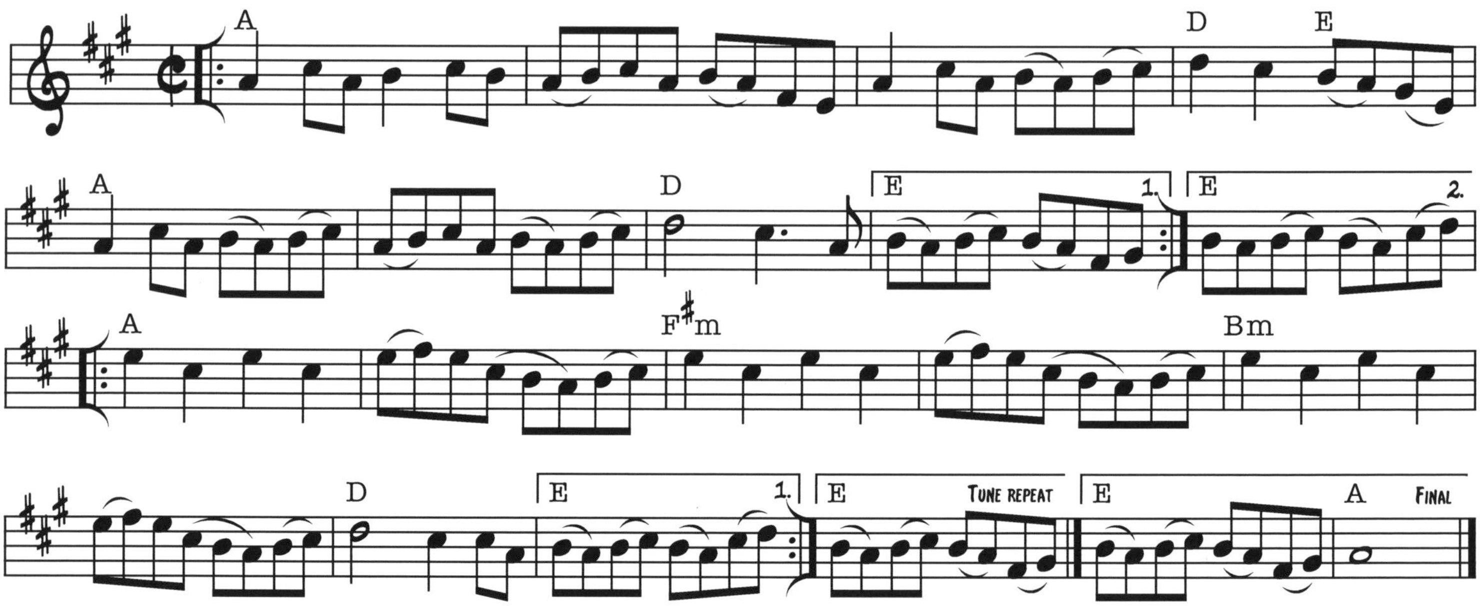

Johnny Cope

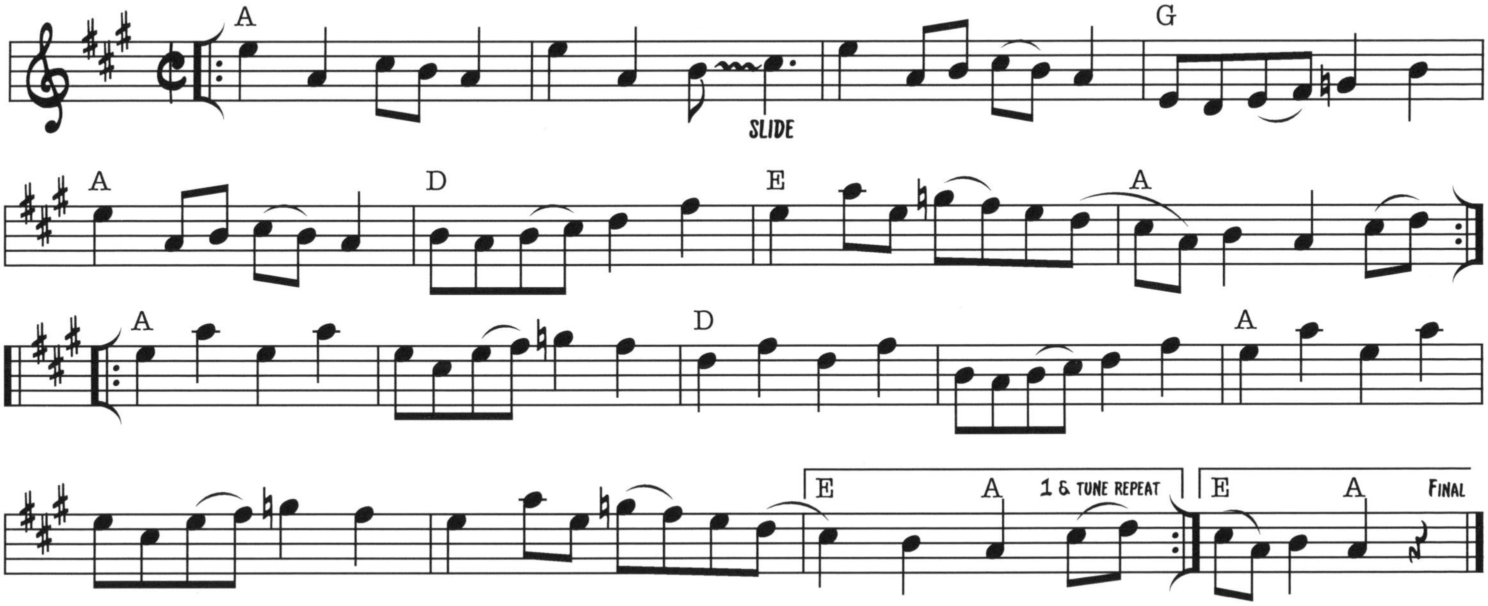

Johnny Don't Get Drunk

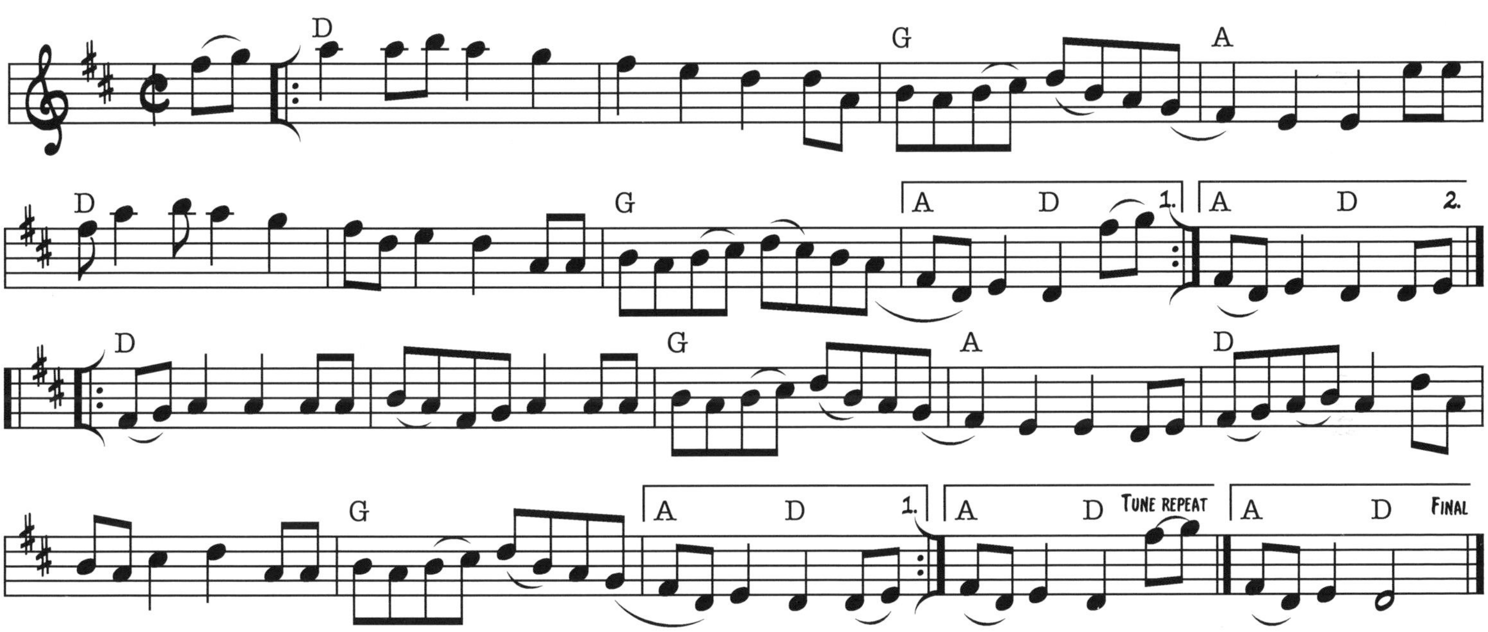

Johnson Boys

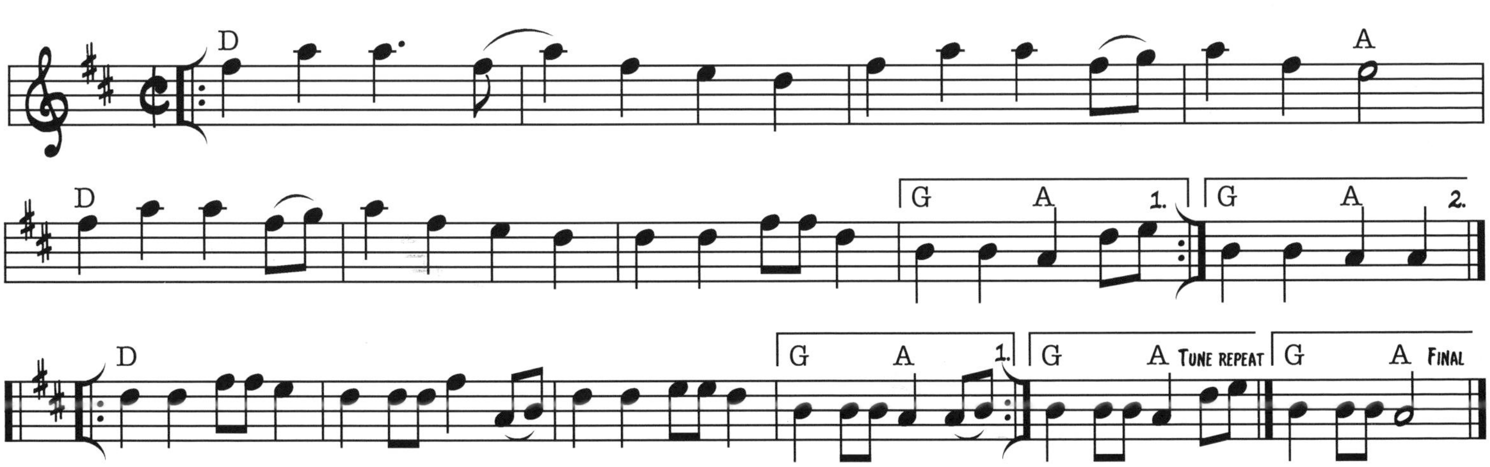

Johnson Gals

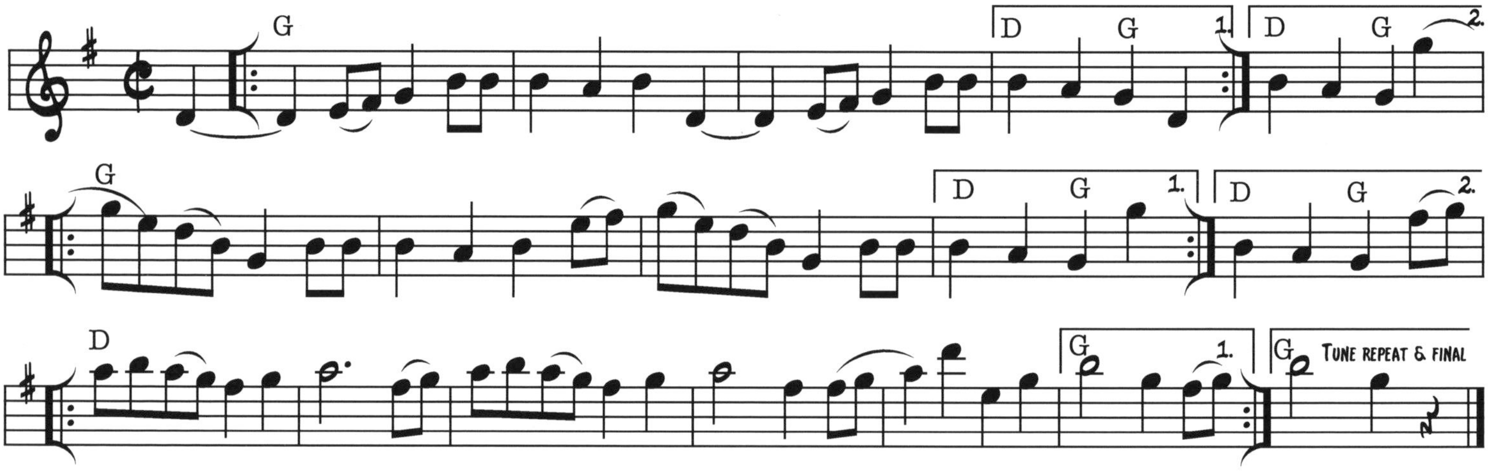

Jonah in the Windstorm

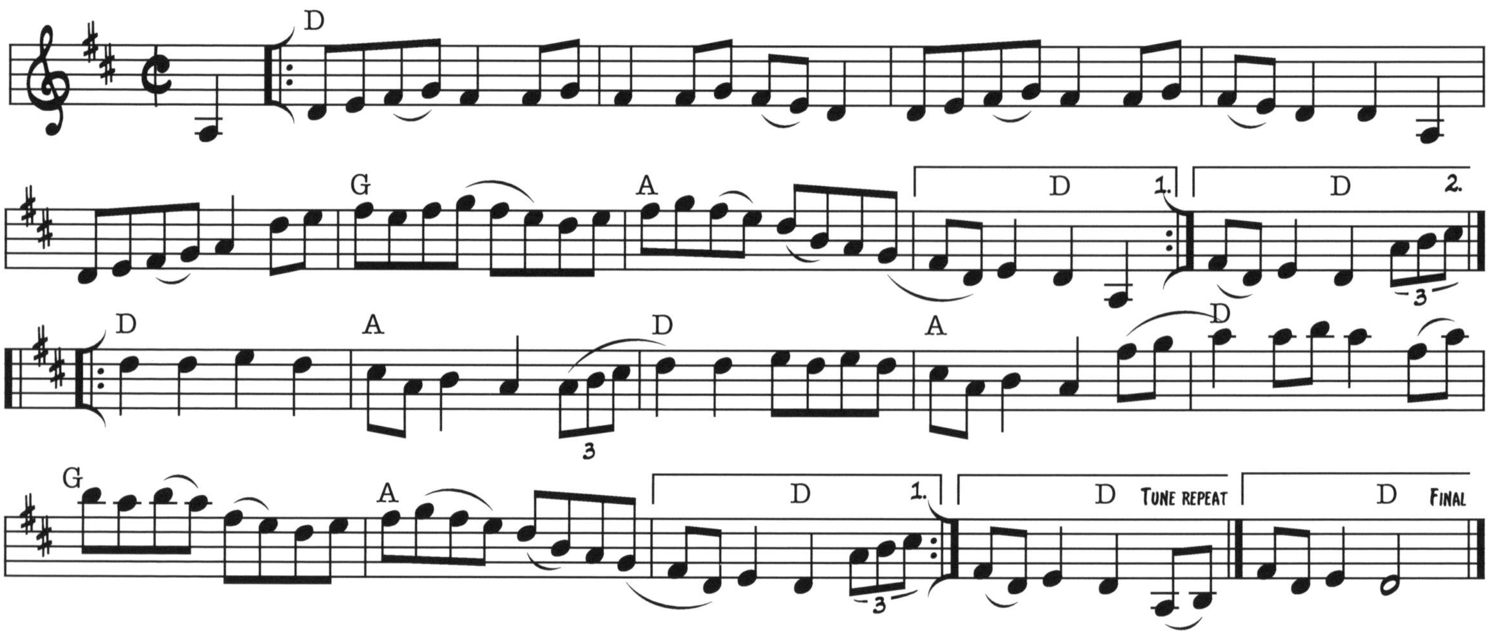

Juliann Johnson

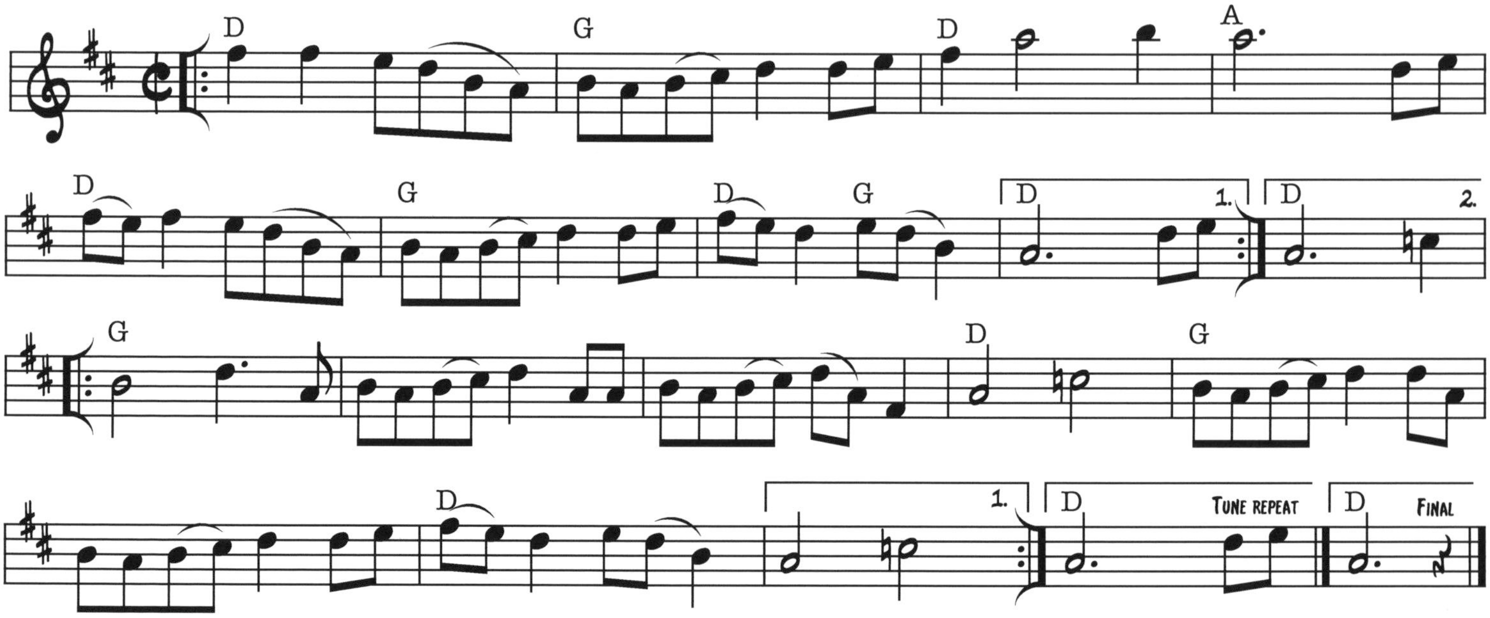

Jump in the Well My Pretty Little Miss

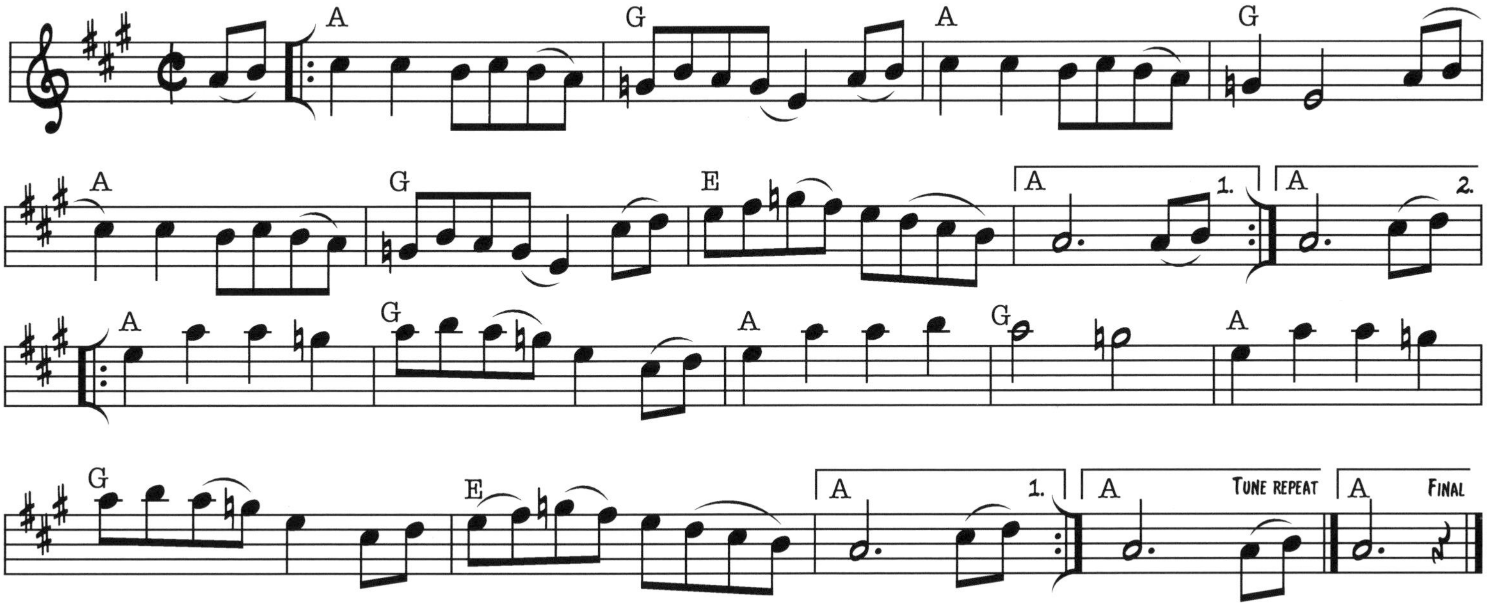

Jump Jim Crow

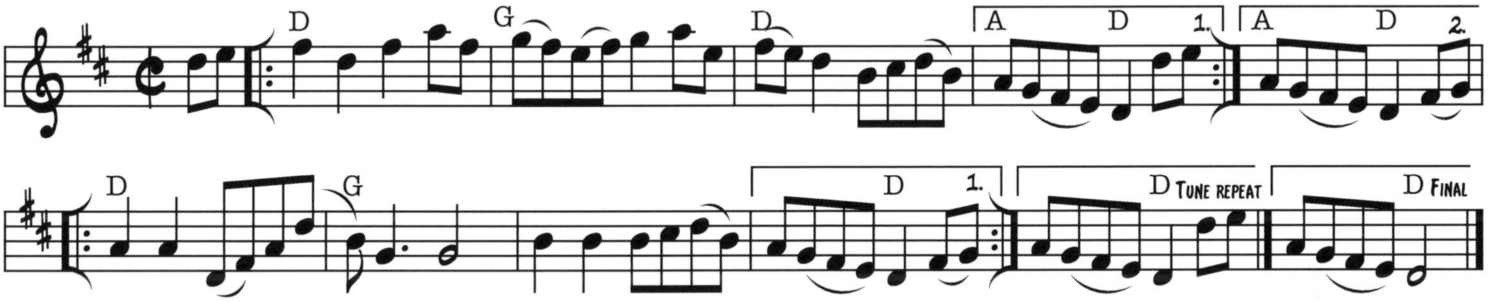

Kash Kersey

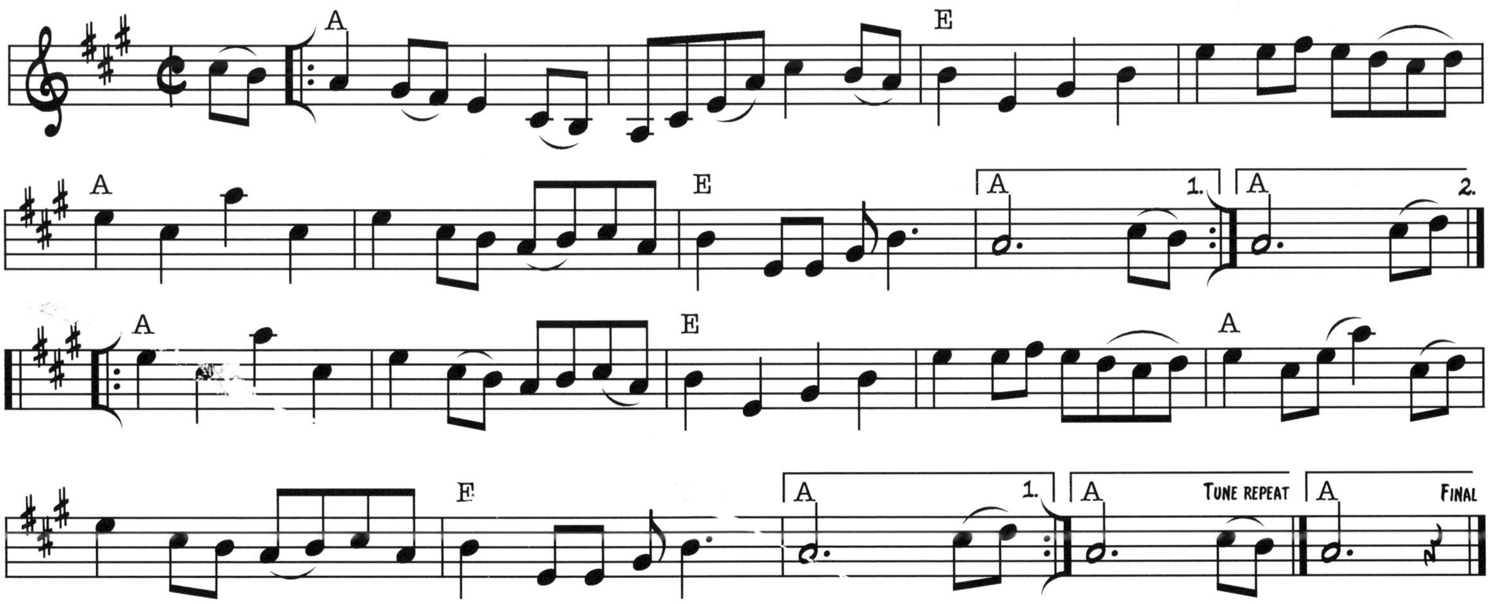

Just From the Fountain

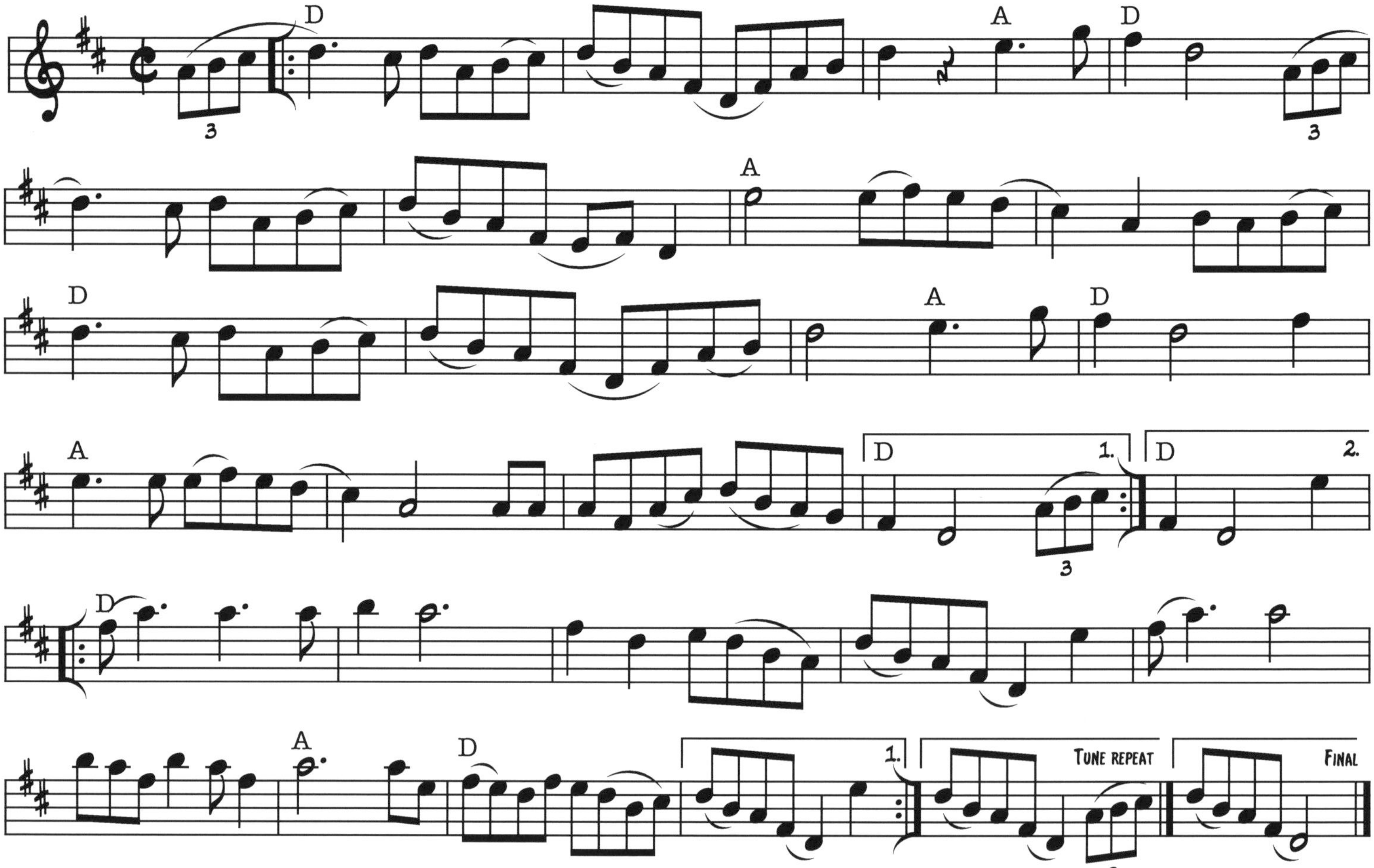

Katy Hill

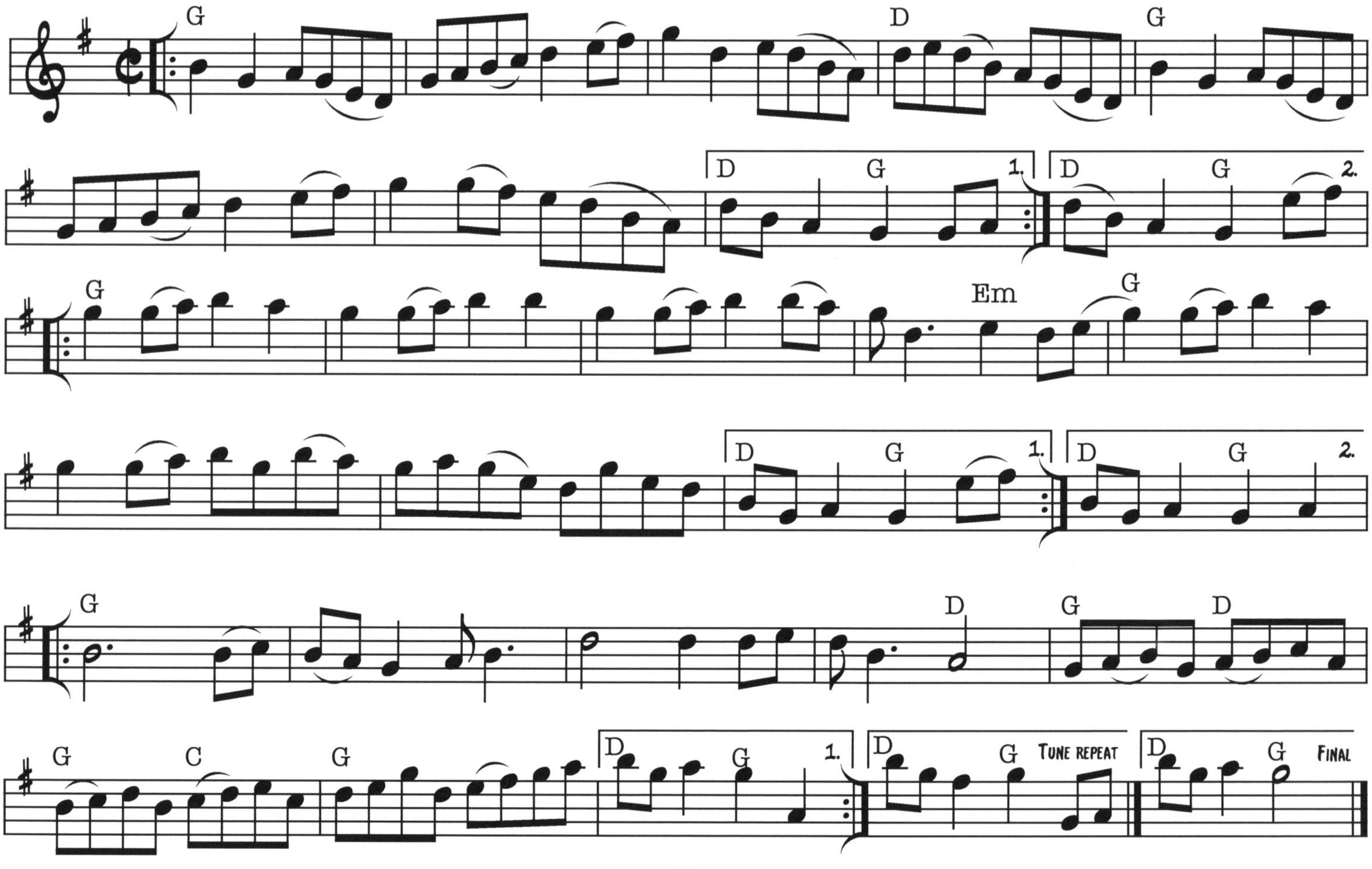

Kansas City Reel

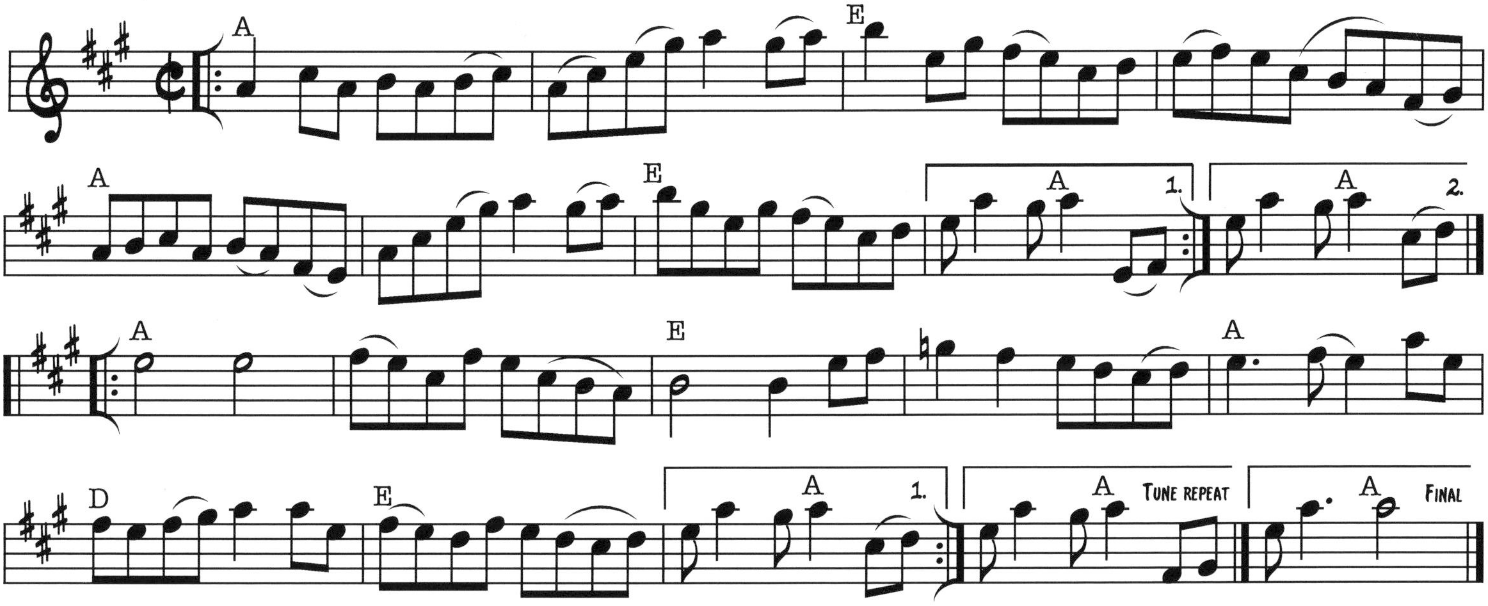

Lady of the Lake 1

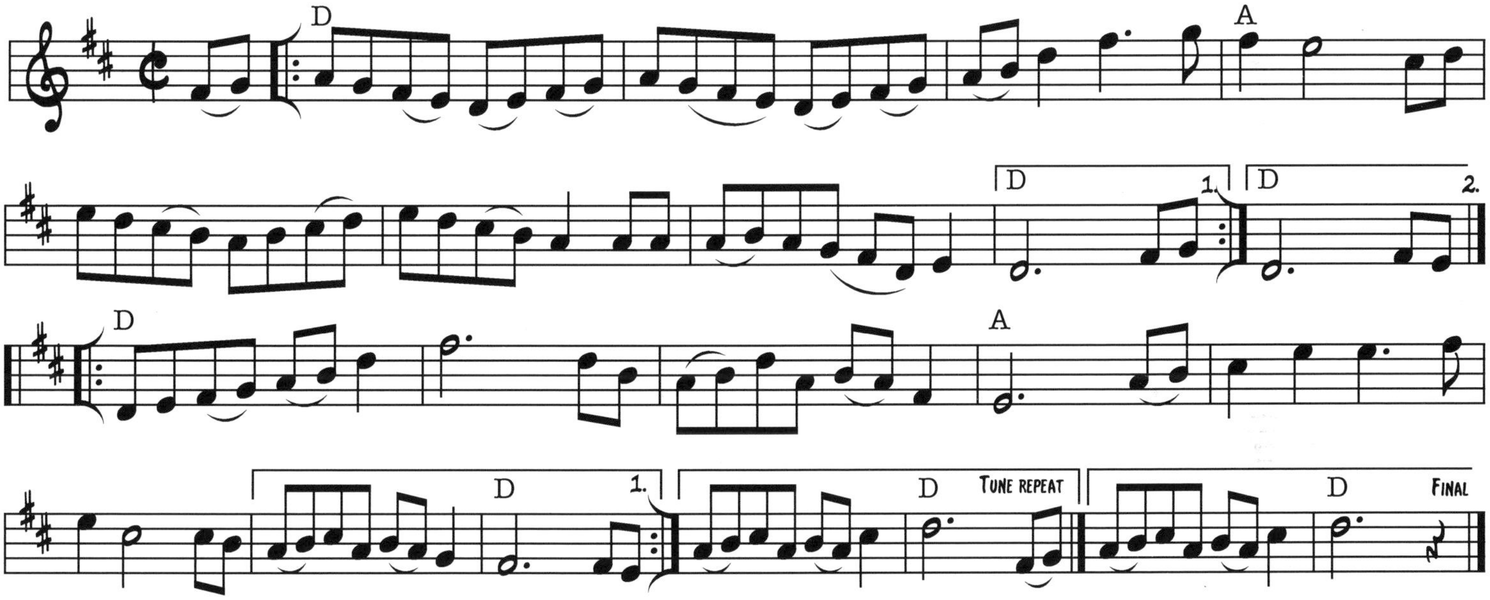

Lady of the Lake 2

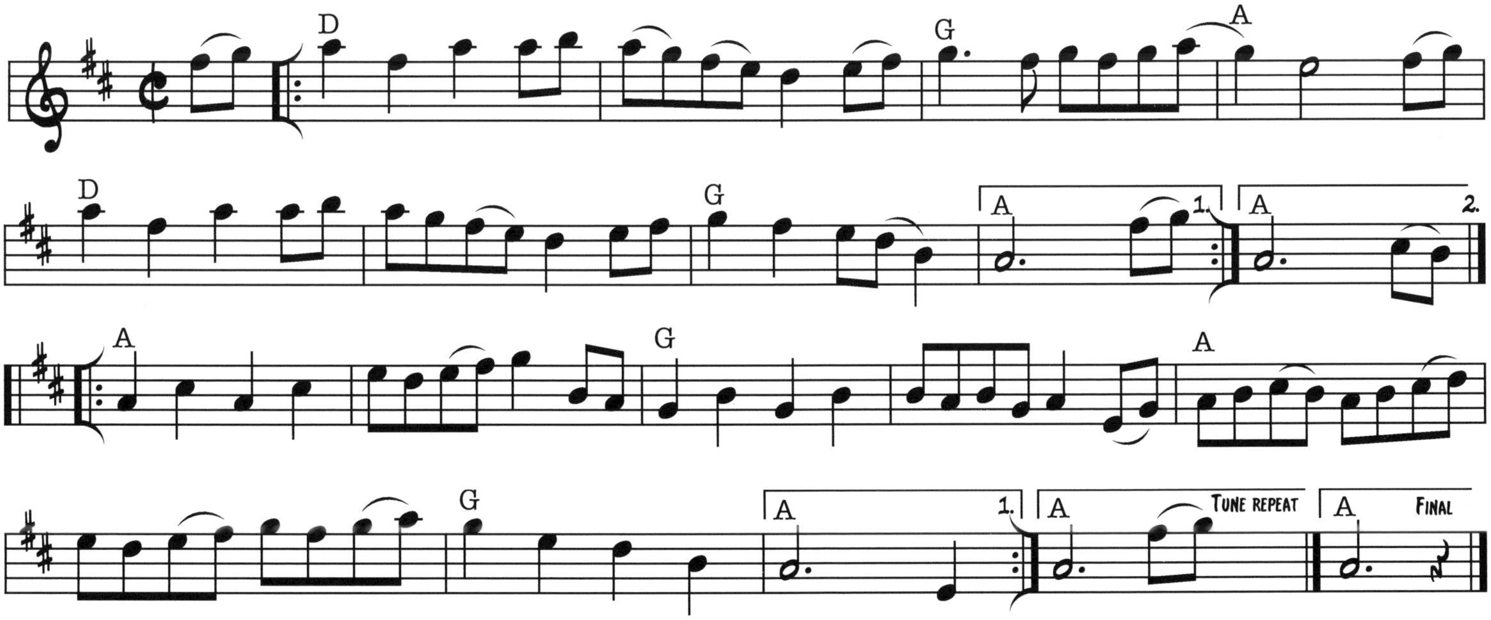

Ladies on the Steamboat

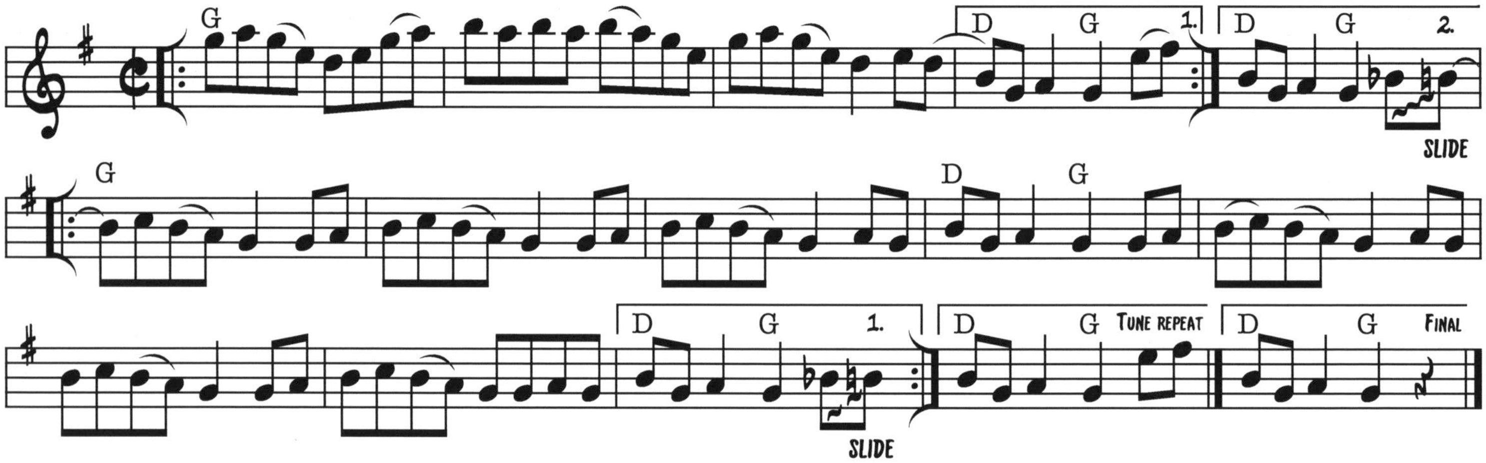

Leather Britches

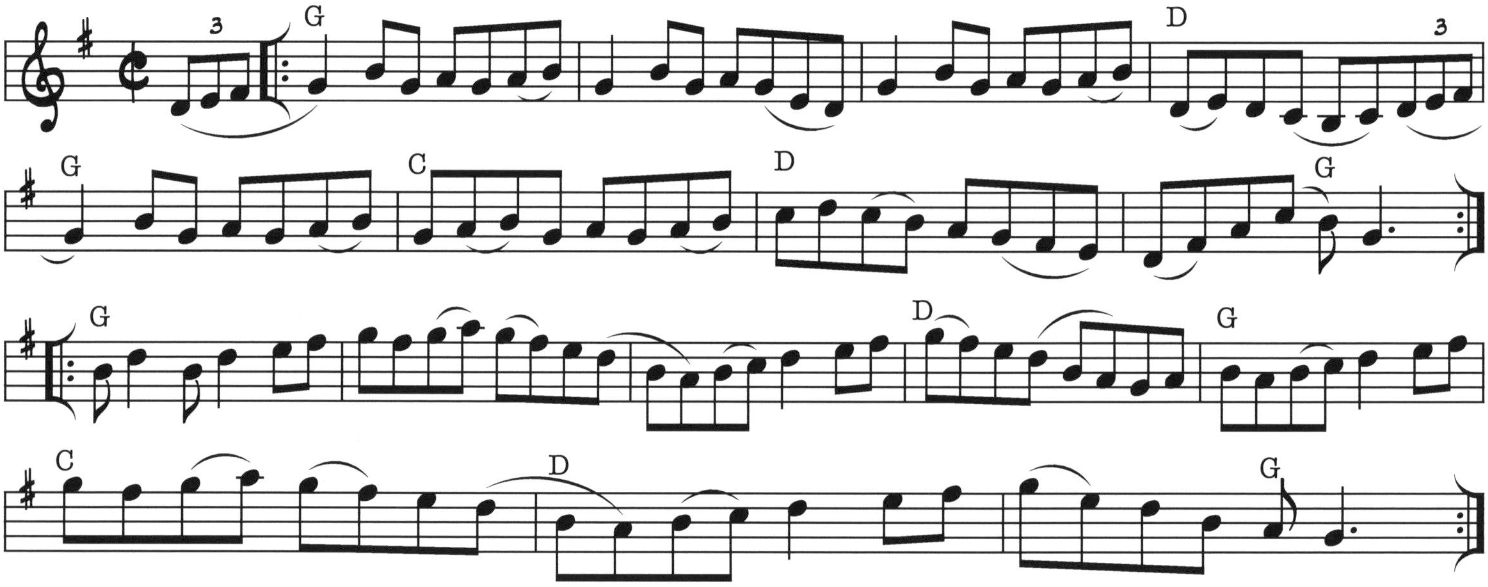

Liberty

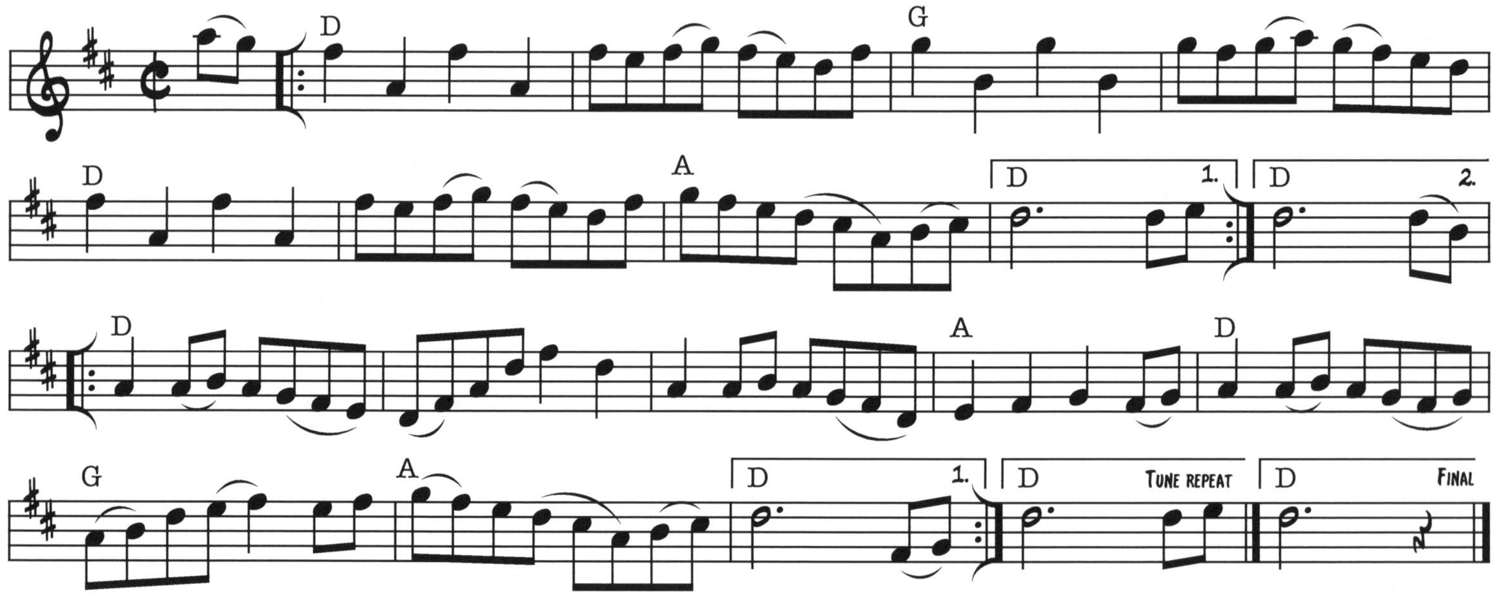

Little Burnt Potato

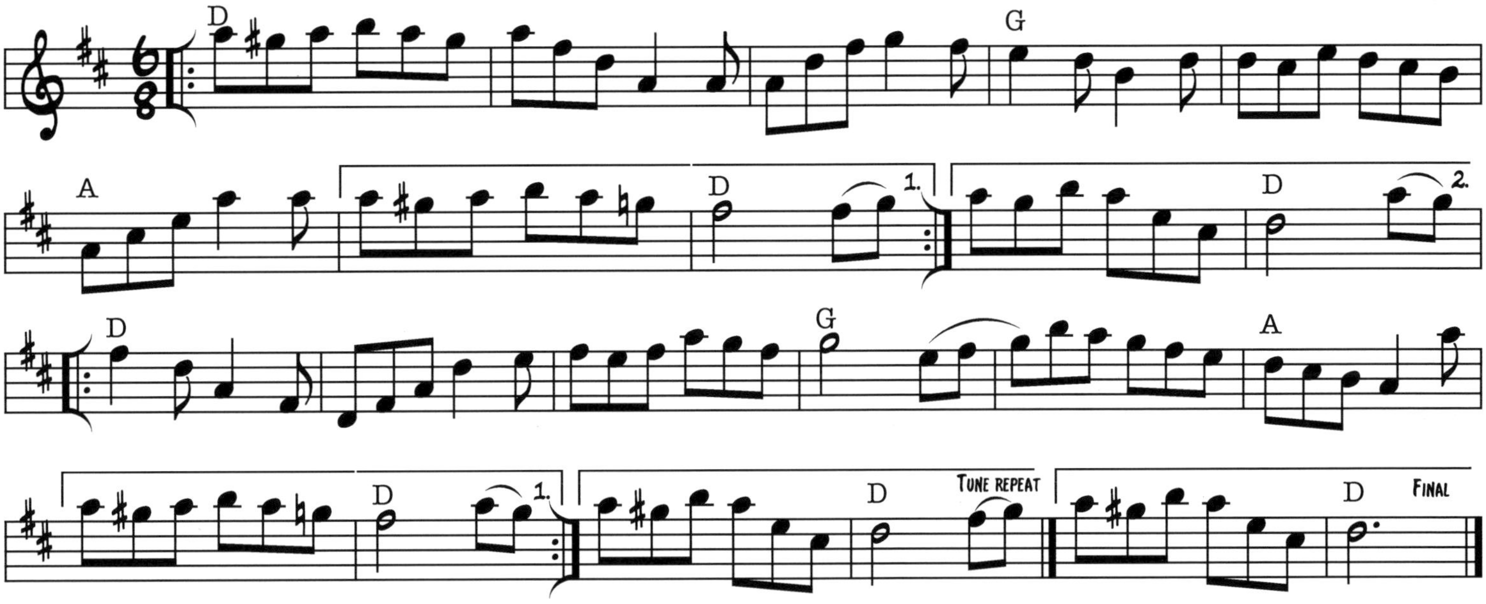

Little Betty Brown

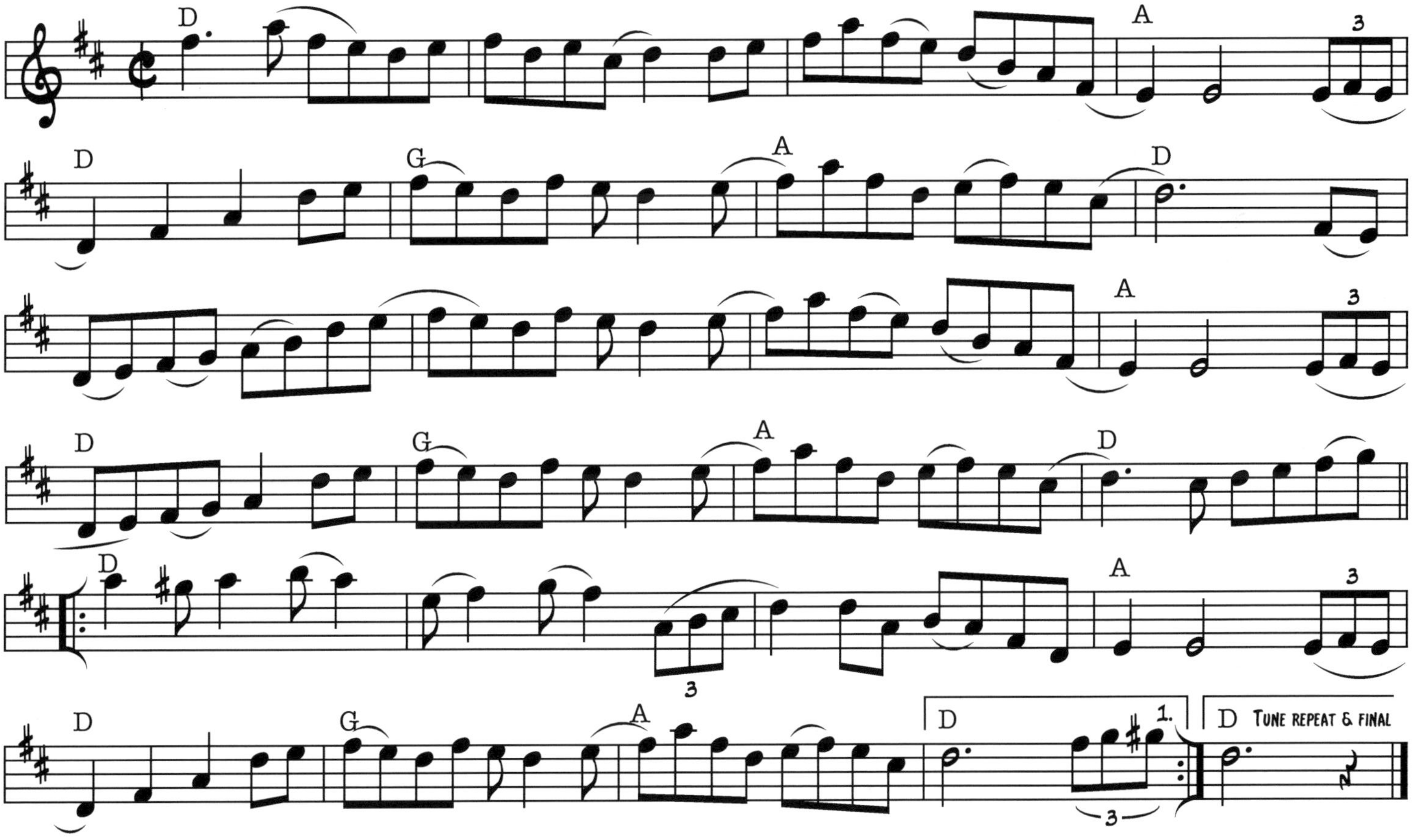

Little Billy Wilson

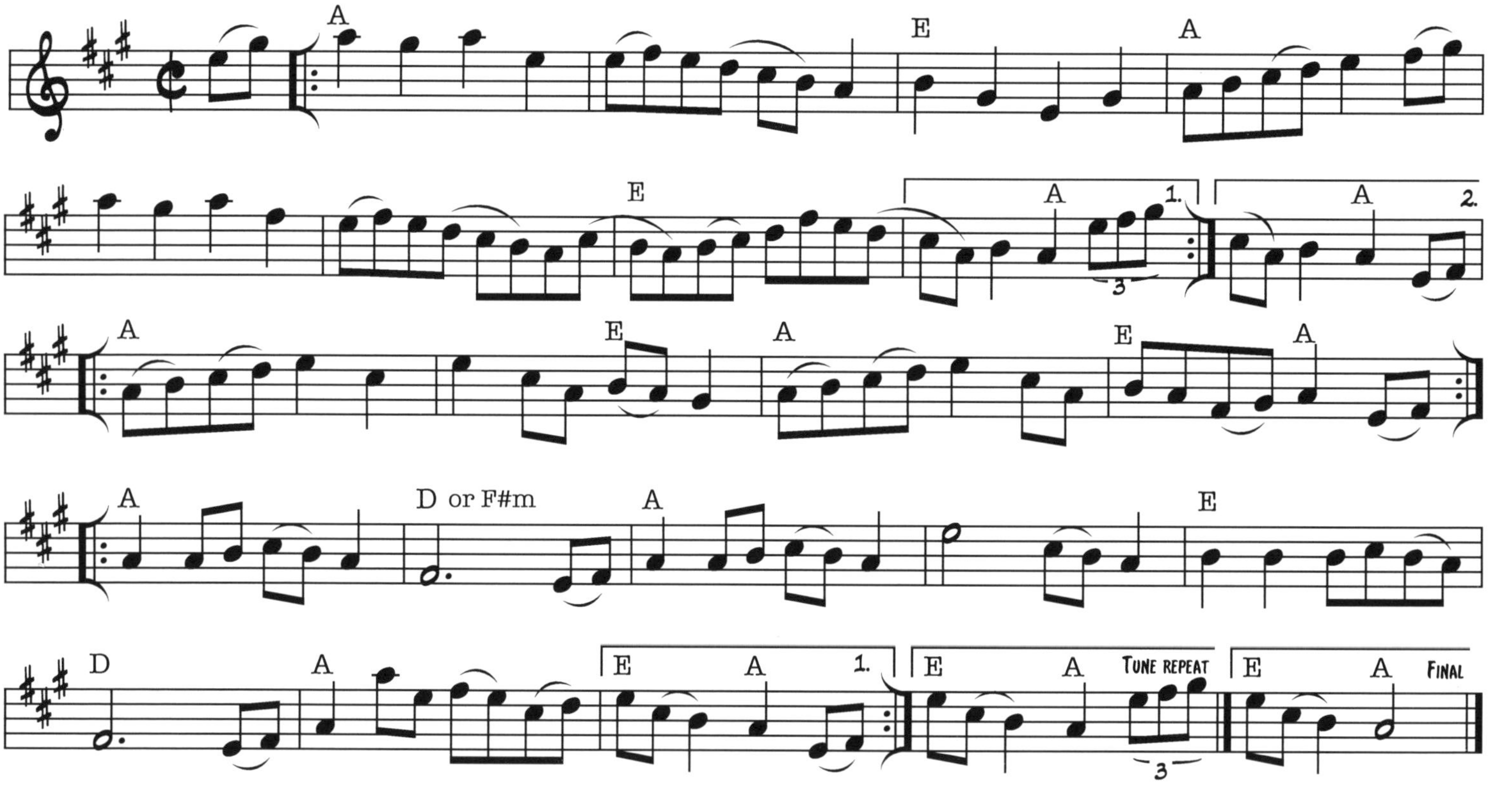

Little Dutch Girl

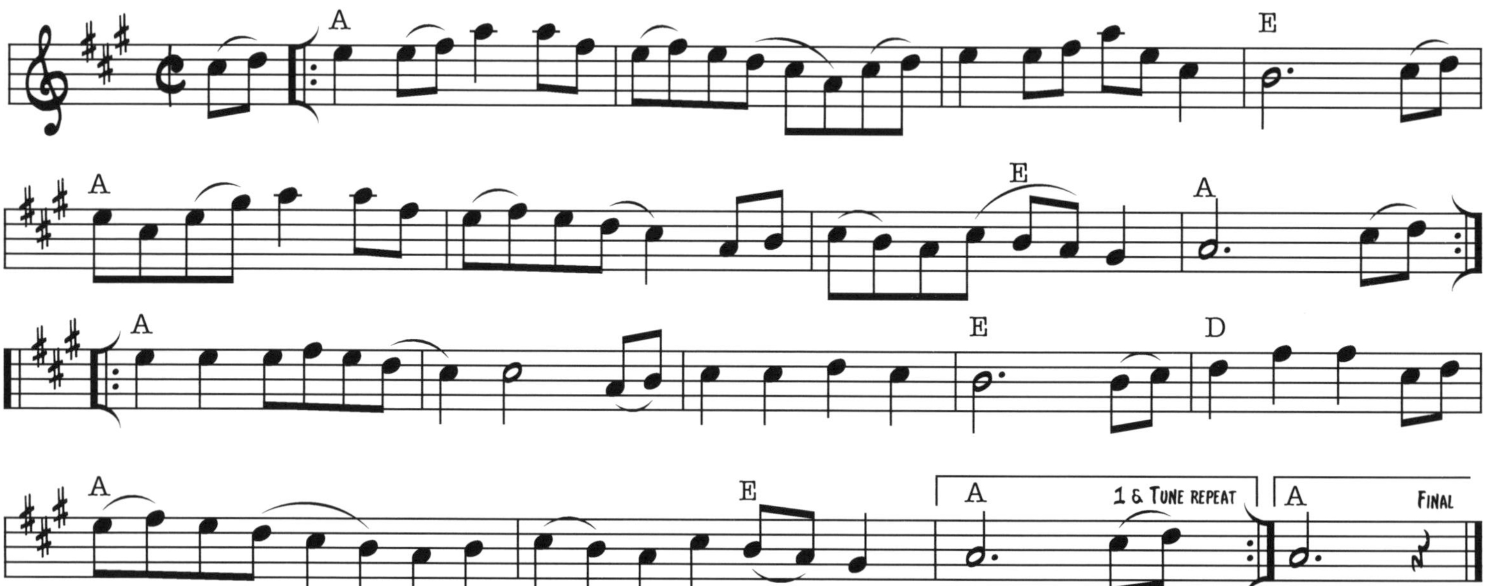

Little Girl with Her Hair Down Behind

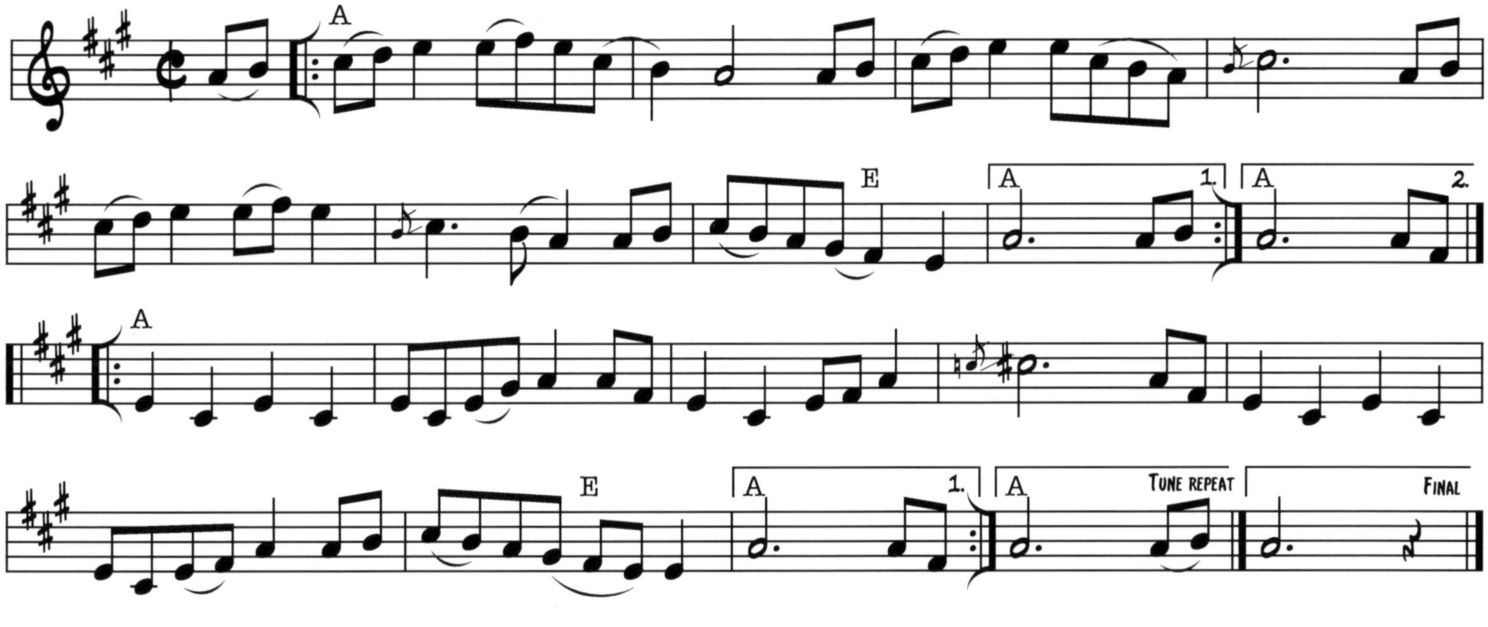

Little Sadie

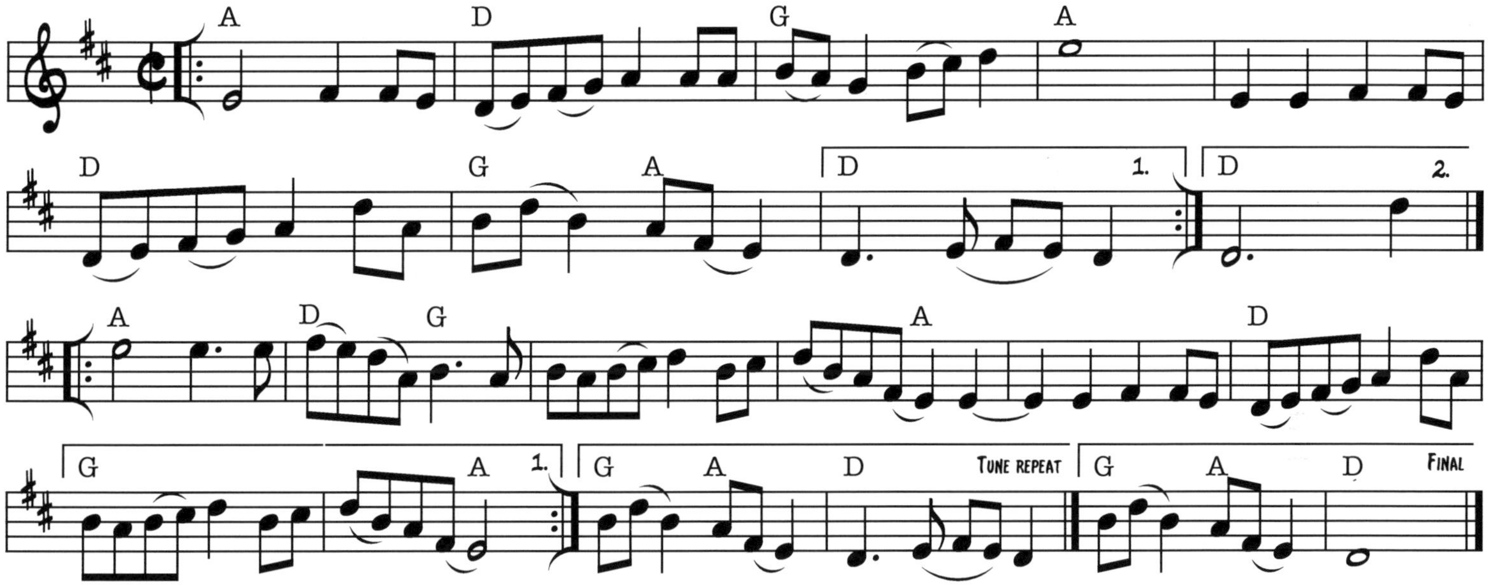

Log Chain

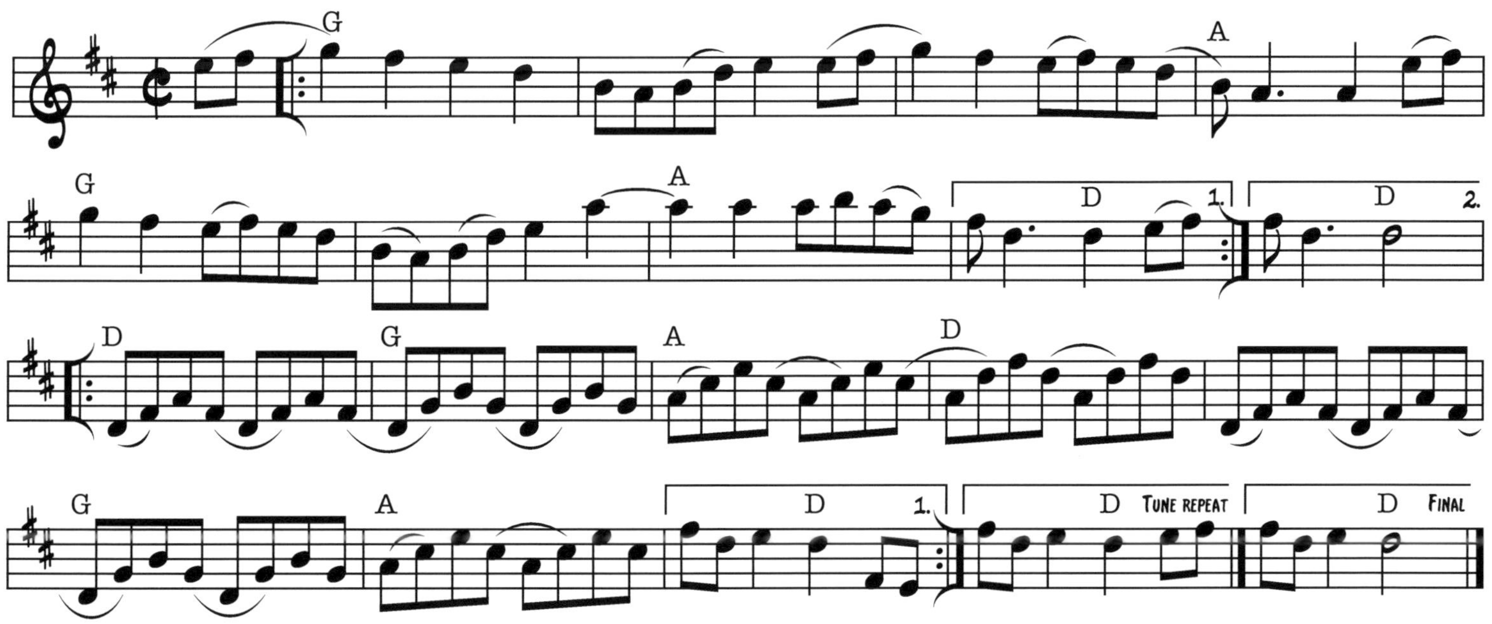

Logan County Blues

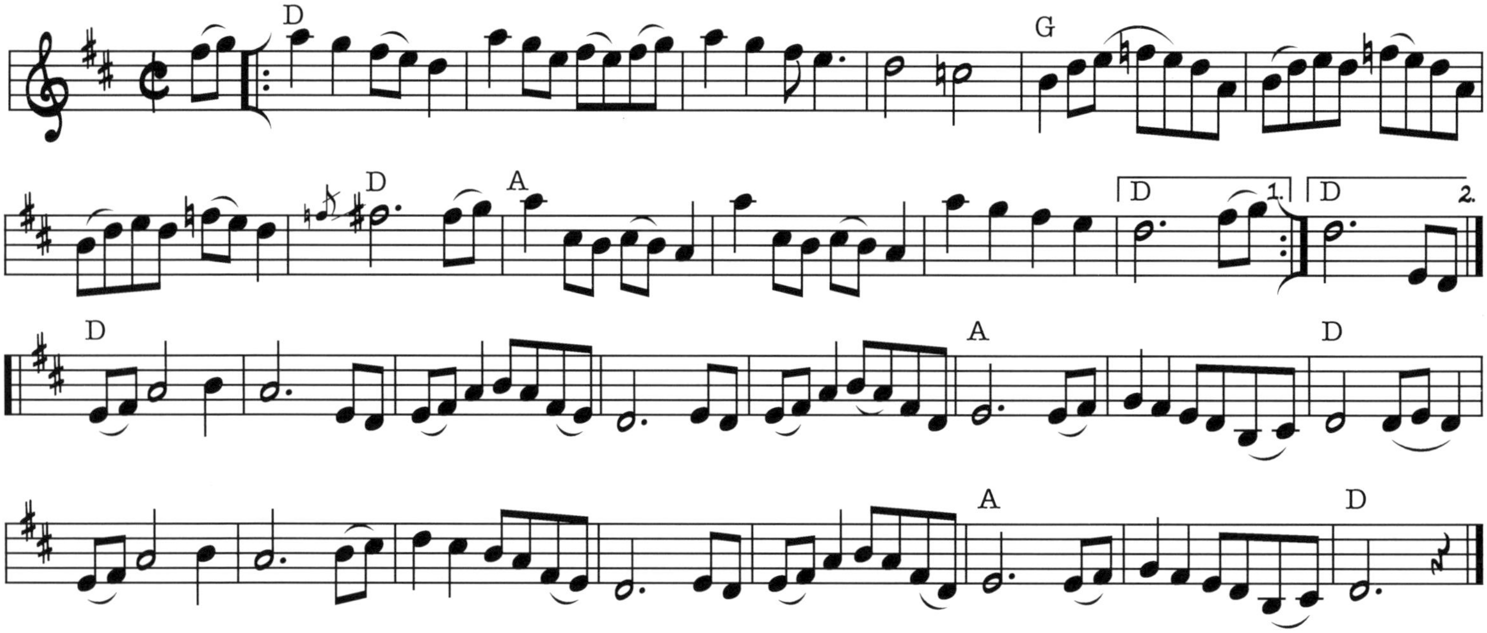

Love Somebody

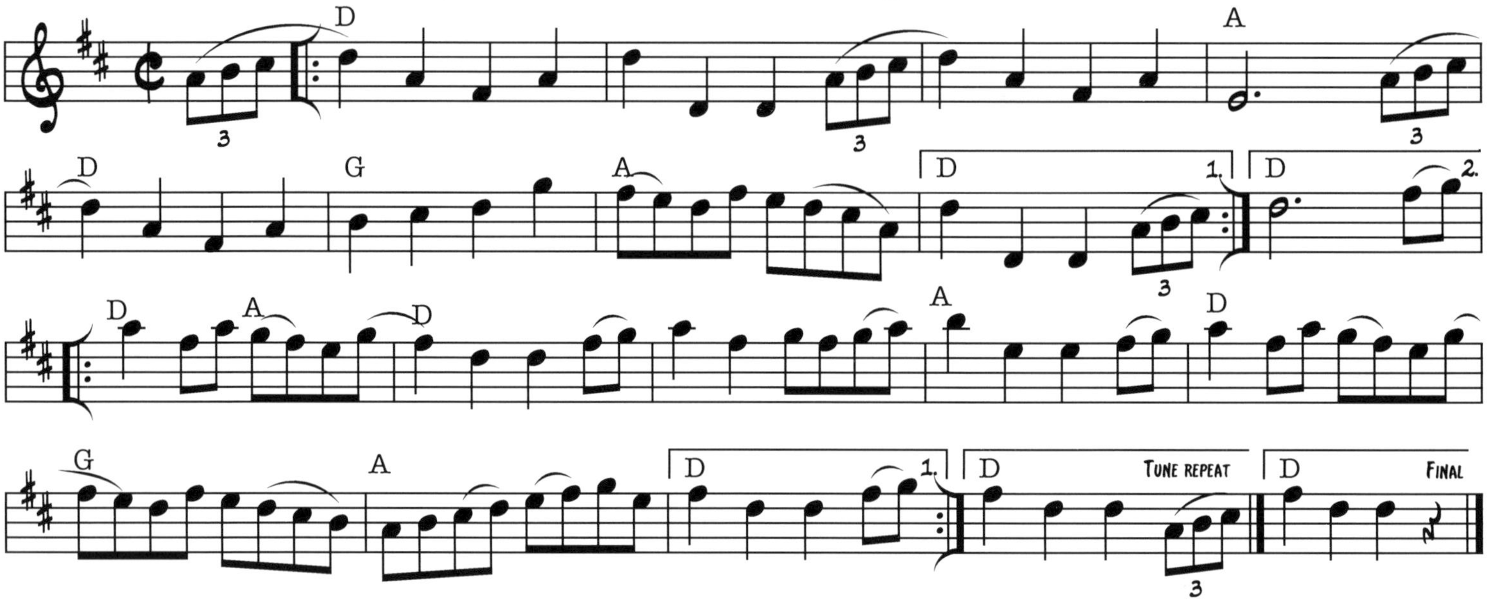

Lonesome Train

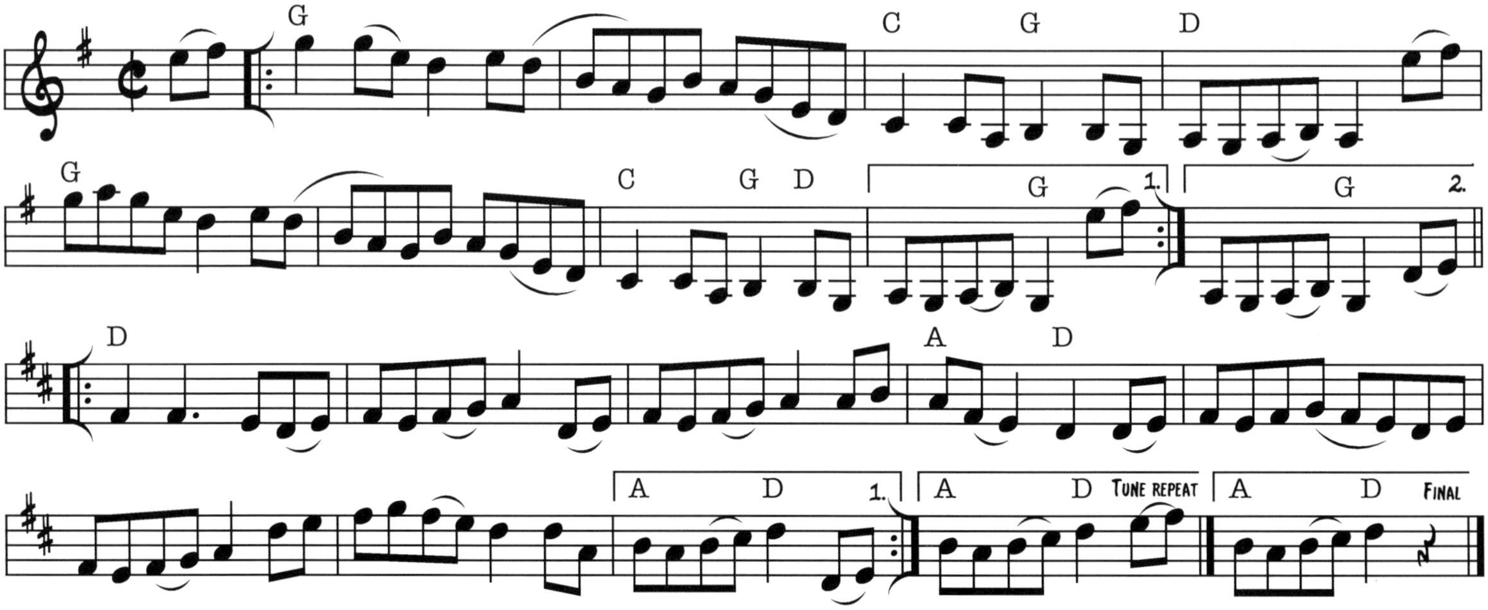

Lost Indian (Ed Haley)

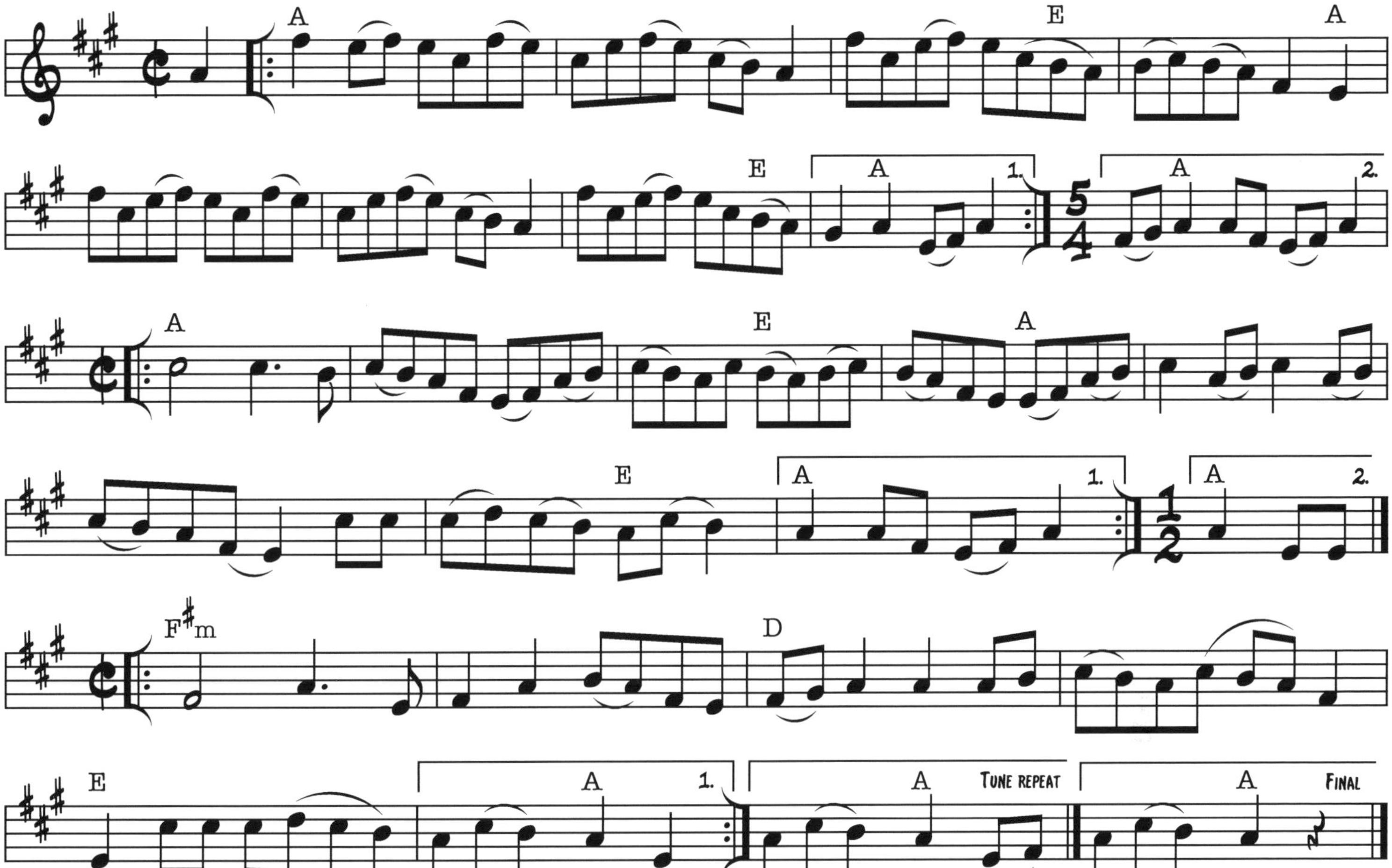

Maggots in the Sheep Hide

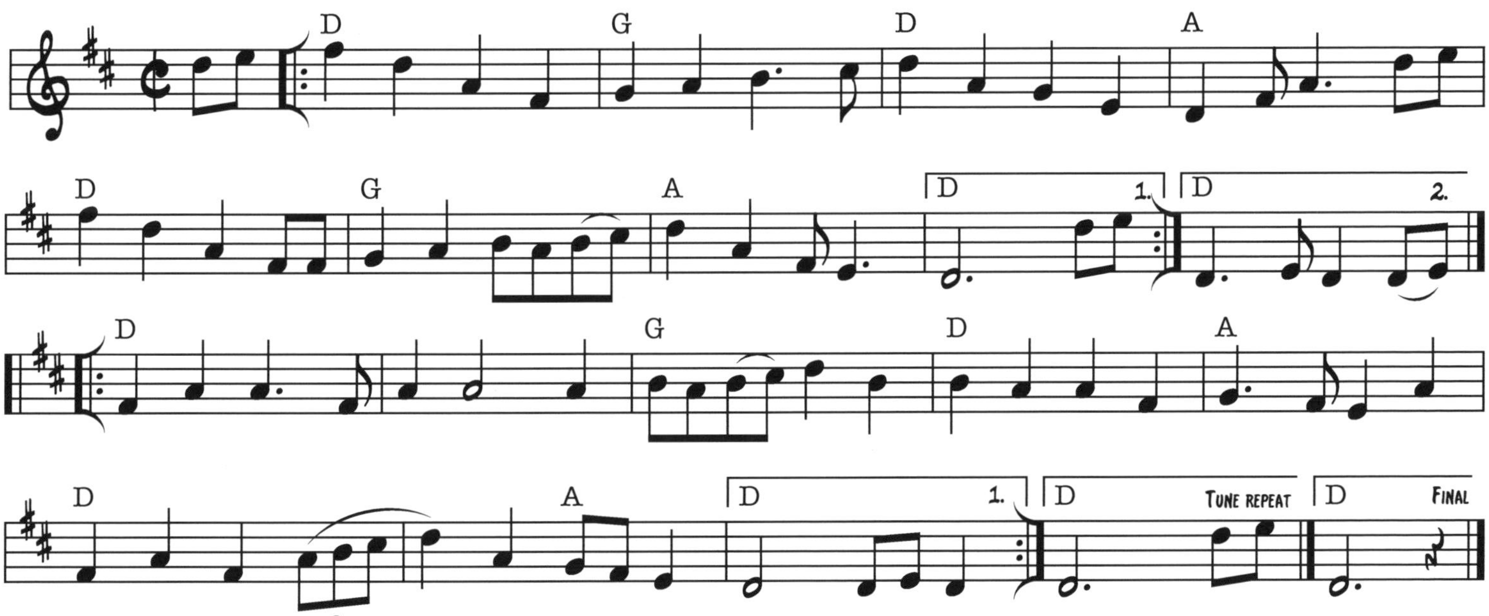

Magpie

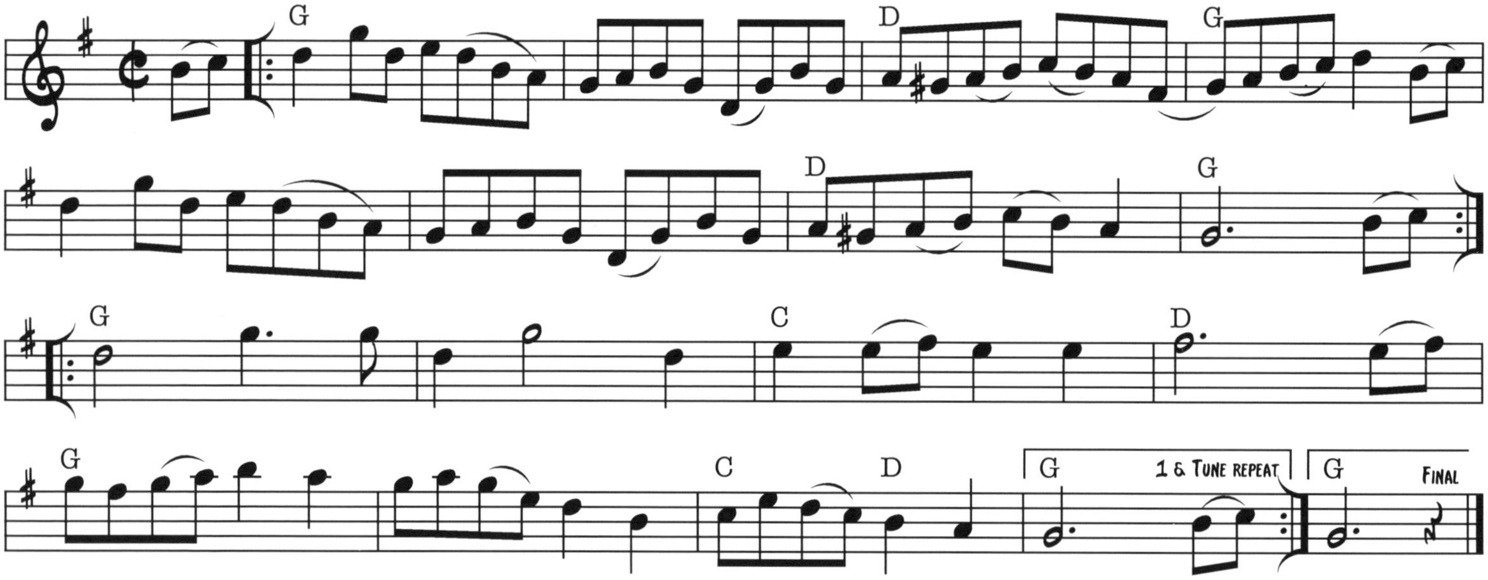

Martha Campbell

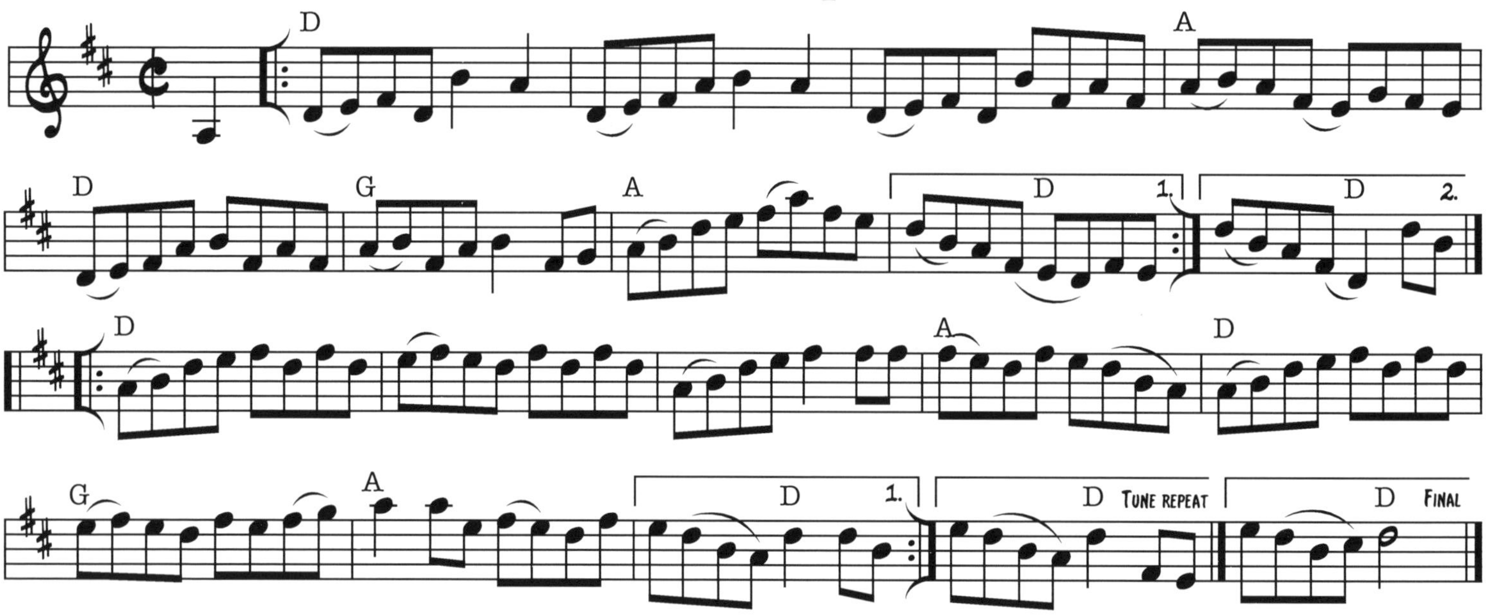

Meadow Prancer (Ryck Kaiser - used by permission)

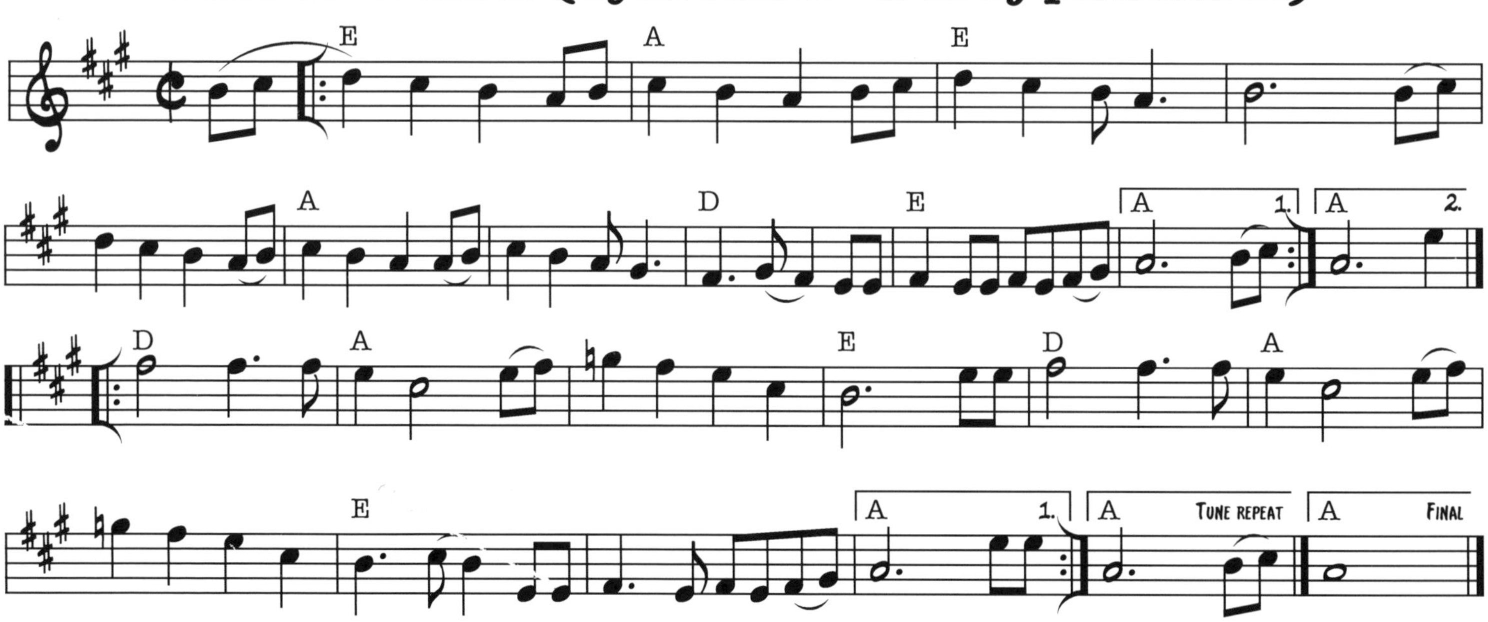

Merry Blacksmith

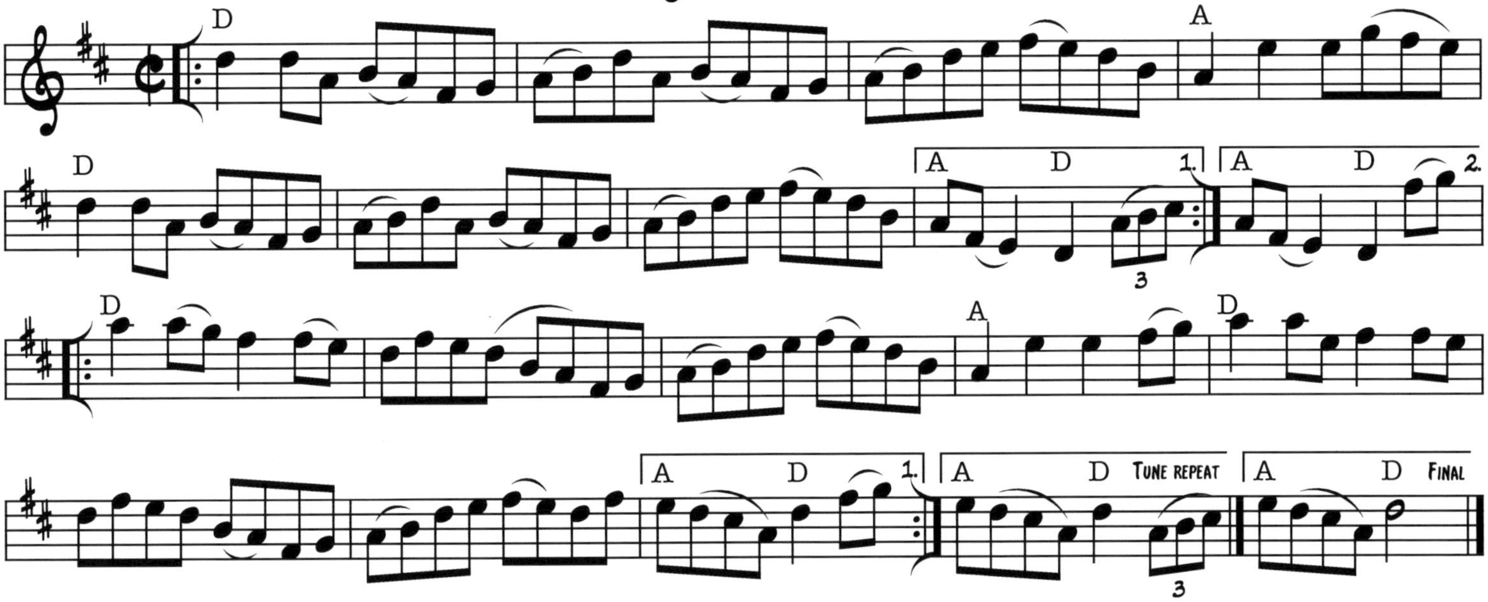

McMichen's Reel (aka Hog Trough Reel)

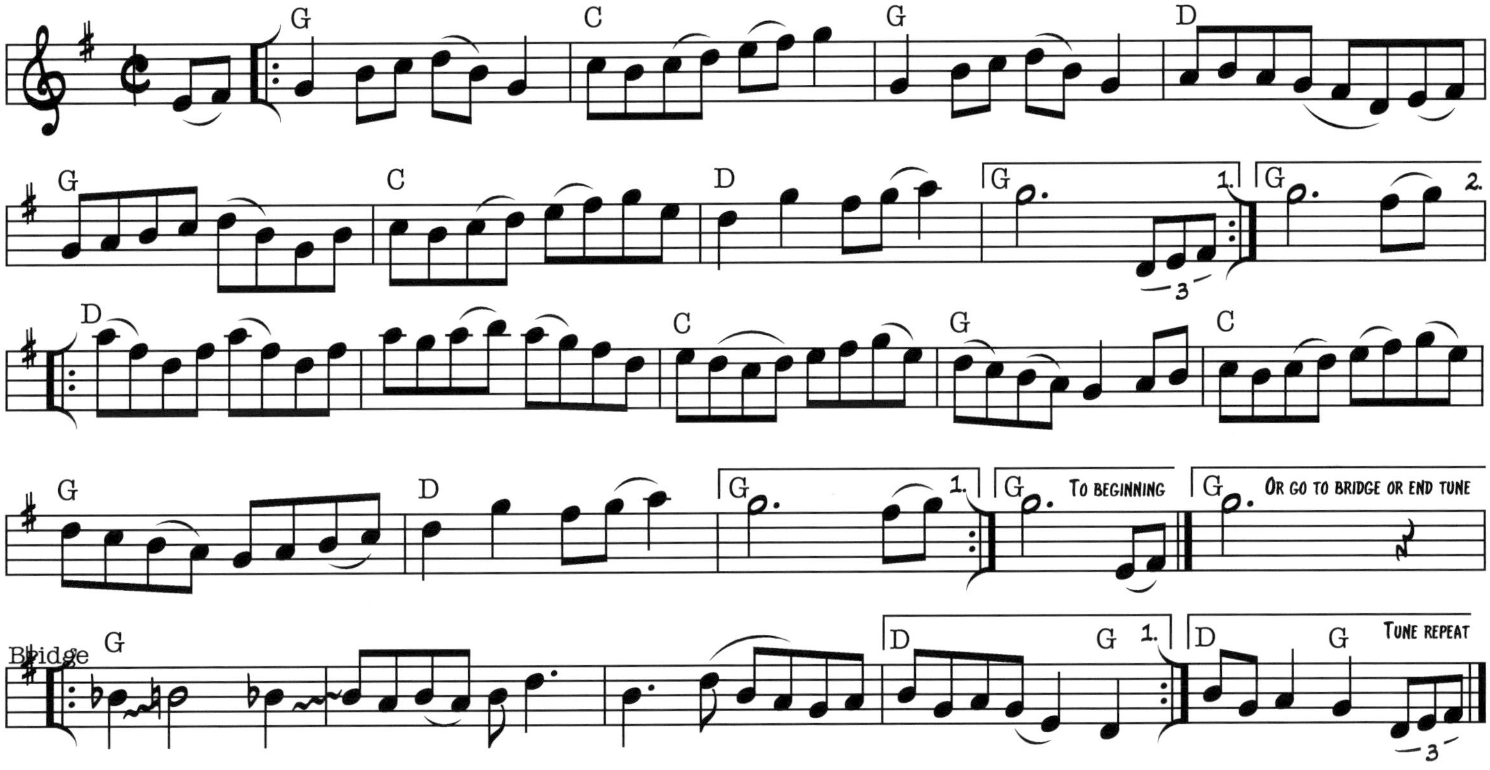

Mike in the Wilderness

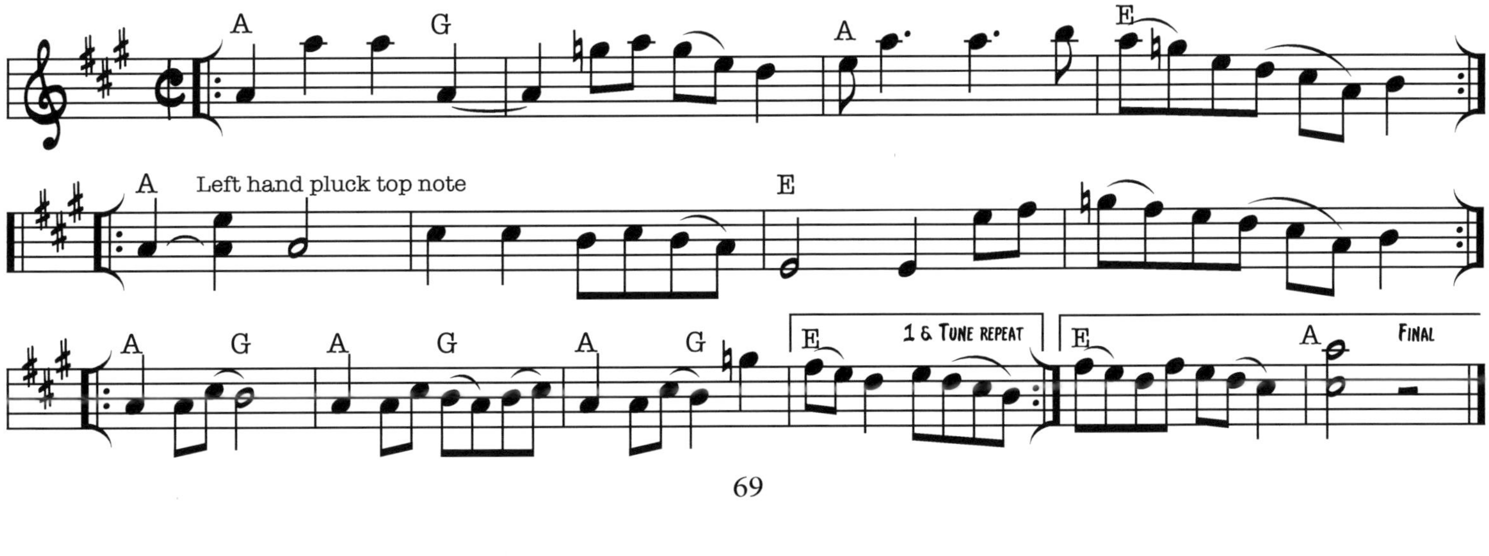

Mississippi Sawyer

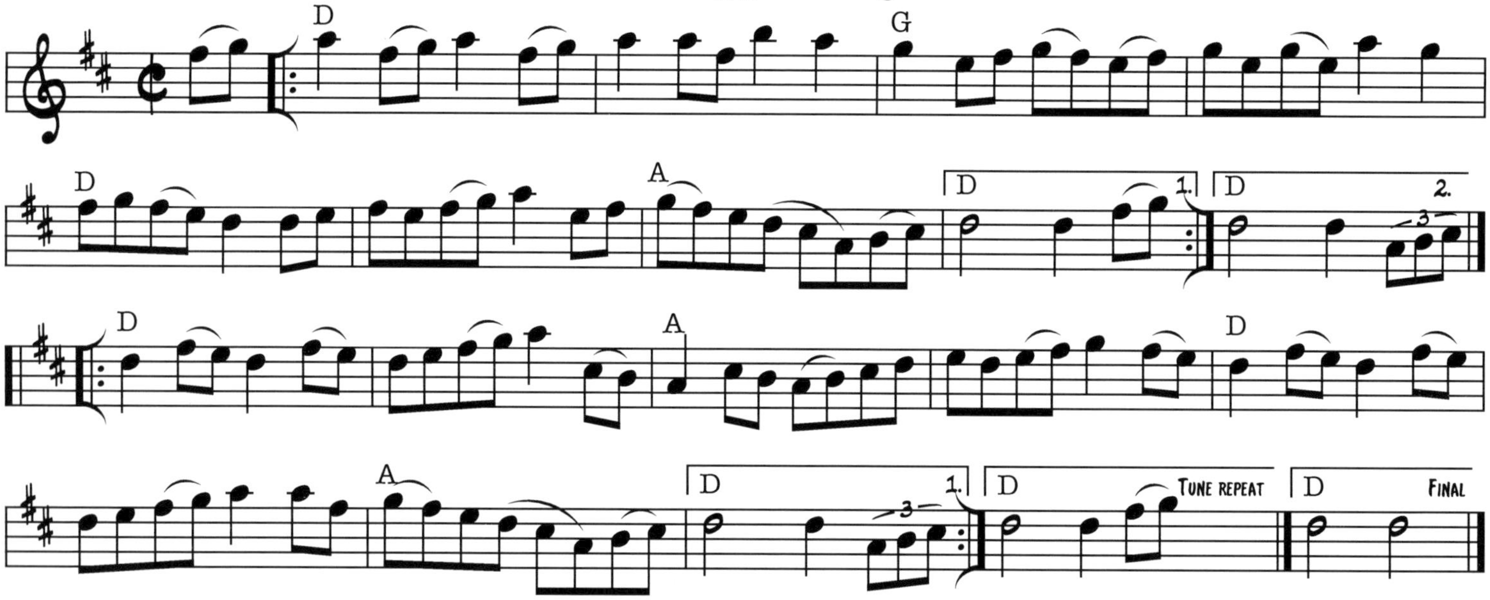

Mole in the Ground

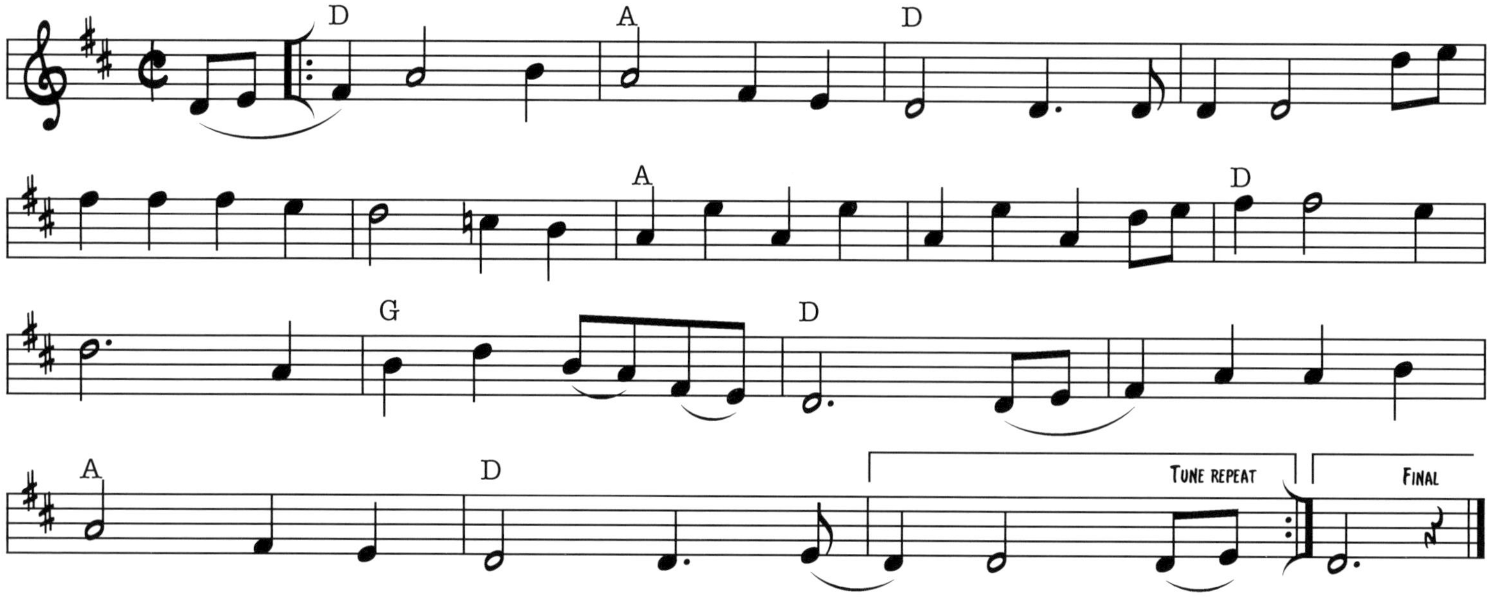

Monkey on a Dogcart

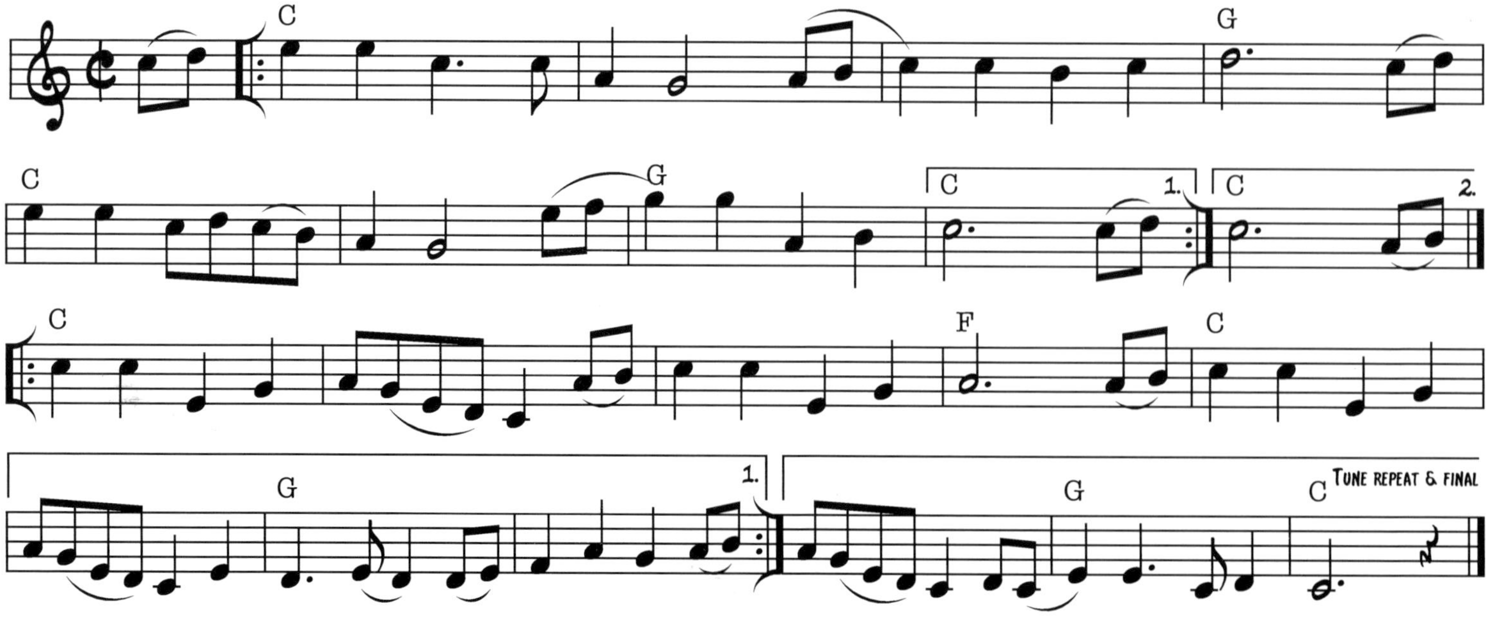

Money Musk

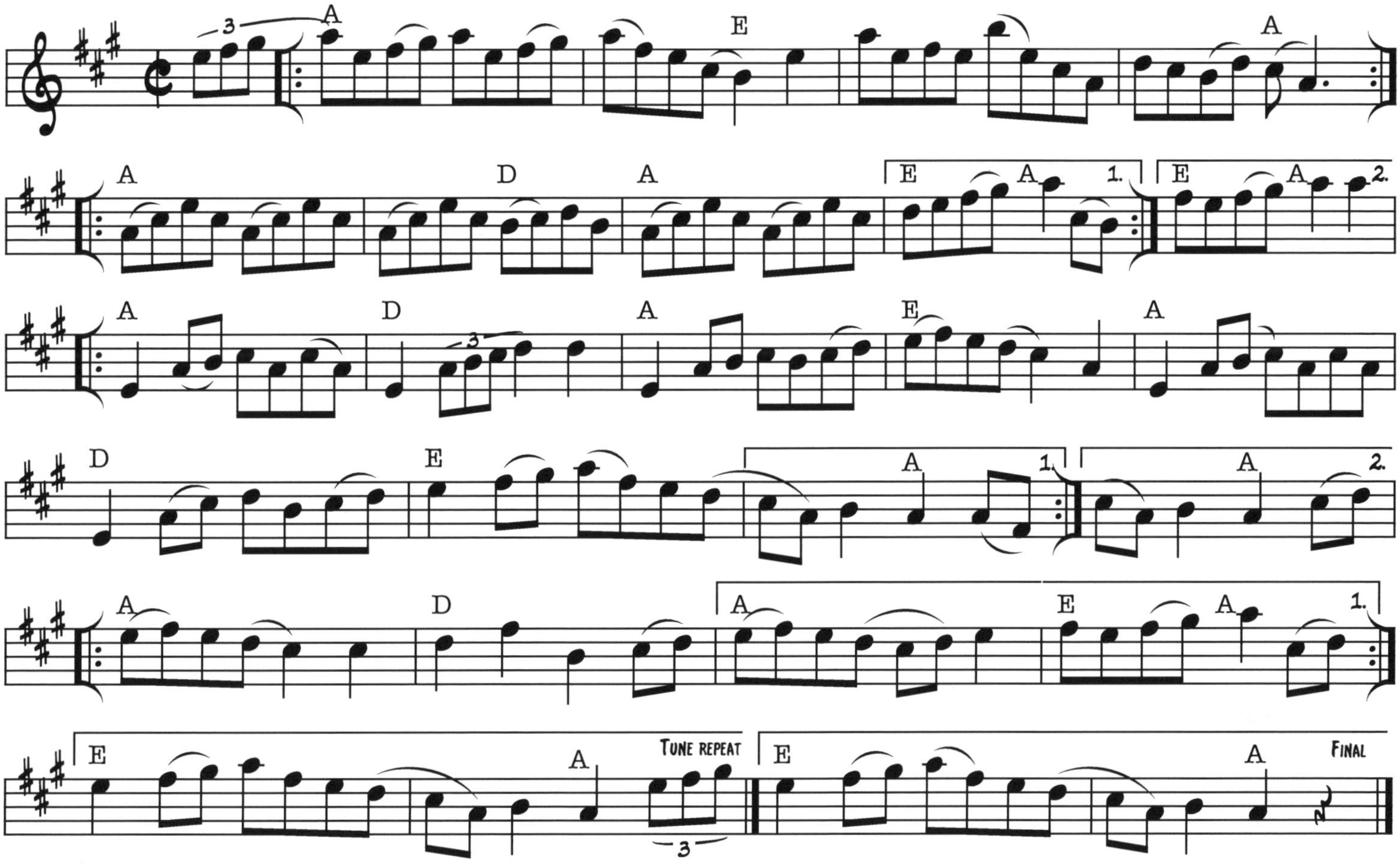

Money Musk (Wooliver's)

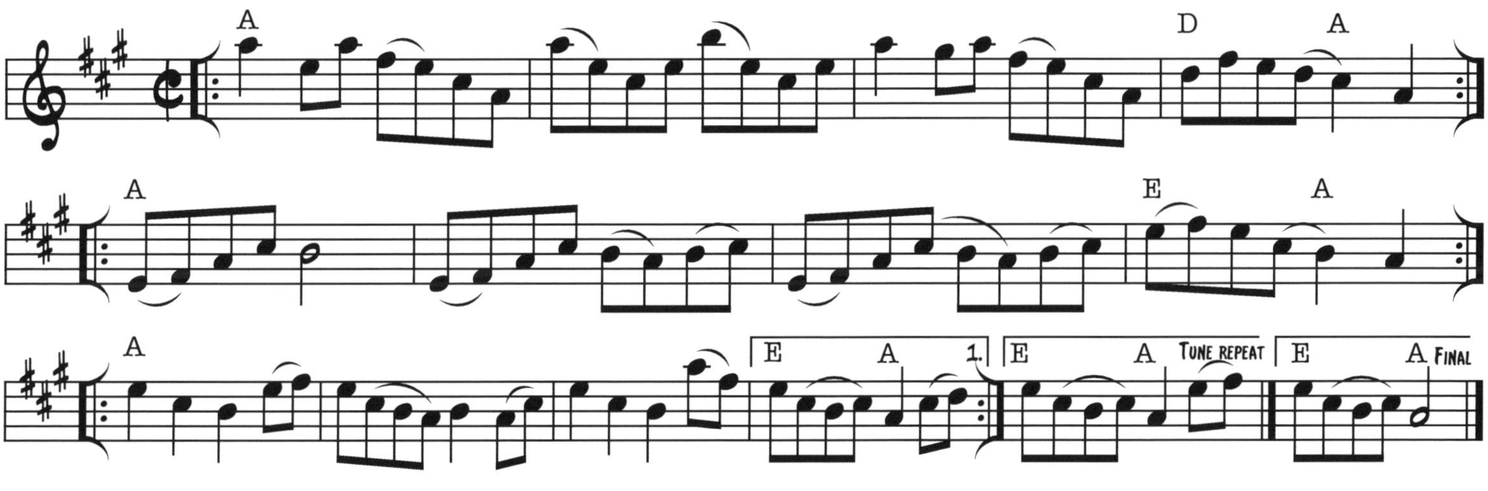

Moses Hoe the Corn

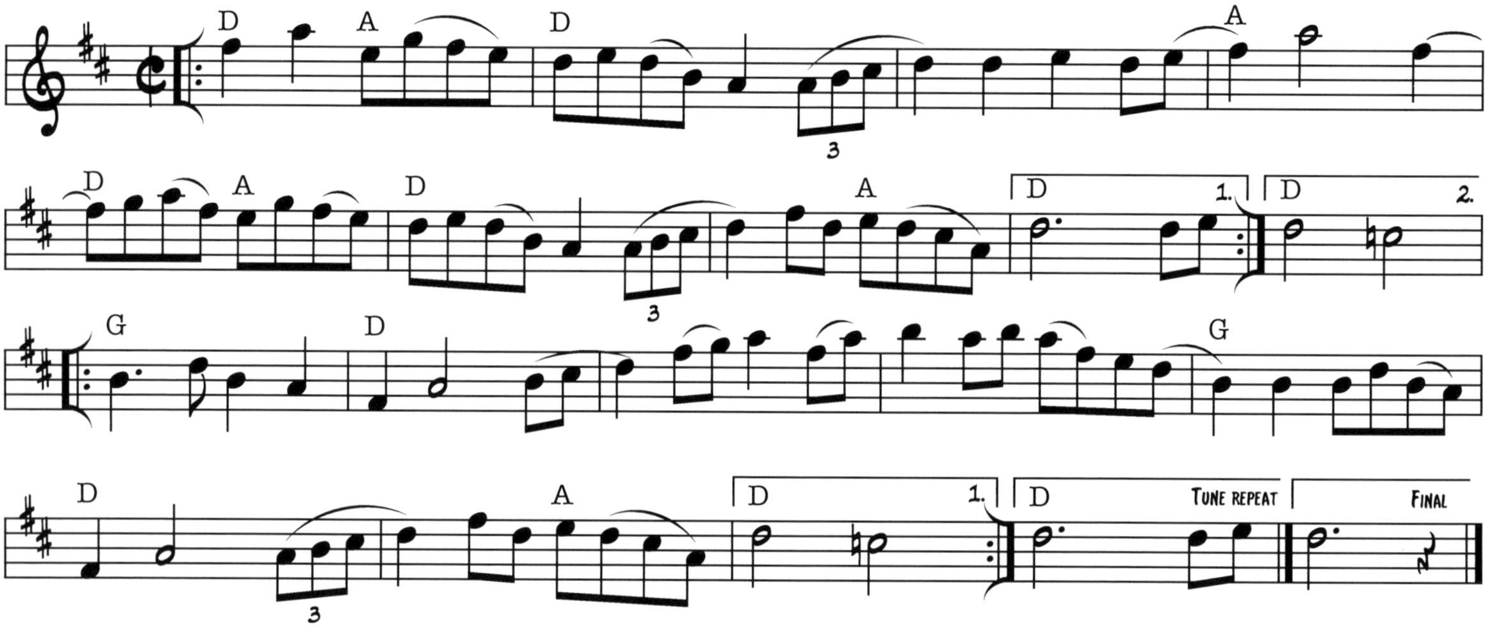

Muddy Roads

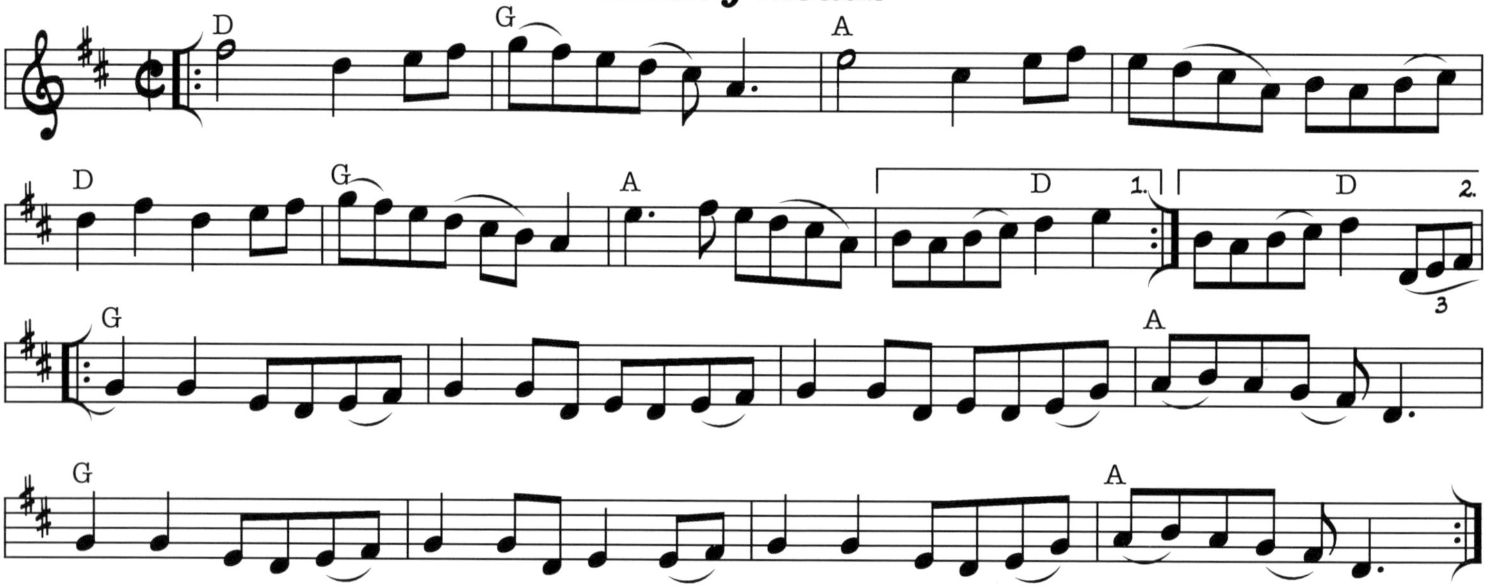

Natchez Under the Hill

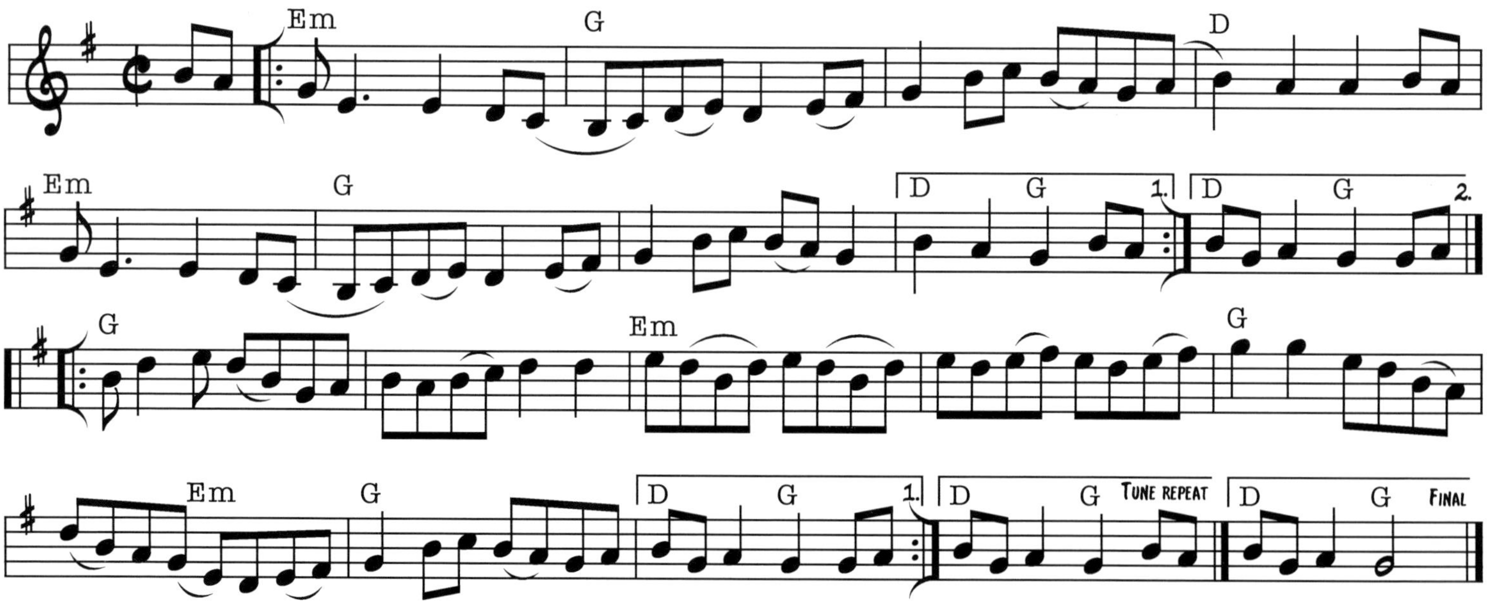

Needlecase (aka Latch Key)

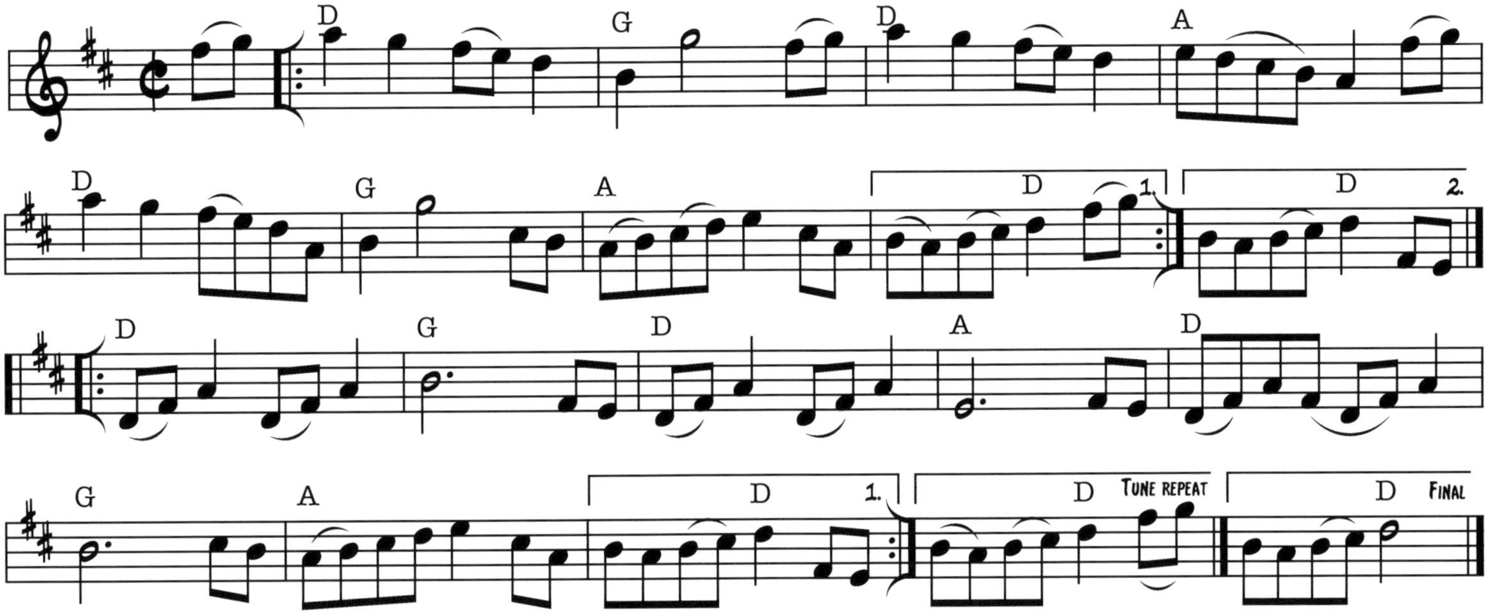

New Five Cents

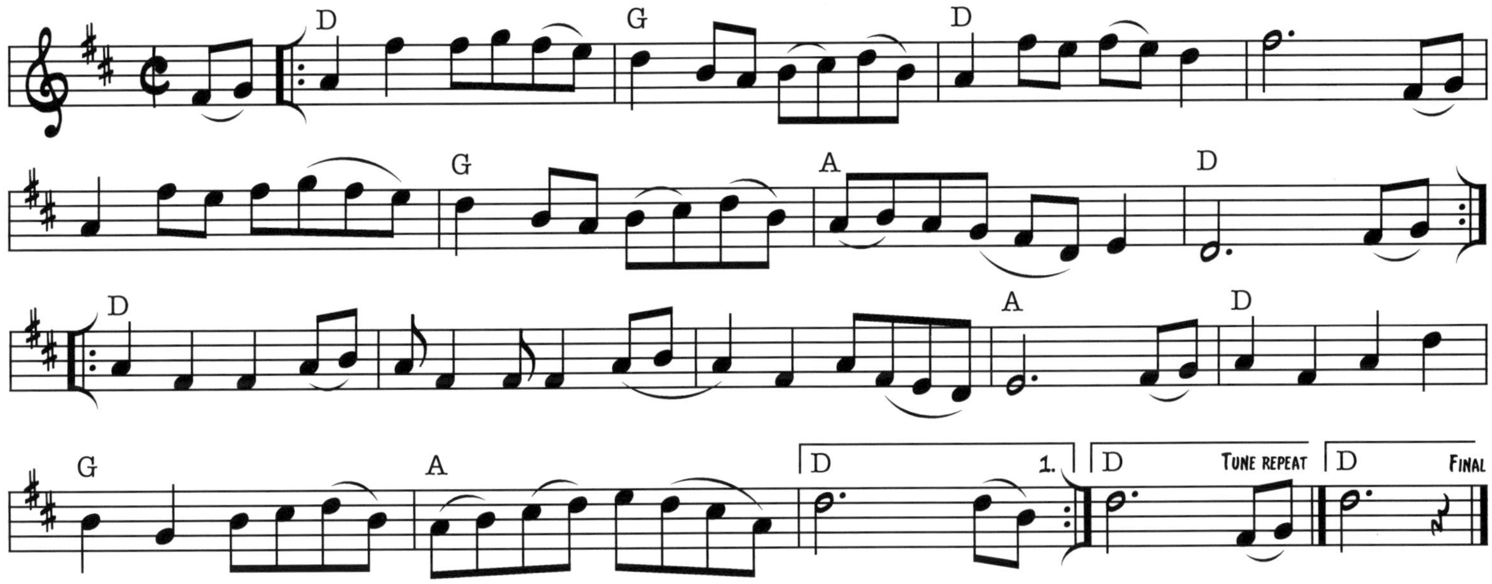

New Money

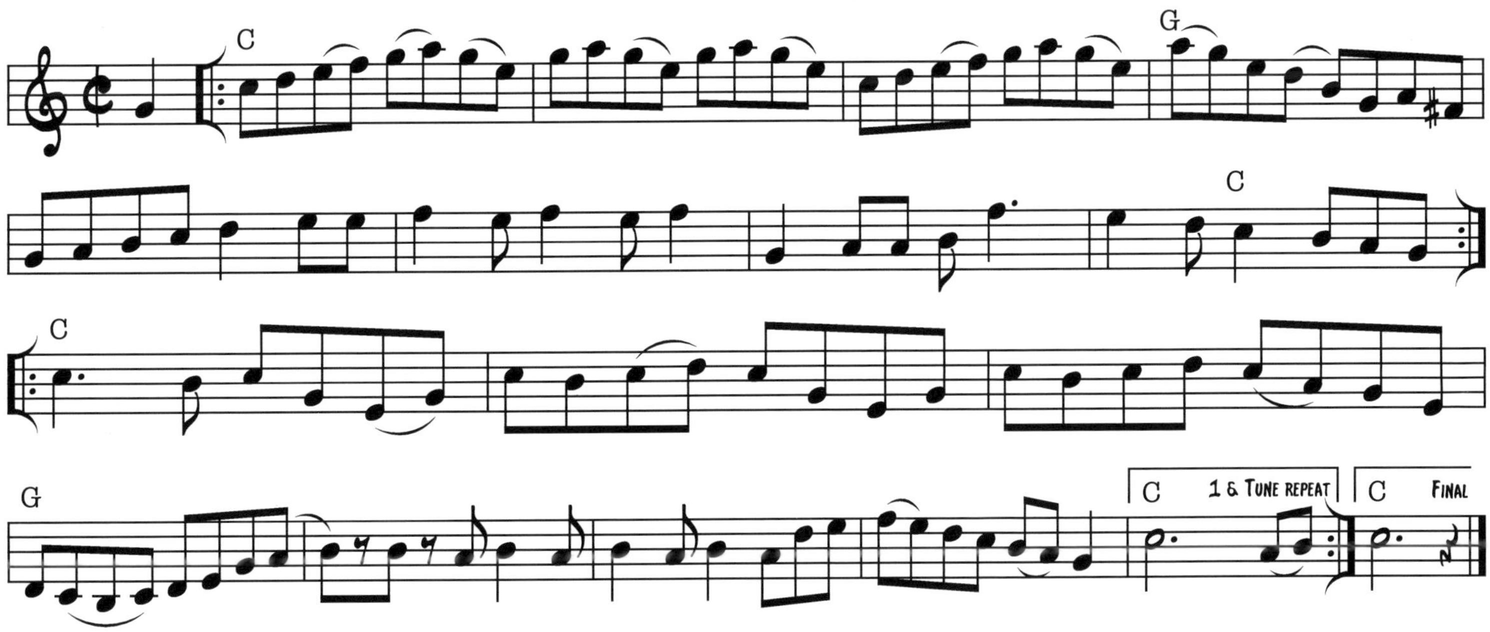

Nixon's Farewell (Curtis Bouterse used by permission)

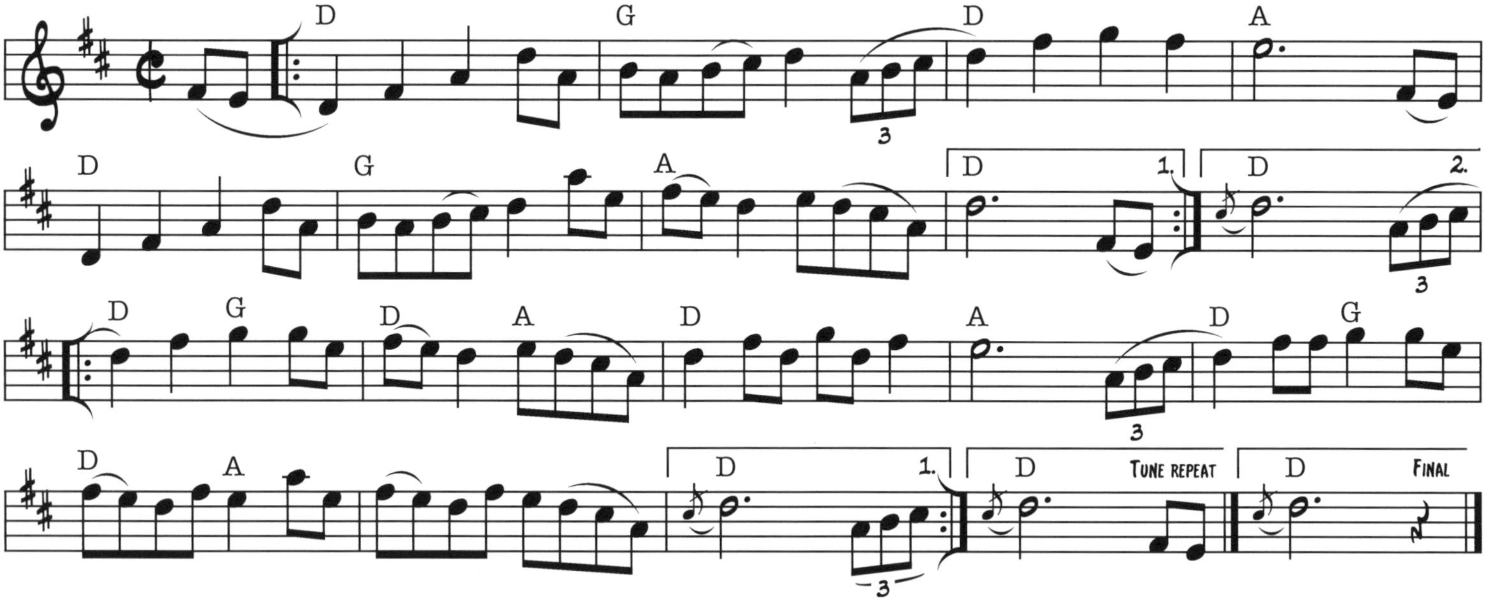

North Carolina Breakdown

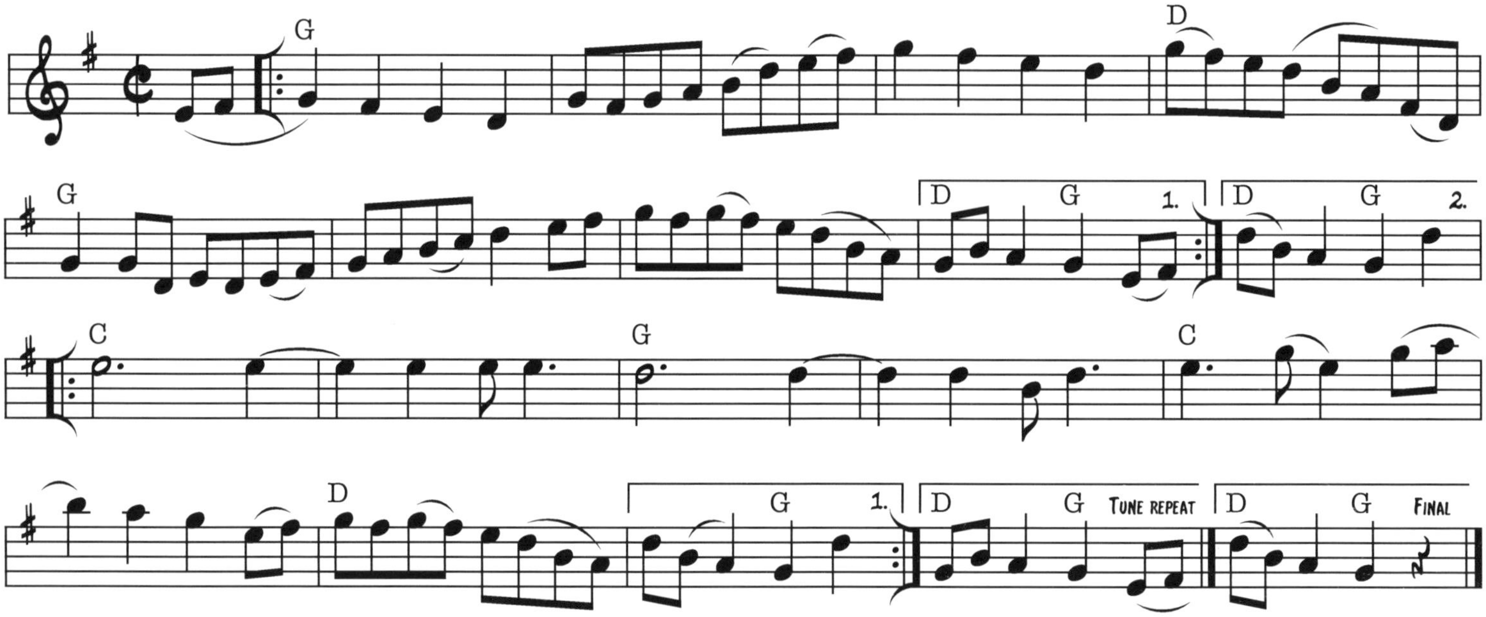

Oh My Little Darling

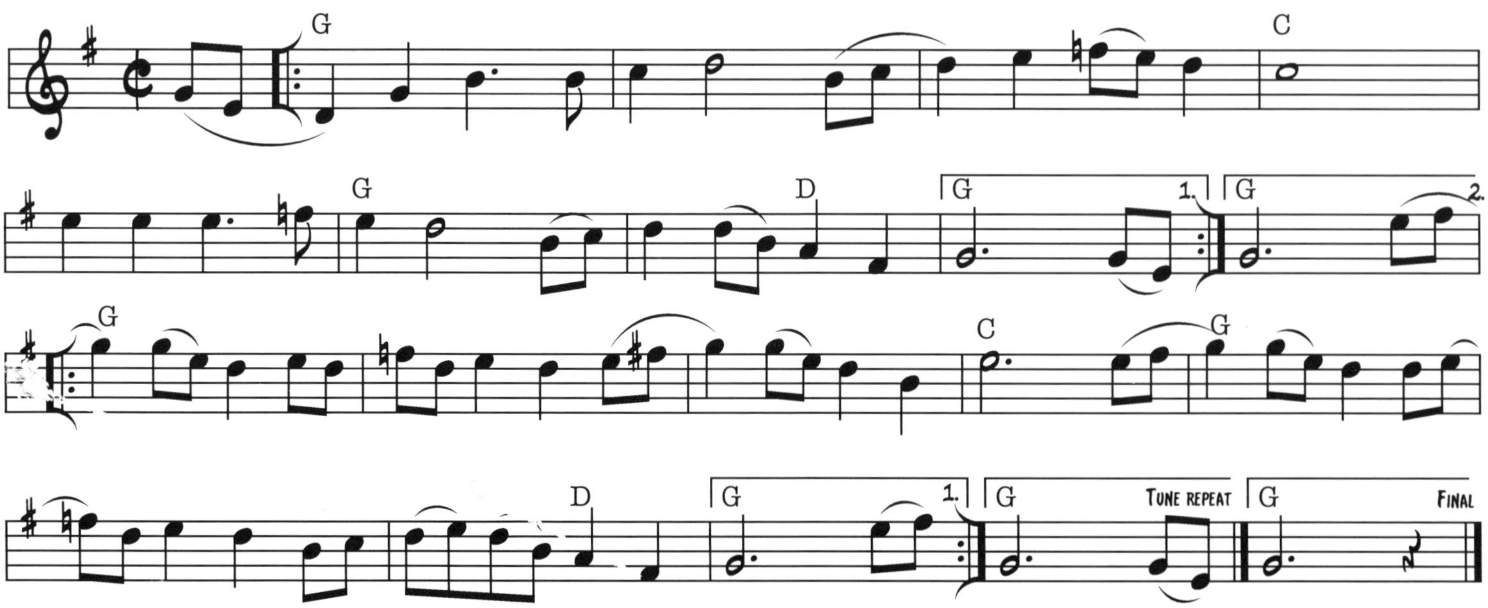

Oklahoma Rooster

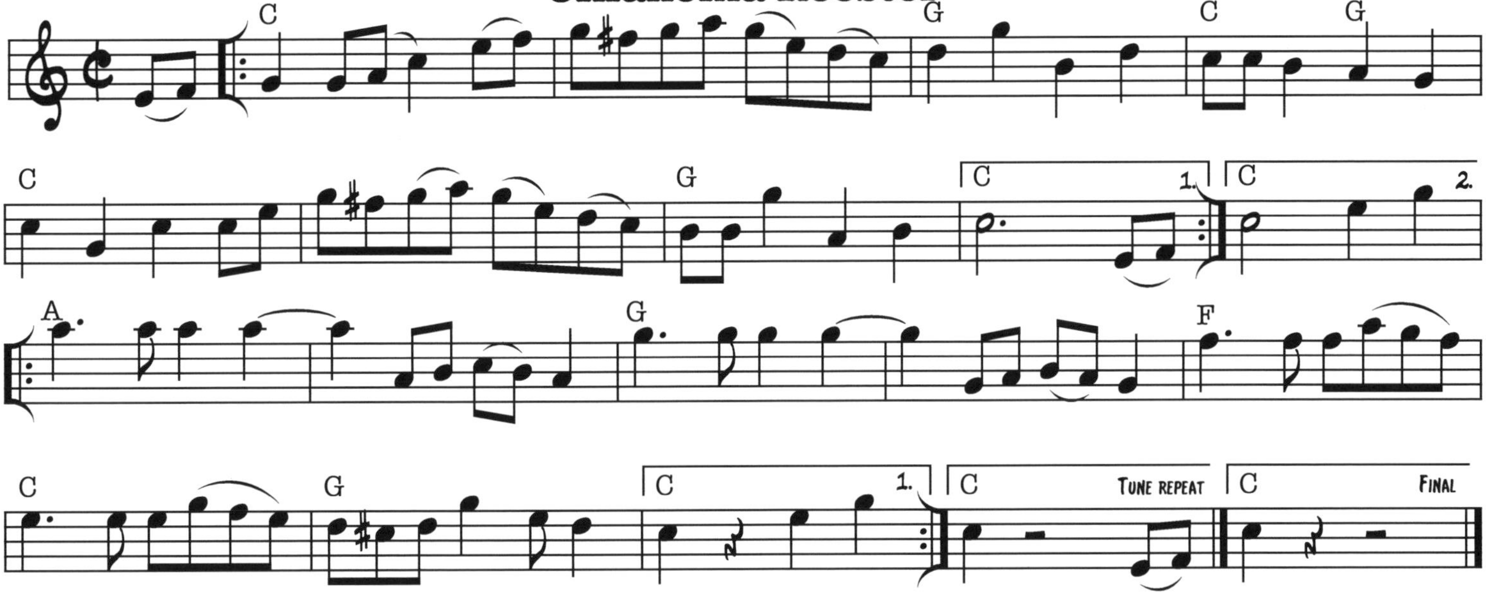

Old Belle Cow (2 part)

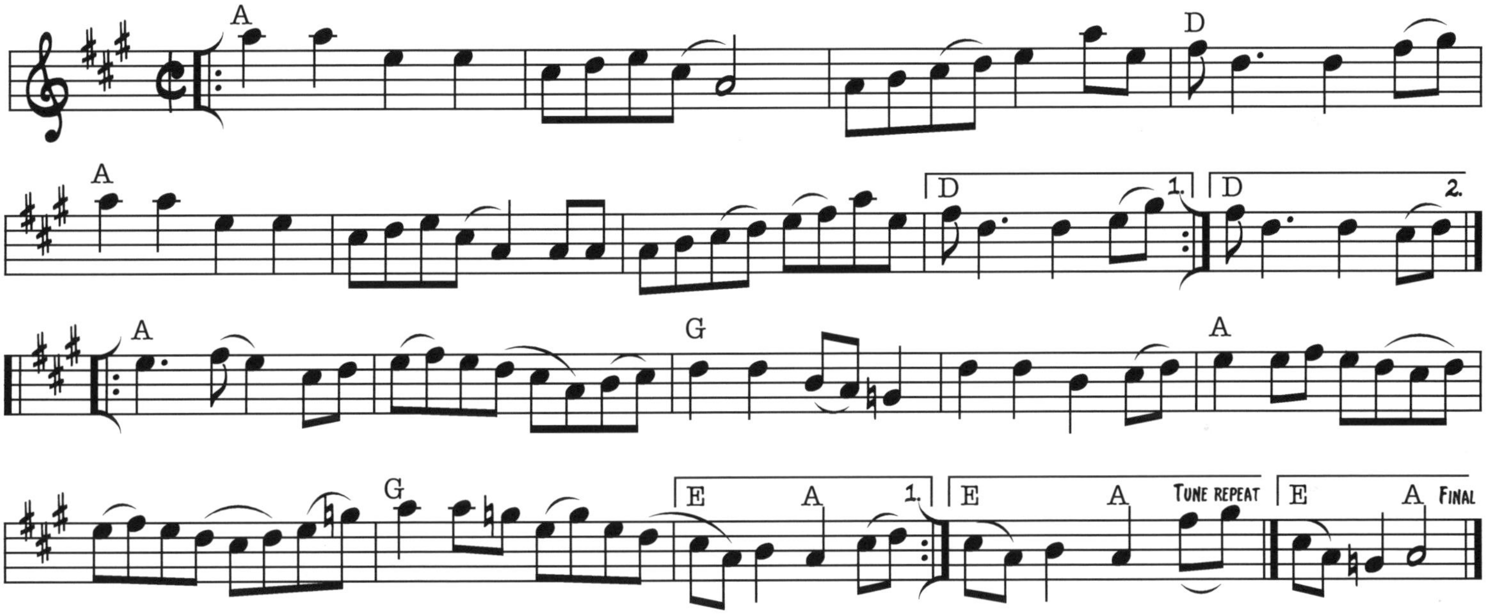

Old Belle Cow (3 part)

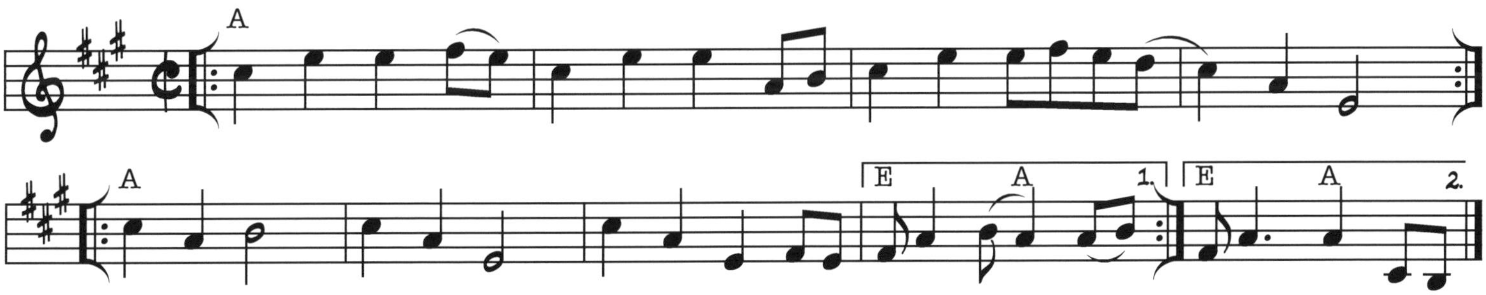

Pluck the C# and A with your left hand if you have retuned to Calico (AEac#)

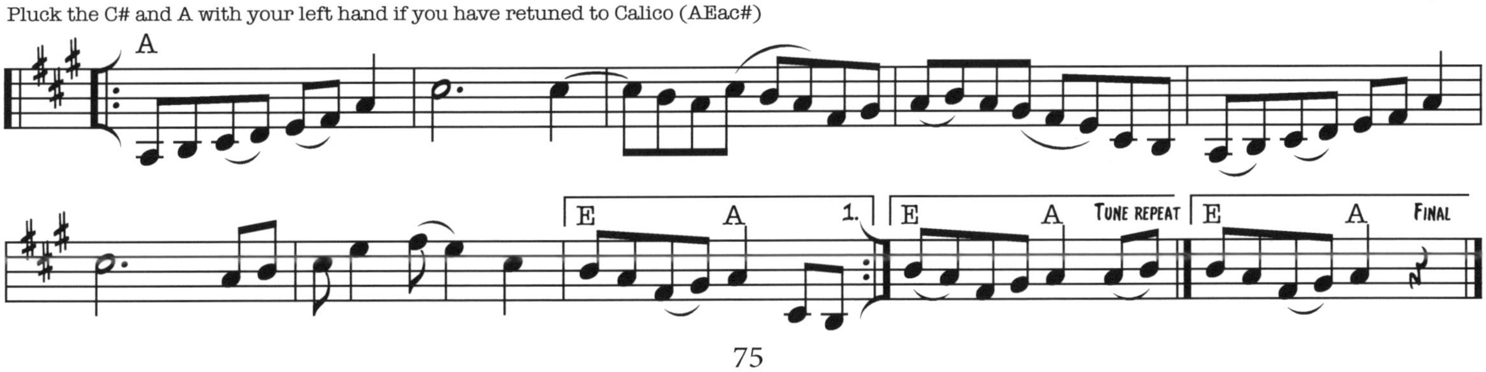

Old Bunch of Keys

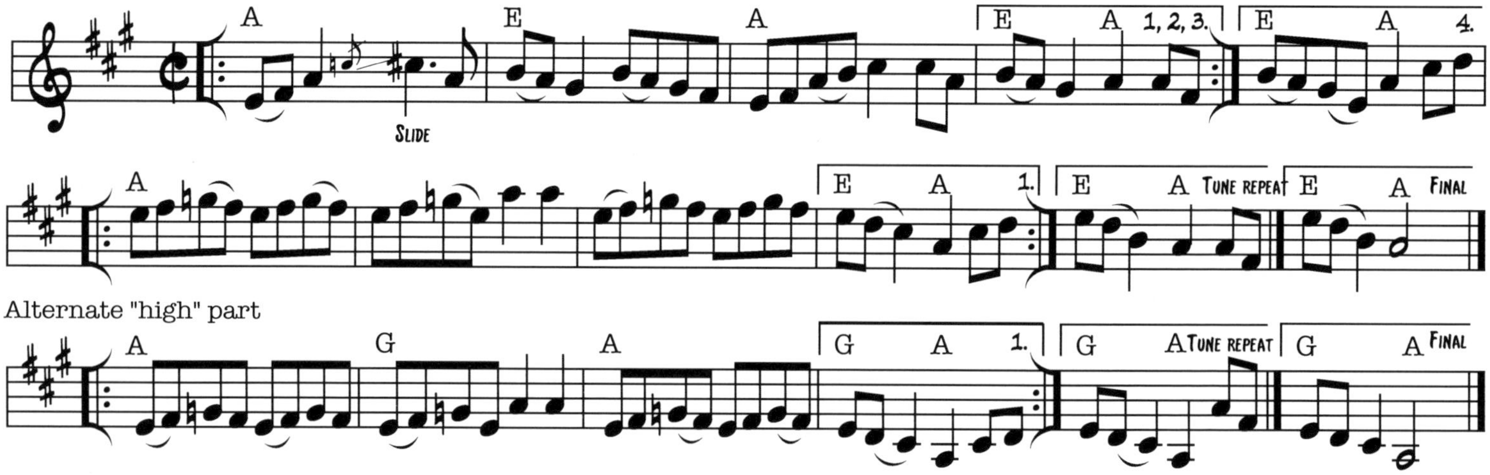

Old Horse and Buggy

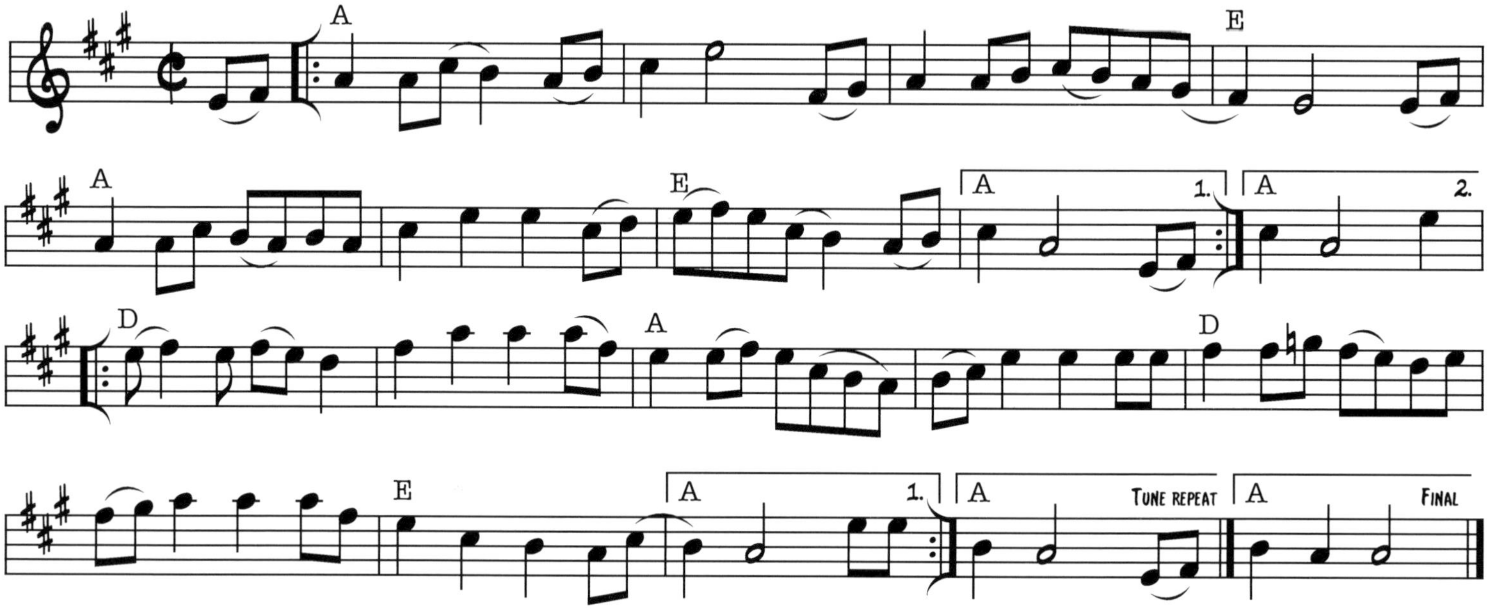

Old Joe Clark

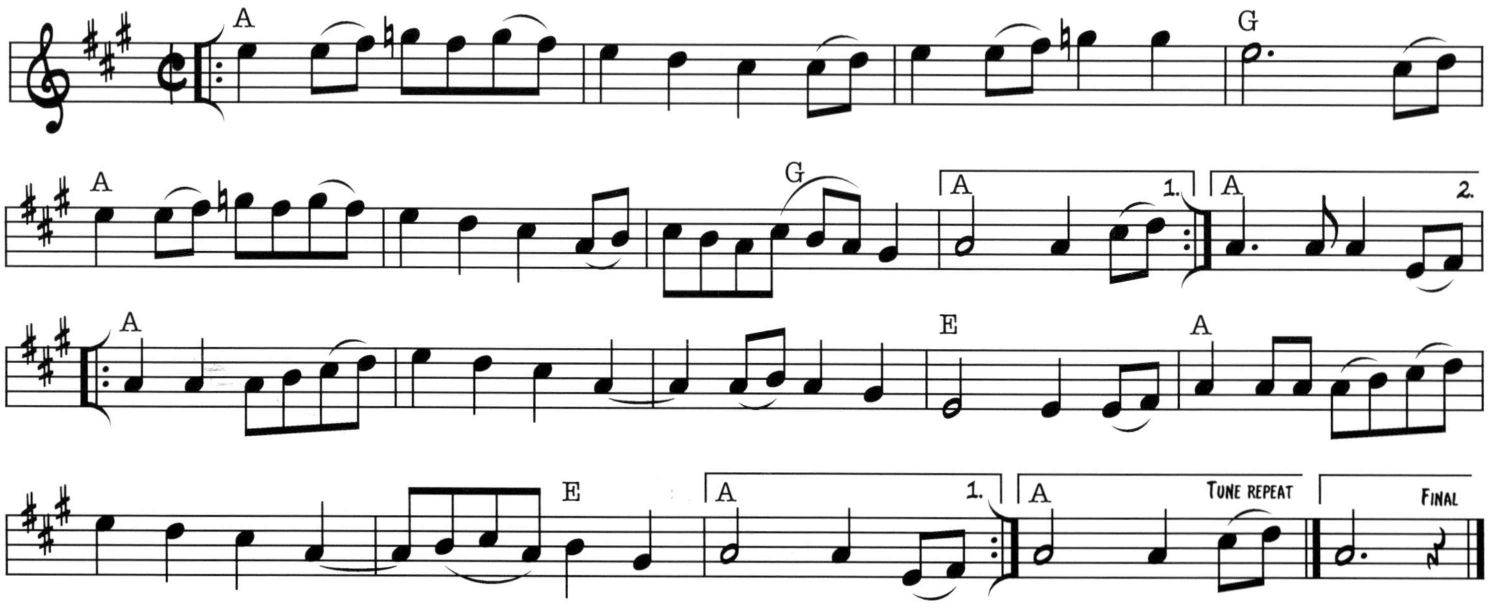

Old Melinda

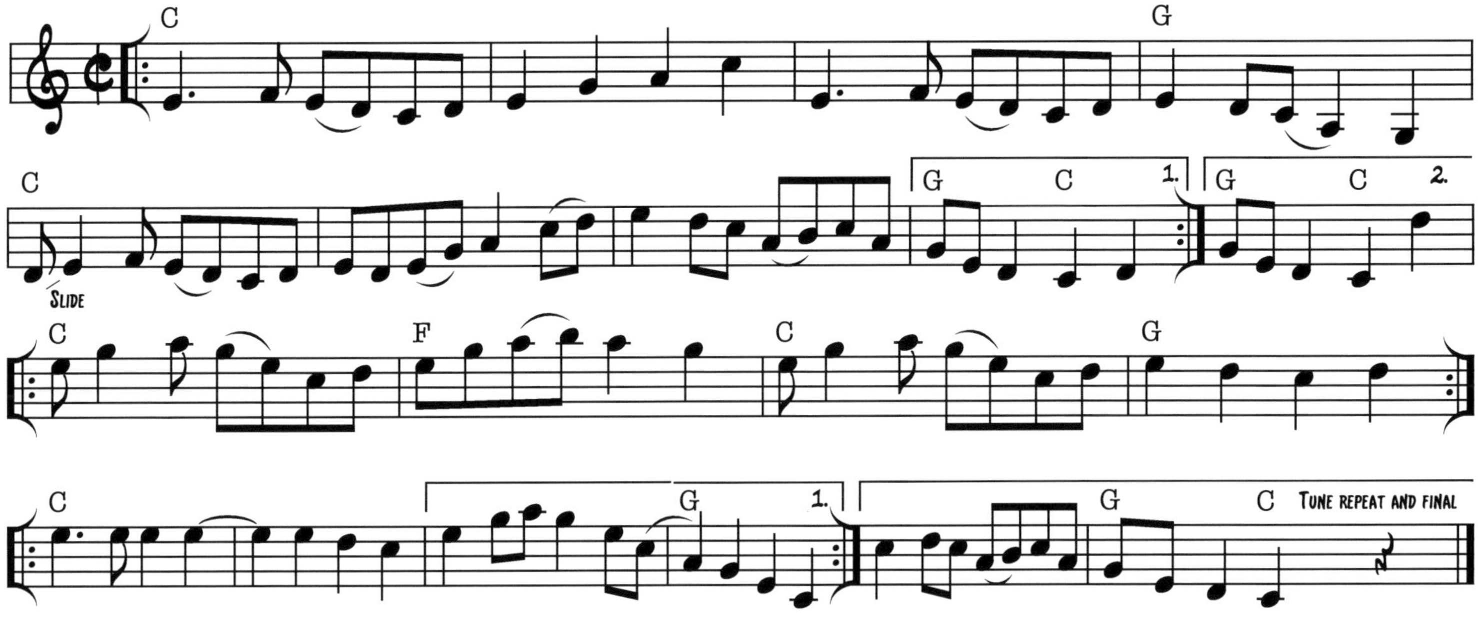

Old Molly Hare

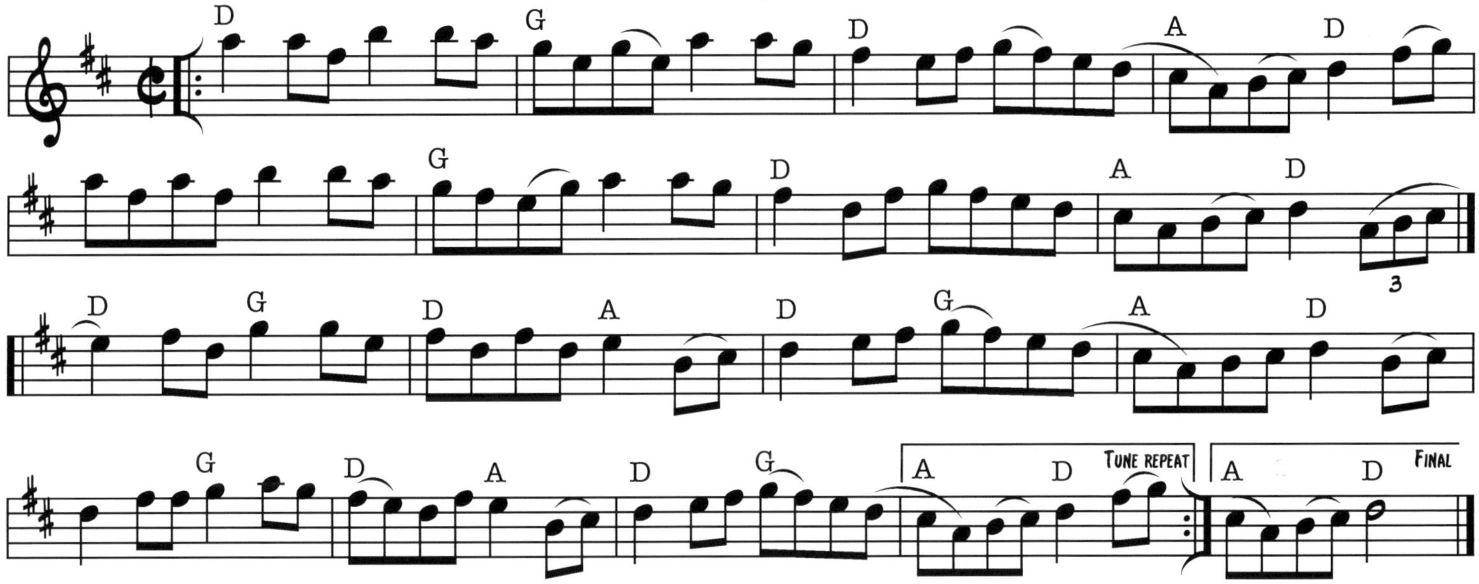

Old Mother Flannigan

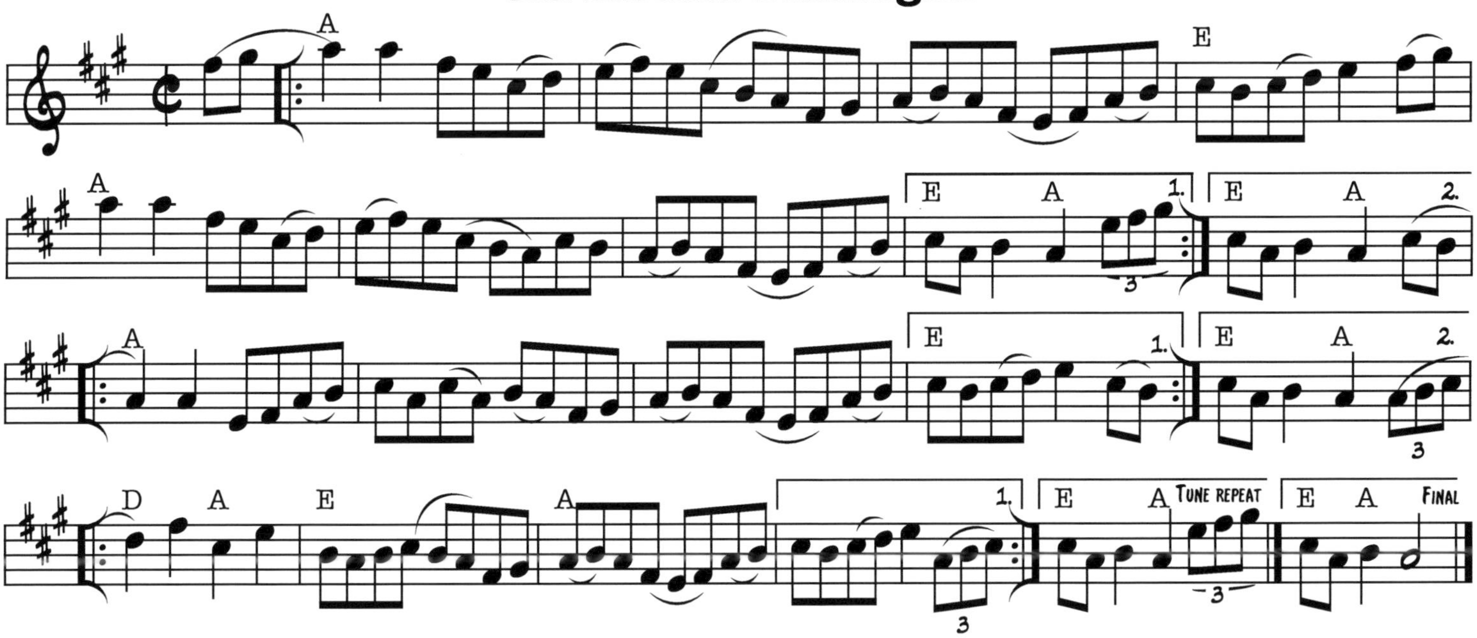

Old Savannah (Beverly Smith used by permission)

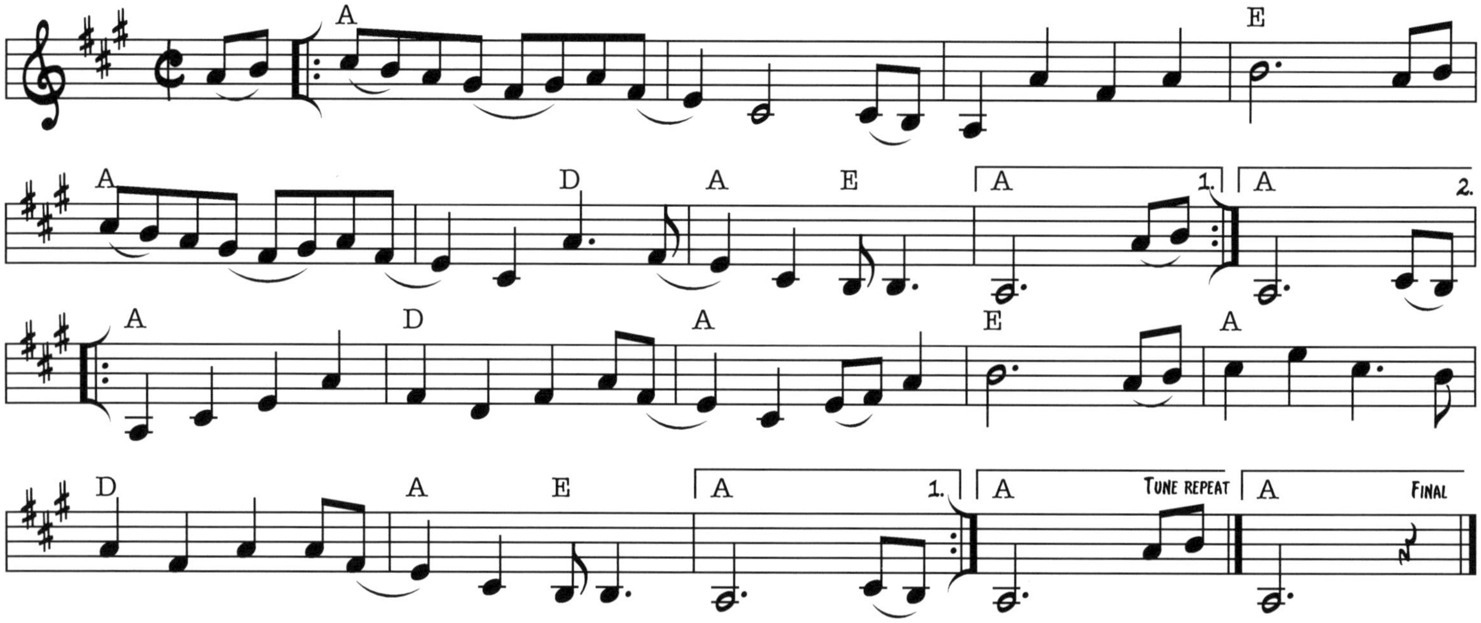

Old Yellow Dog Come Trotting Through the Meeting House

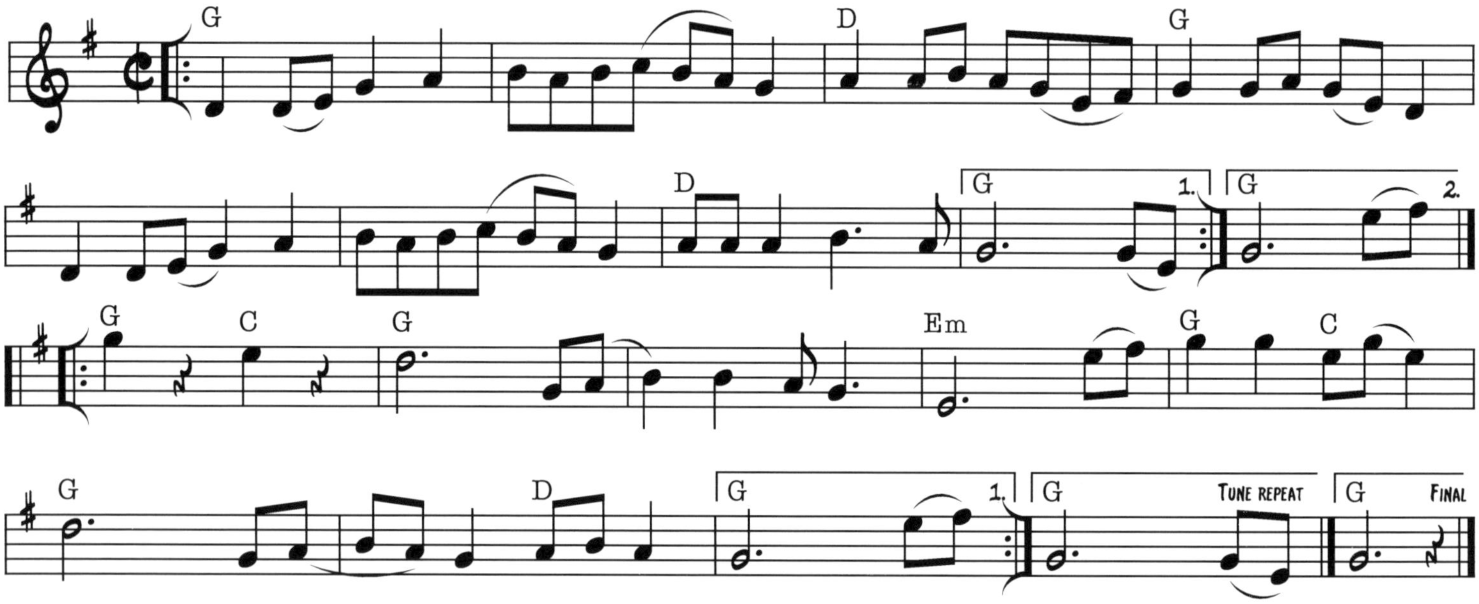

Ora Lee

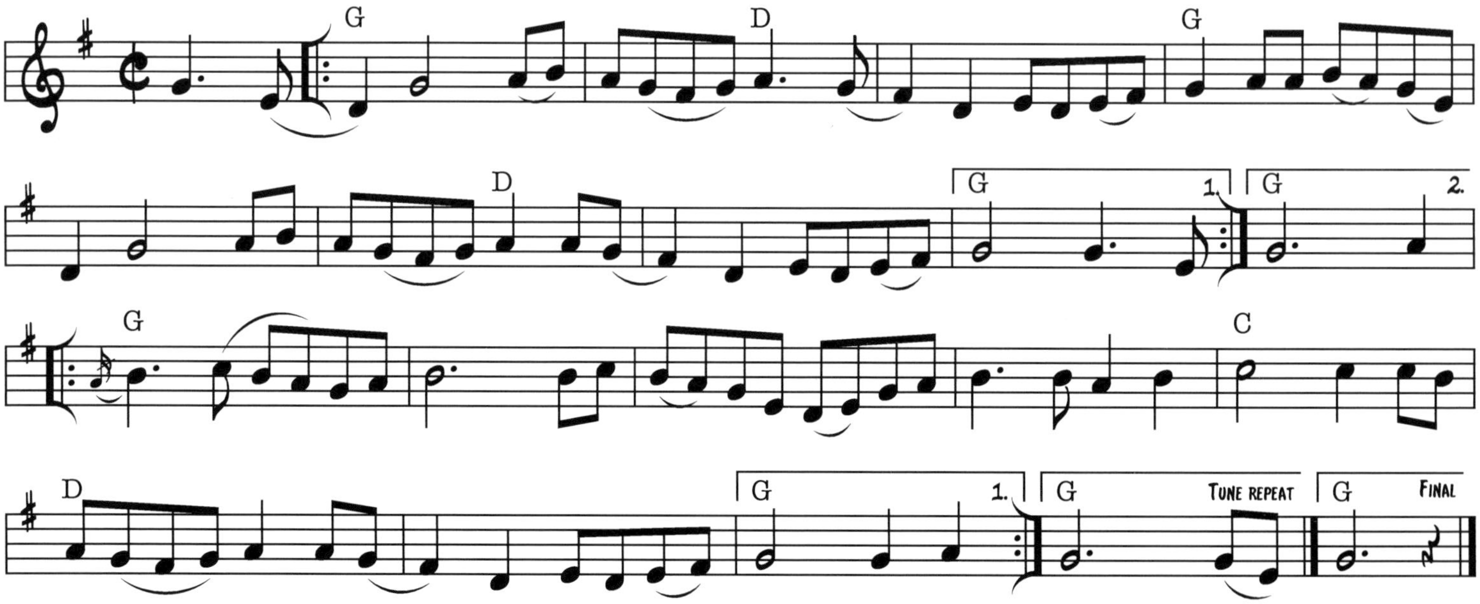

Opera Reel (aka The Celebrated Opera Reel)

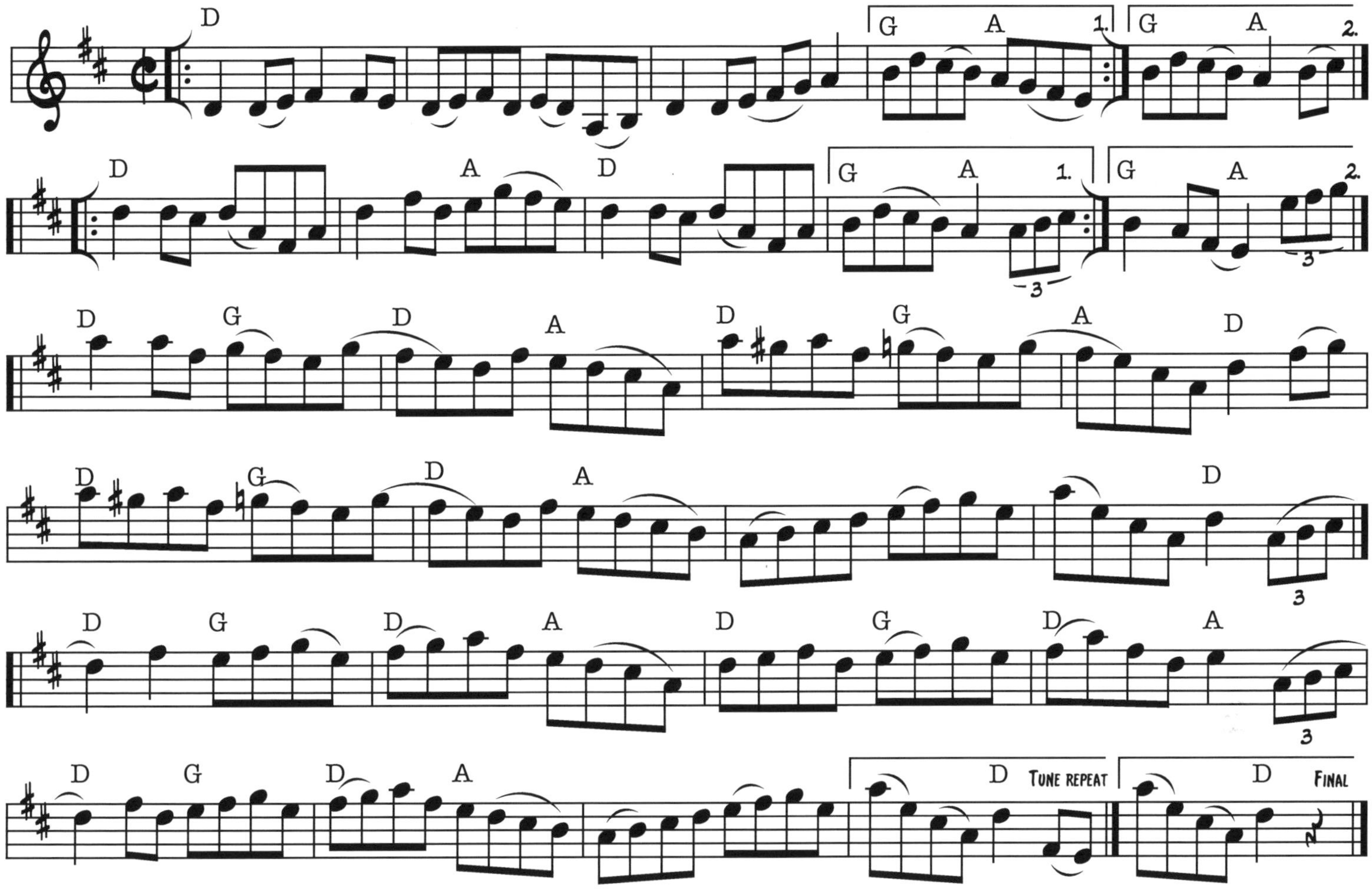

Orvetta Waltz

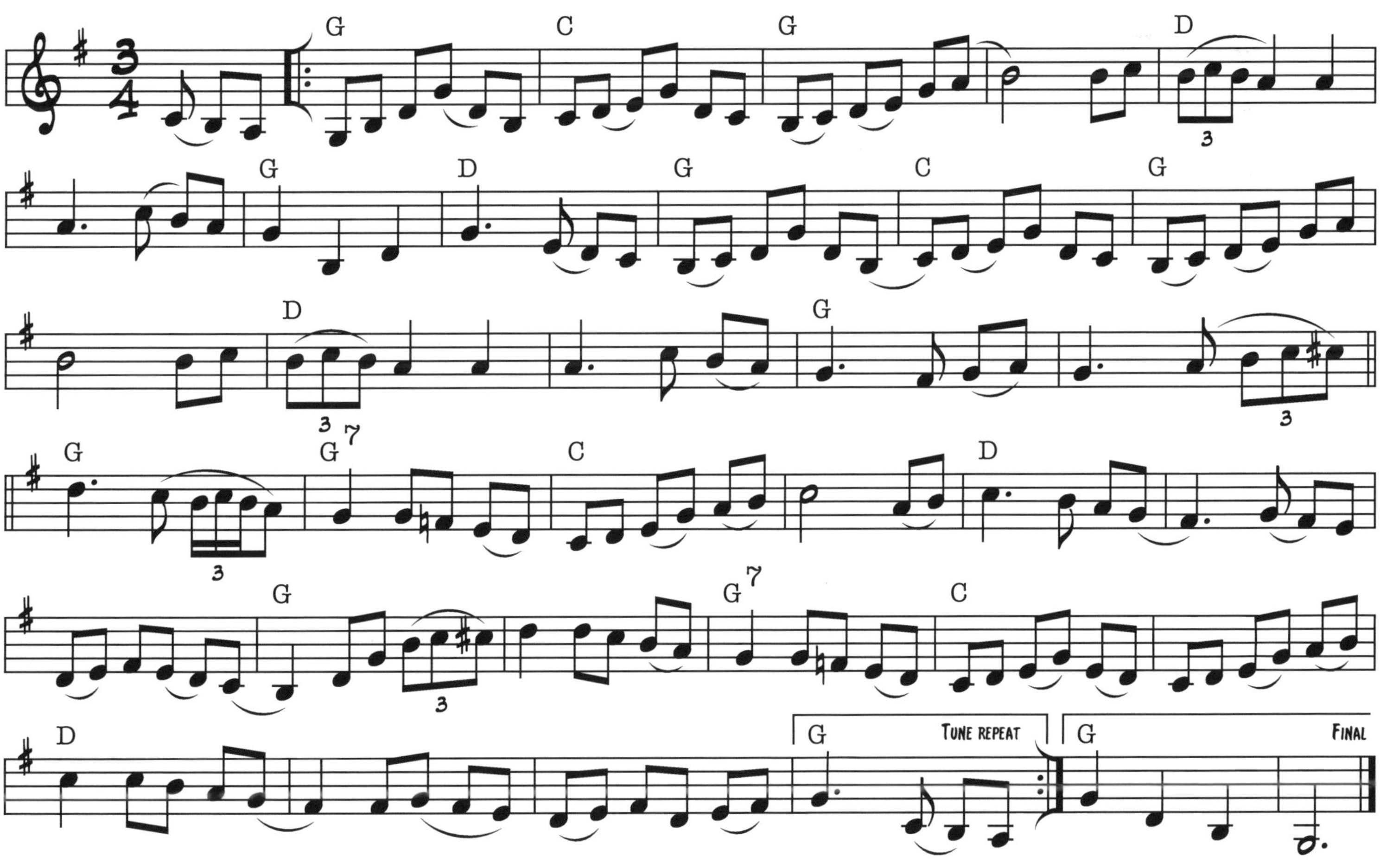

Over the Waterfall

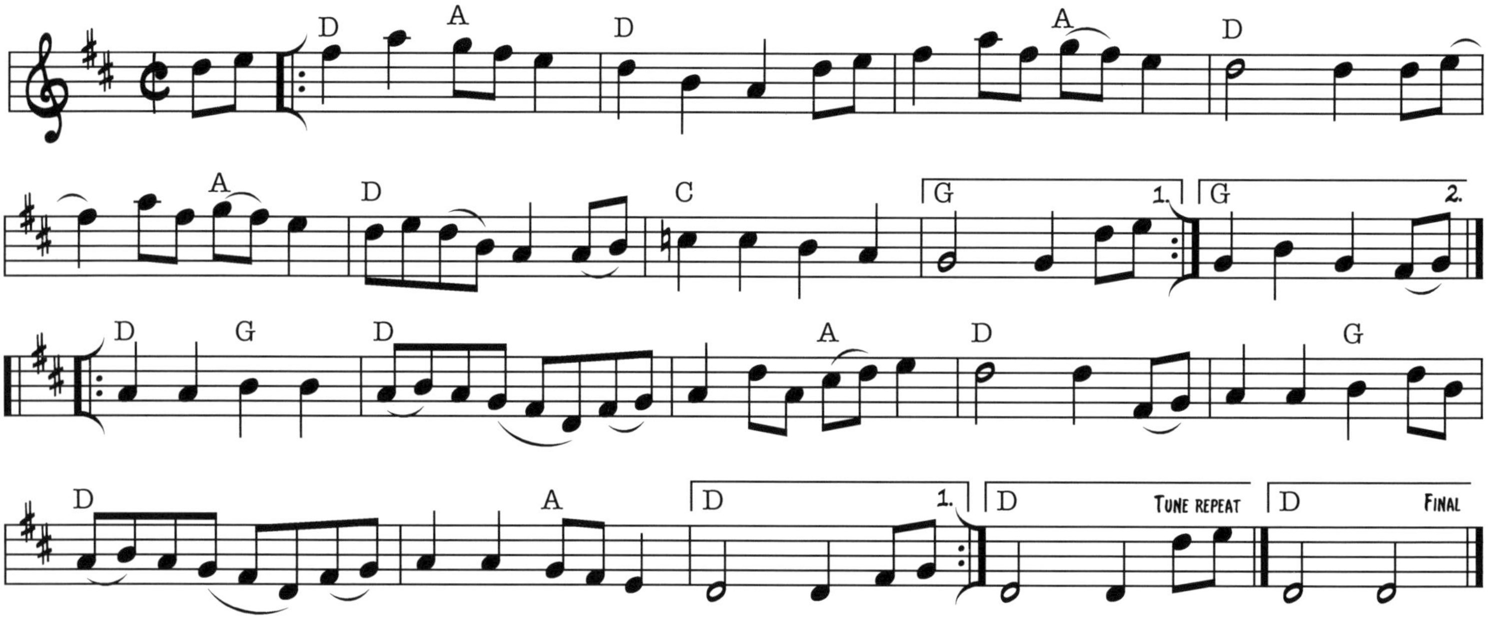

Pikes Peak

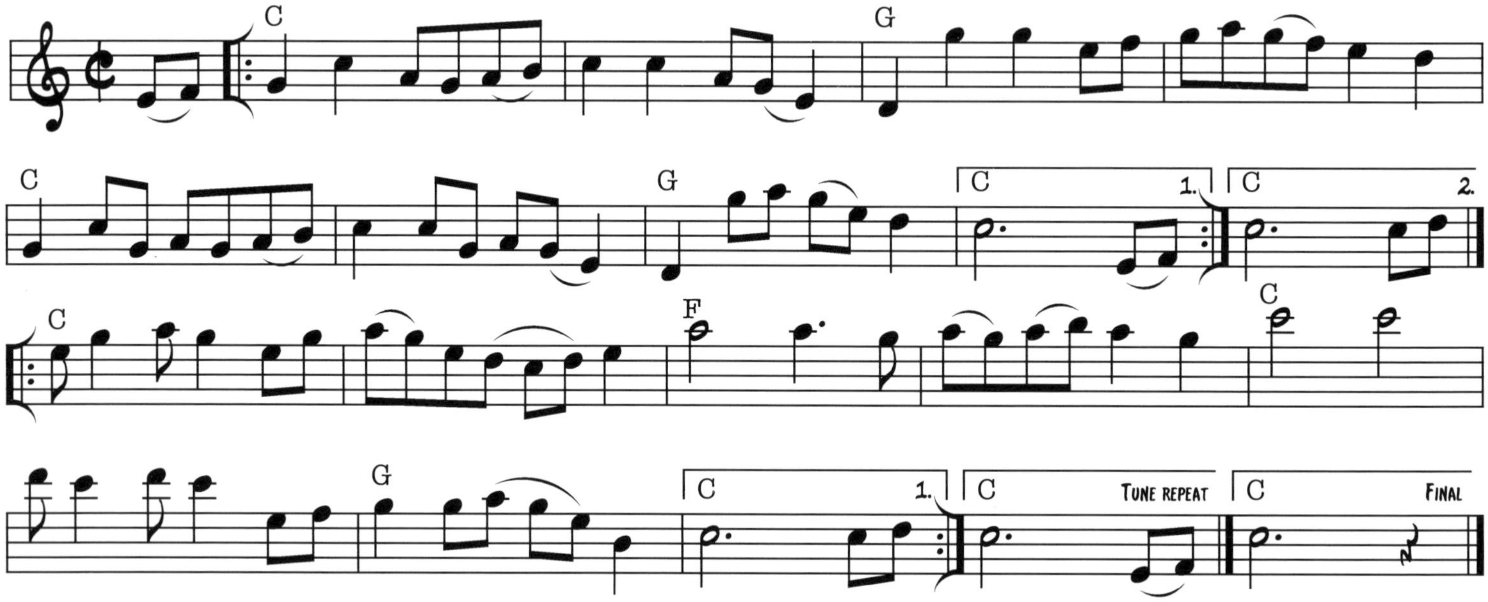

Polly Put the Kettle On

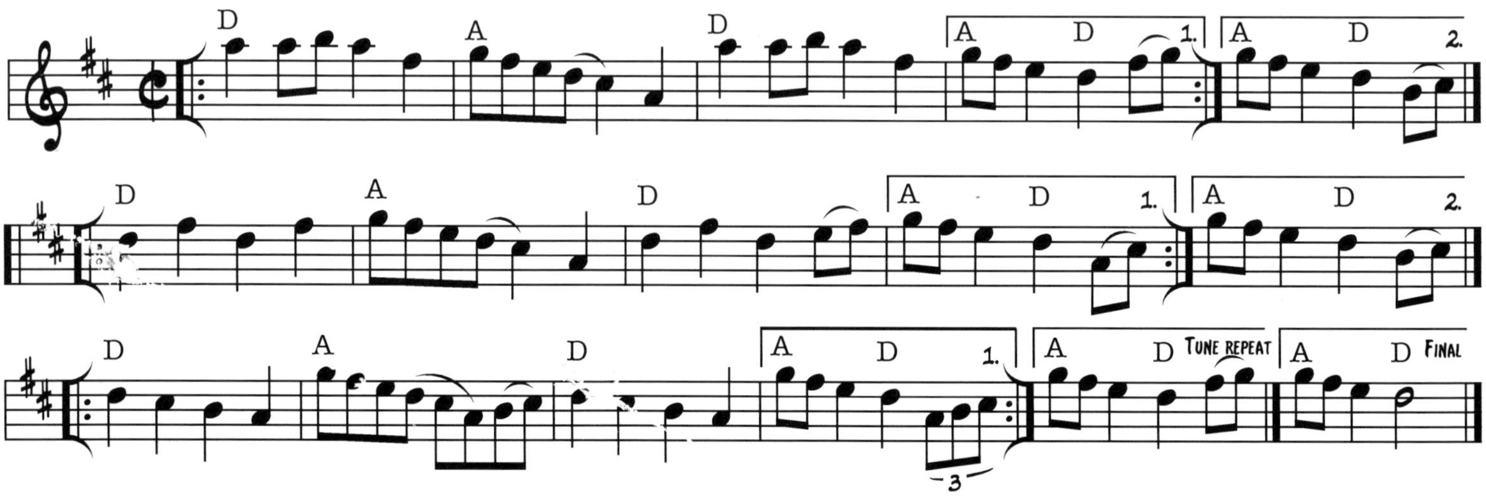

Pig Ankle Rag

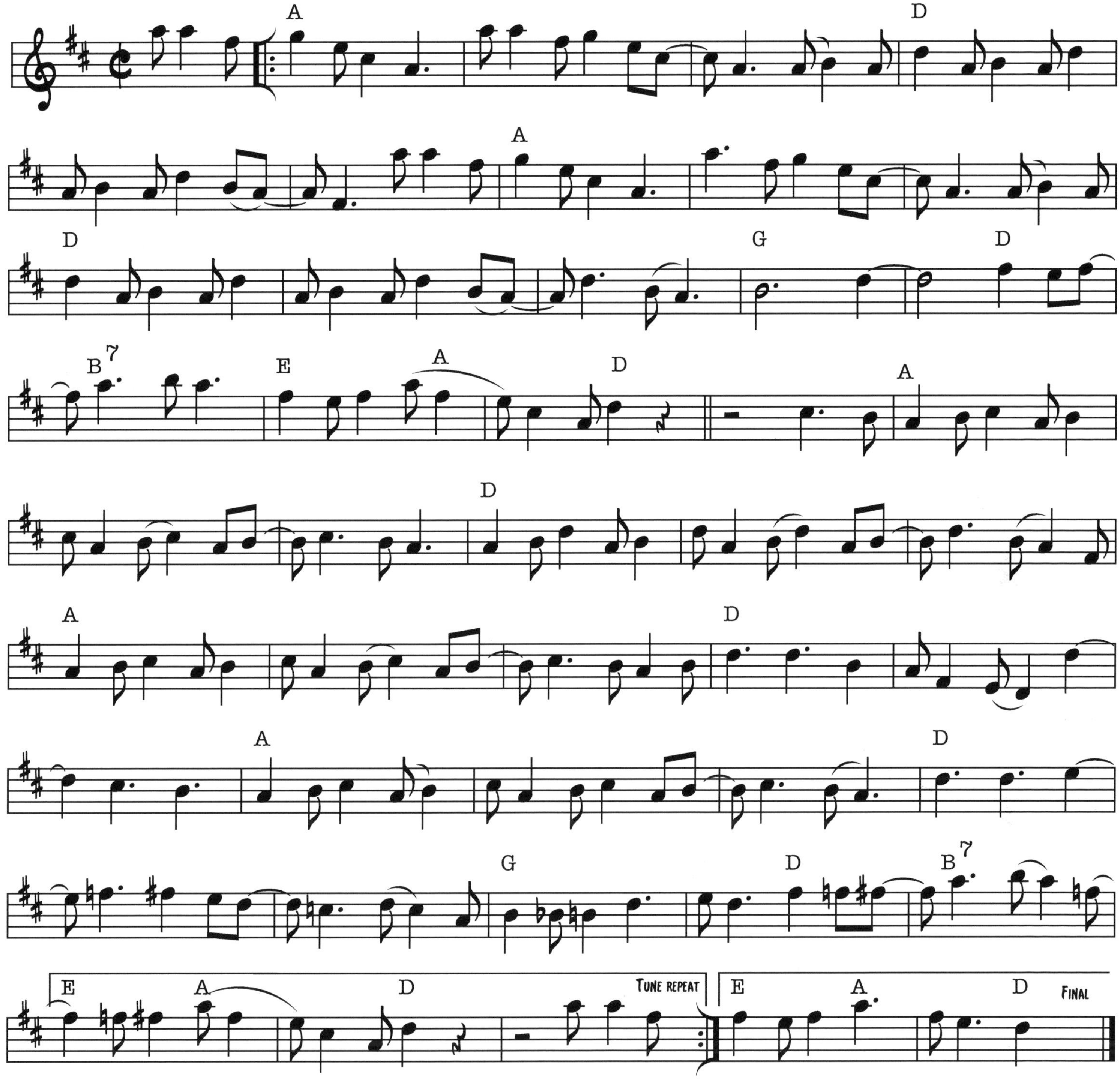

Policeman

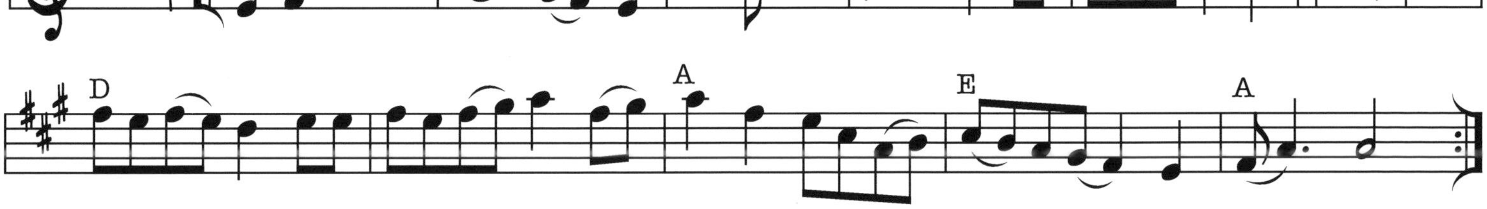

Possum in the Well

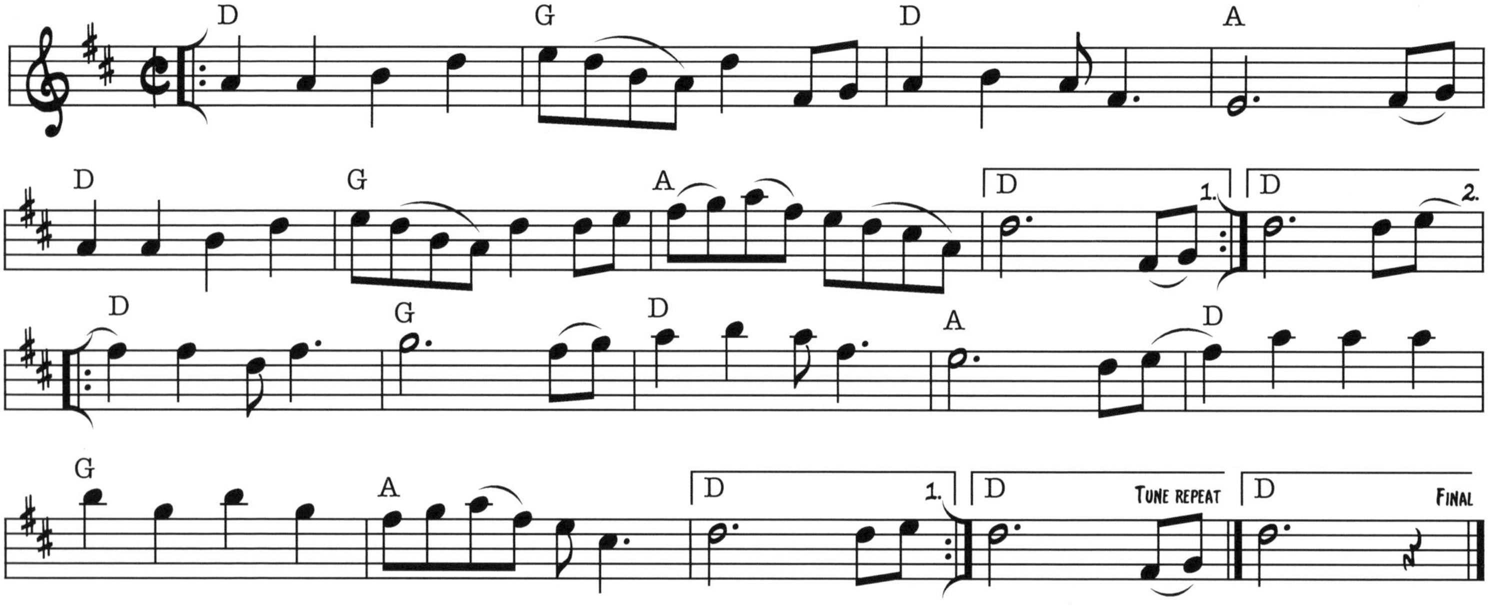

Possum on a Rail

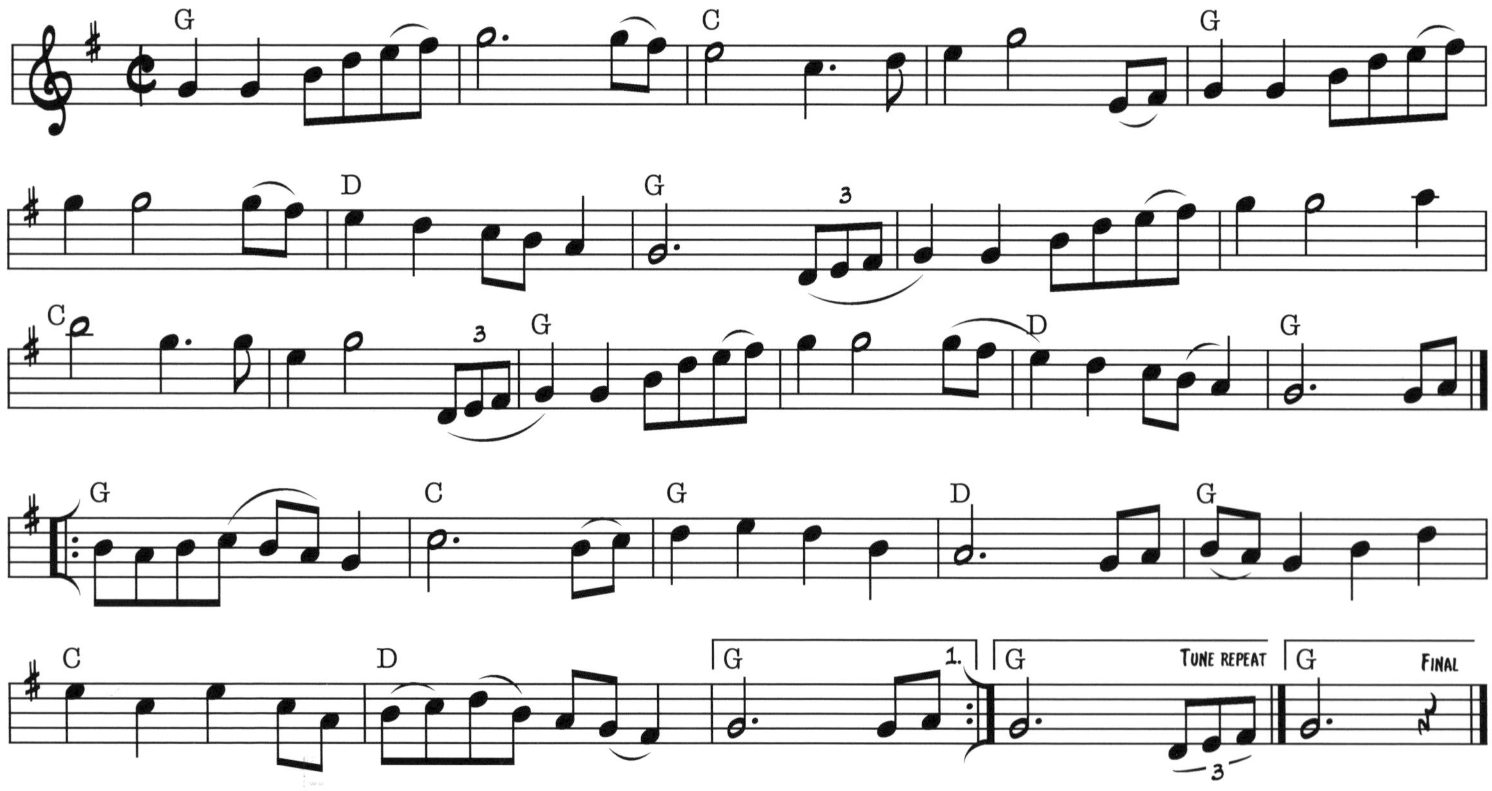

Porter's Reel

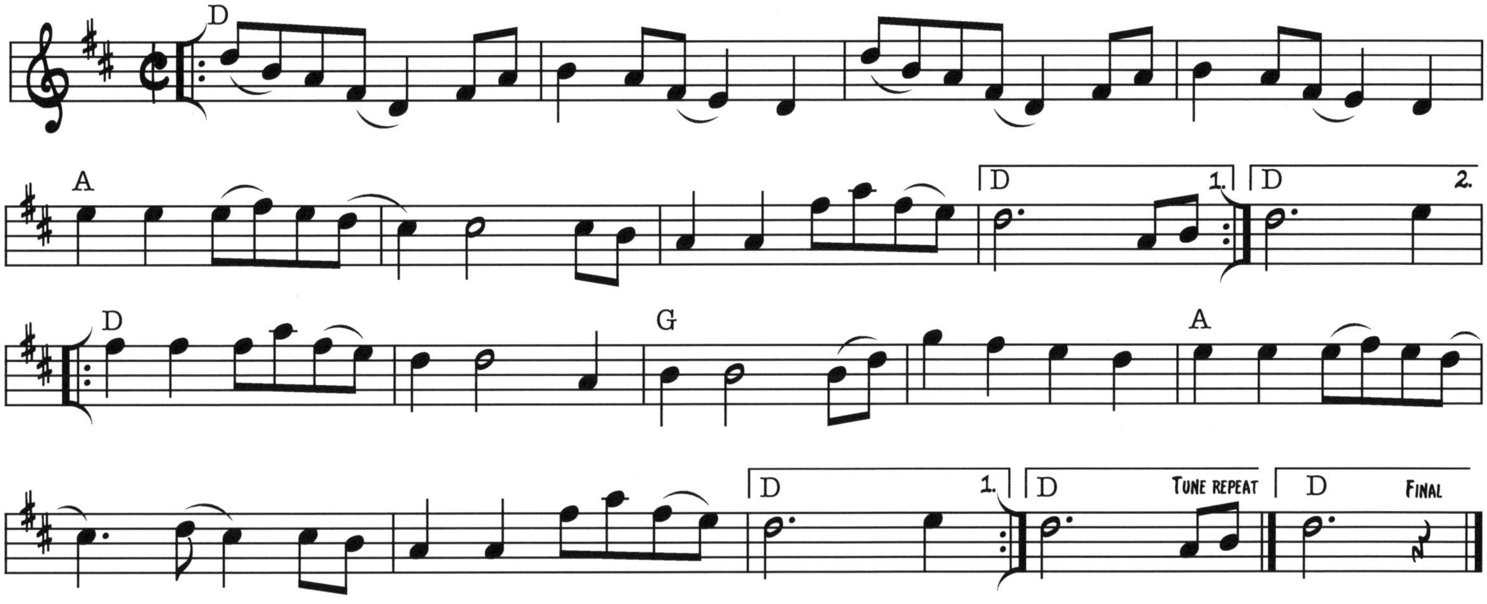

Quince Dillon's High D

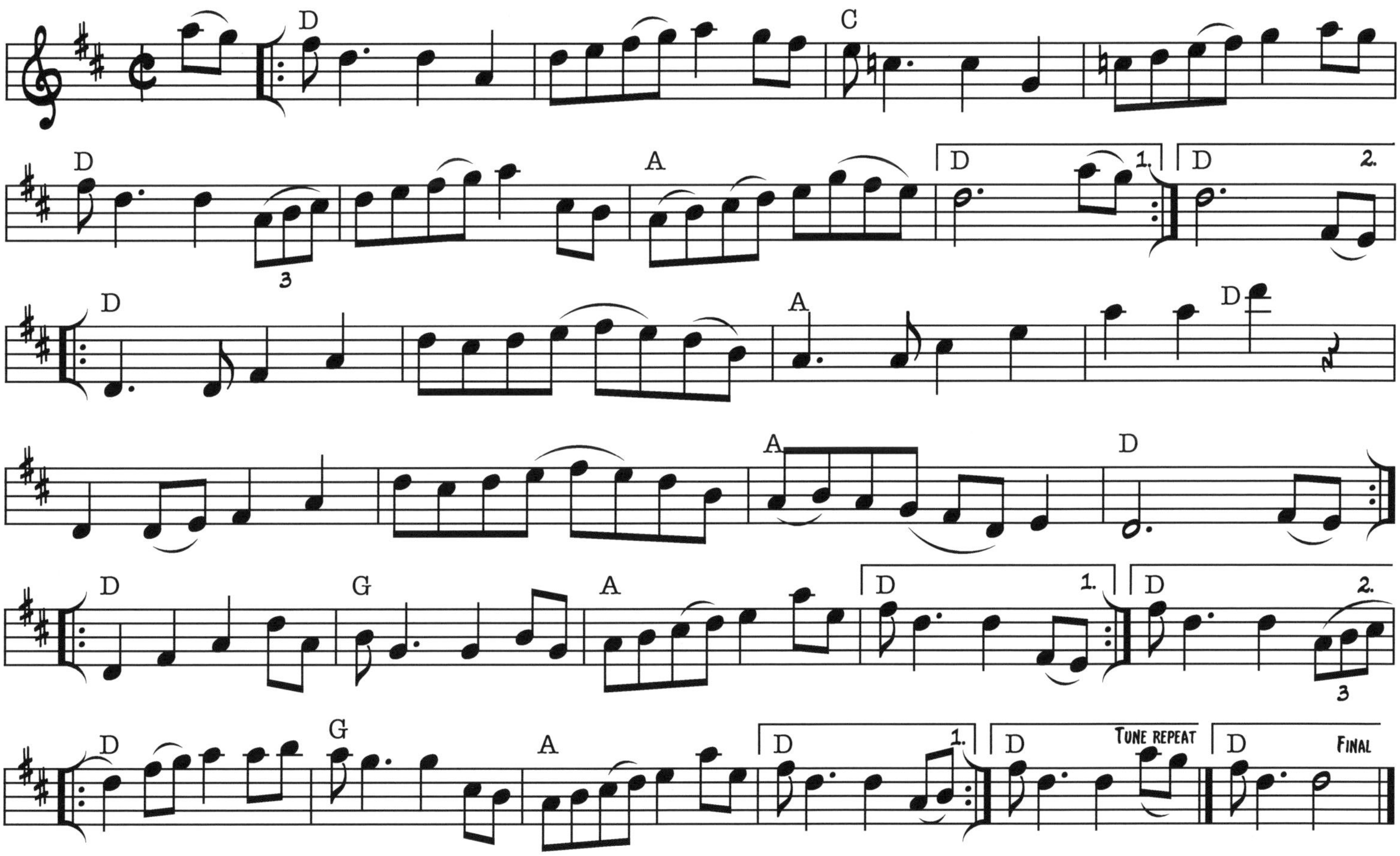

Ragtime Annie

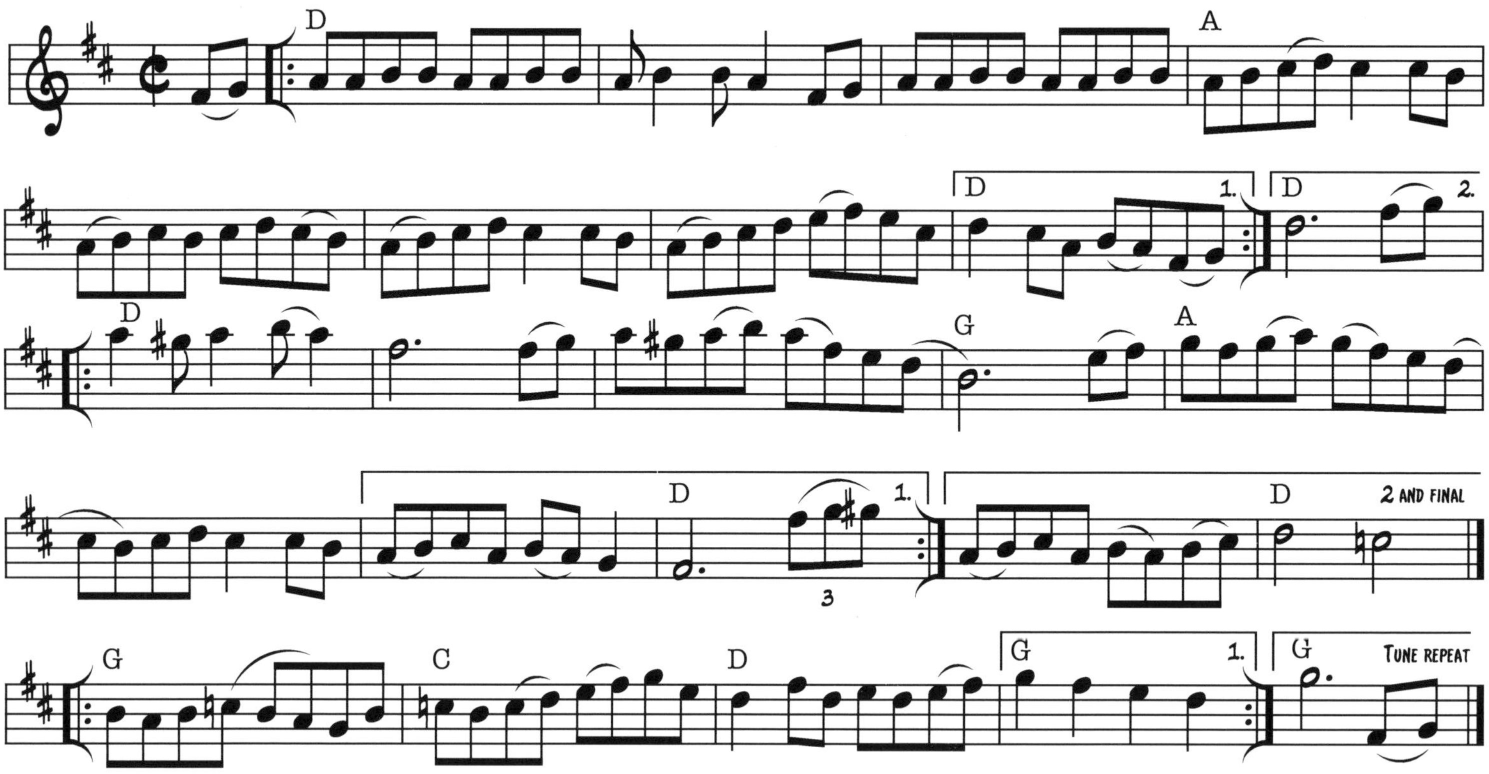

Railroad Through the Rocky Mountains (aka Marmaduke's Hornpipe)

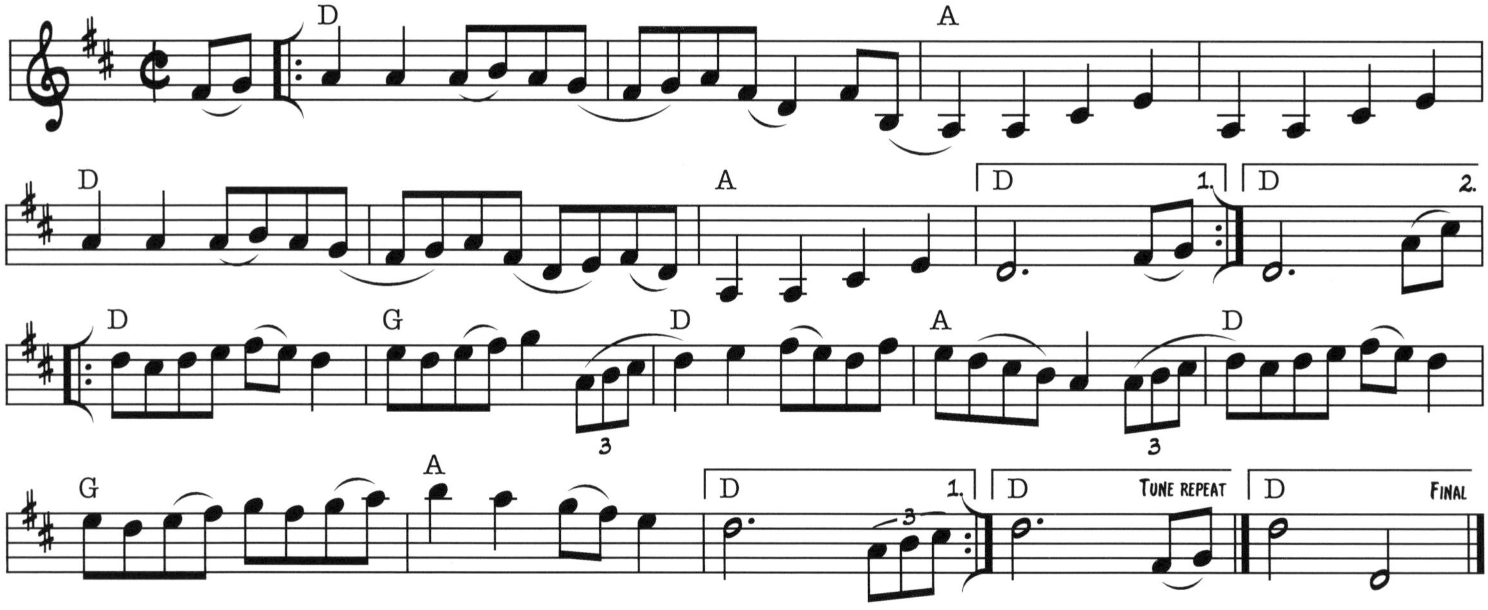

Rainy Day

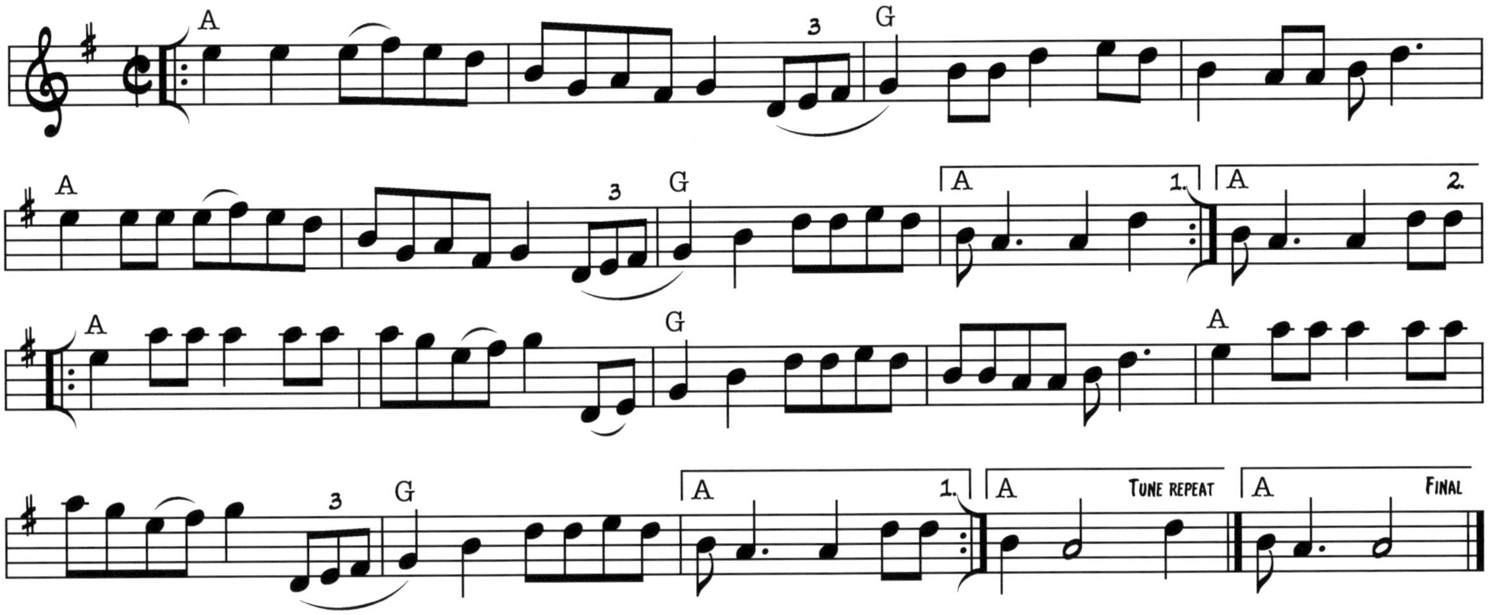

(The) Rattlesnake

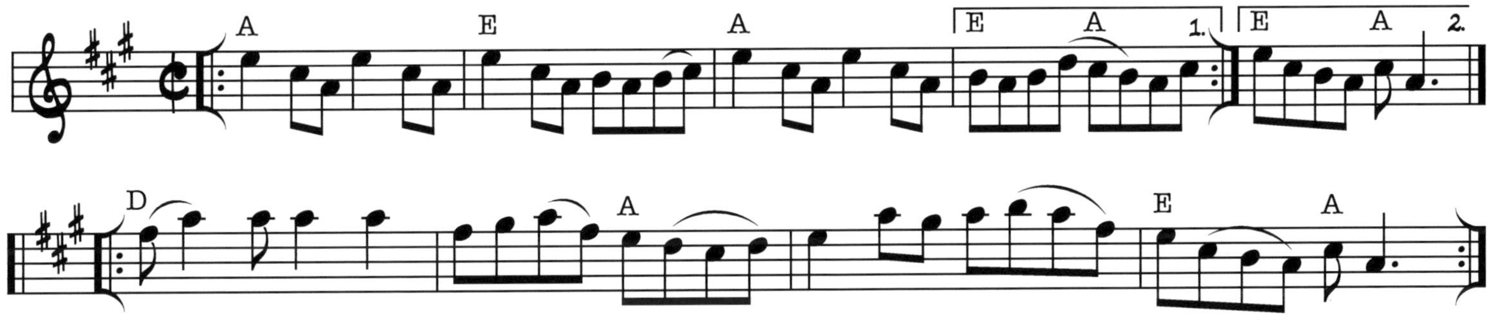

Rattlesnake Bit the Baby

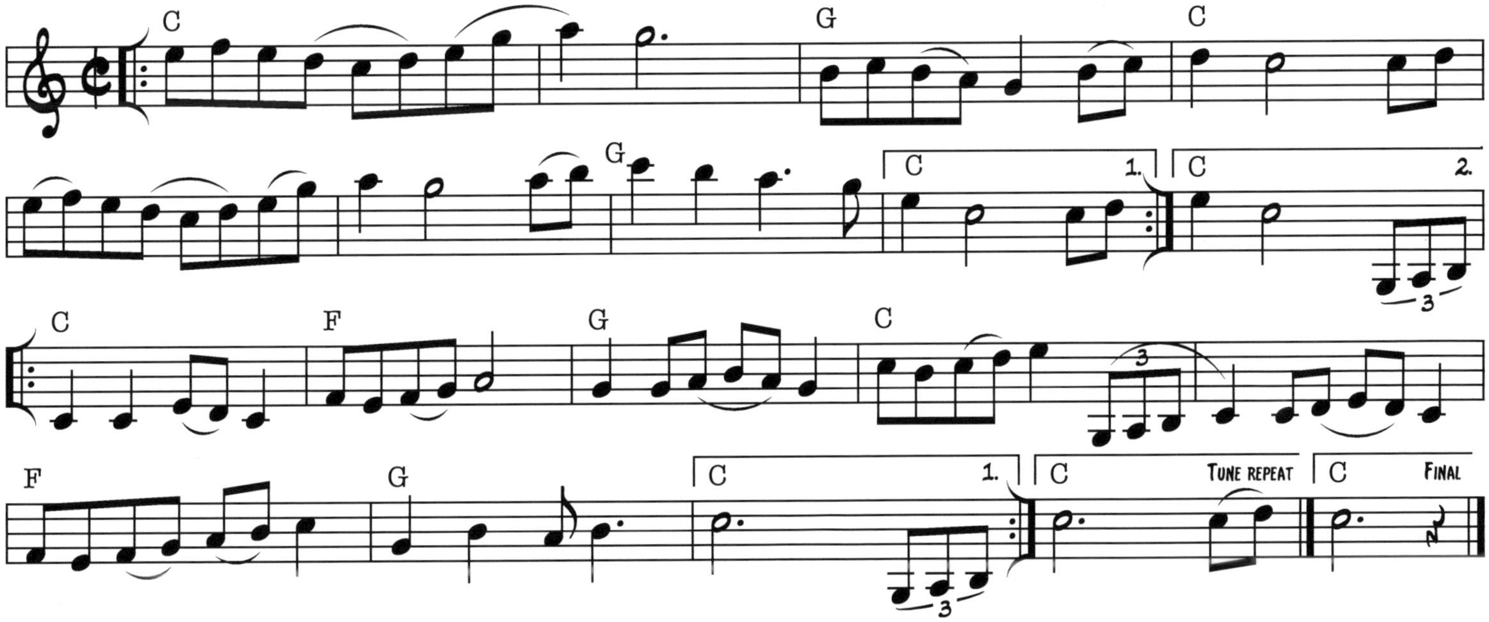

Red Bird

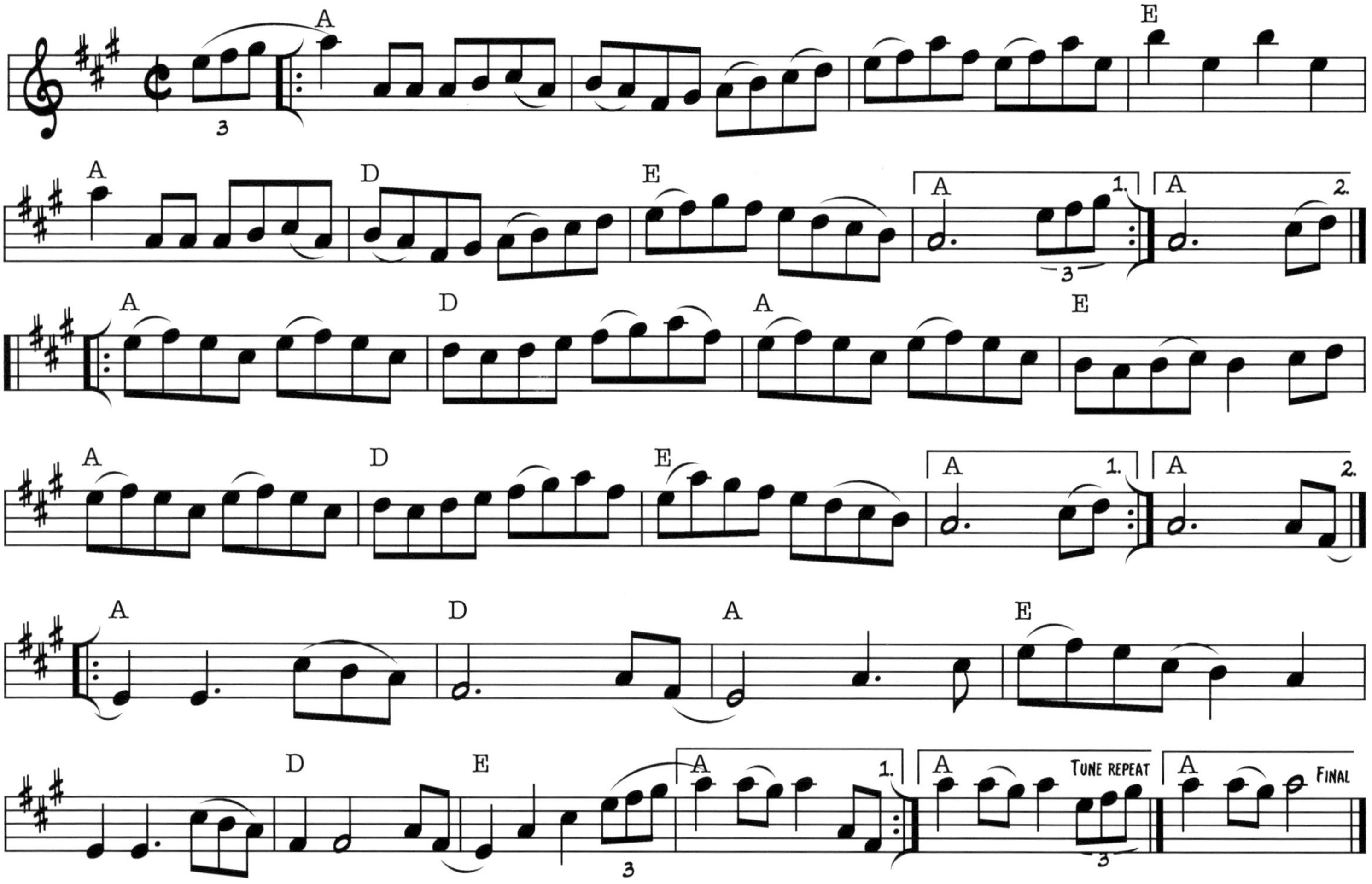

Red Fox Waltz

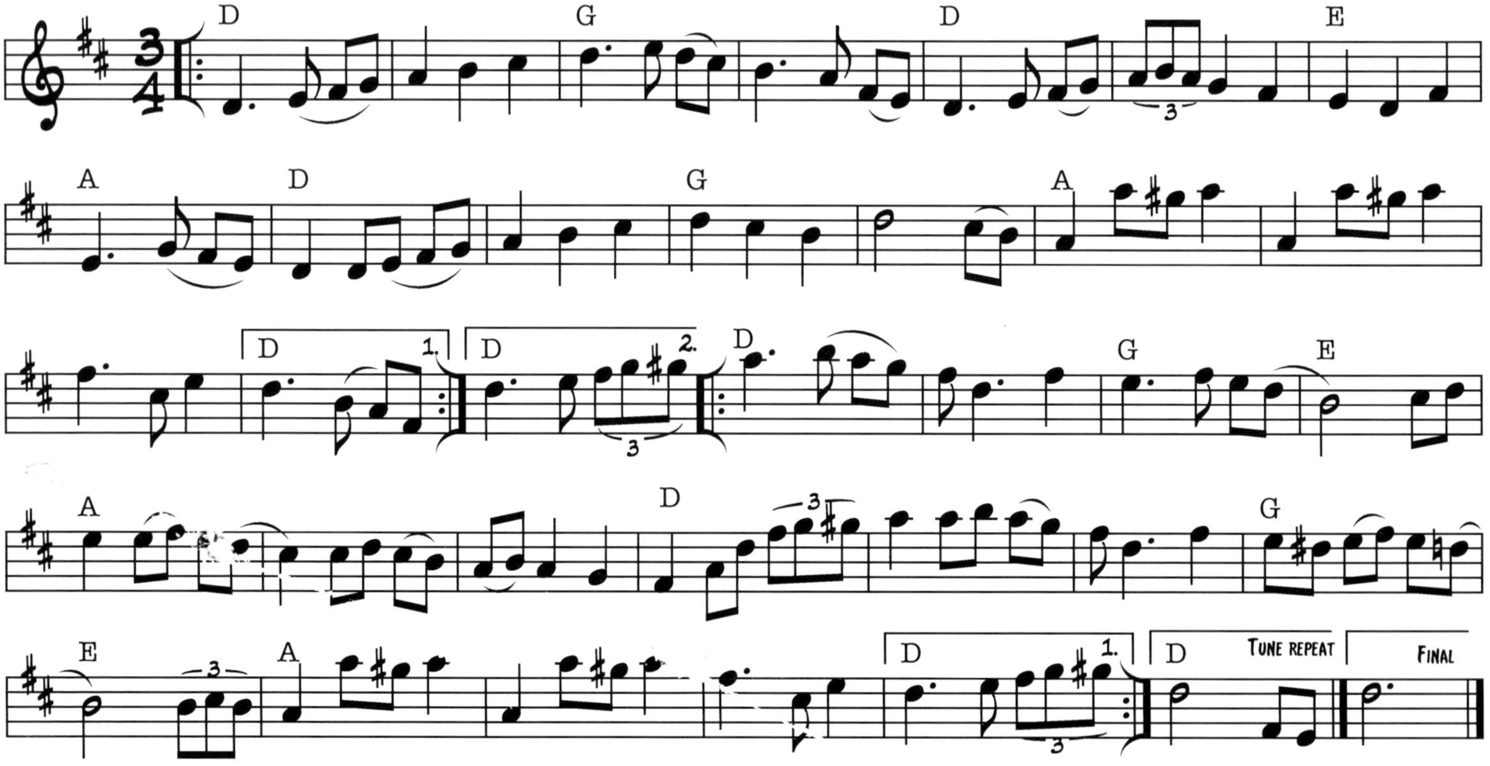

Red Haired Boy (aka Little Begger Man)

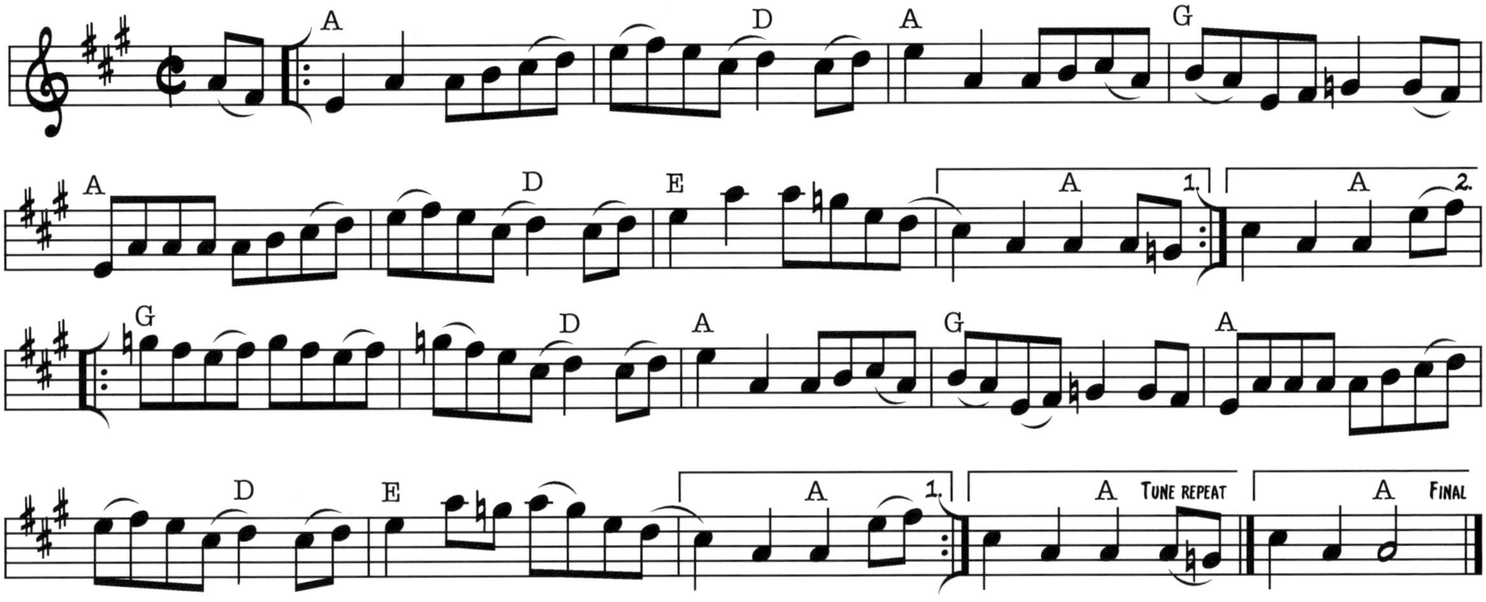

Richmond Cotillion

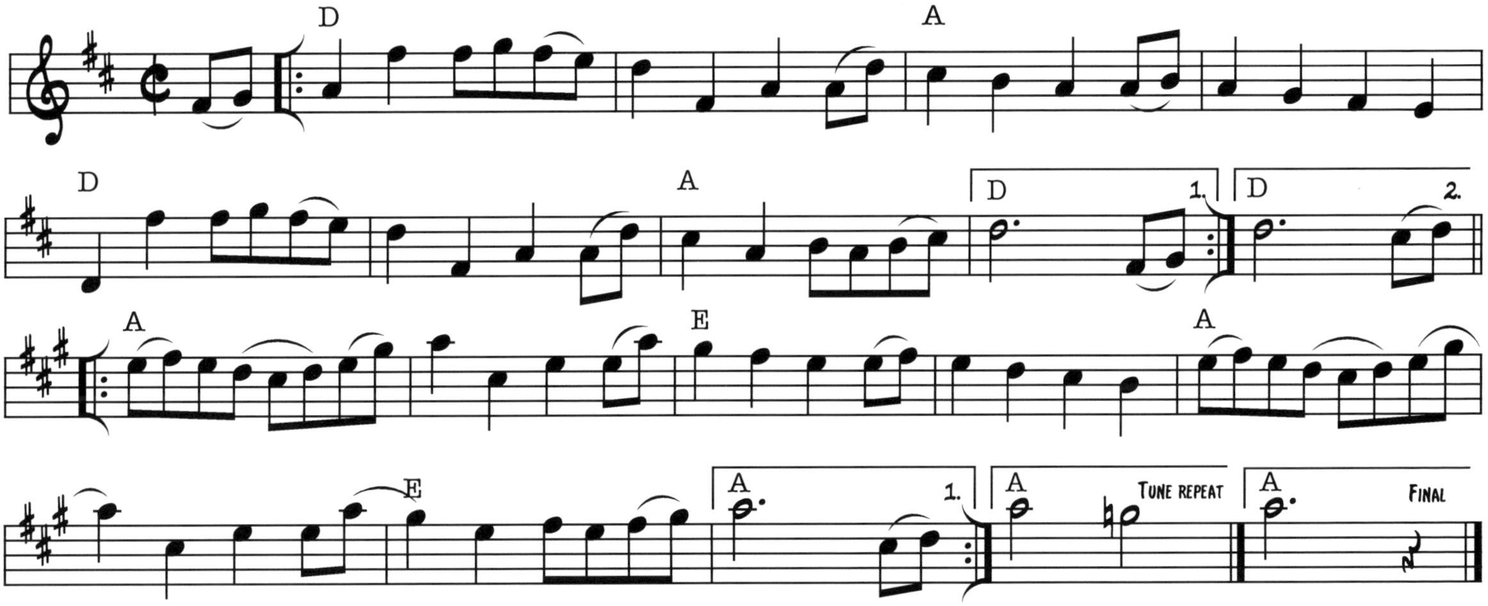

Rickett's Hornpipe

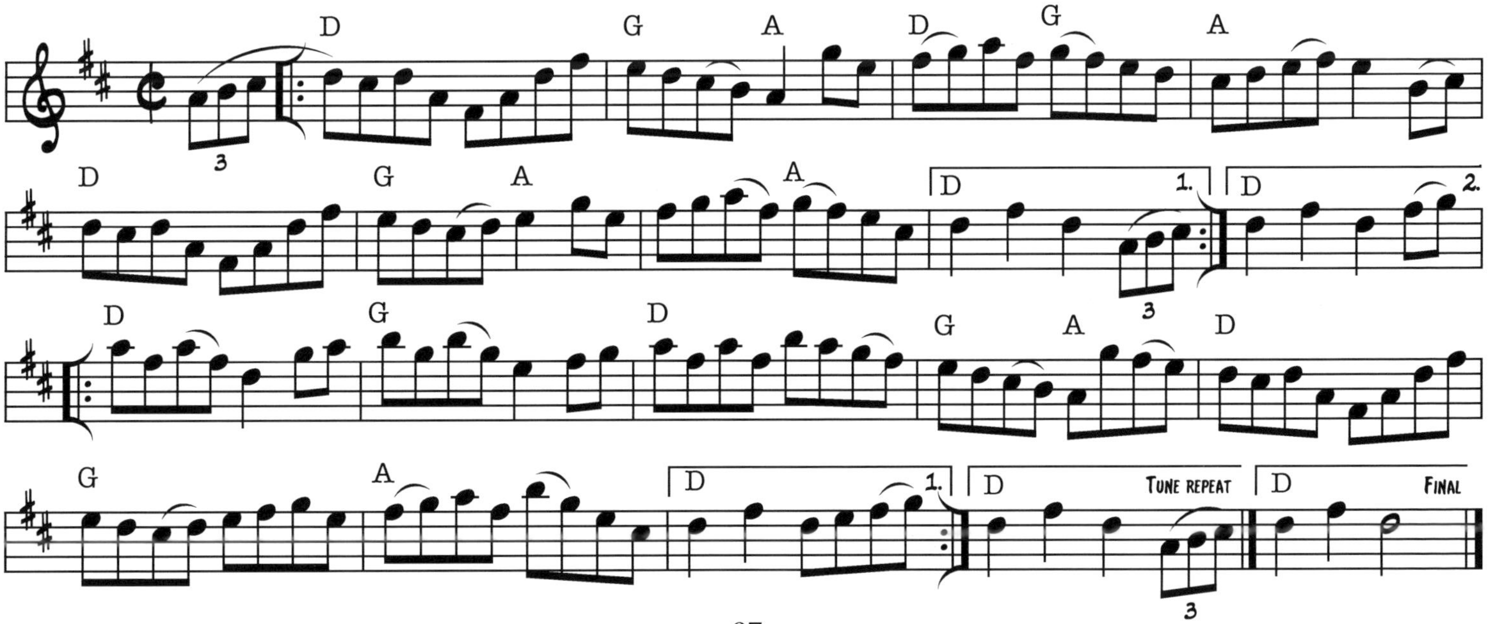

Rock That Cradle Lucy

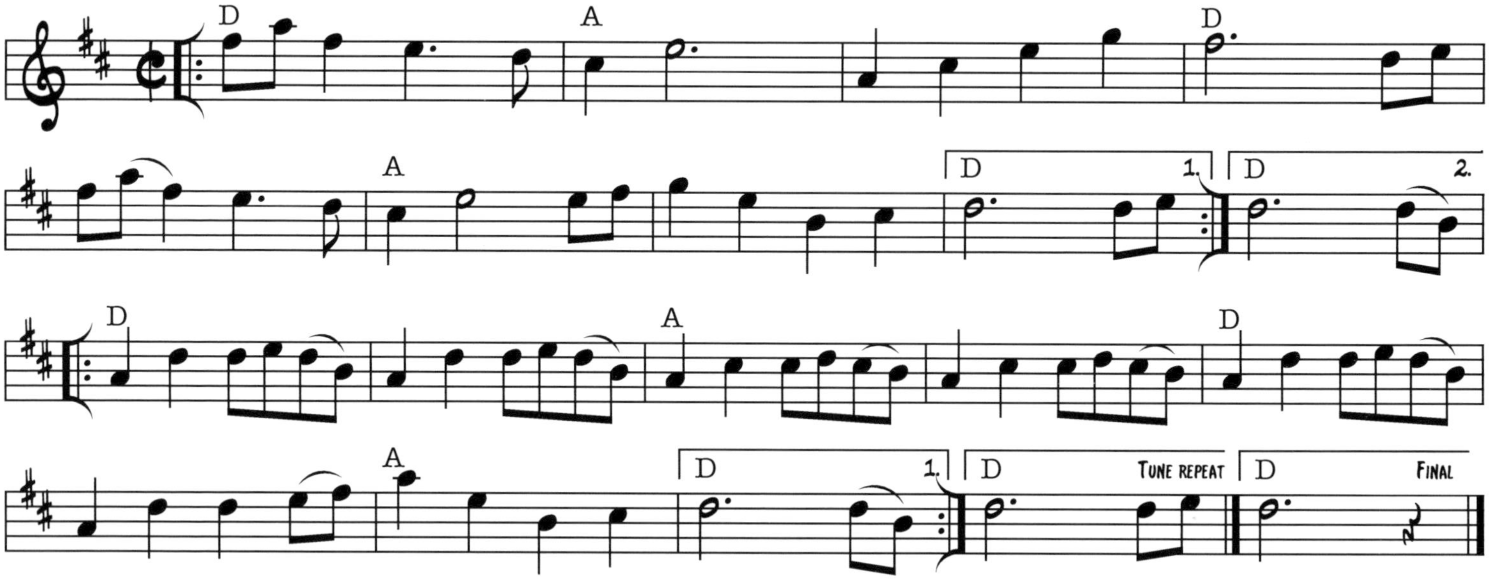

Rock the Cradle Joe (1)

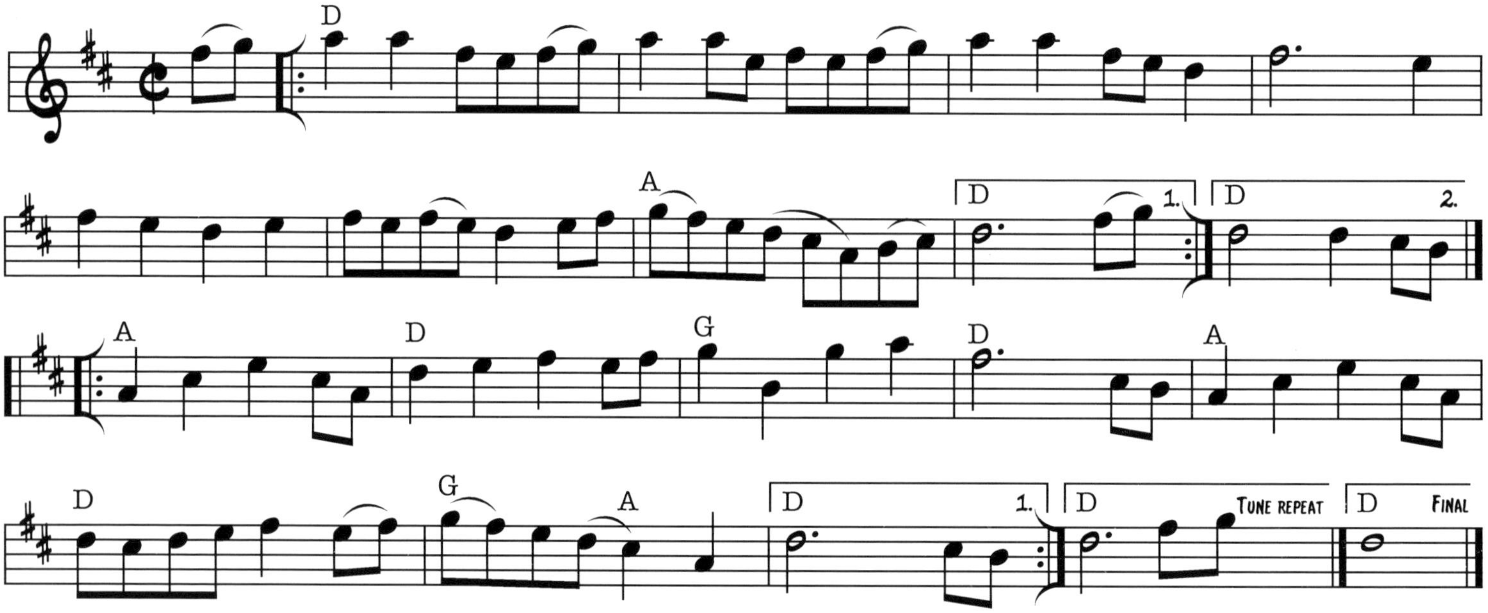

Rock the Cradle Joe (2)

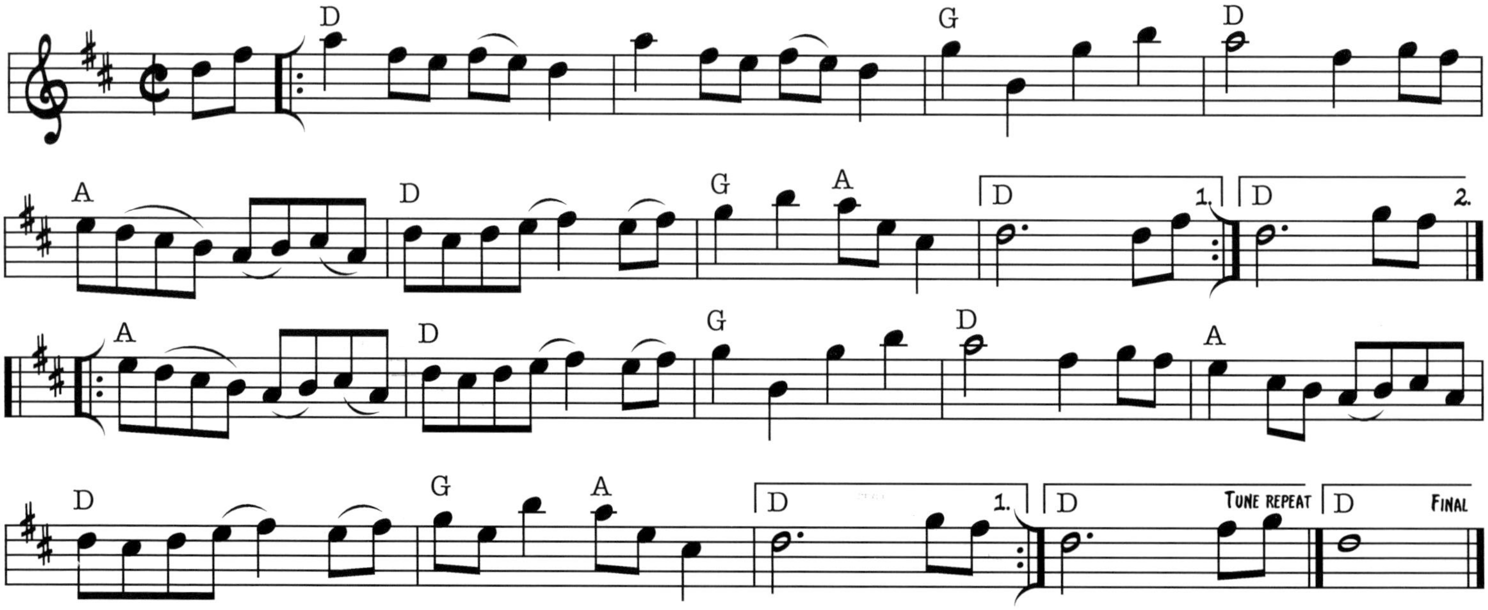

Roaring River

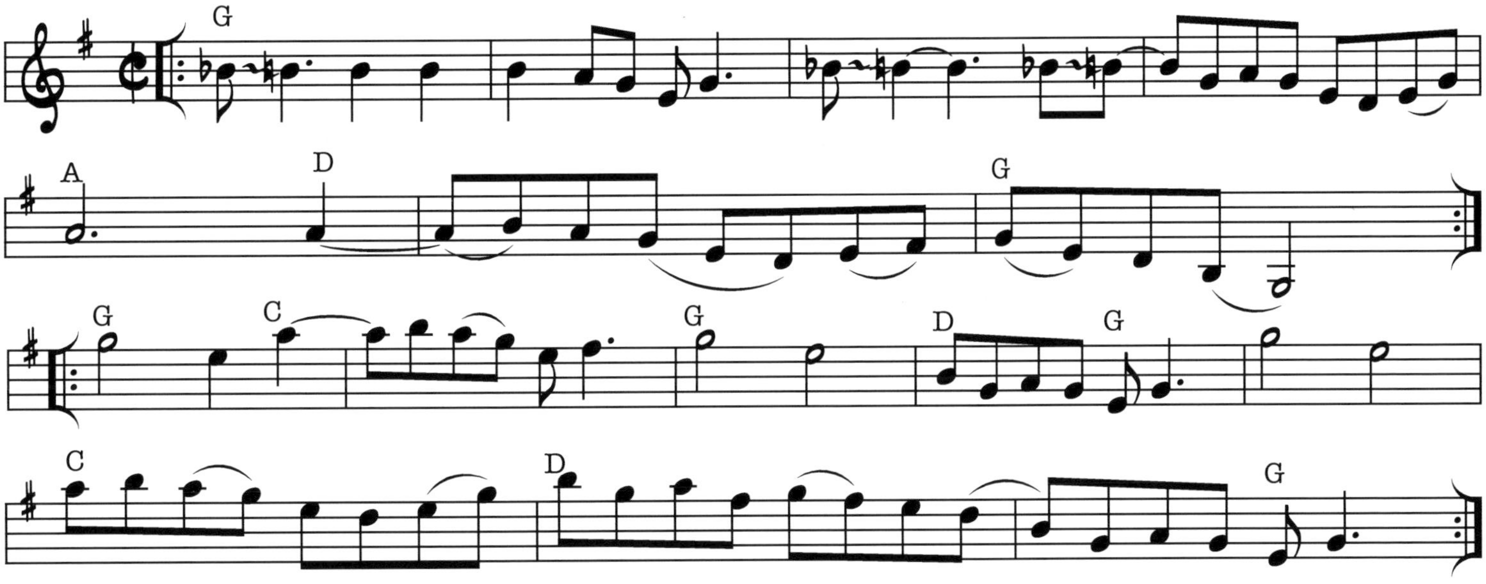

Rochester Schottische

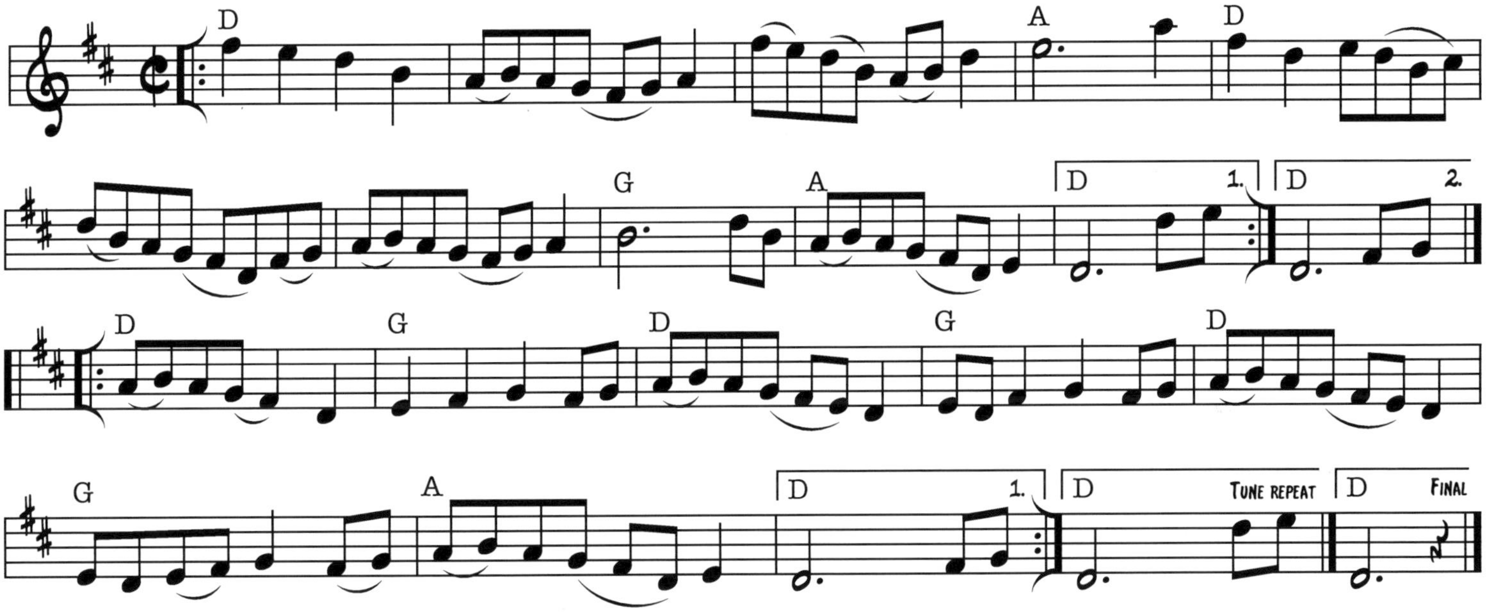

Rocky Mountain Goat

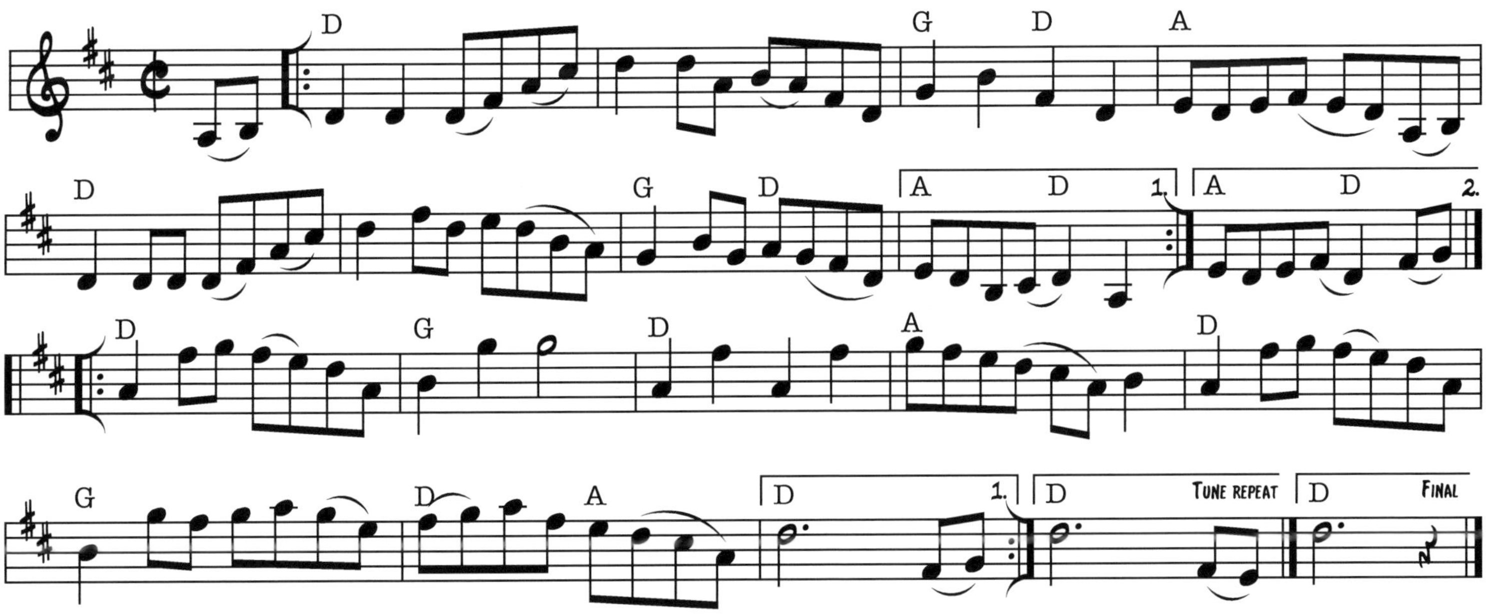

Rocky Mountain Hornpipe

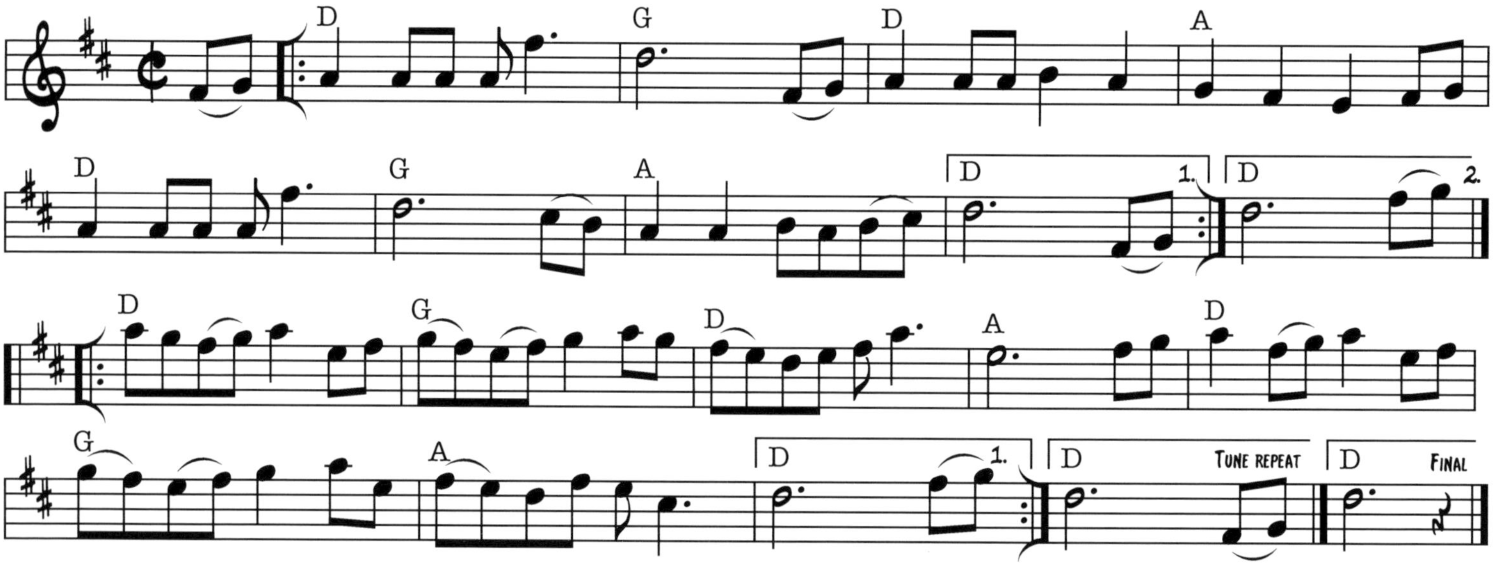

Rocky Pallet

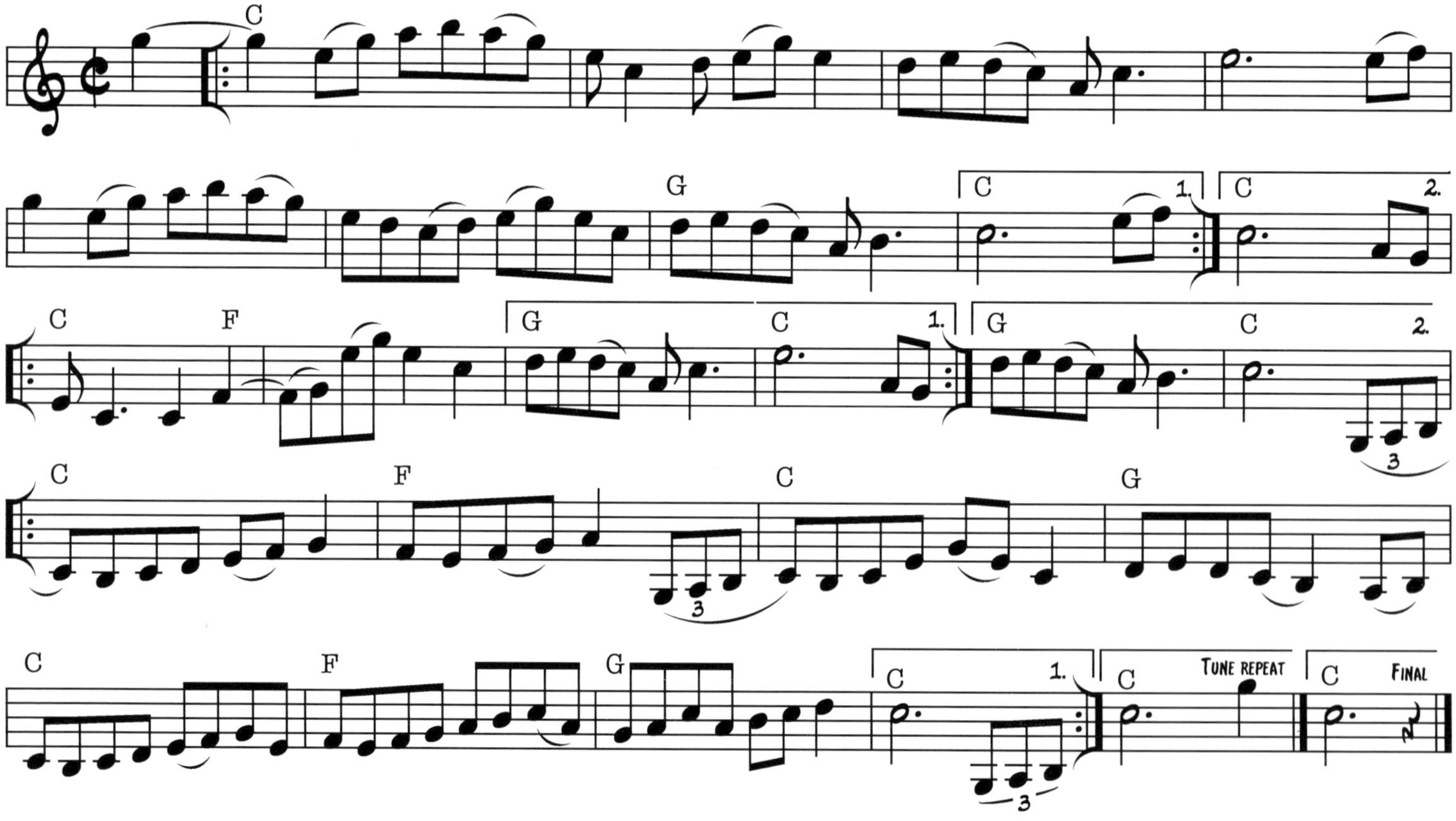

Rocky Road to Jordan

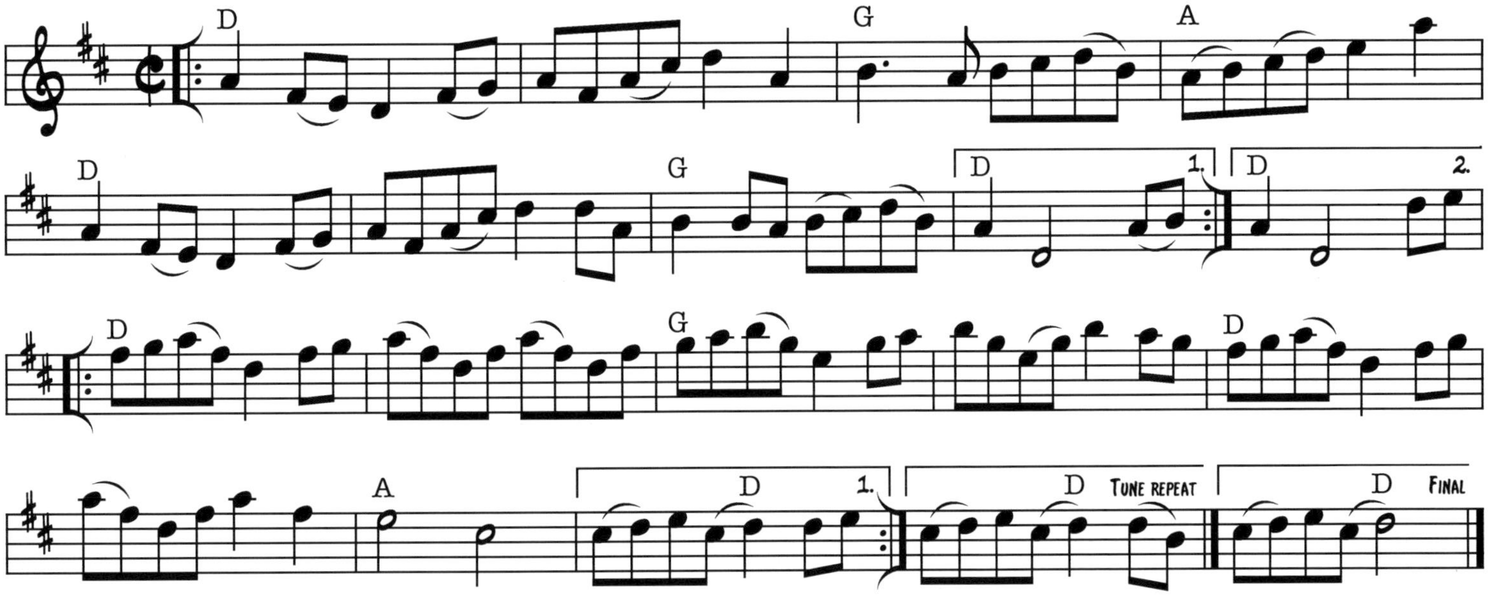

Rolling River

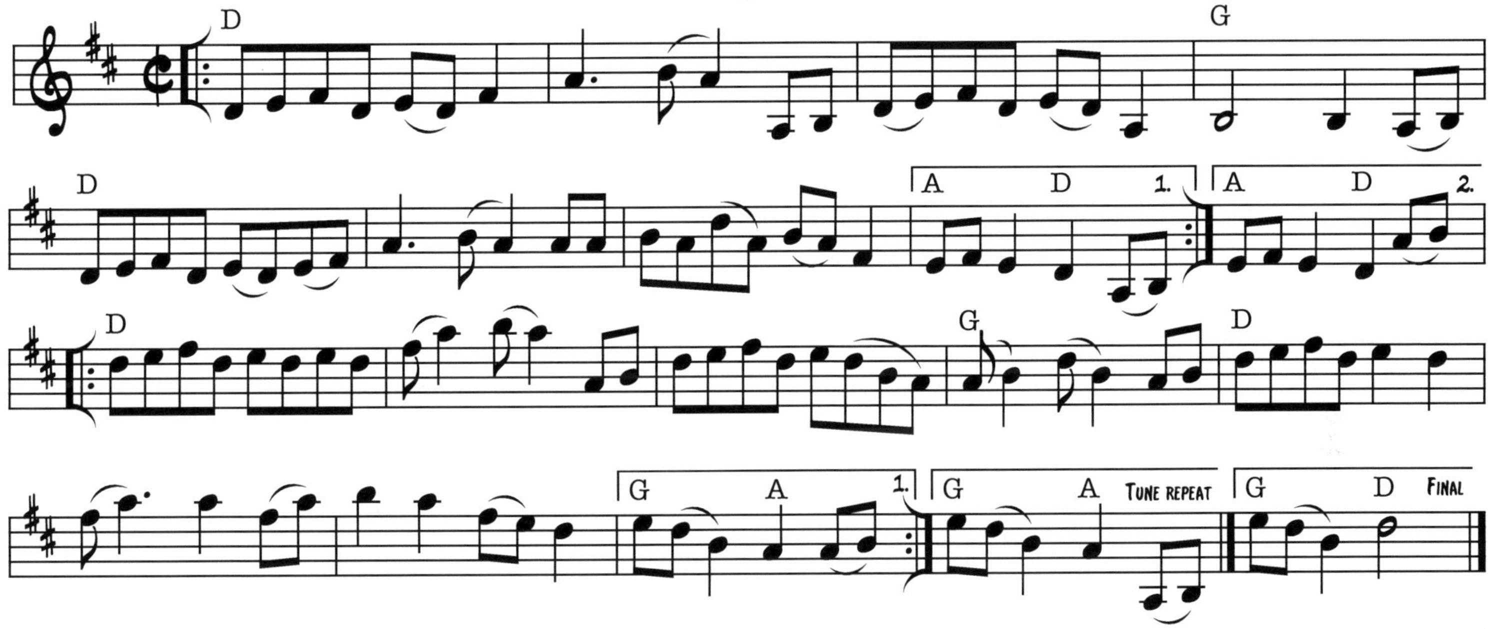

Roscoe

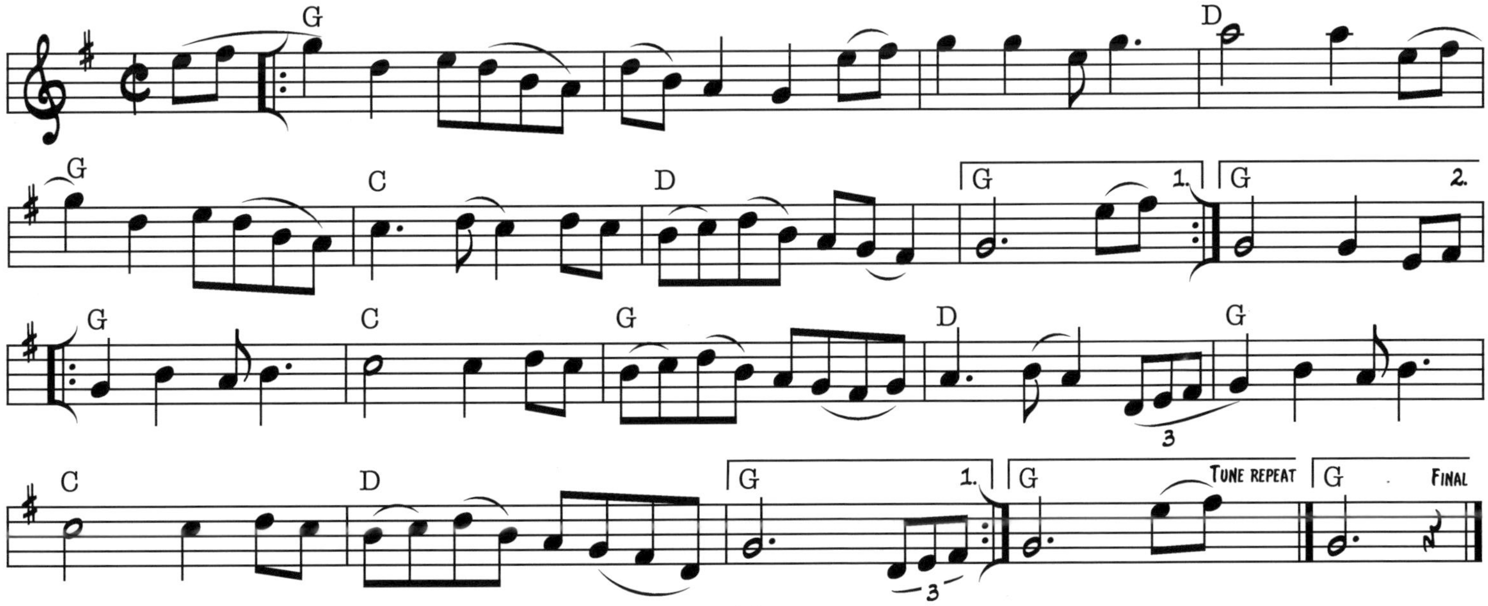

Run Down Boot

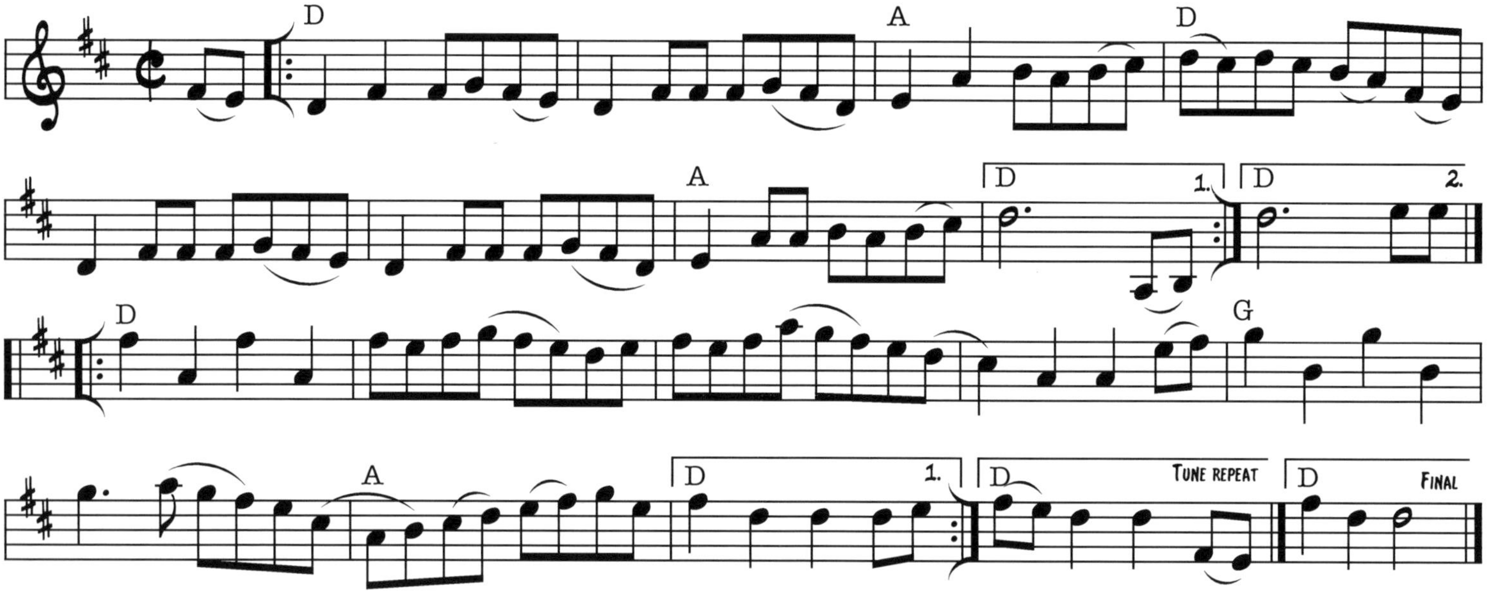

Run Rabbit Run

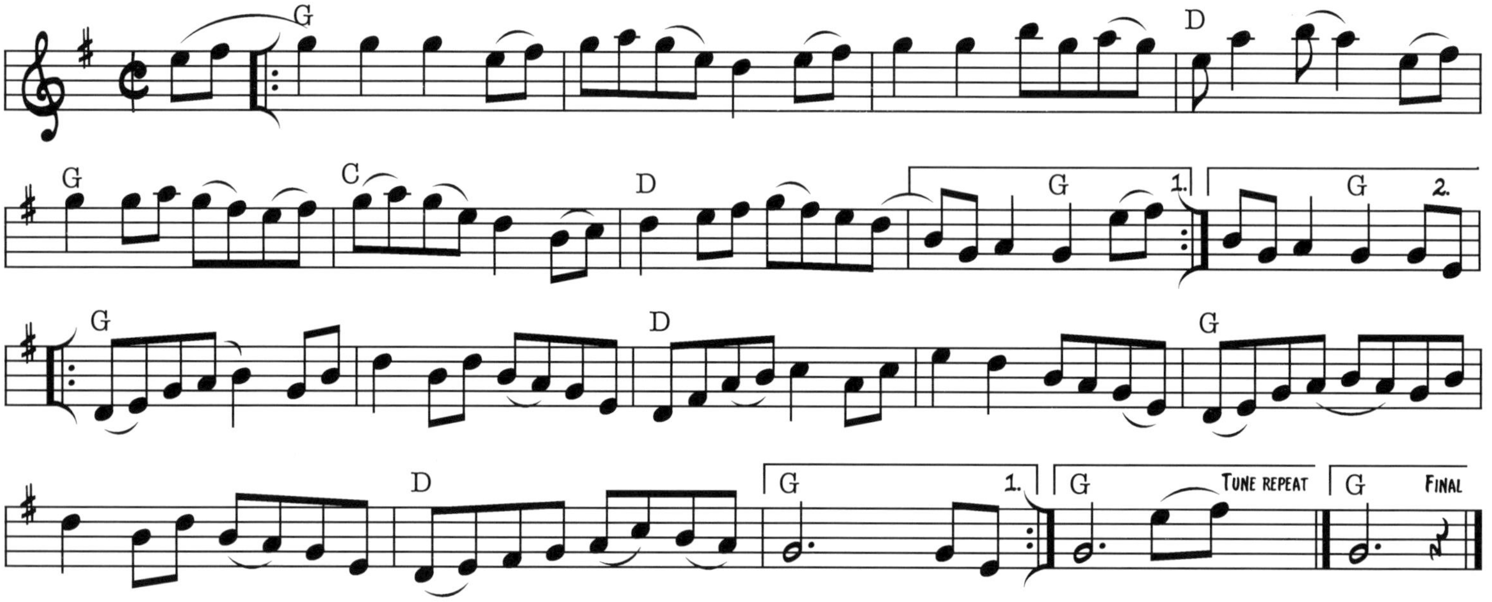

Rye Straw (aka Joke on the Puppy)

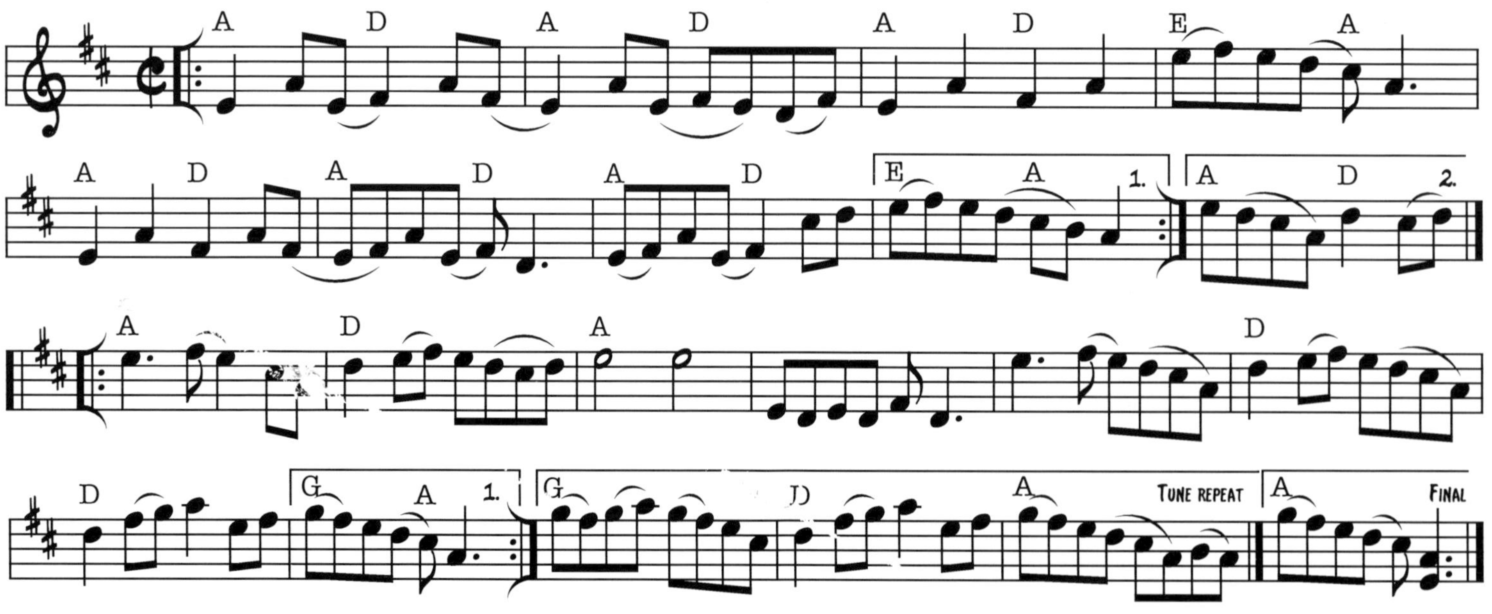

Saddle Up the Gray

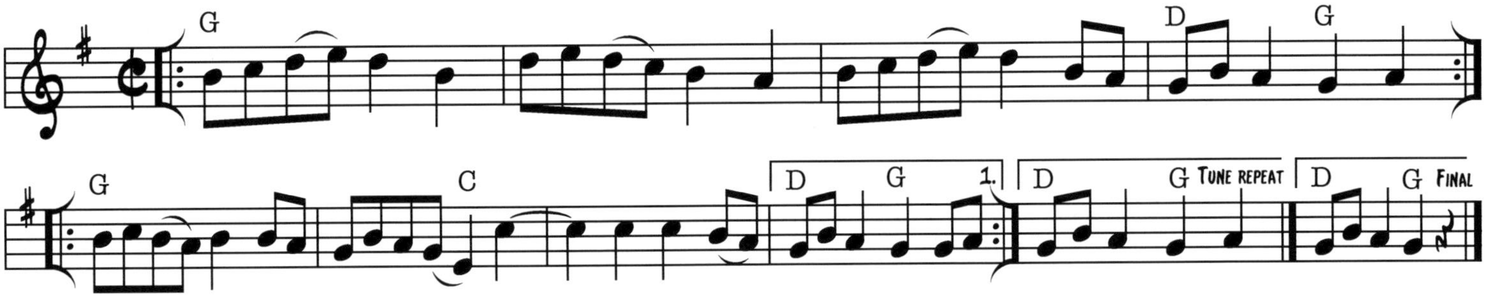

Sailing Over England

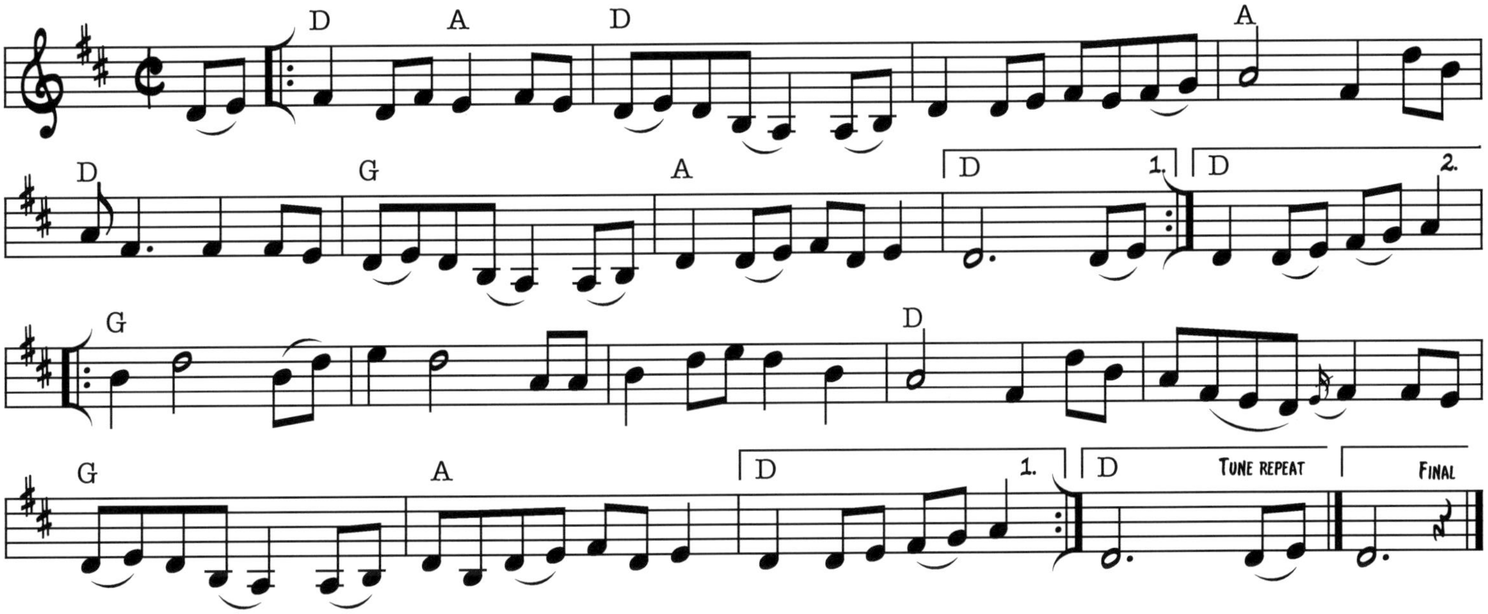

Saint Anne's Reel

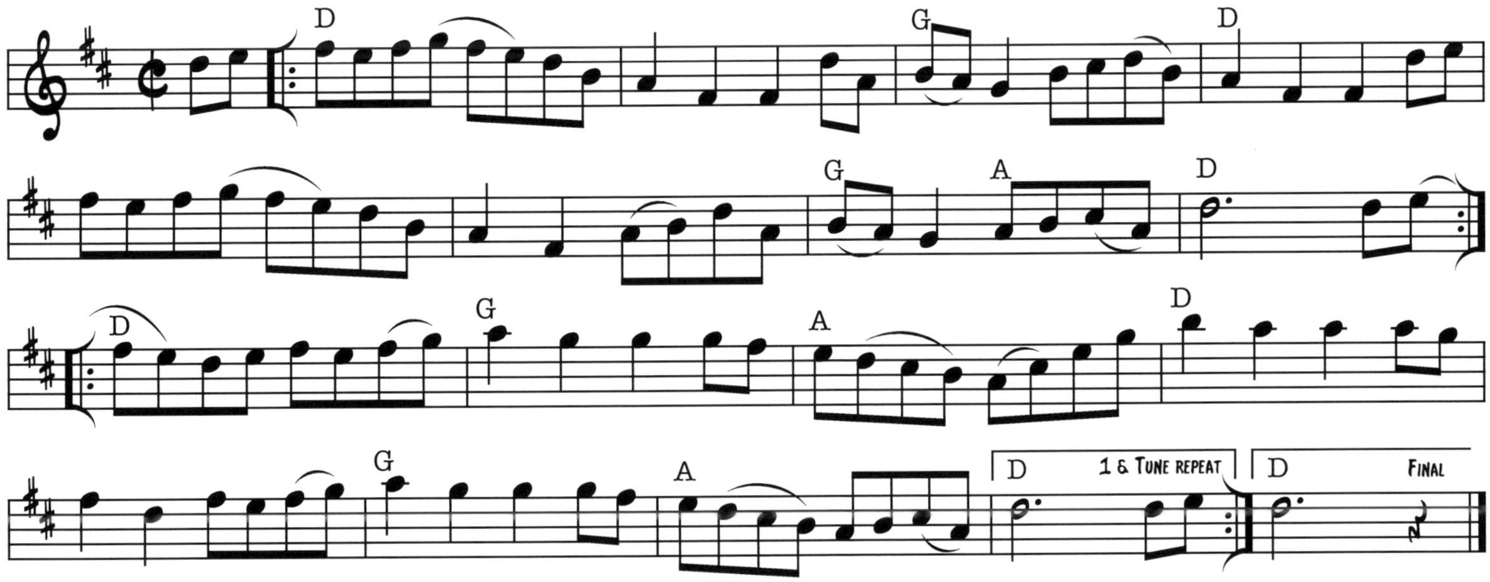

Sally Anne Johnson

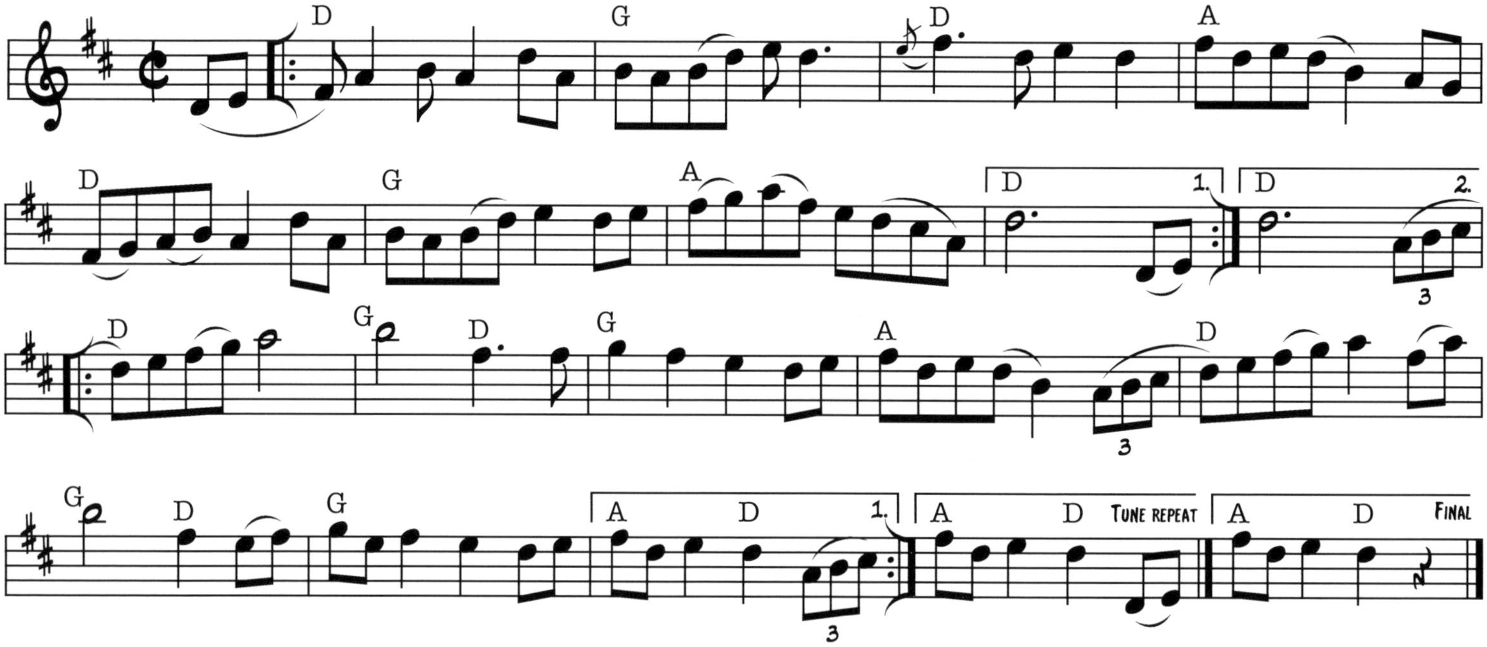

Sal's Got Mud Between Her Toes

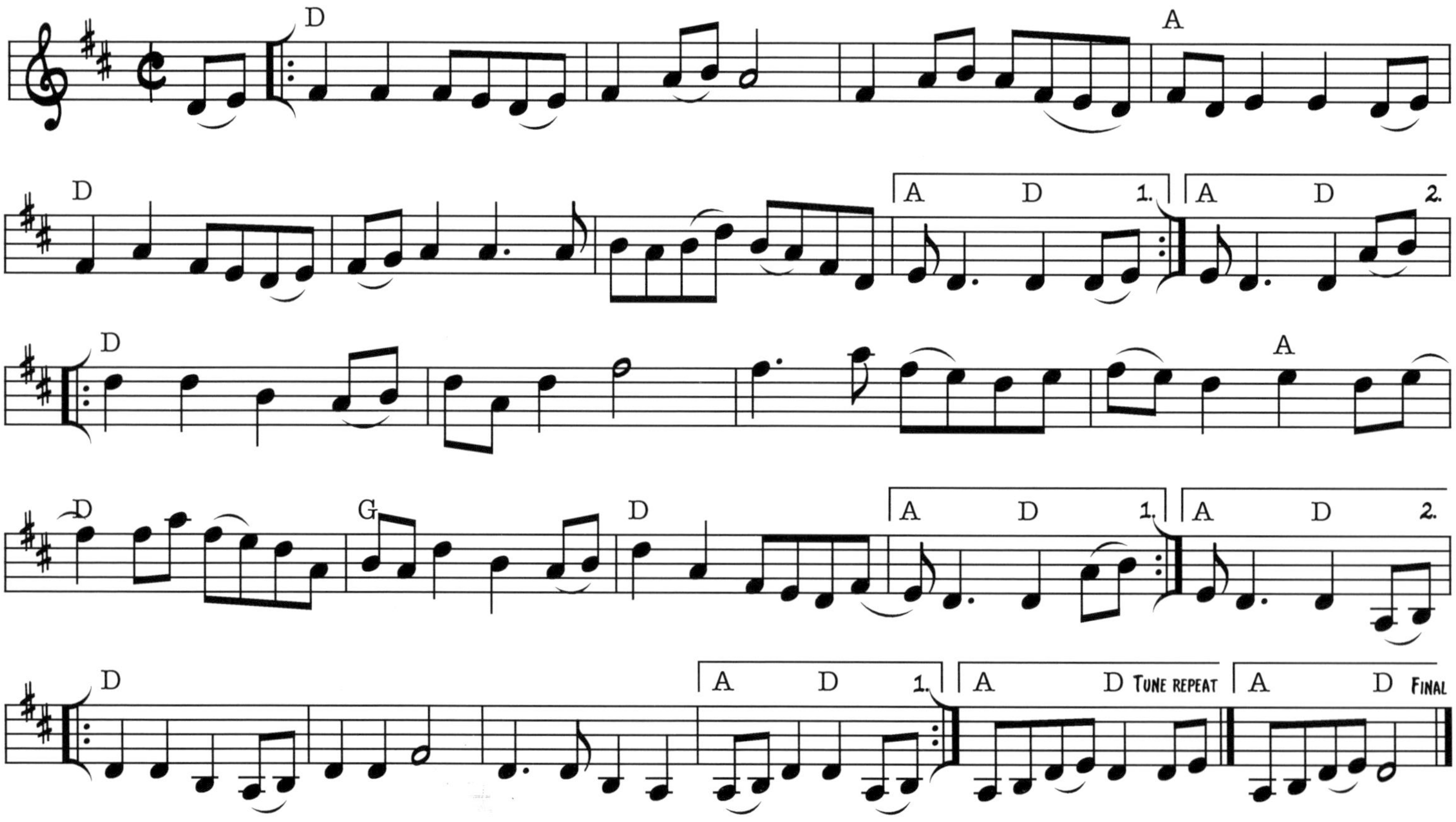

Salty River Reel

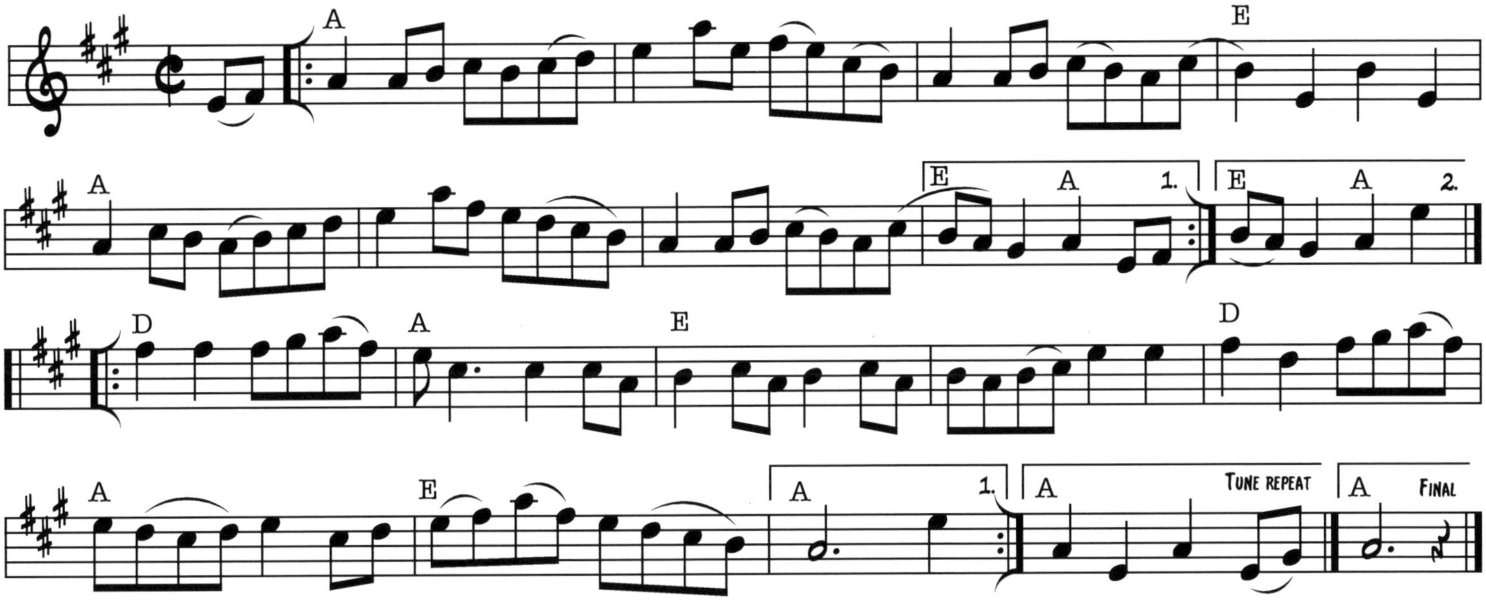

Sandy Boys

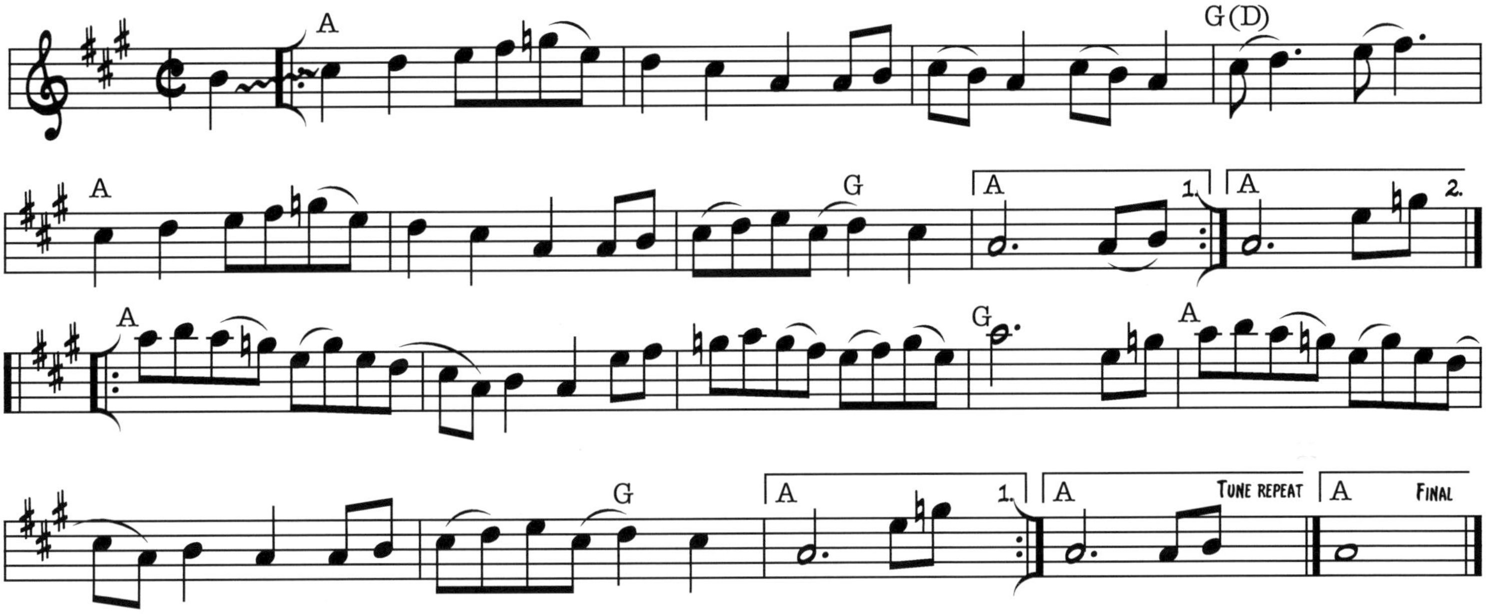

Sandy River Belle

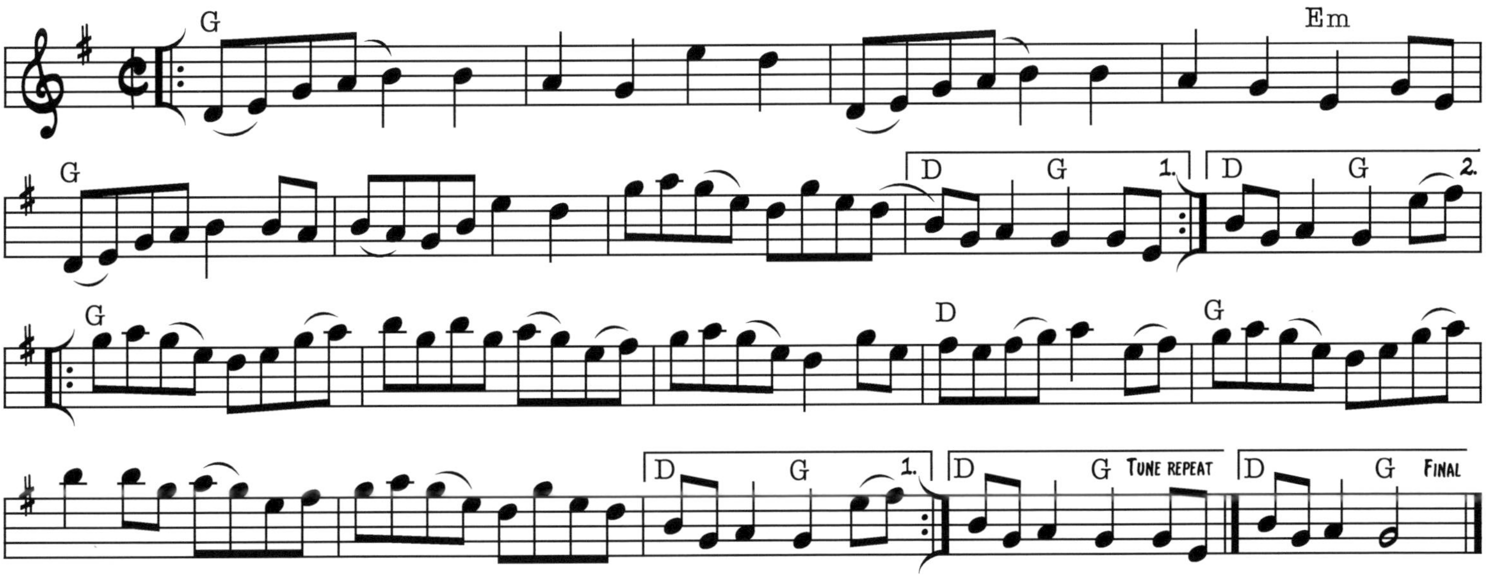

Sarah Armstrong (collected as Old Reel)

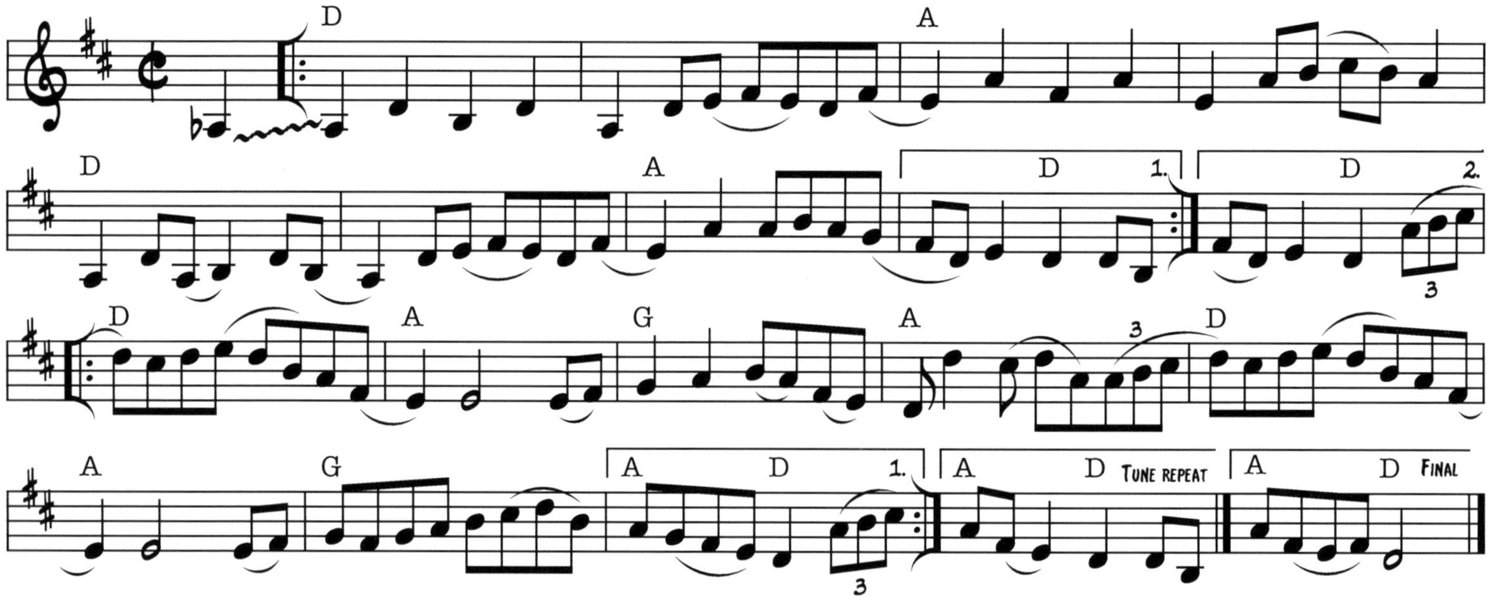

Saturday Night Breakdown

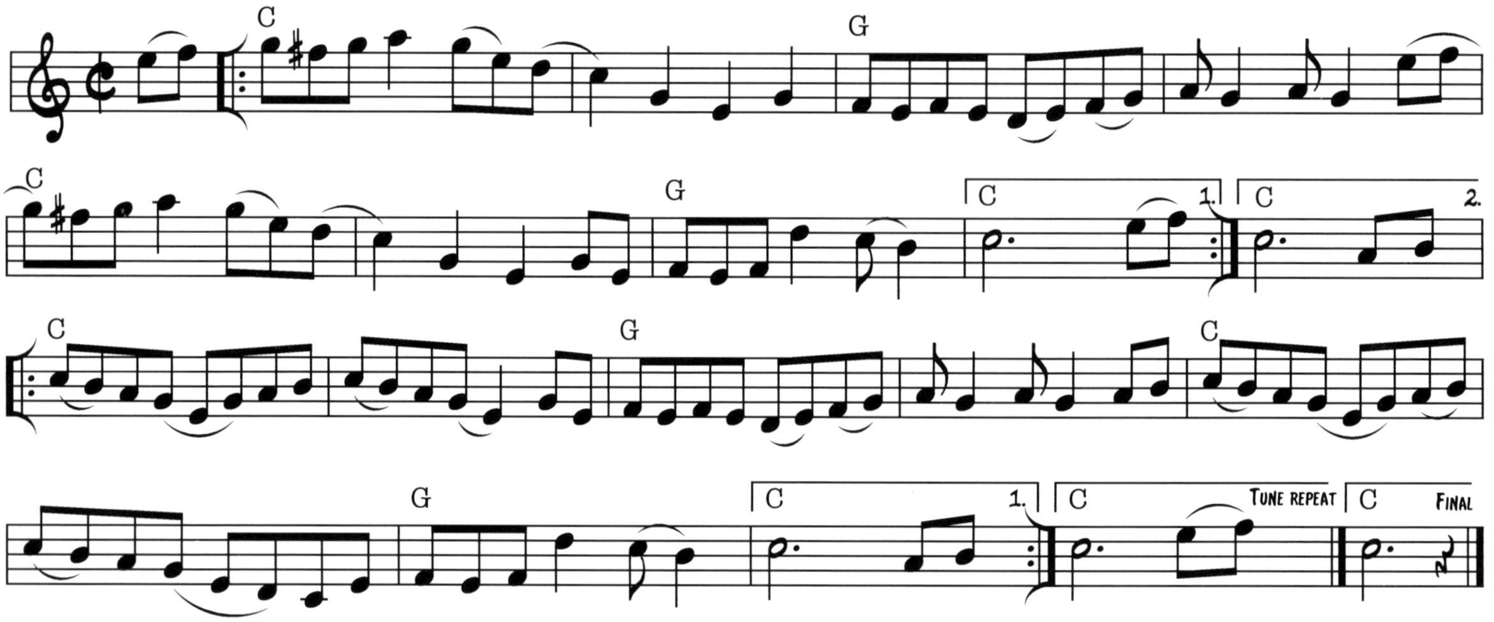

Seneca Square Dance

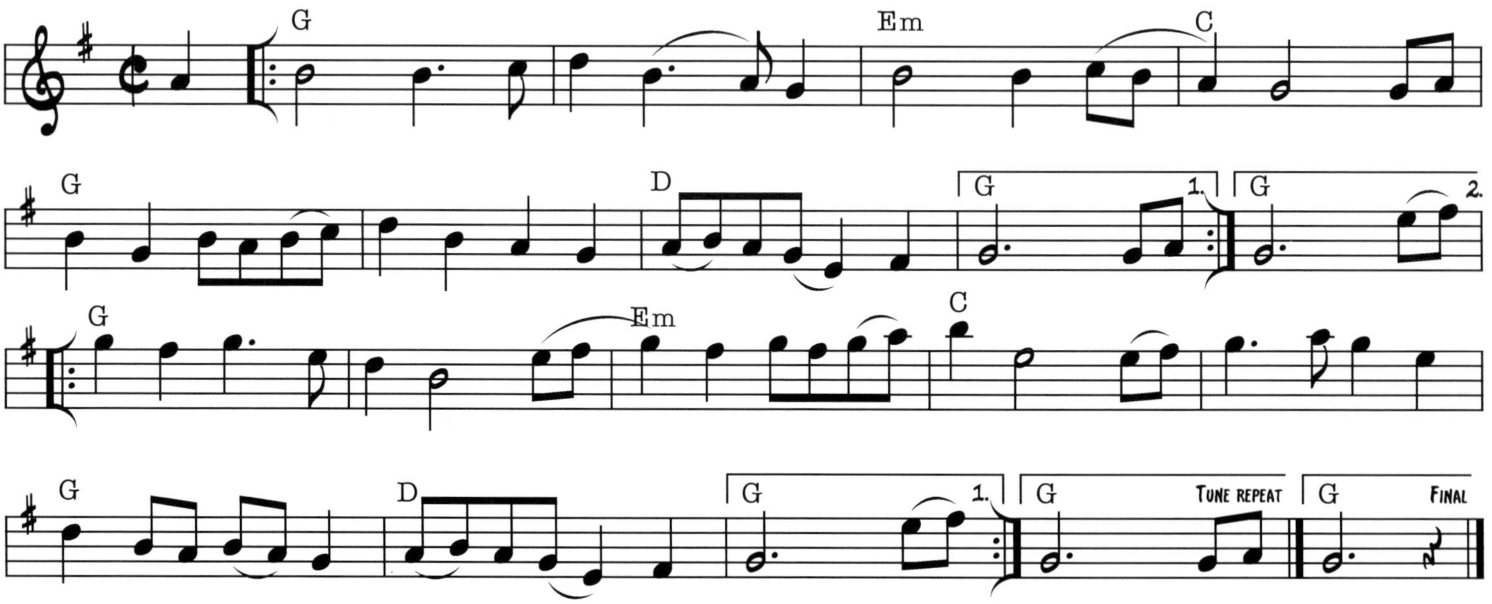

Shepherd's Walk

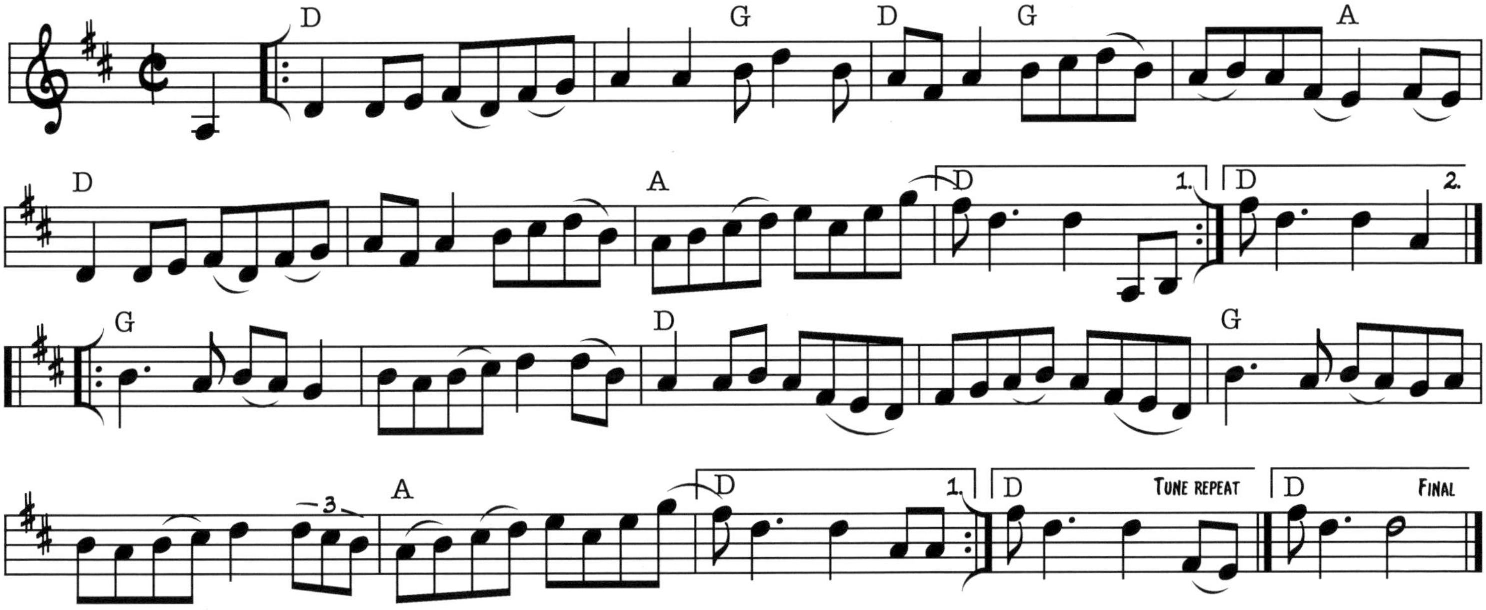

Shoes and Stockings

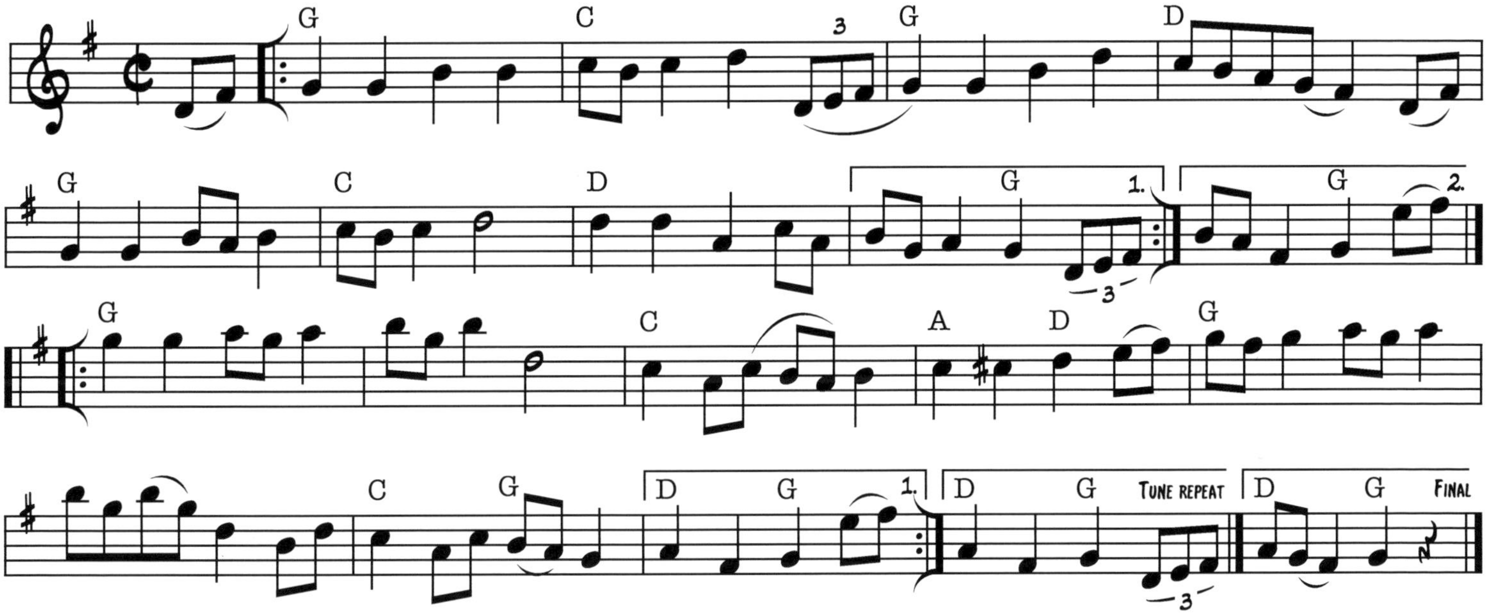

Shoo Fly

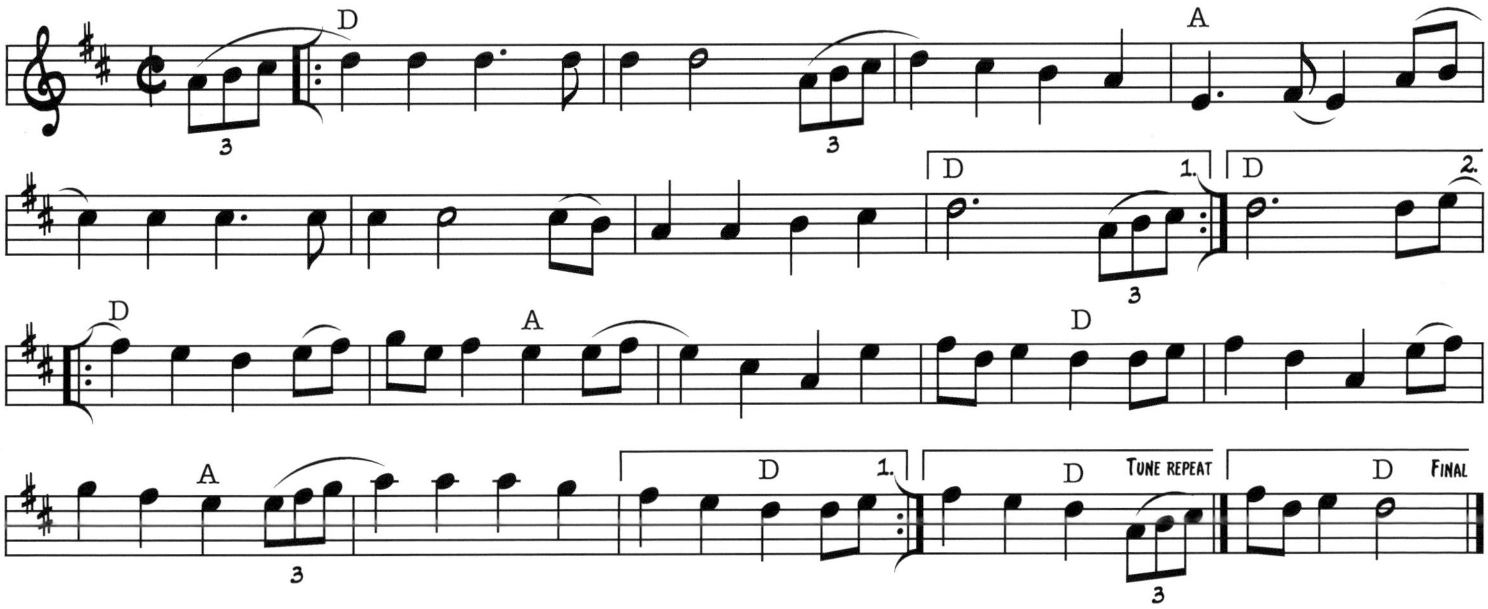

Shortening Bread (Doc Roberts')

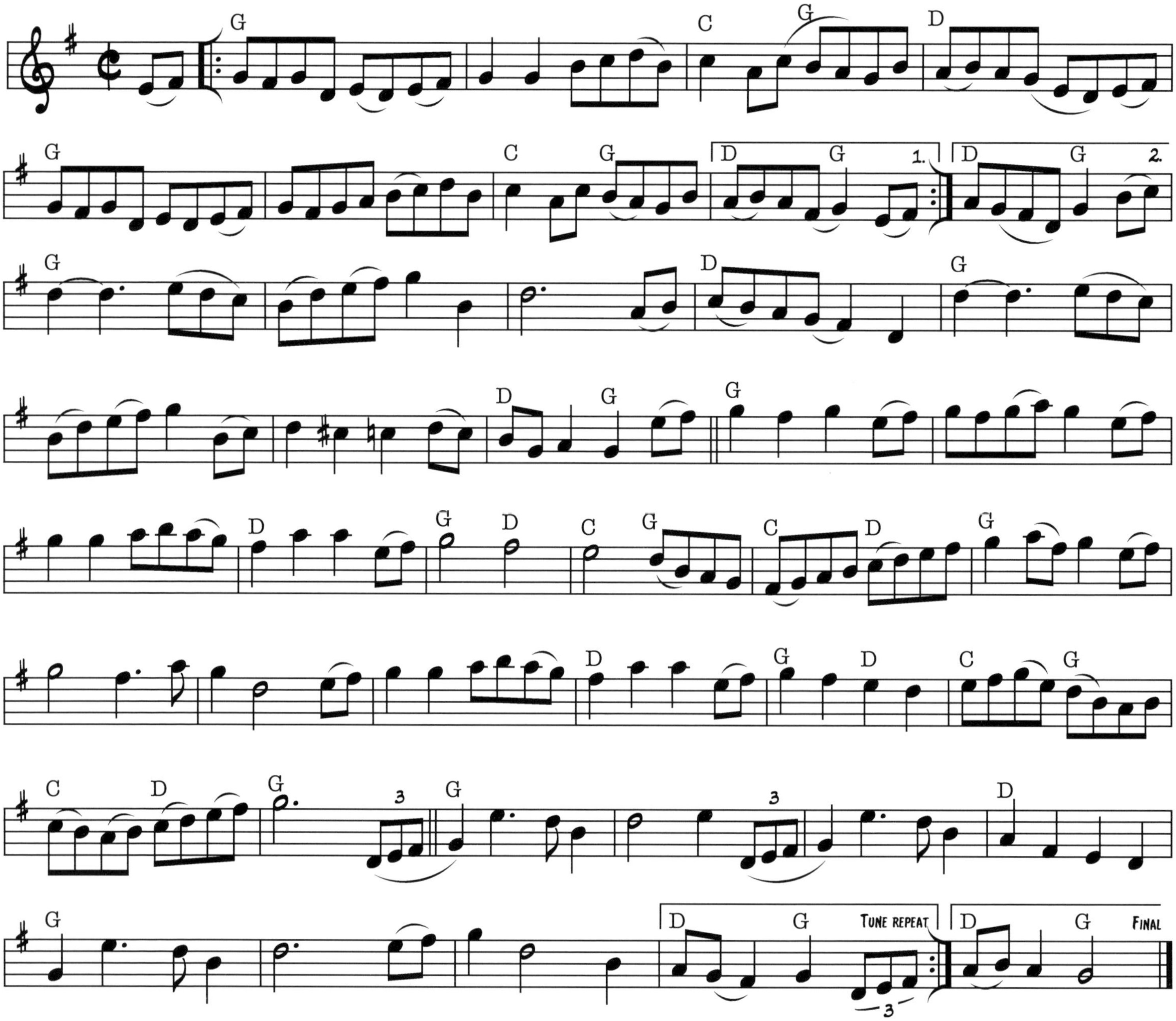

Shove That Pig's Foot a Little Further Into the Fire

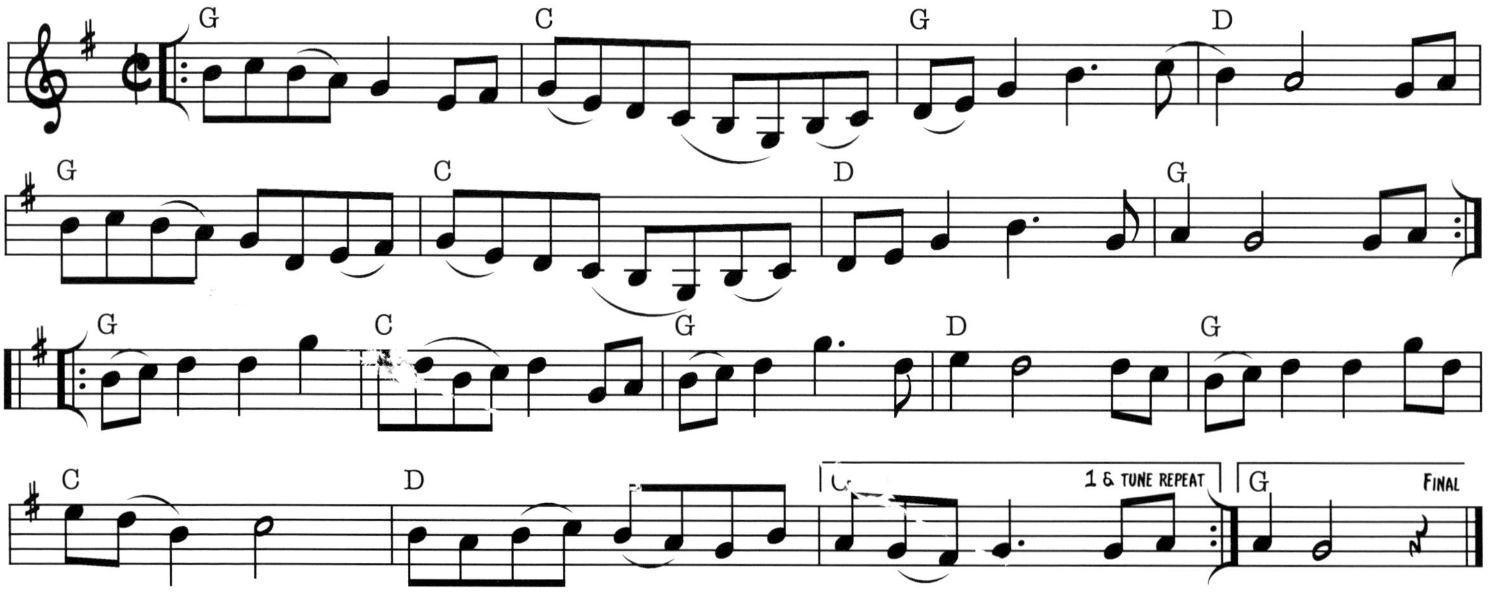

Shuckin' the Brush

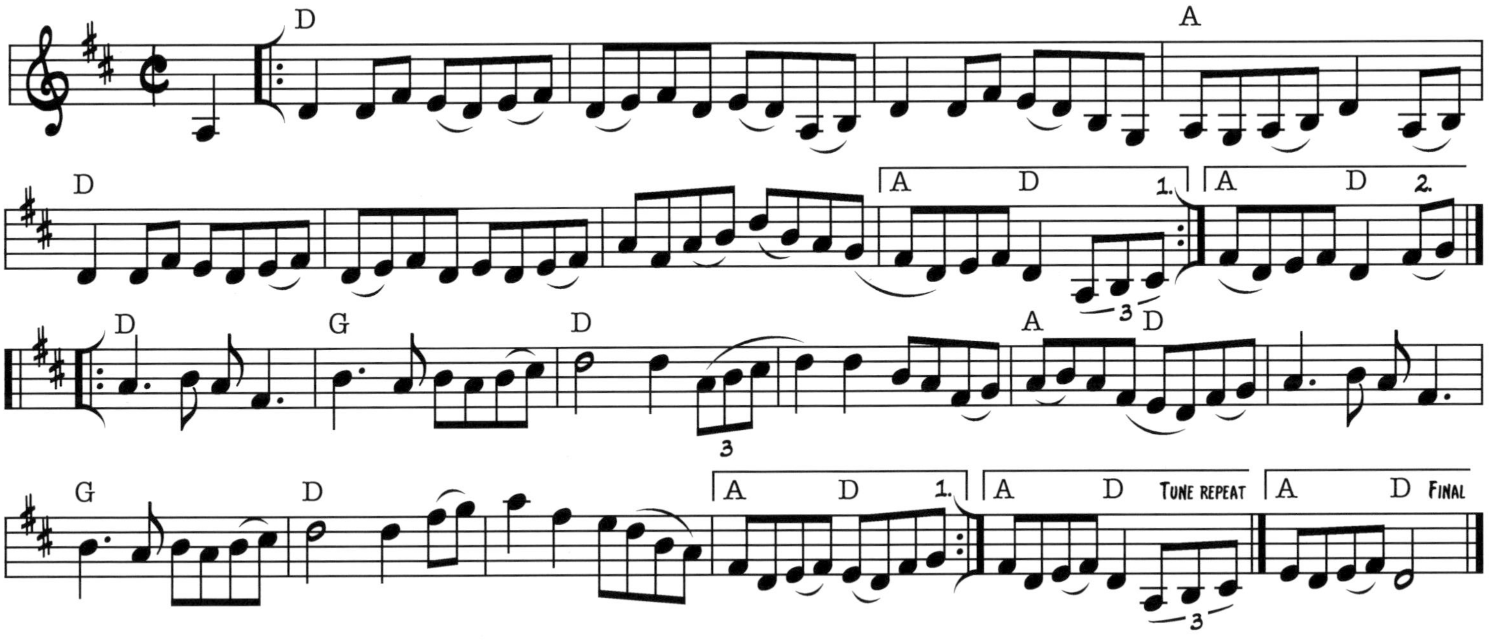

Shuffle About

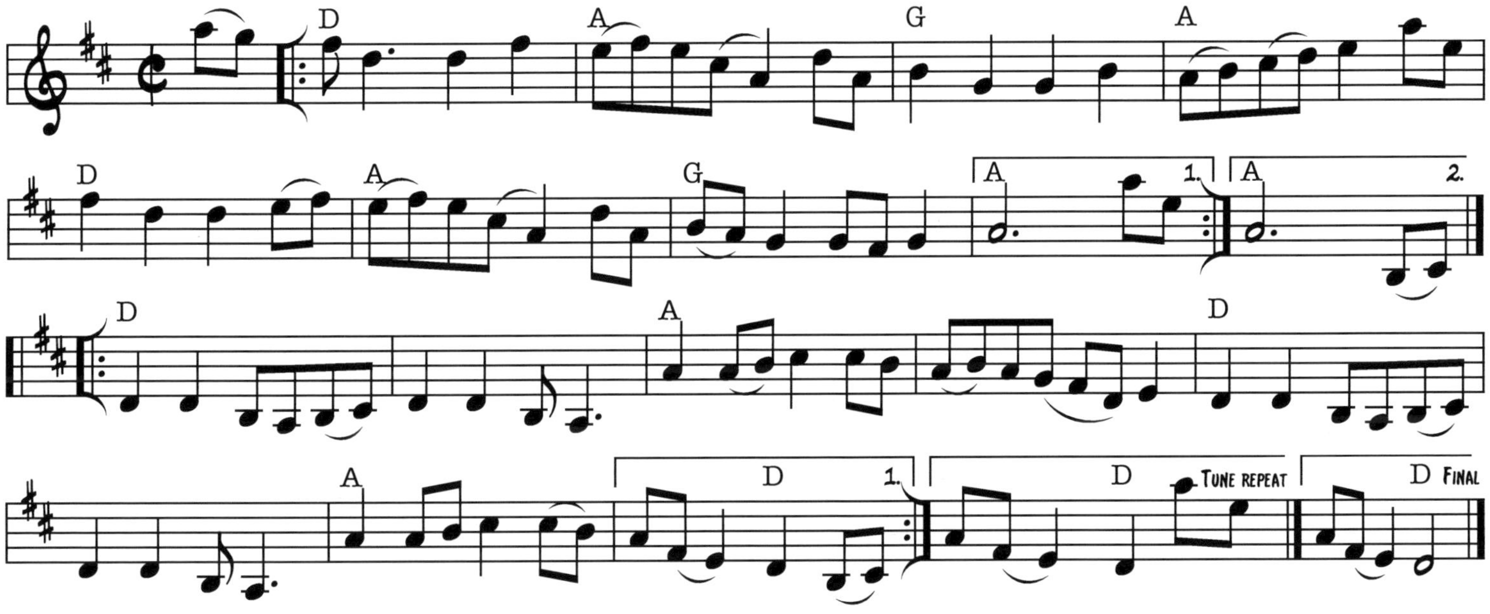

Silly Bill

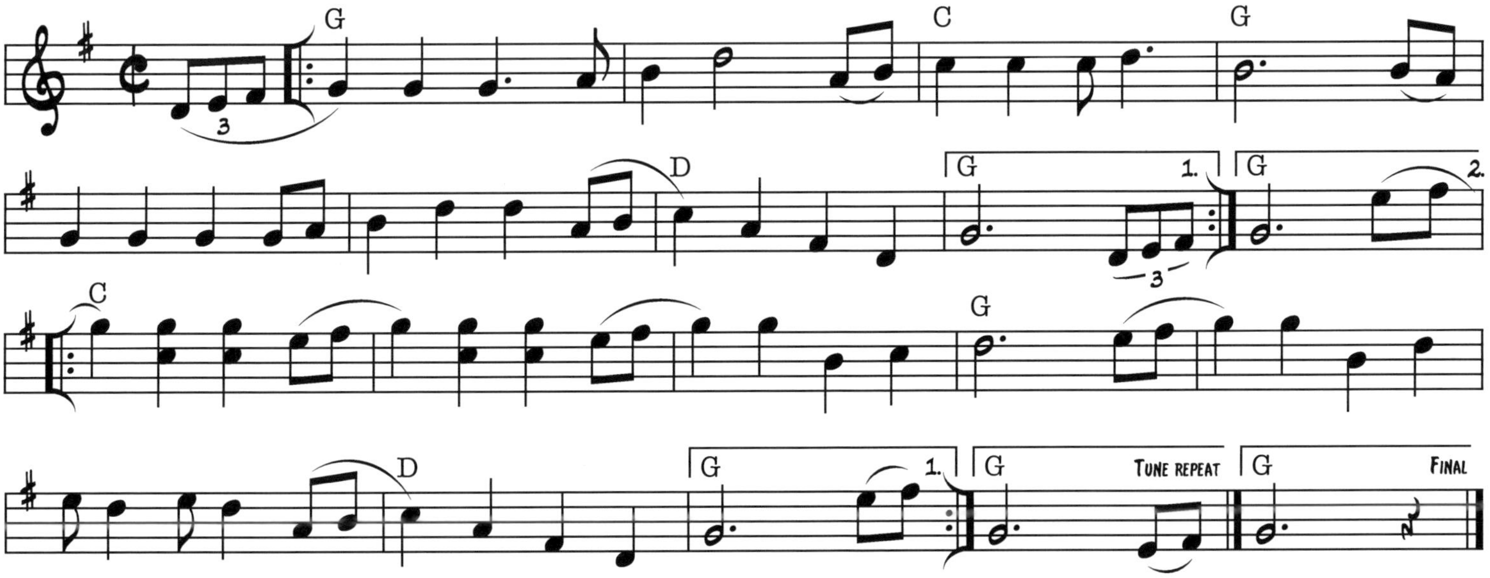

Sleepy Eyed Joe

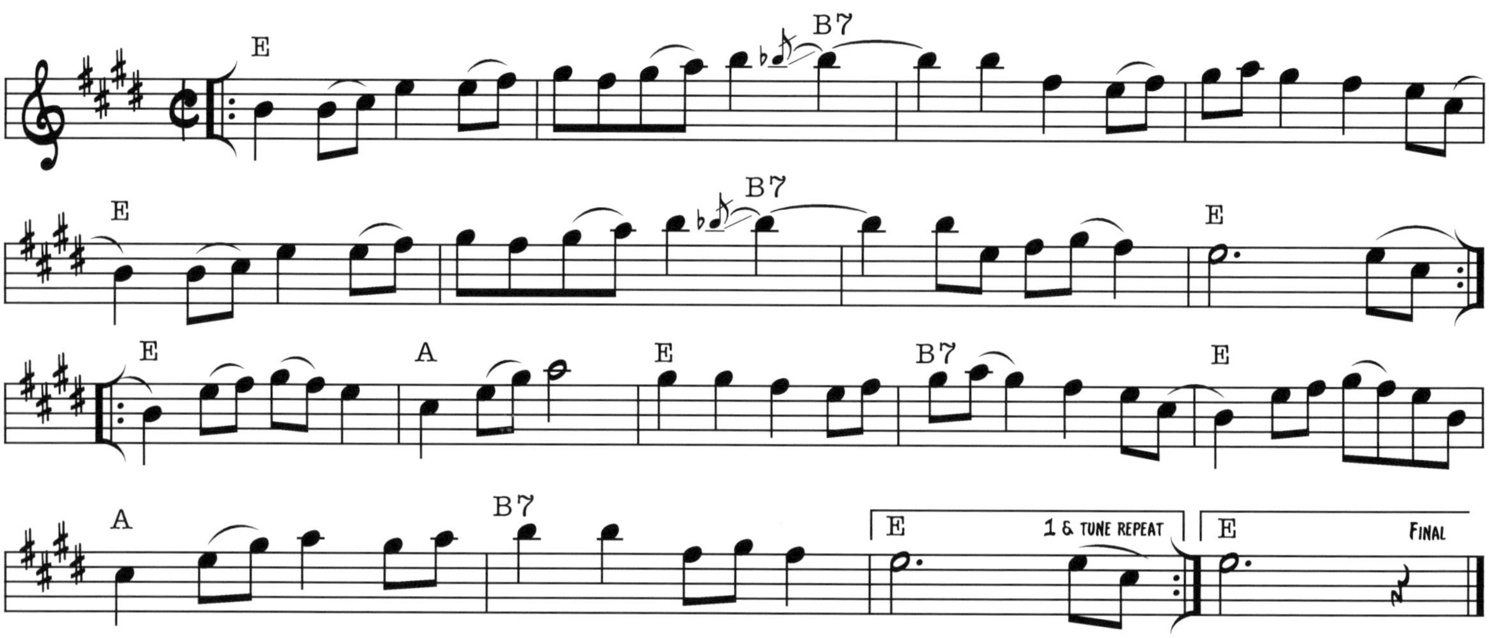

Sleepy Eyed John

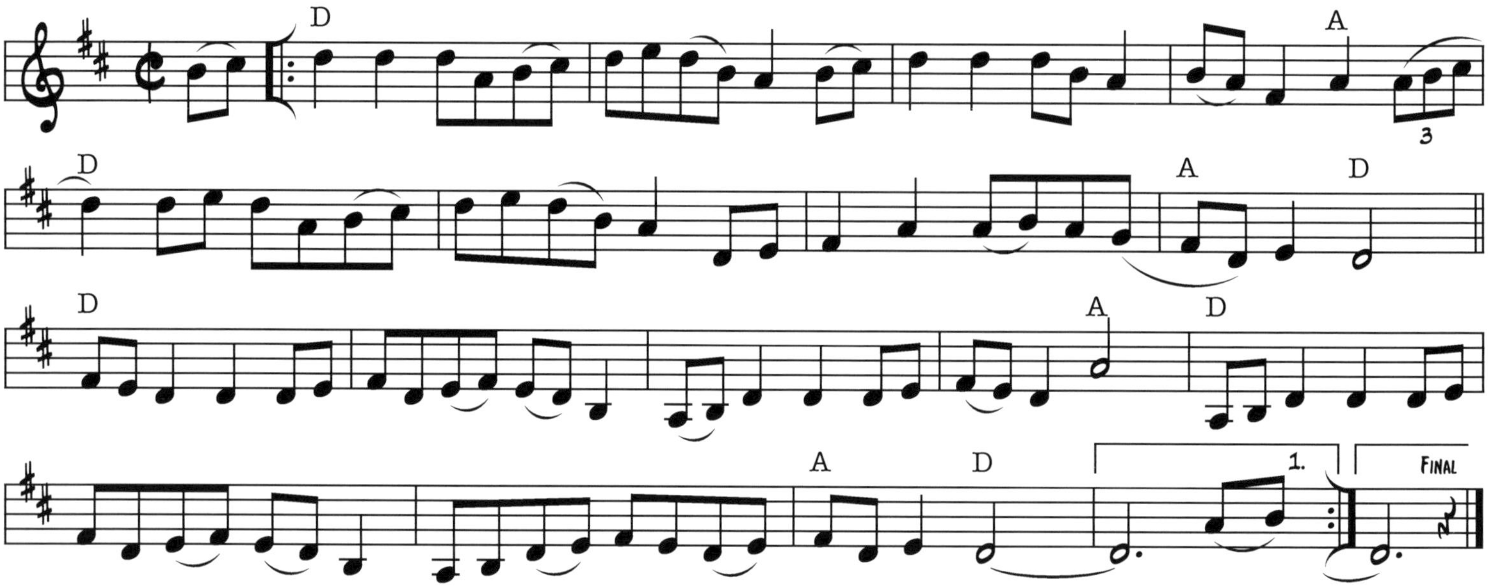

Snake River Reel (Peter Lippincott used by permission)

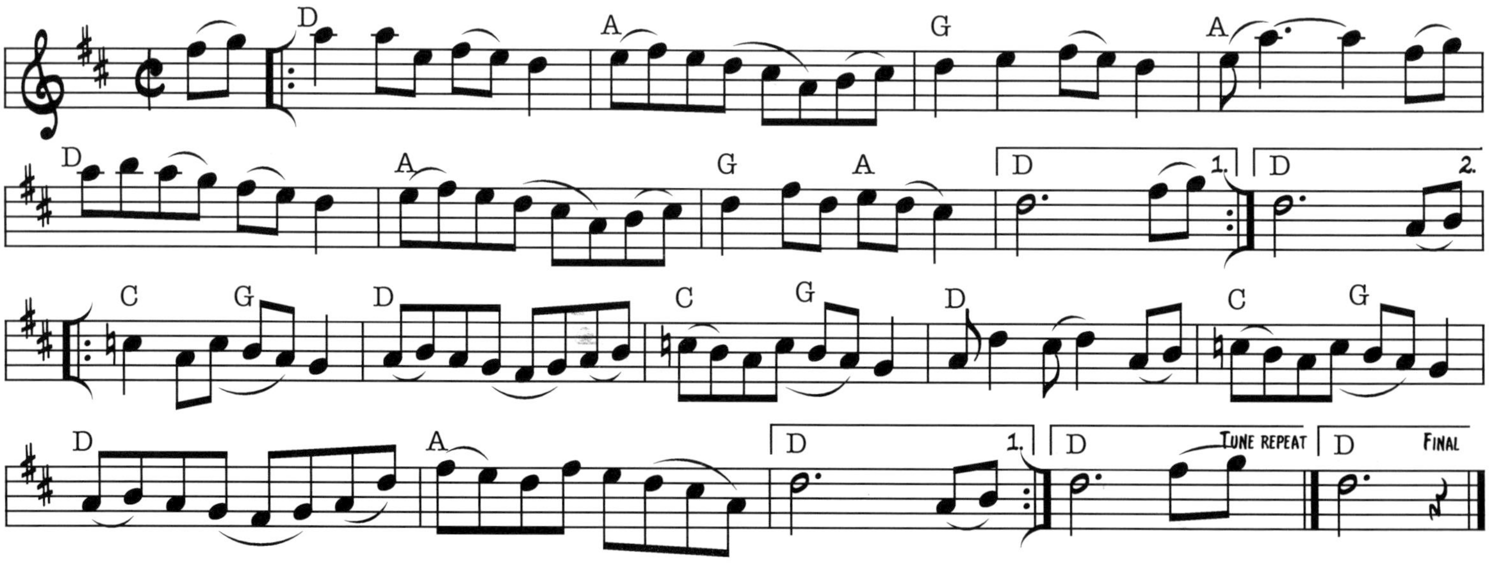

Snowbird

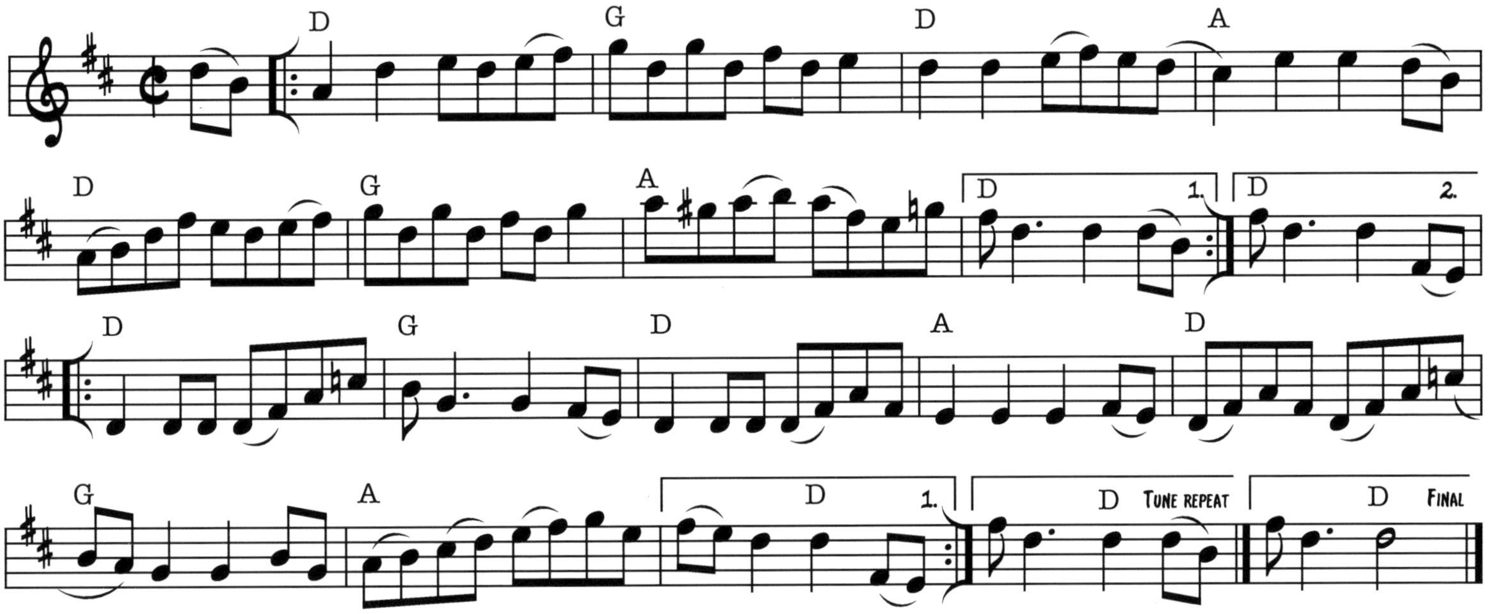

Soldier's Joy

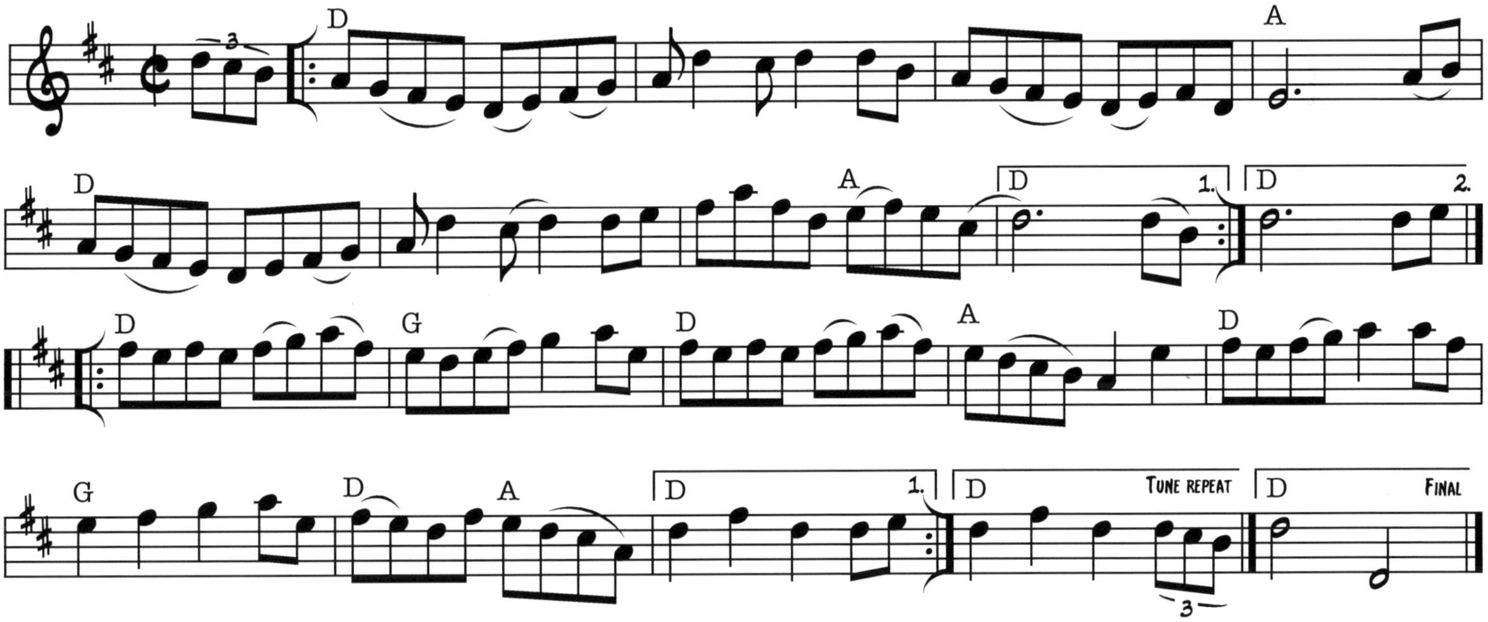

Spotted Pony

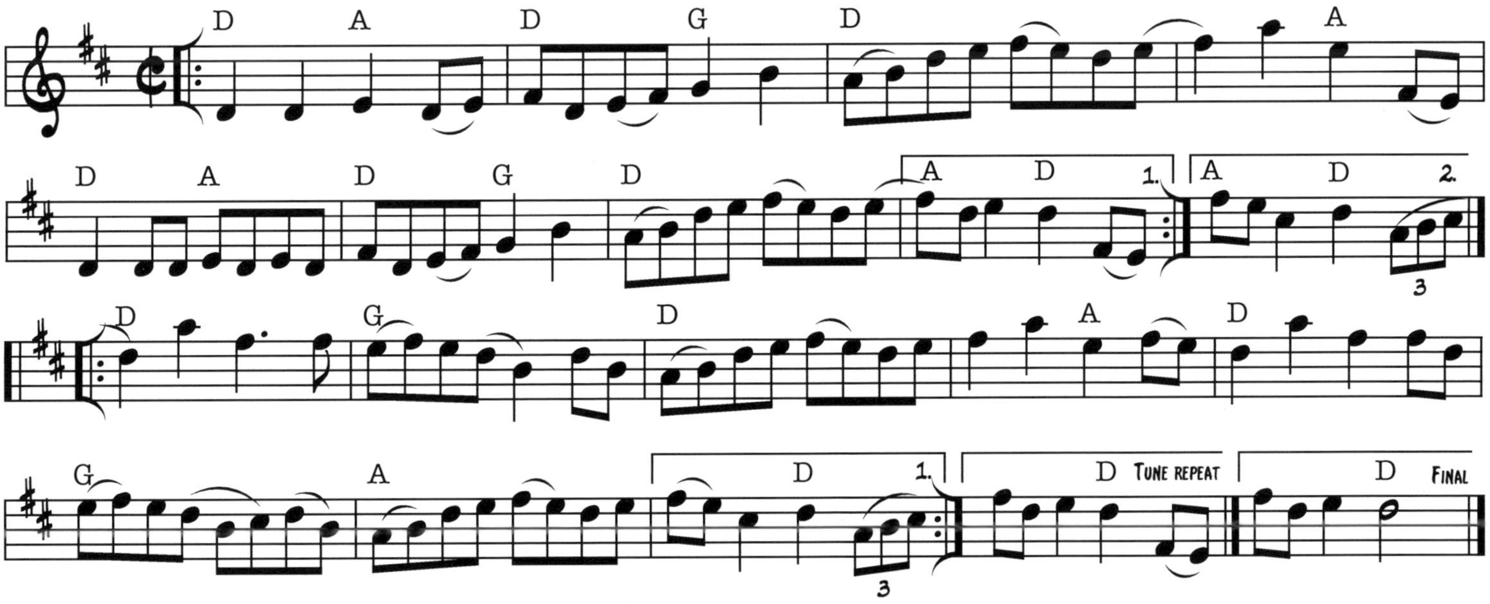

Star of Bethlehem

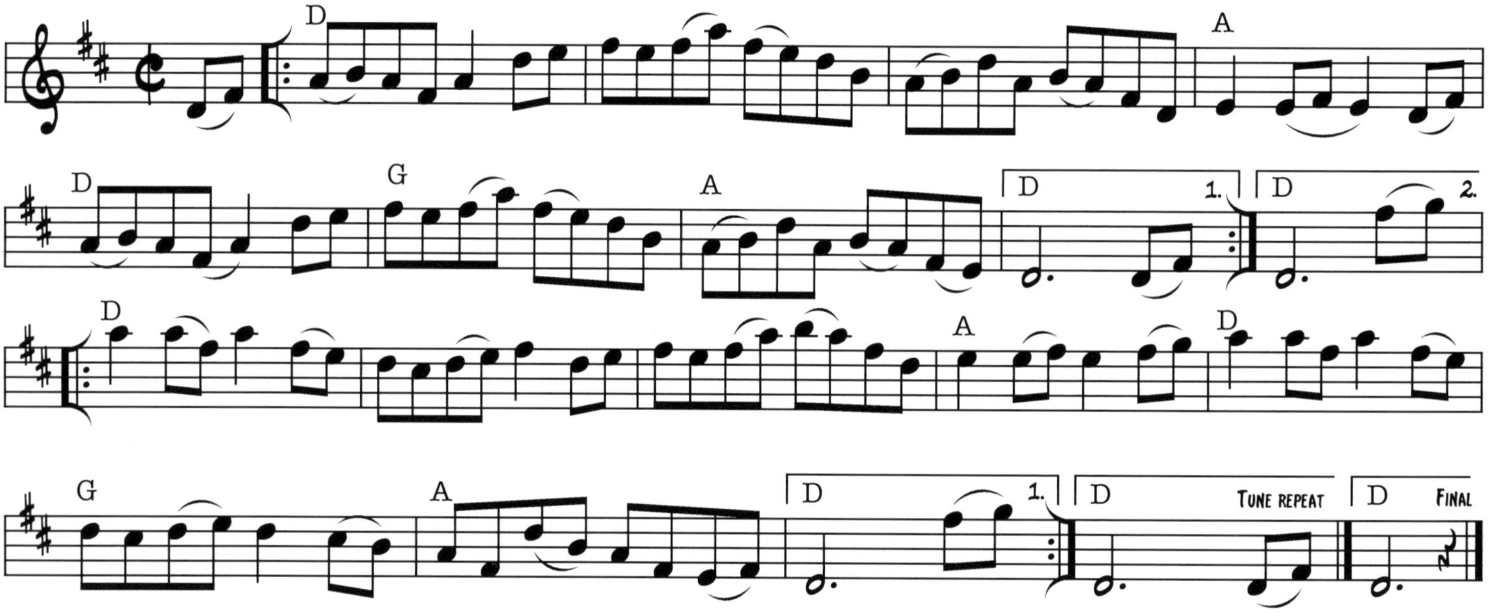

Staten Island Hornpipe

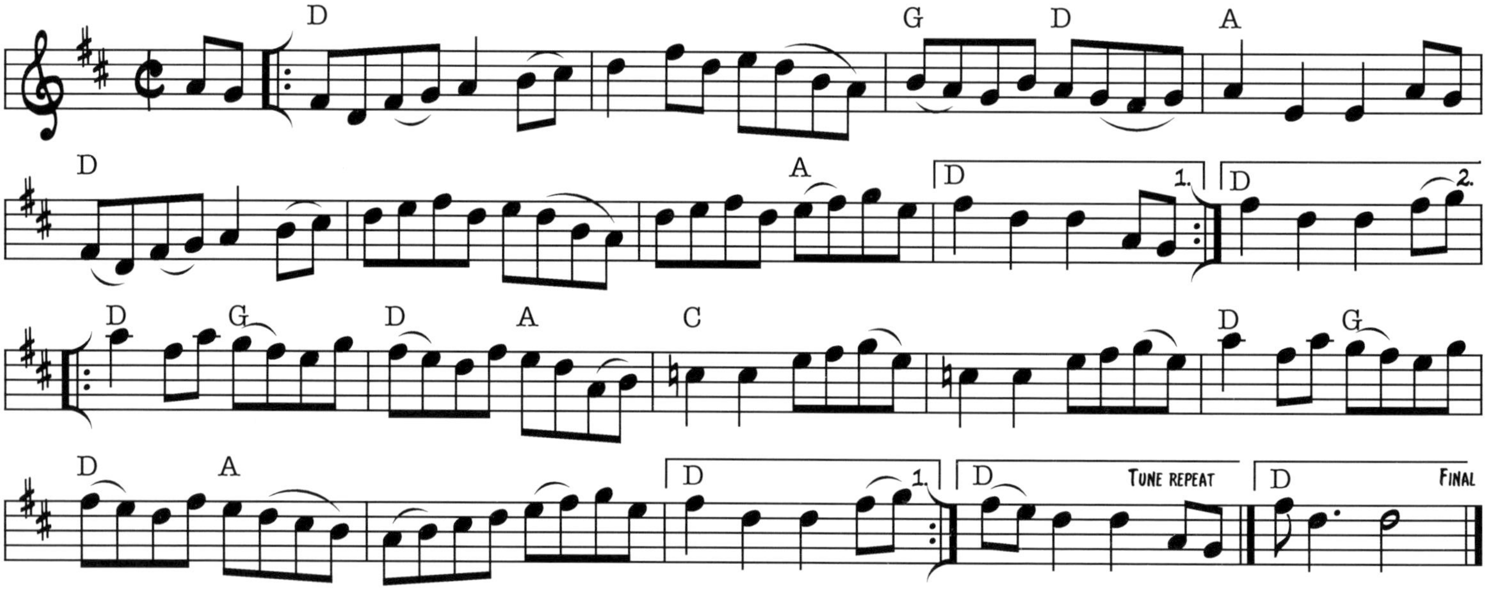

Step Around Johnny

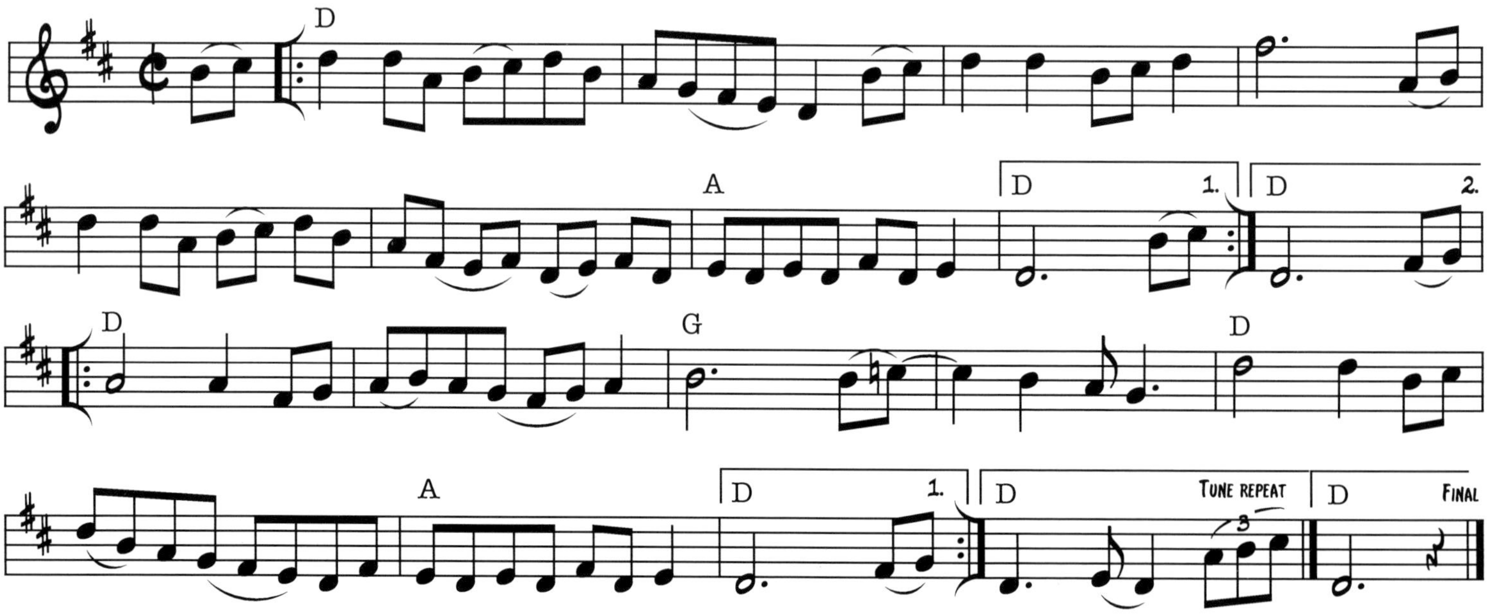

Sugar Hill

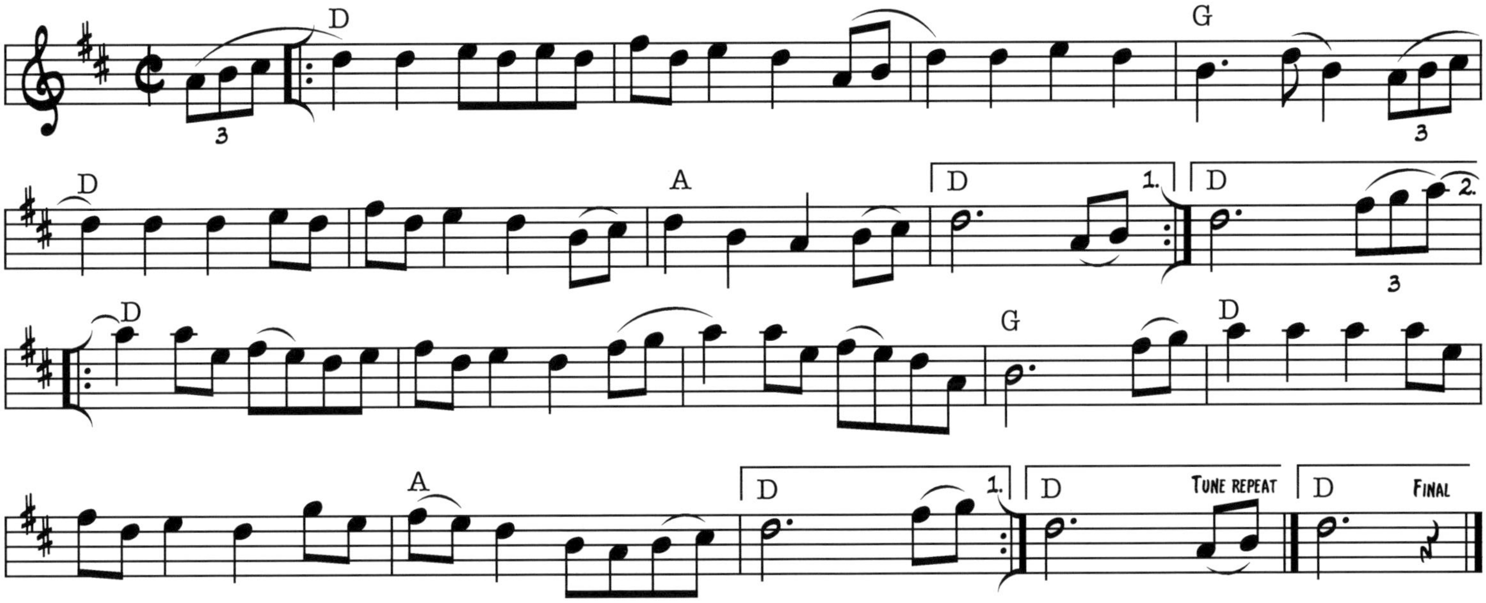

Sugar in the Gourd

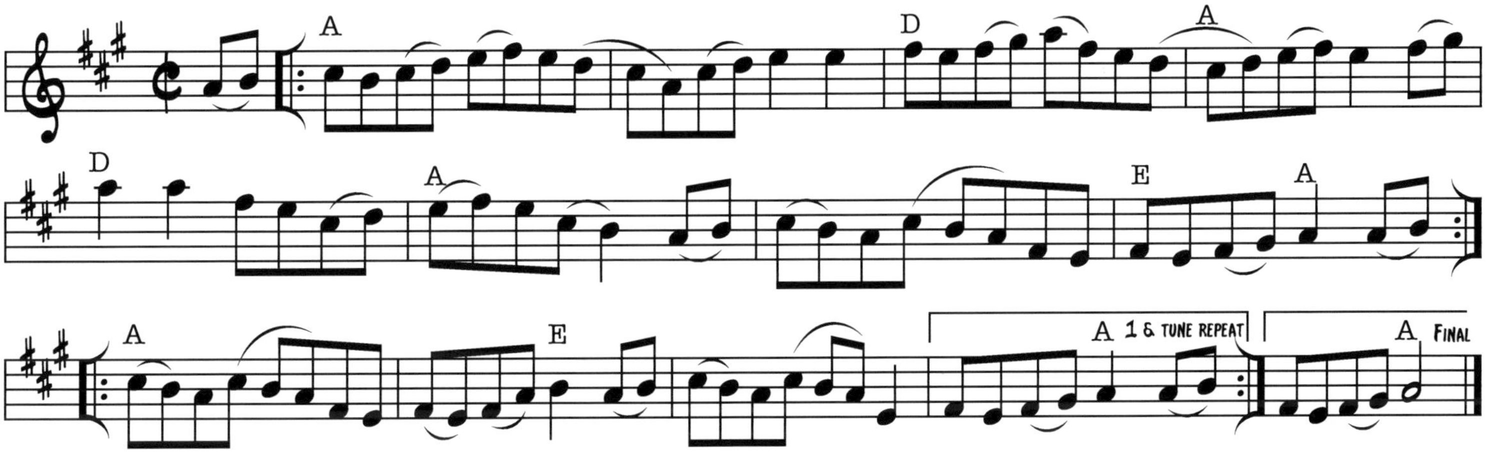

Tater Patch

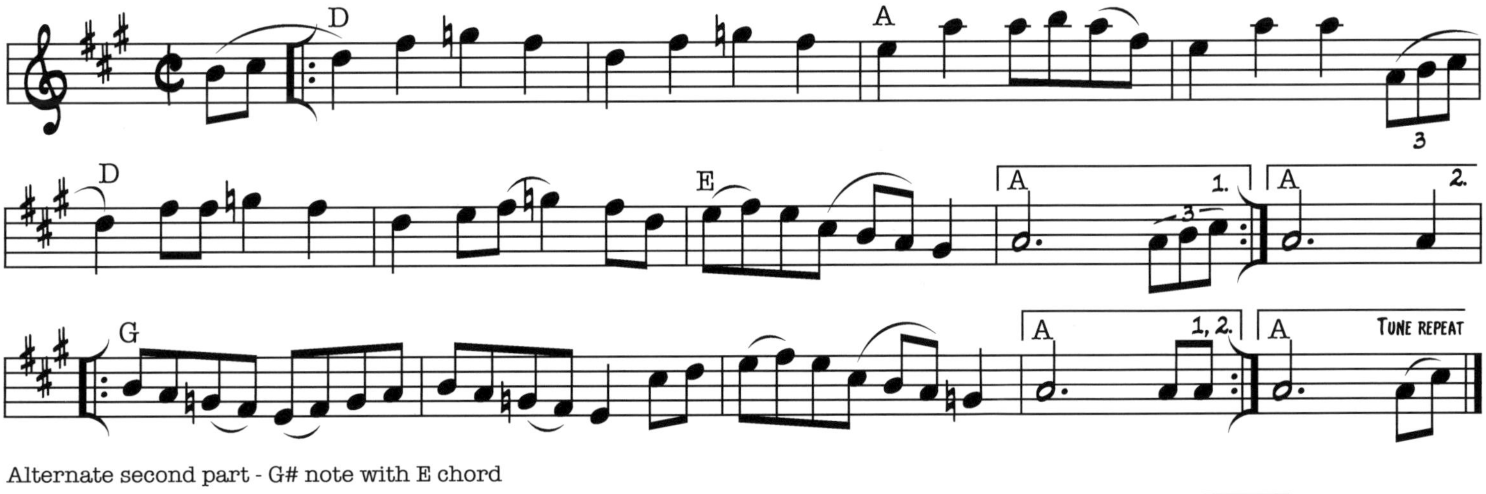

Alternate second part - G# note with E chord

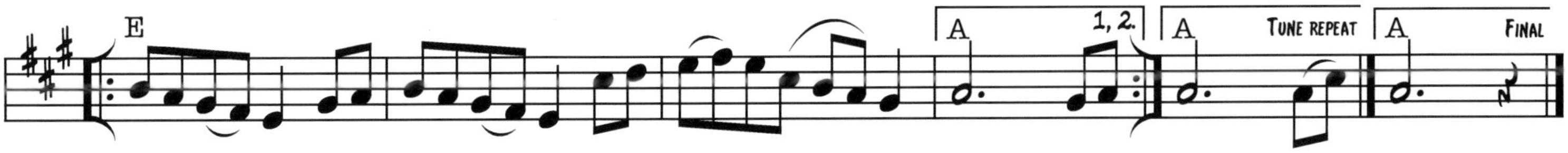

Sugarbaby

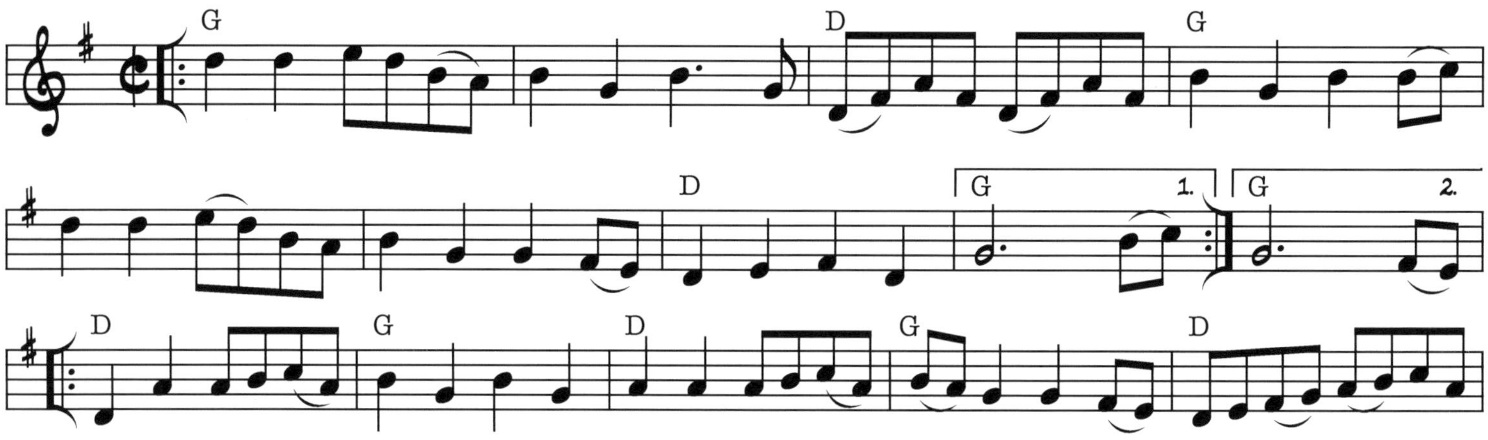

Temperance Reel (aka Teatotalers Reel)

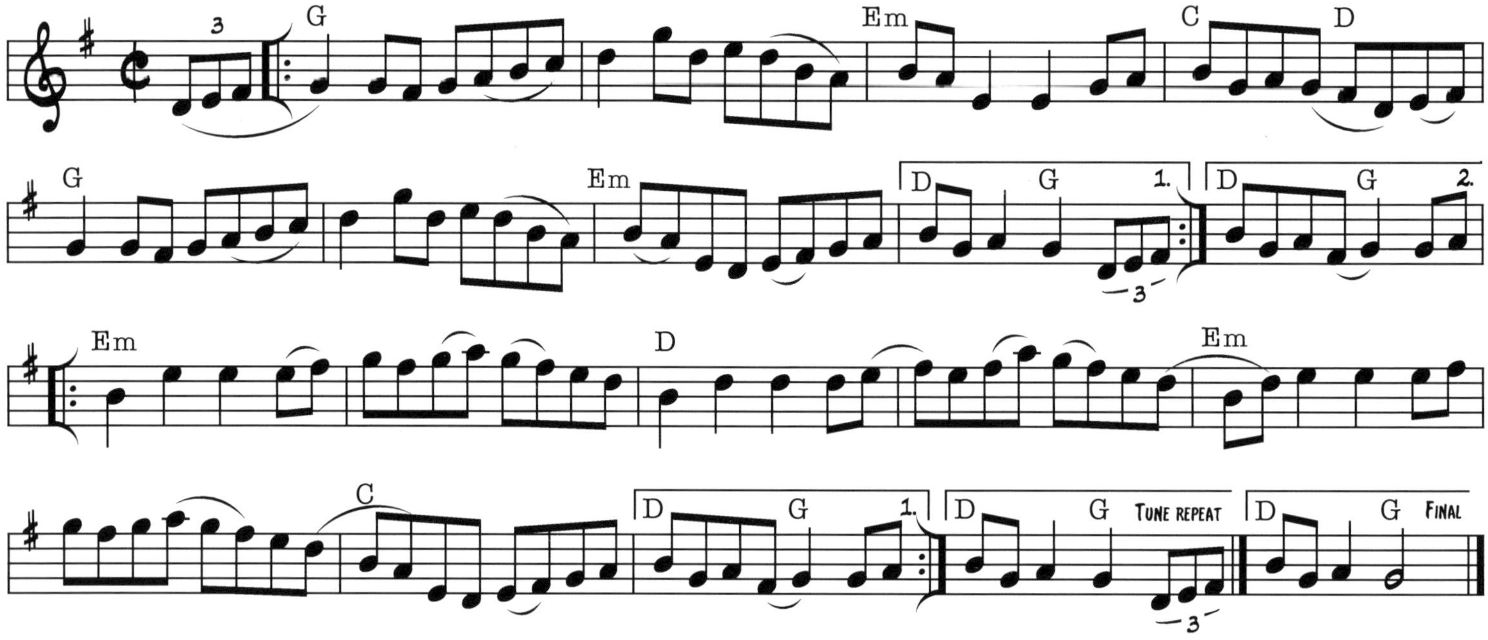

Texas

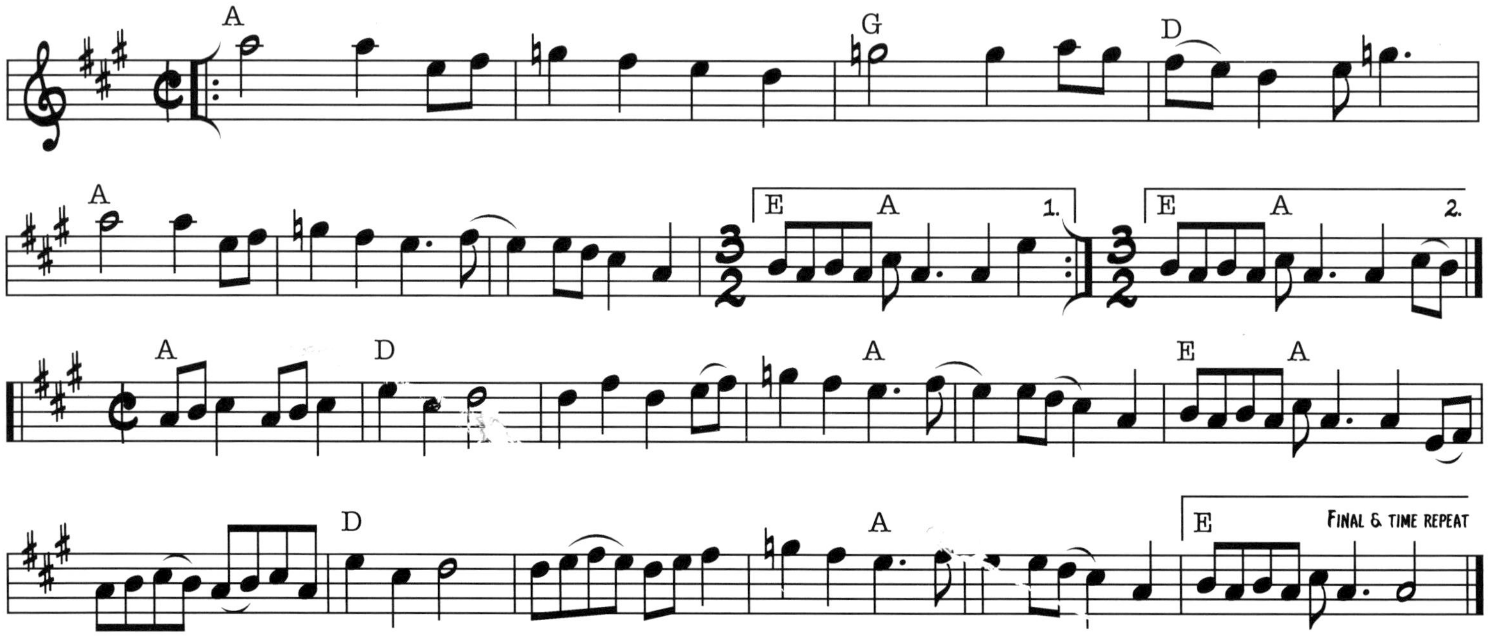

Texas Gals

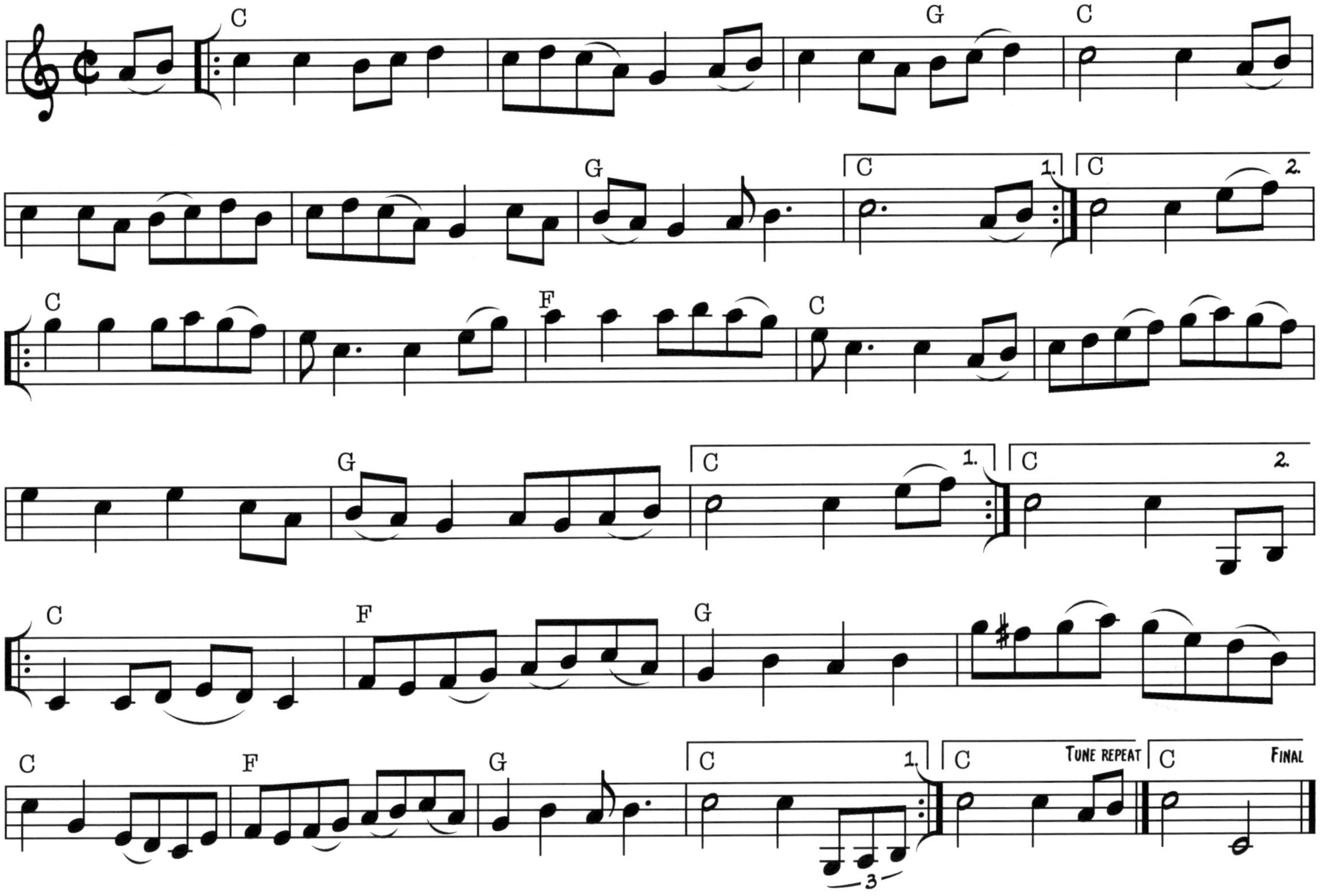

Texas Quick Step (aka Rachael)

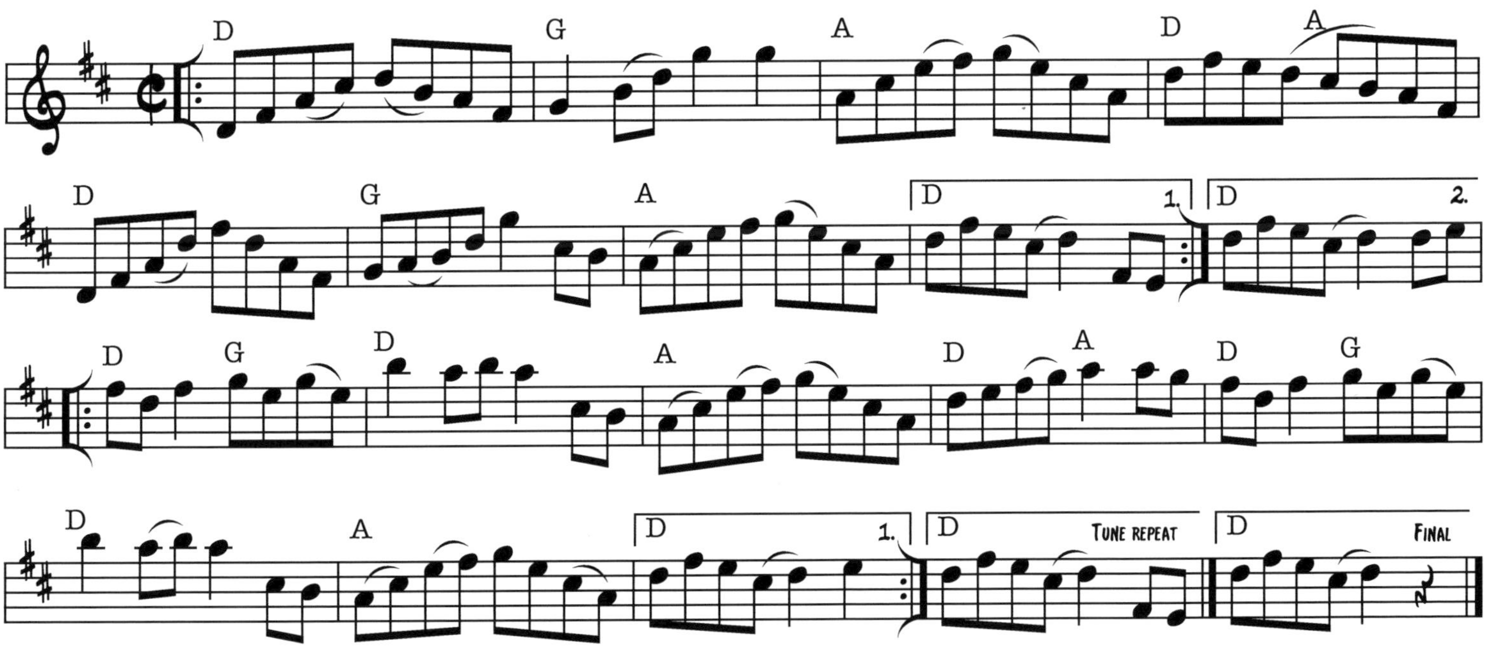

That's My Rabbit, My Dog Caught It

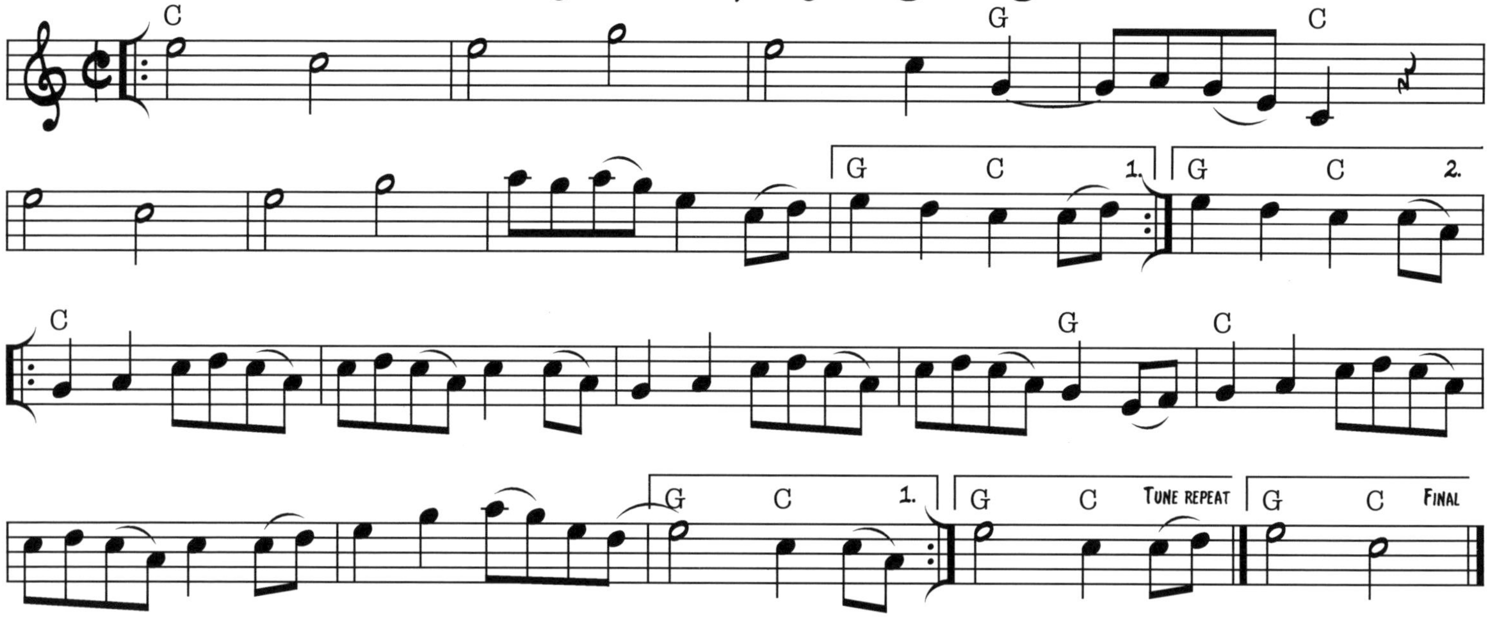

Thread the Needle

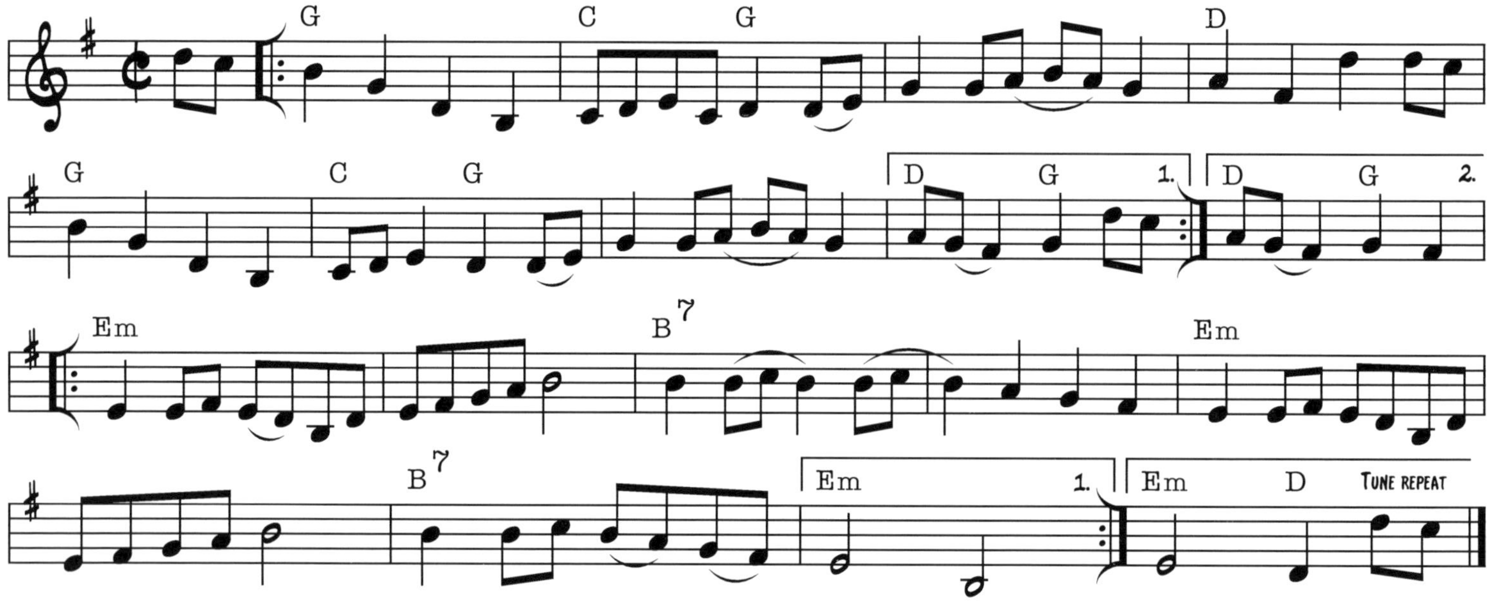

Three Forks of Reedy

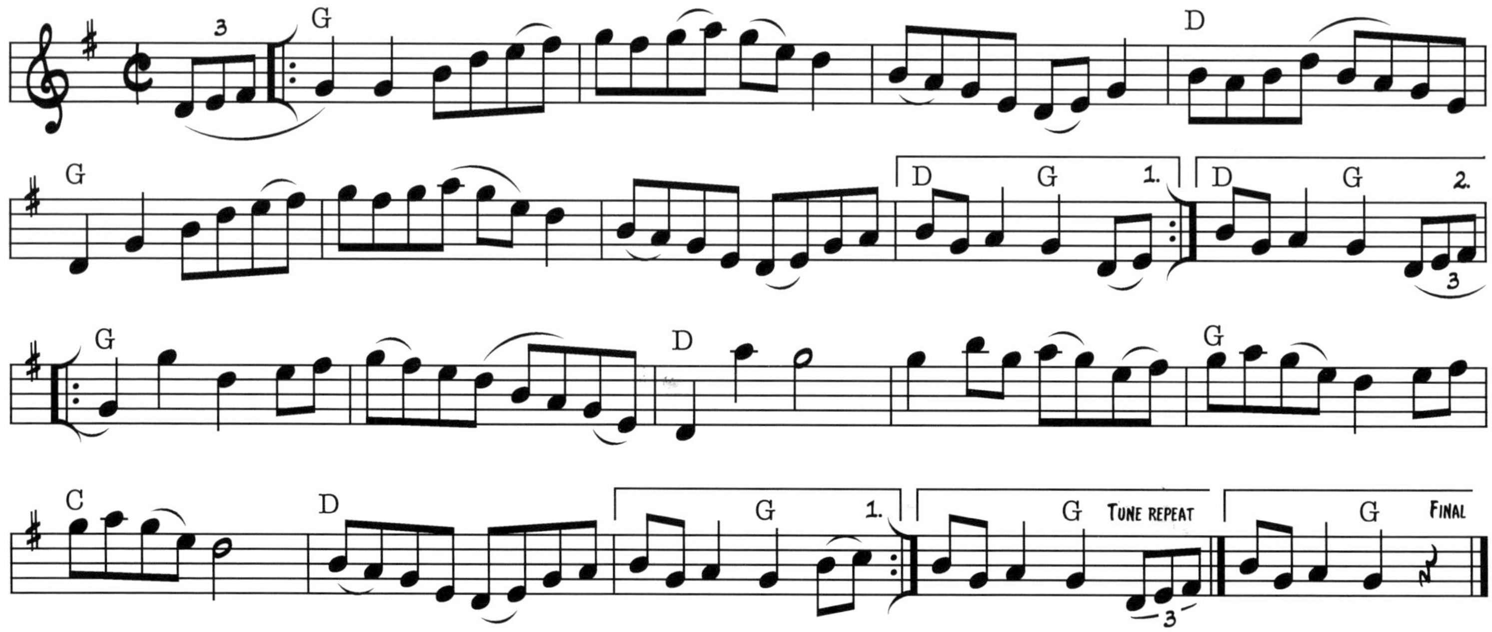

Three Thin Dimes

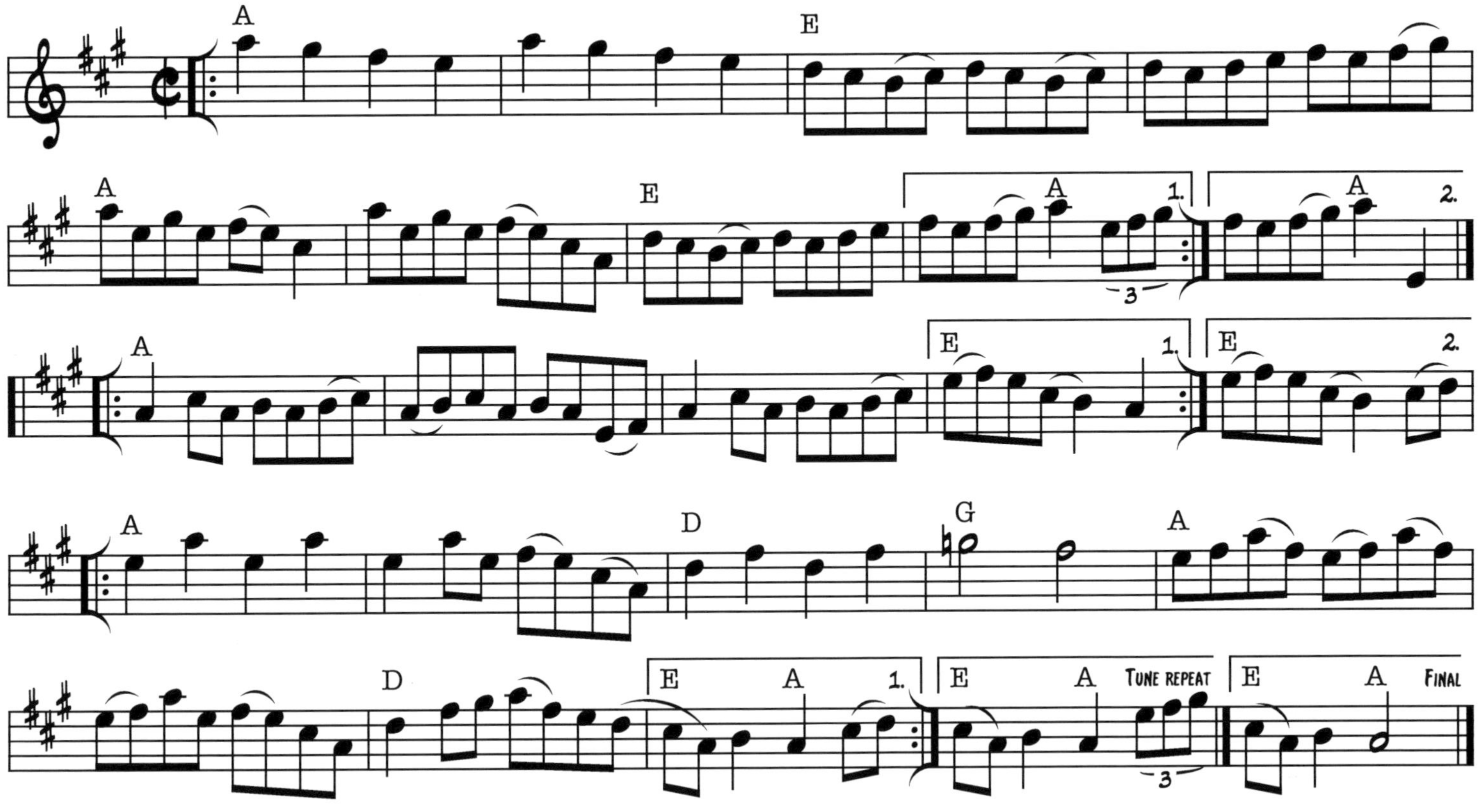

Three Way Hornpipe

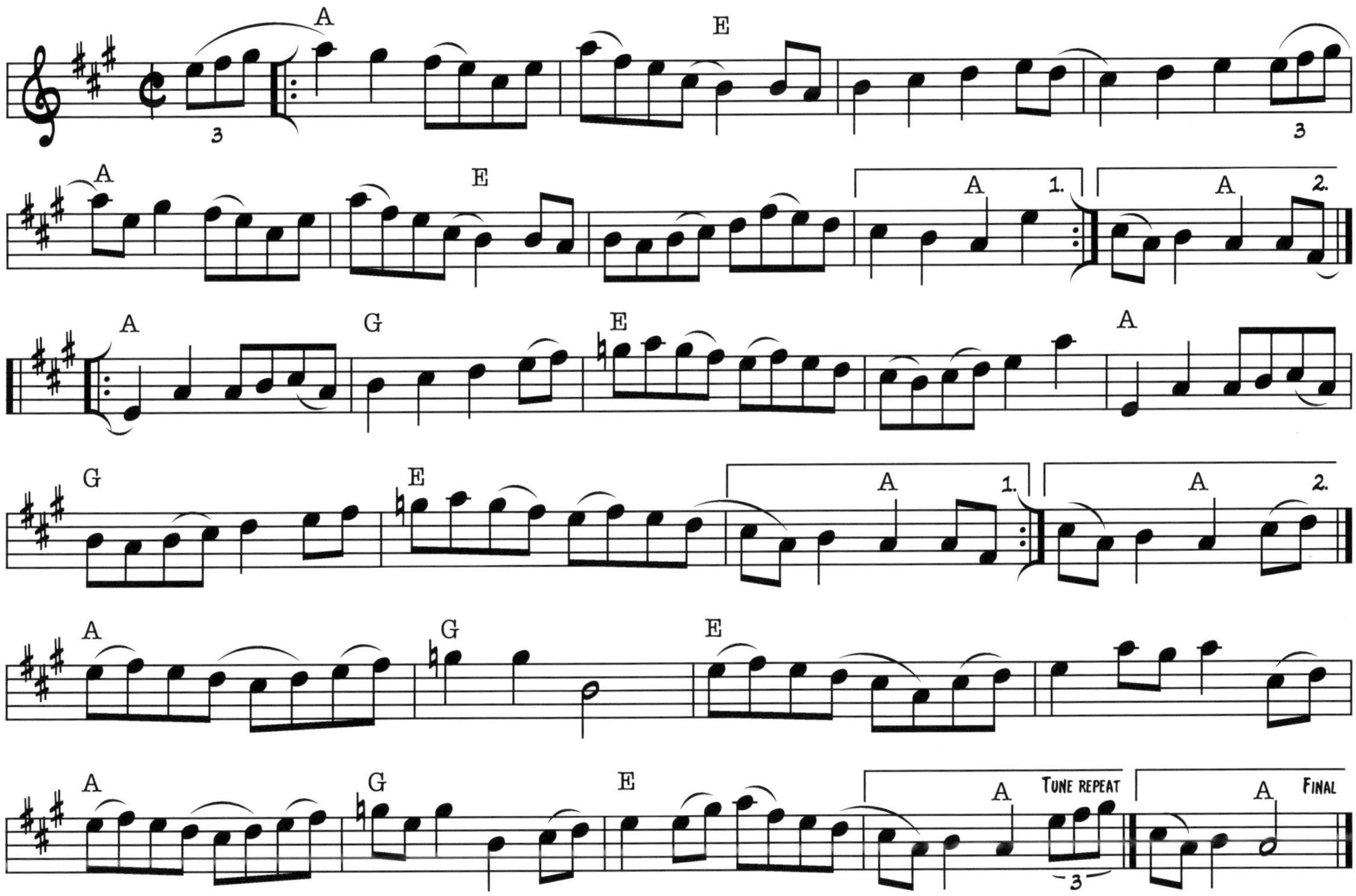

Tom and Jerry

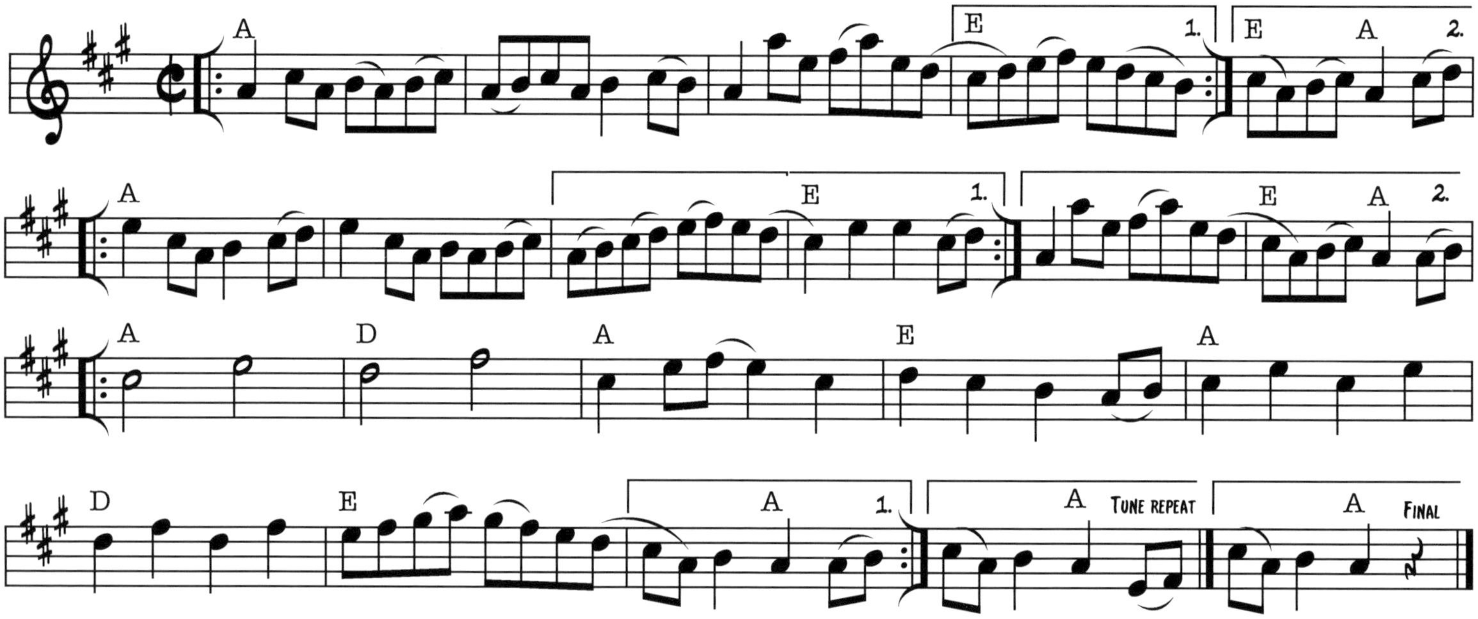

Tomahawk

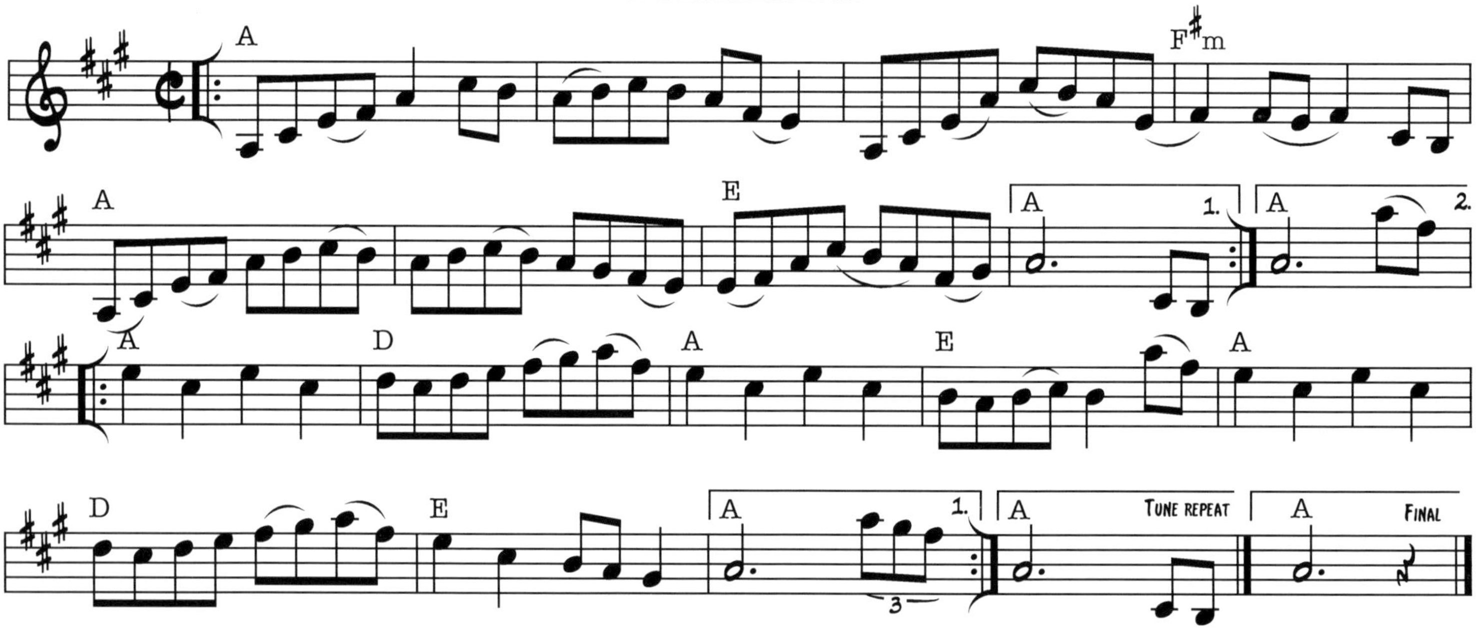

Tombigbee Waltz

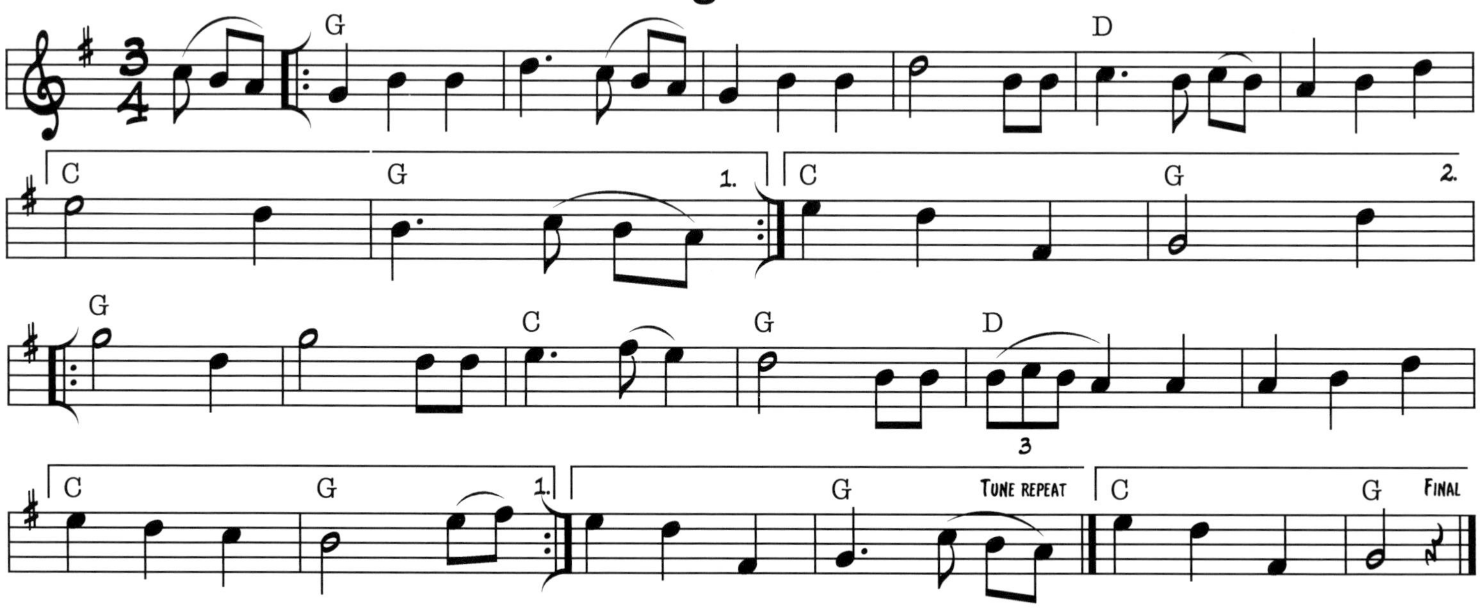

Too Young to Marry (1)

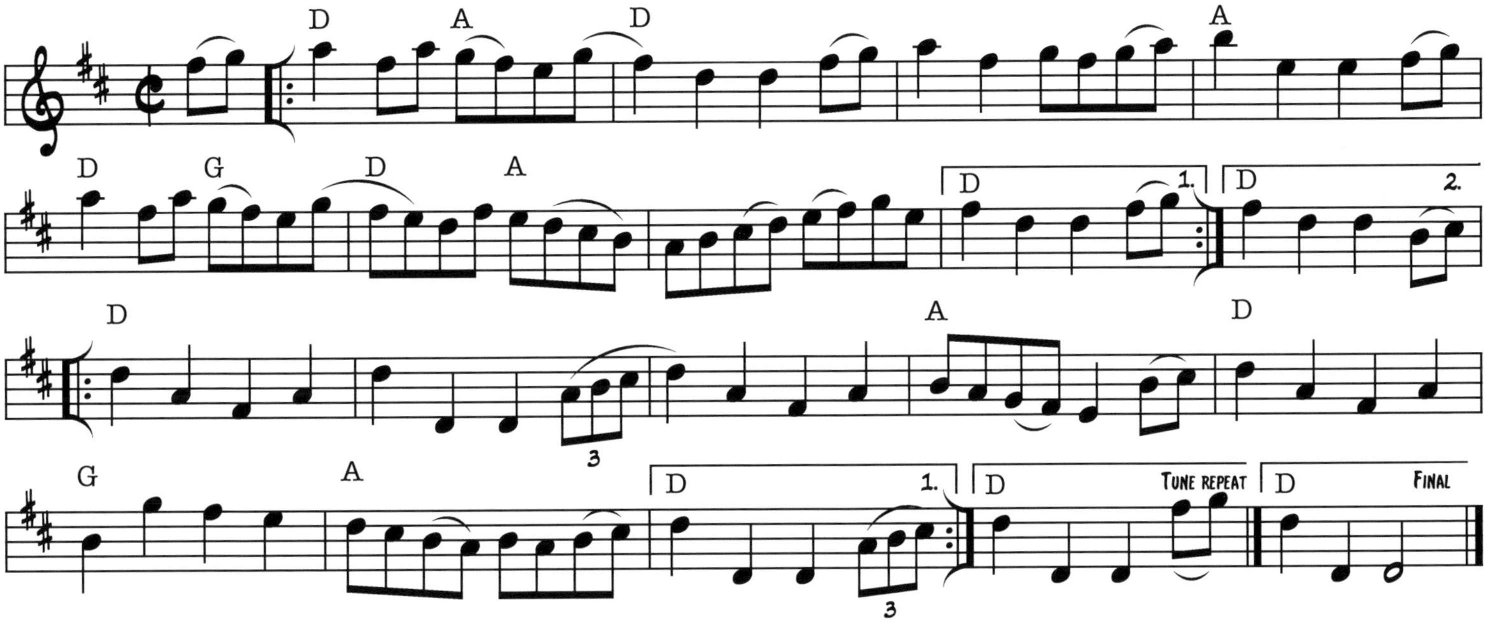

Too Young to Marry (2)

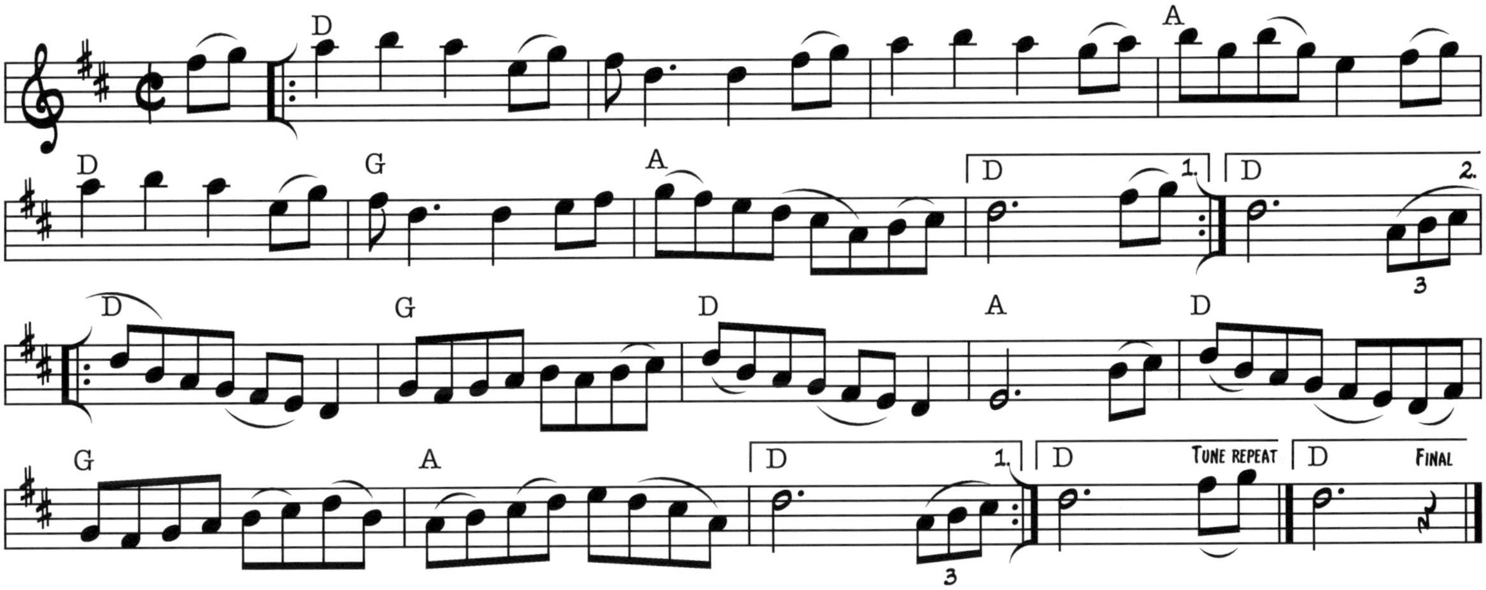

Triangle Blues (misnamed Under the Parasol)

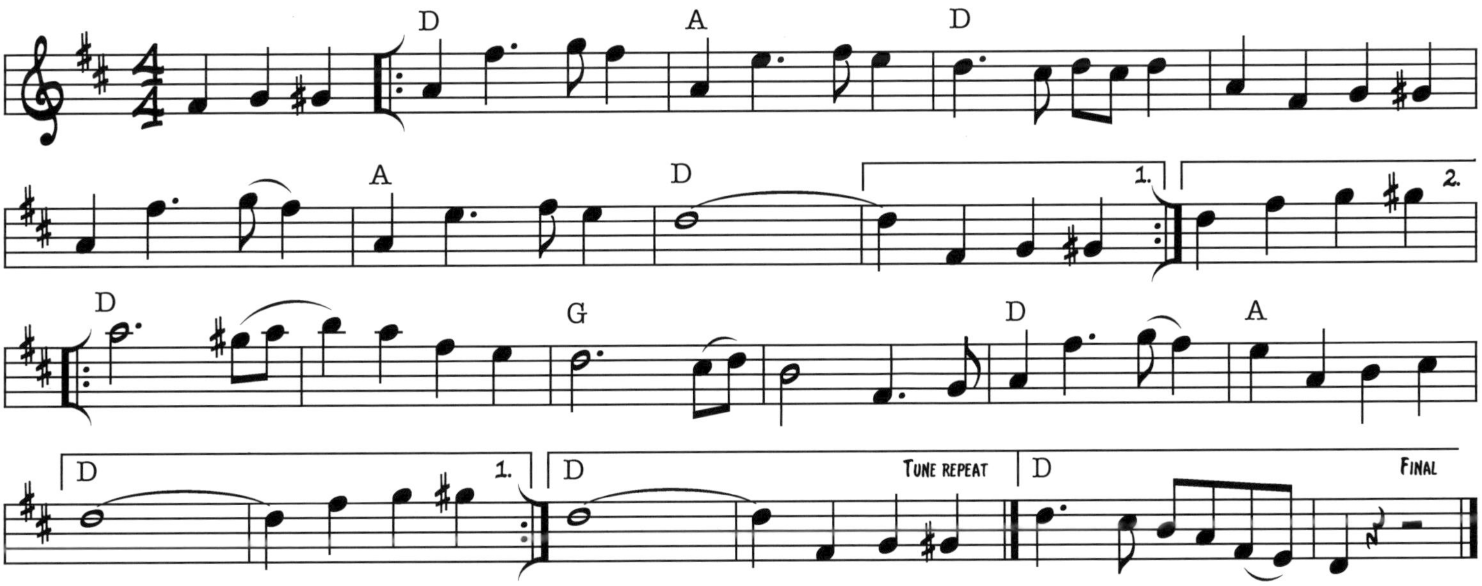

Train on the Island

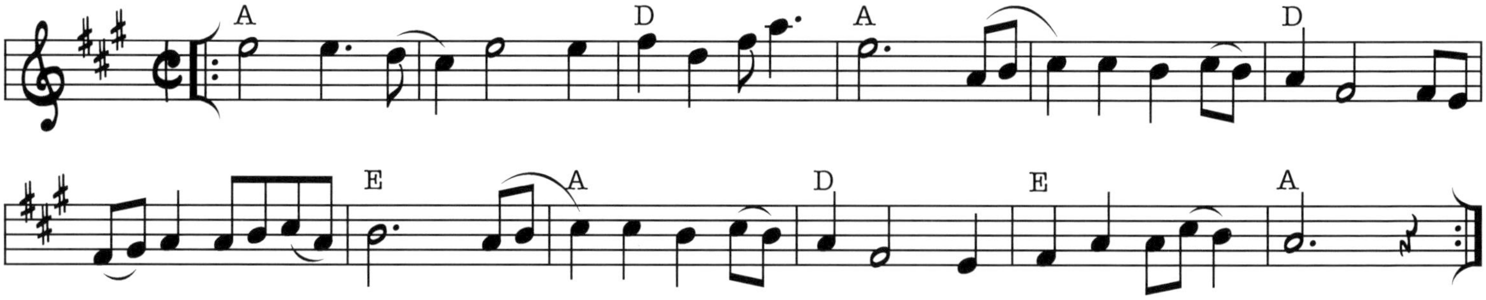

Trot Along My Honey

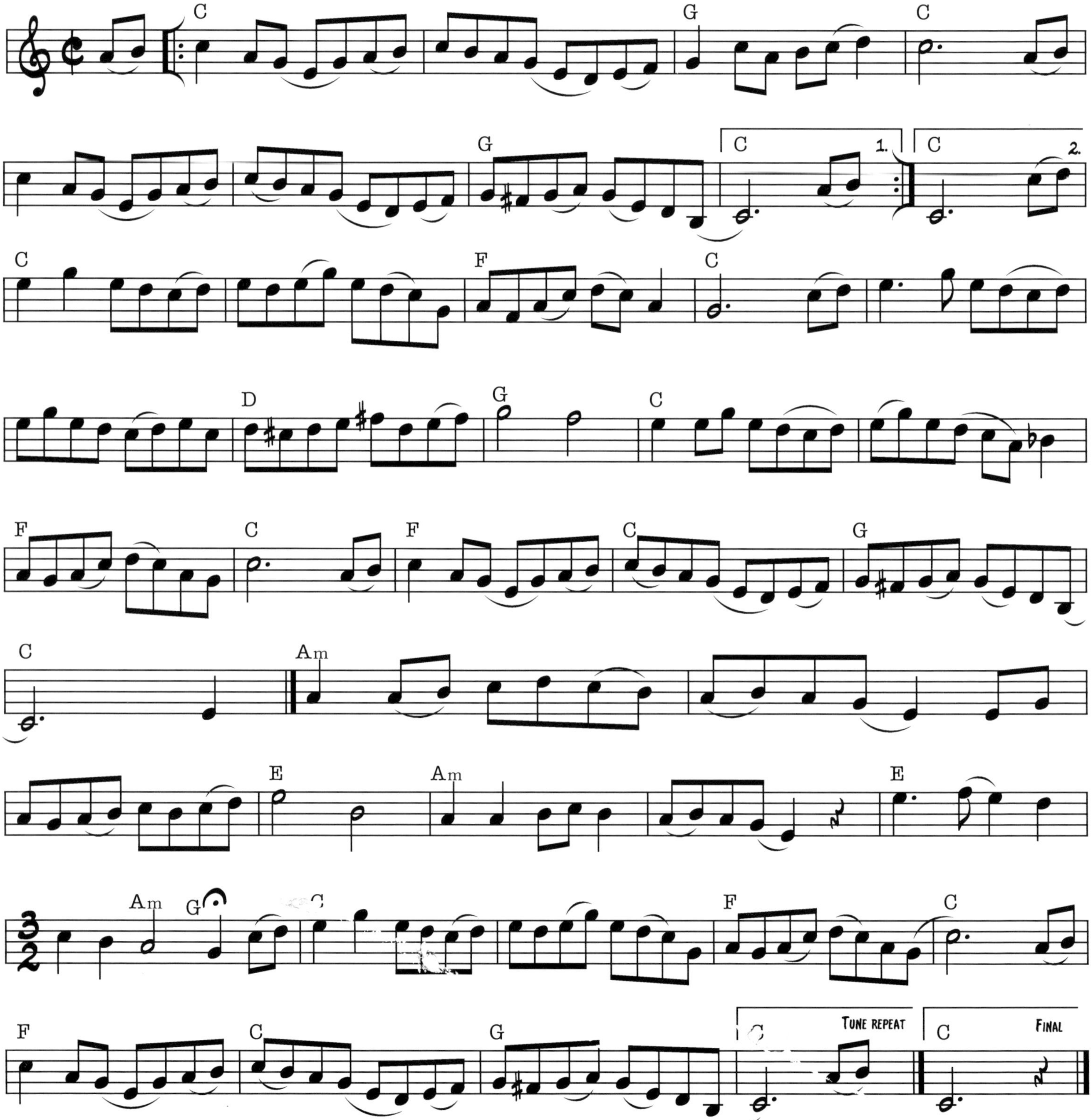

Trouble on My Mind

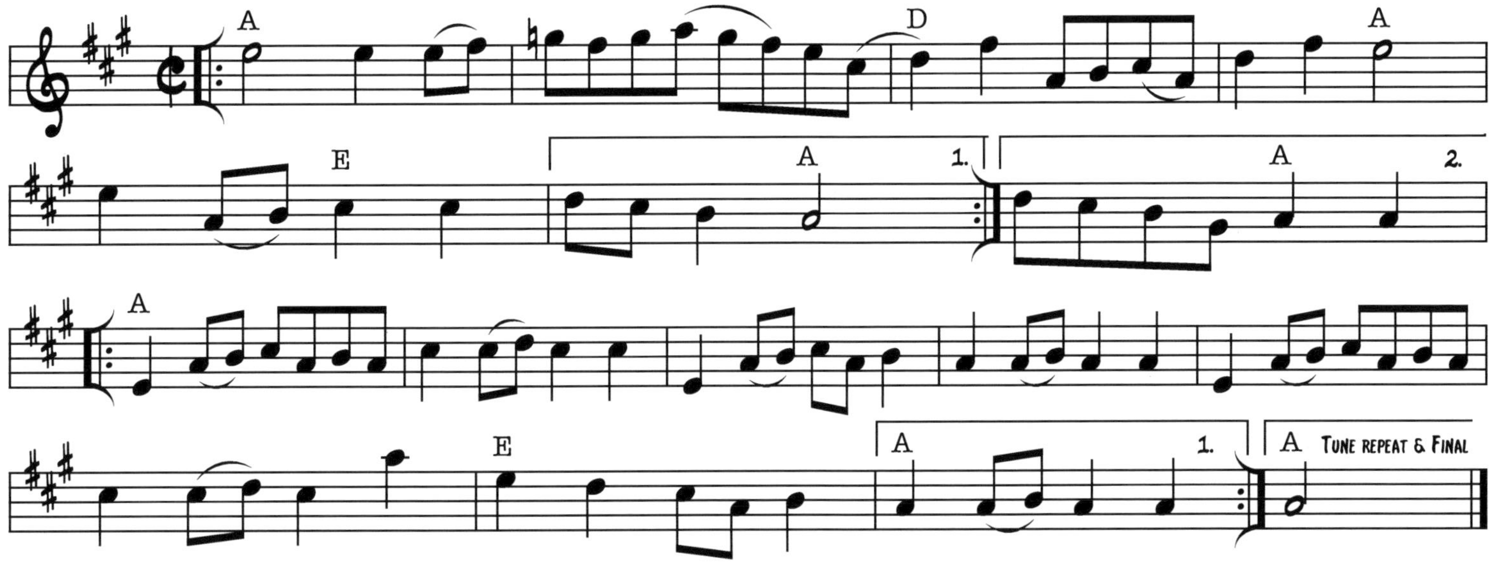

Wake Up Susan (1)

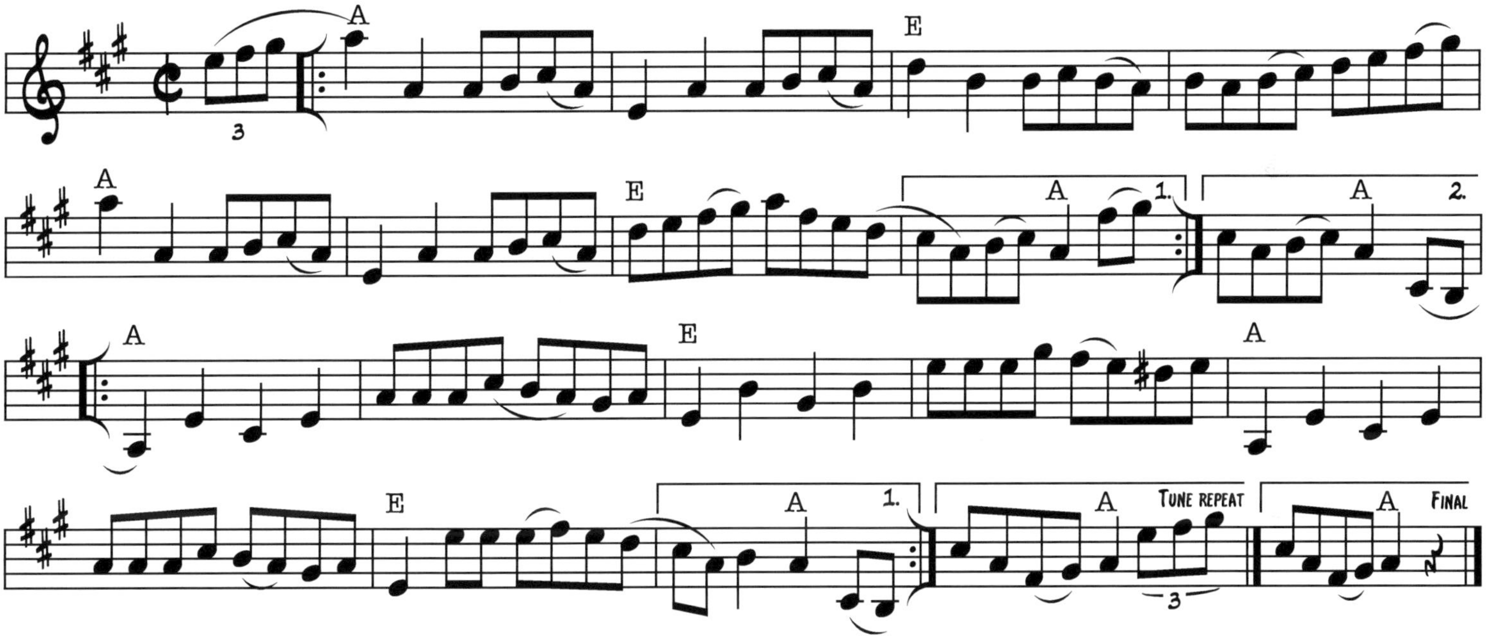

Wake Up Susan (2)

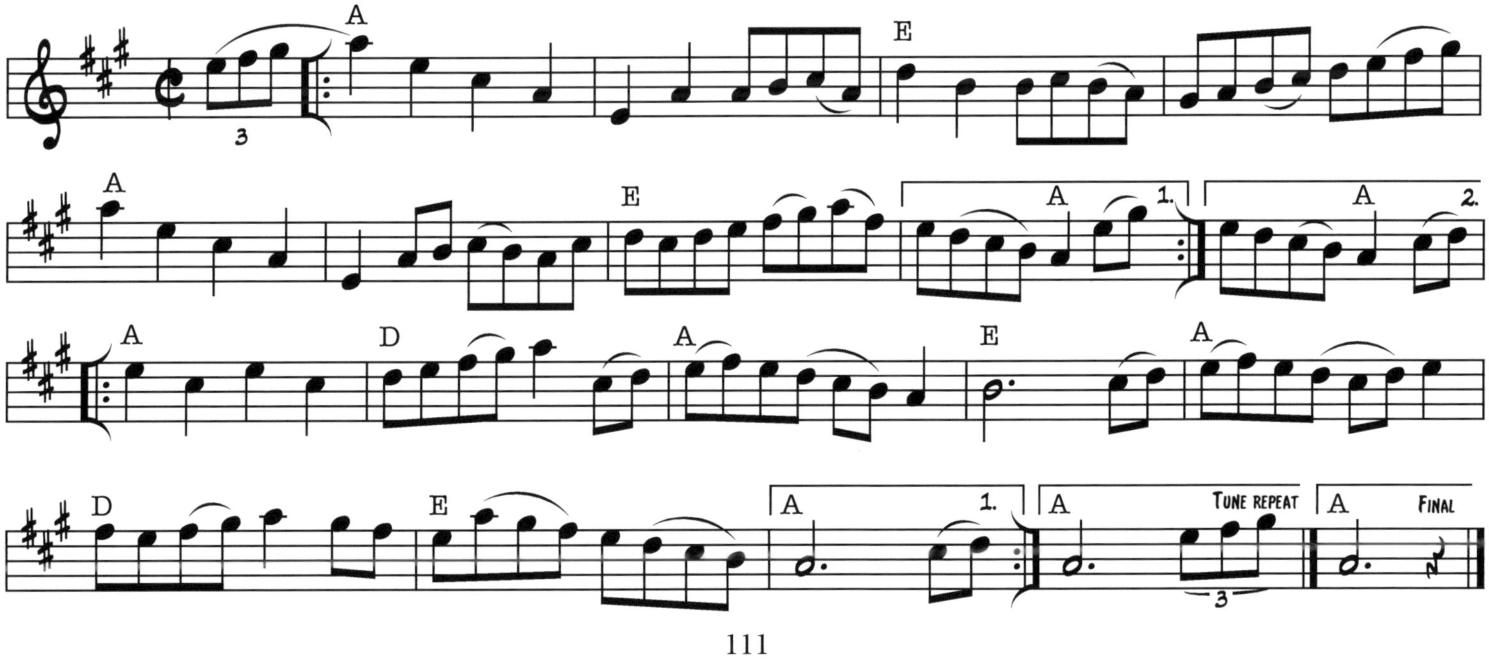

Valley Forge

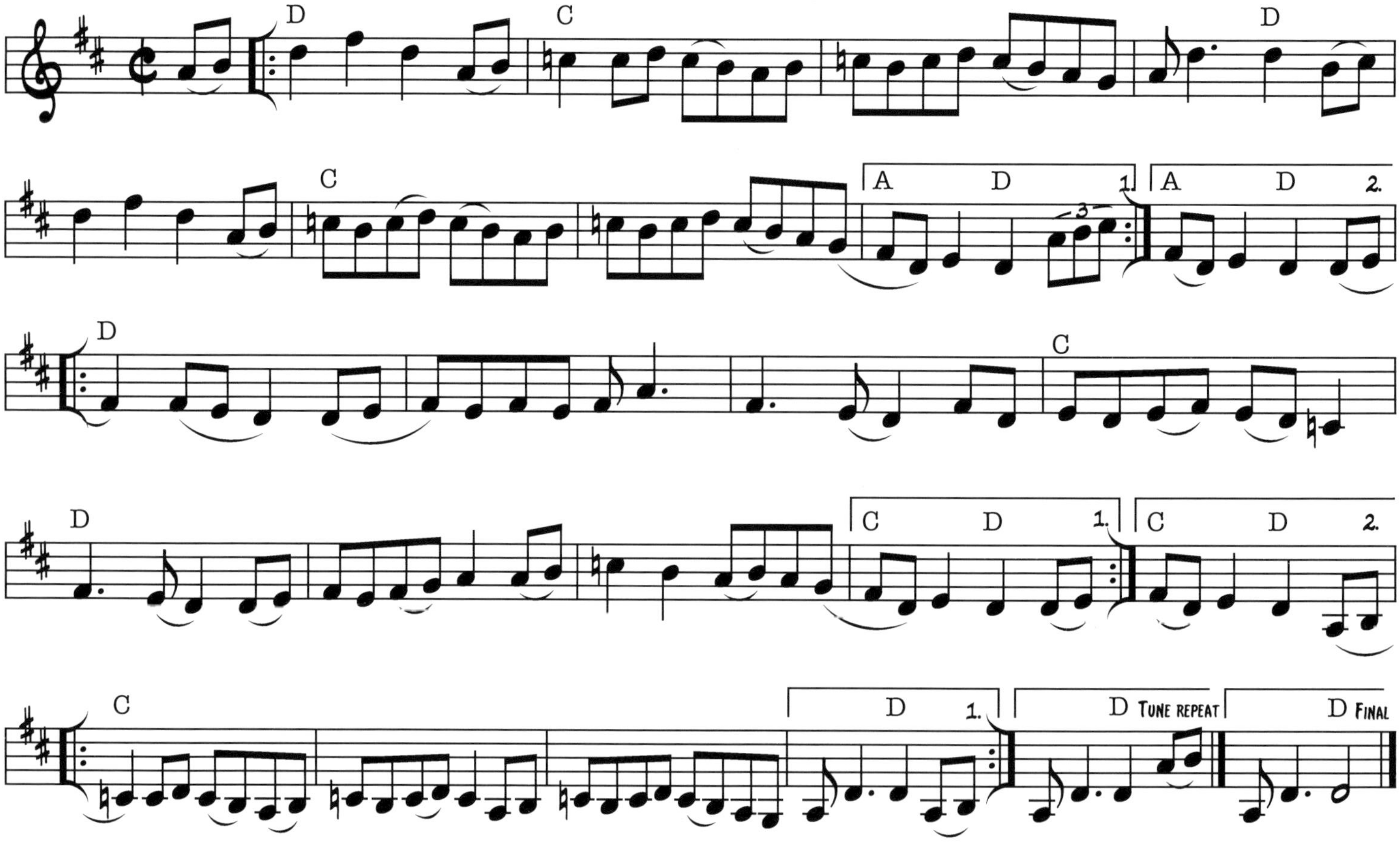

Waiting for the Boatsman

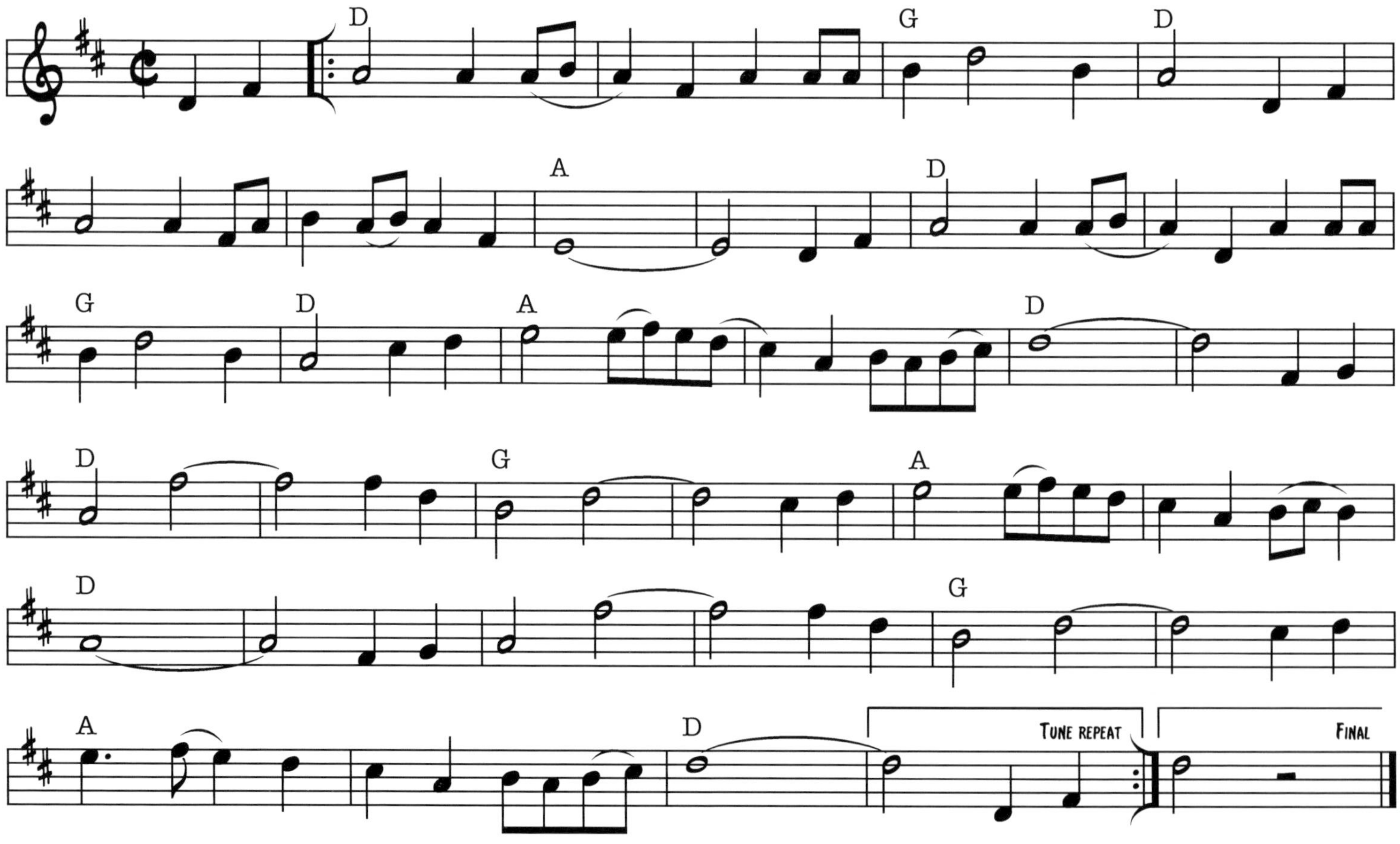

Waldorf Reel

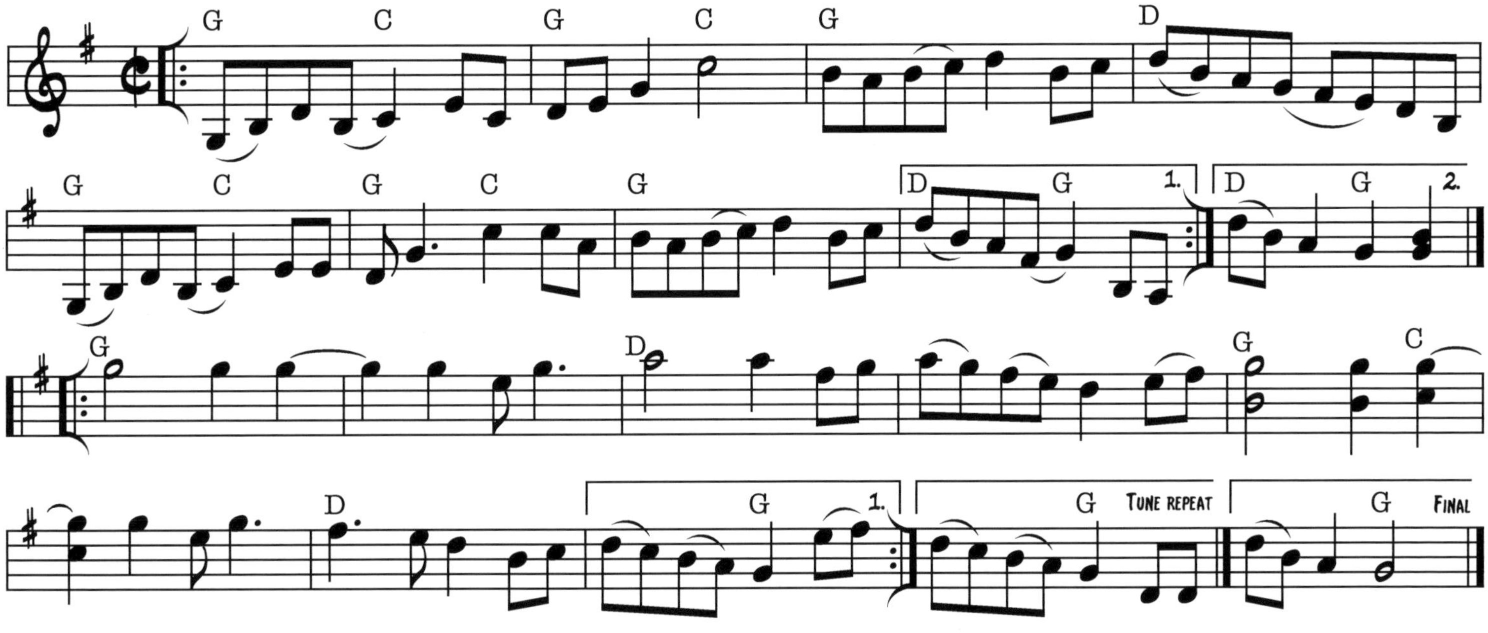

Walk Along John to Kansas

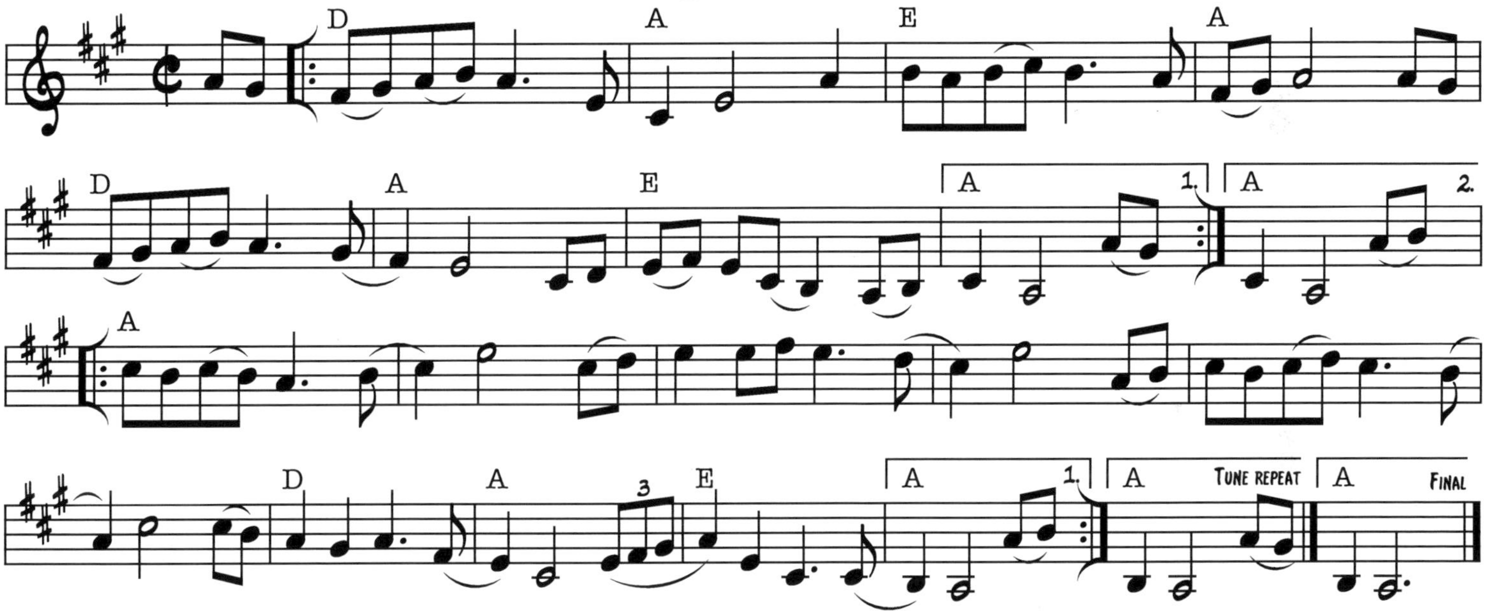

Walk Old Shoe (with a Heel Come a Draggin')

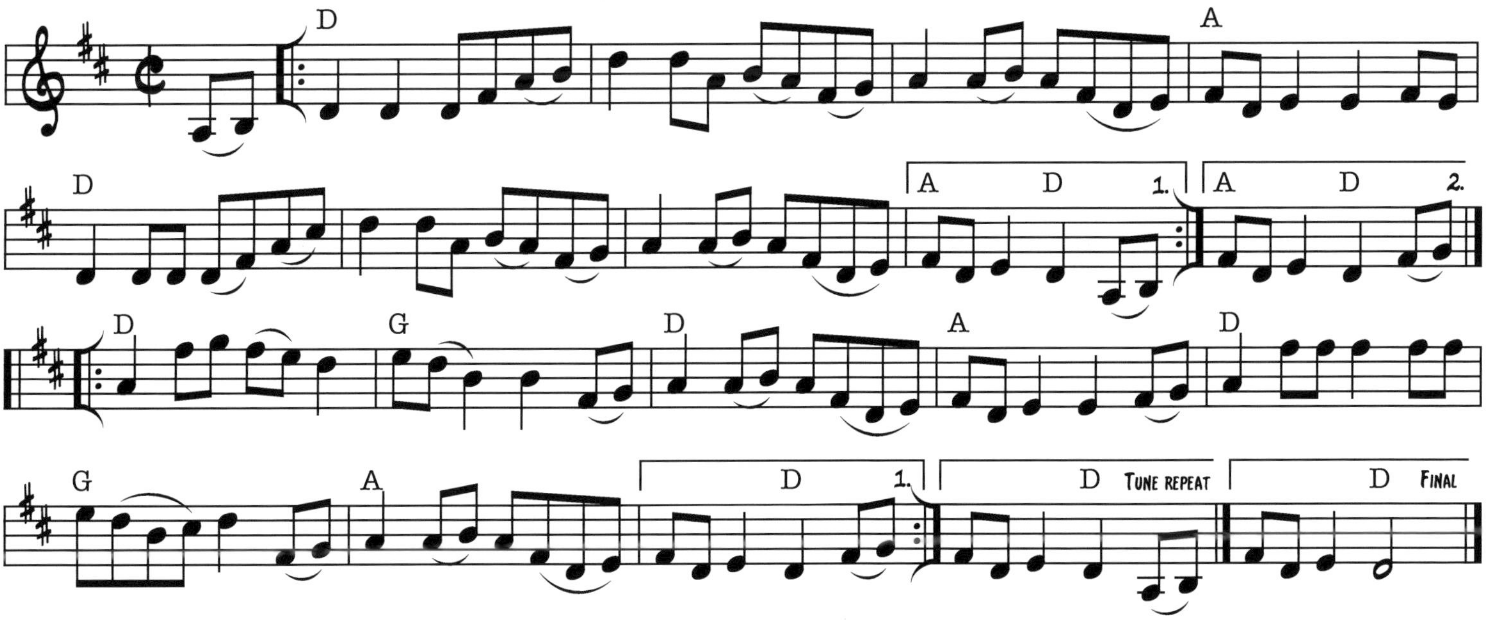

Walking in My Sleep

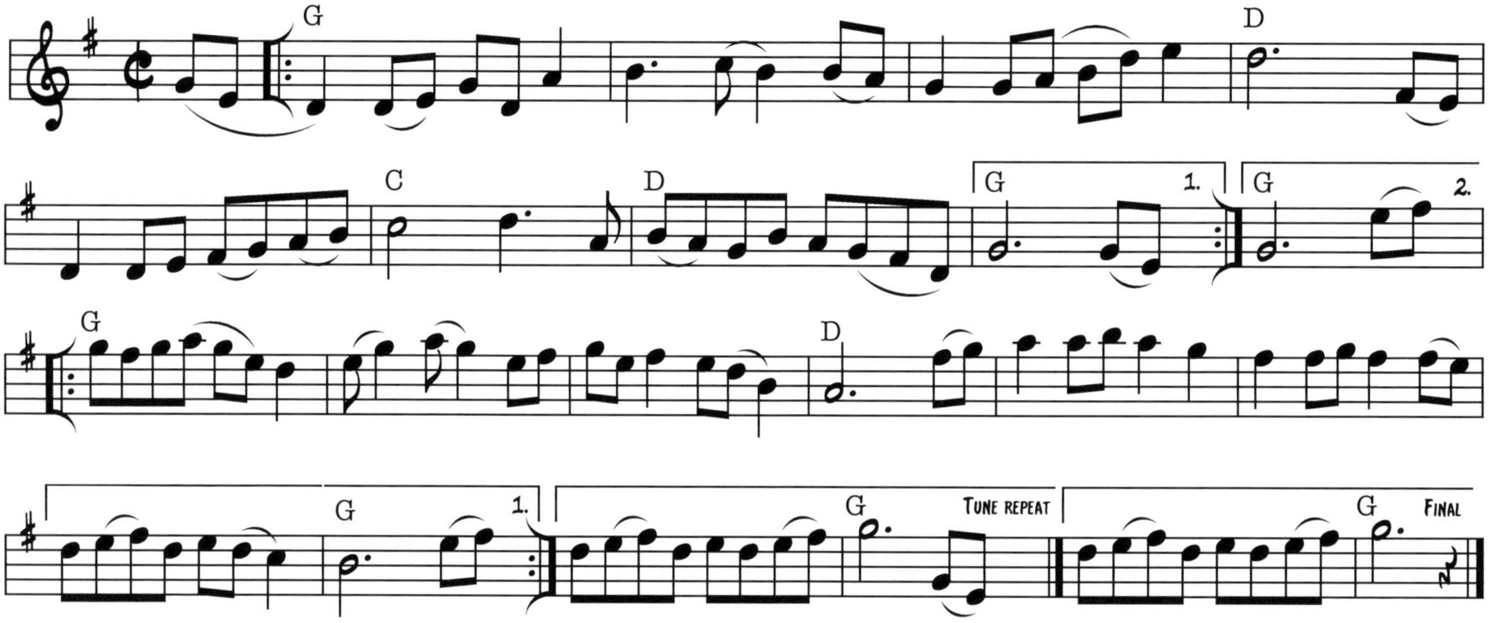

Washington's March

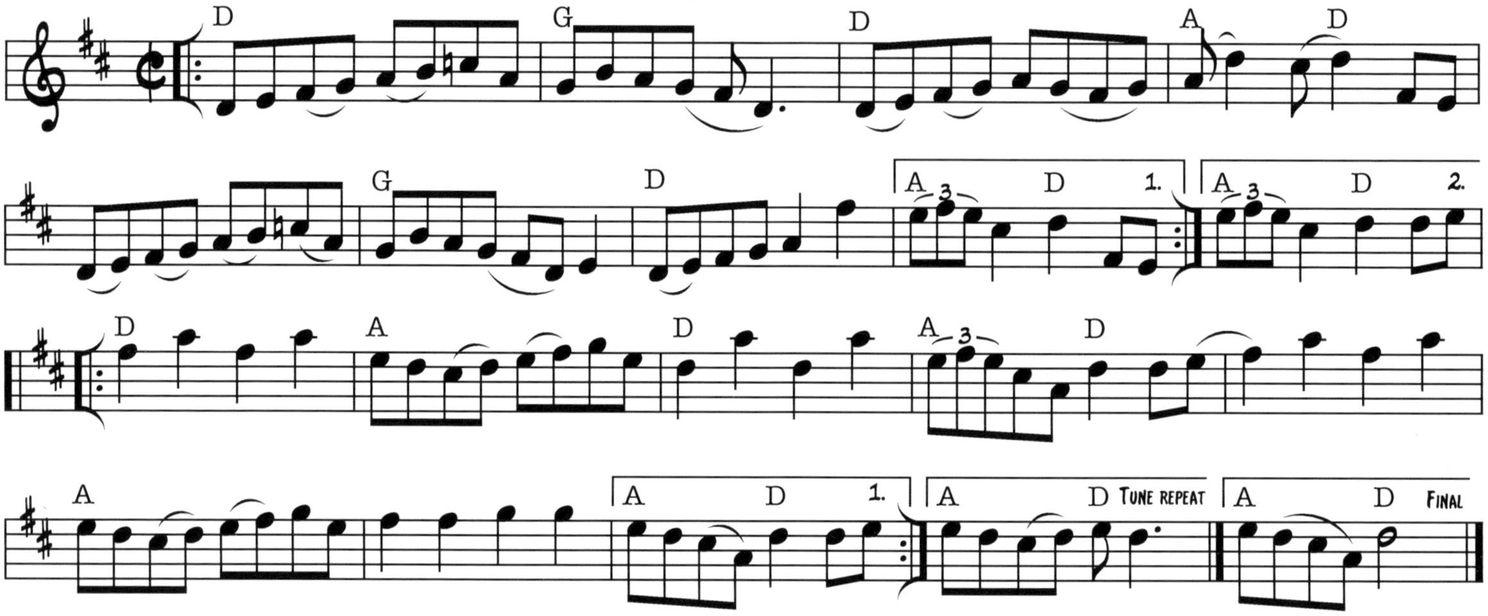

Waterbound

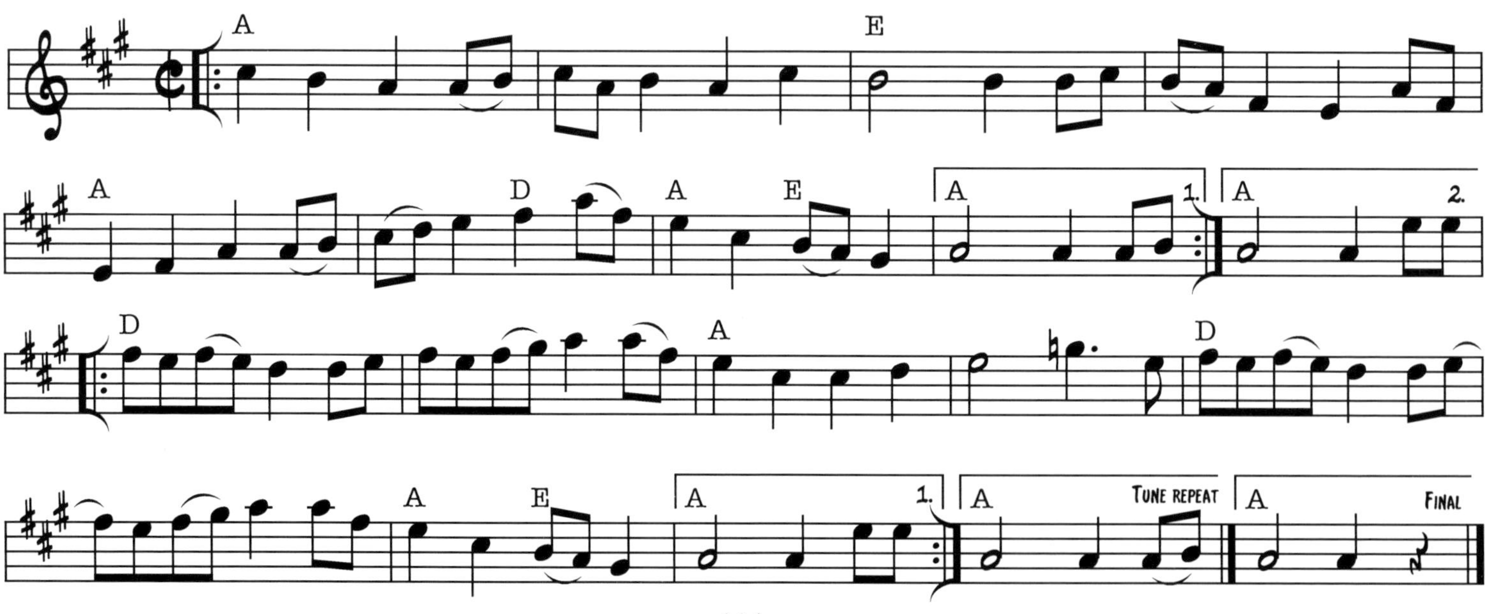

Ways of the World

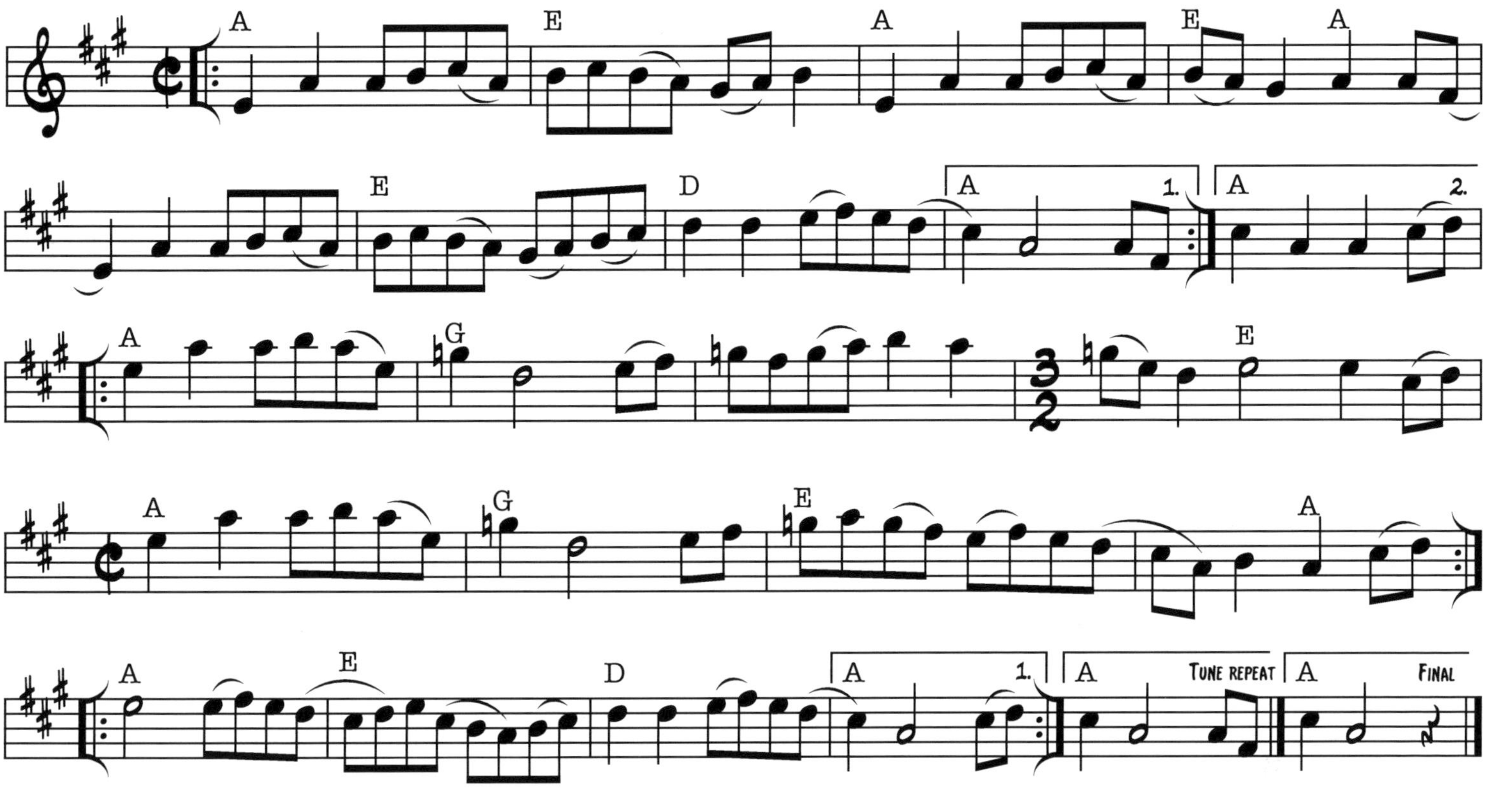

Whistling Rufus (aka Way Down South)

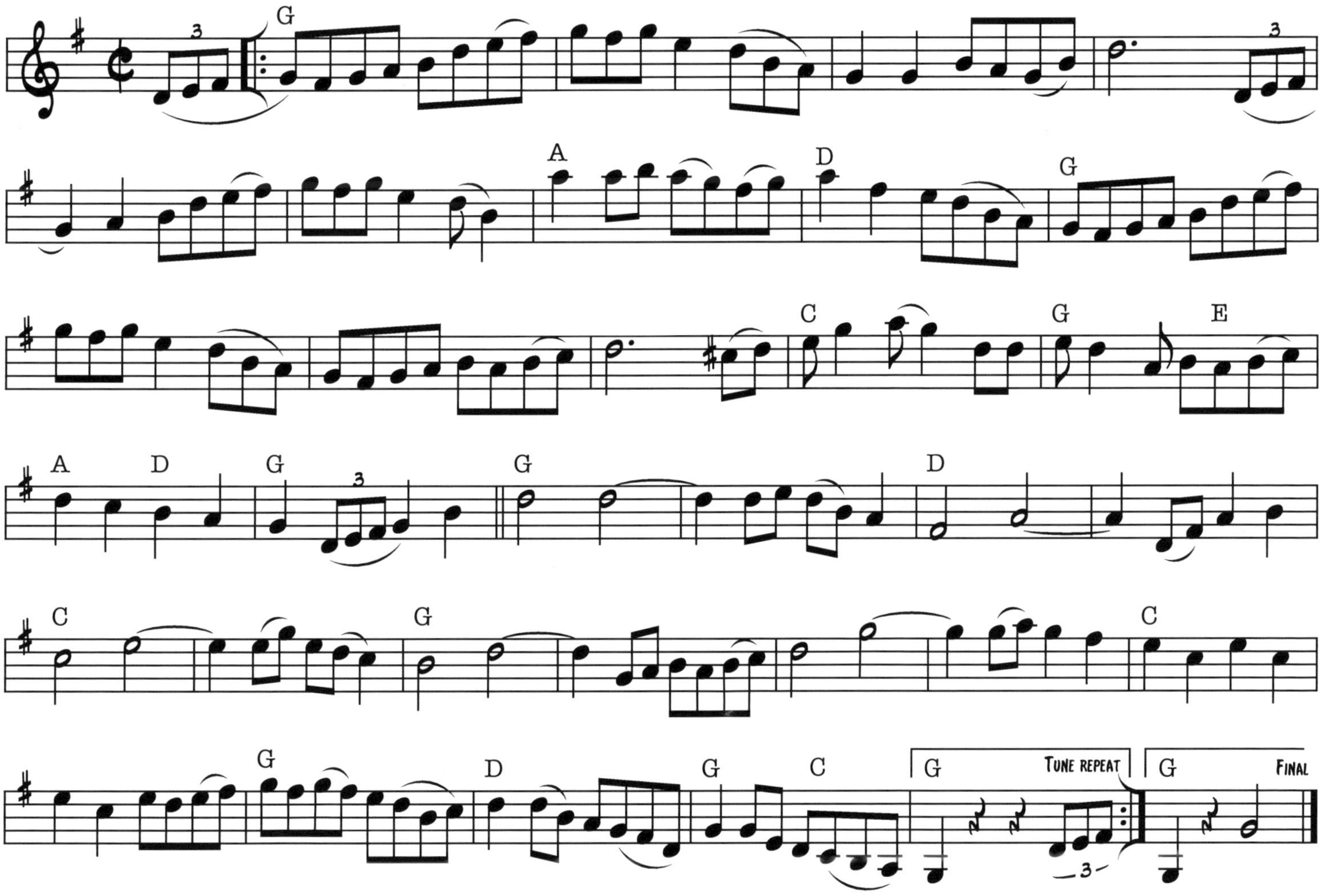

West Fork Gals

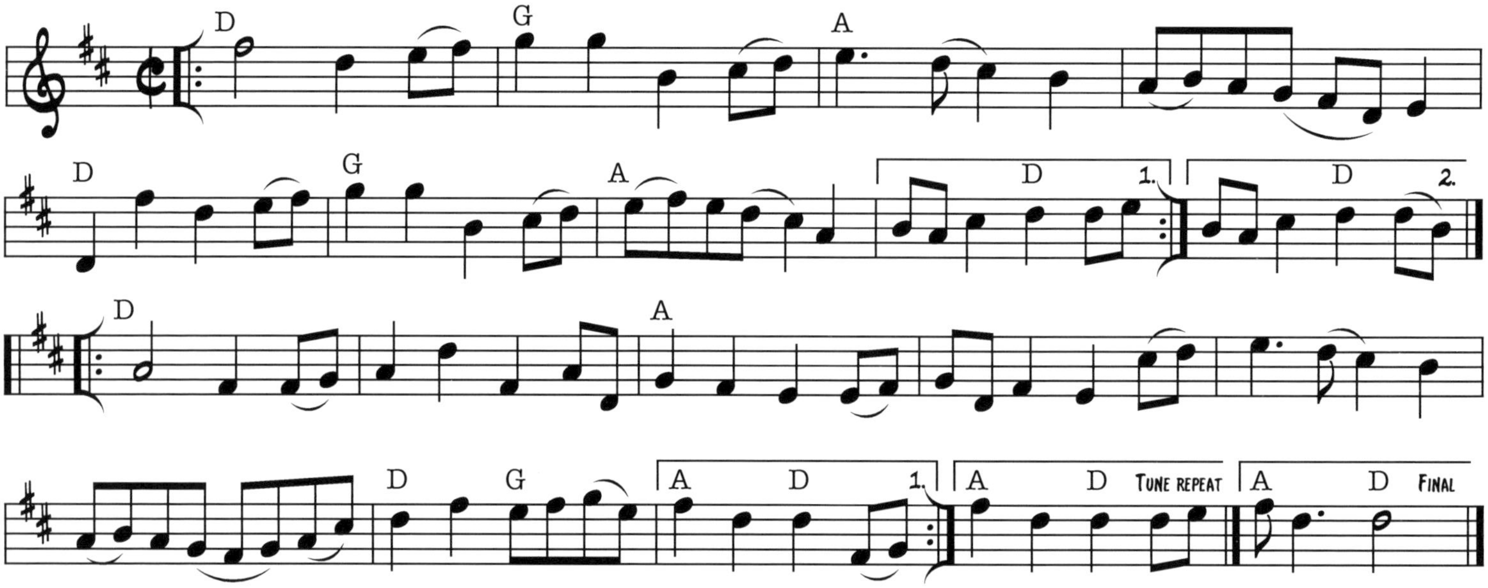

Whiskey Before Breakfast

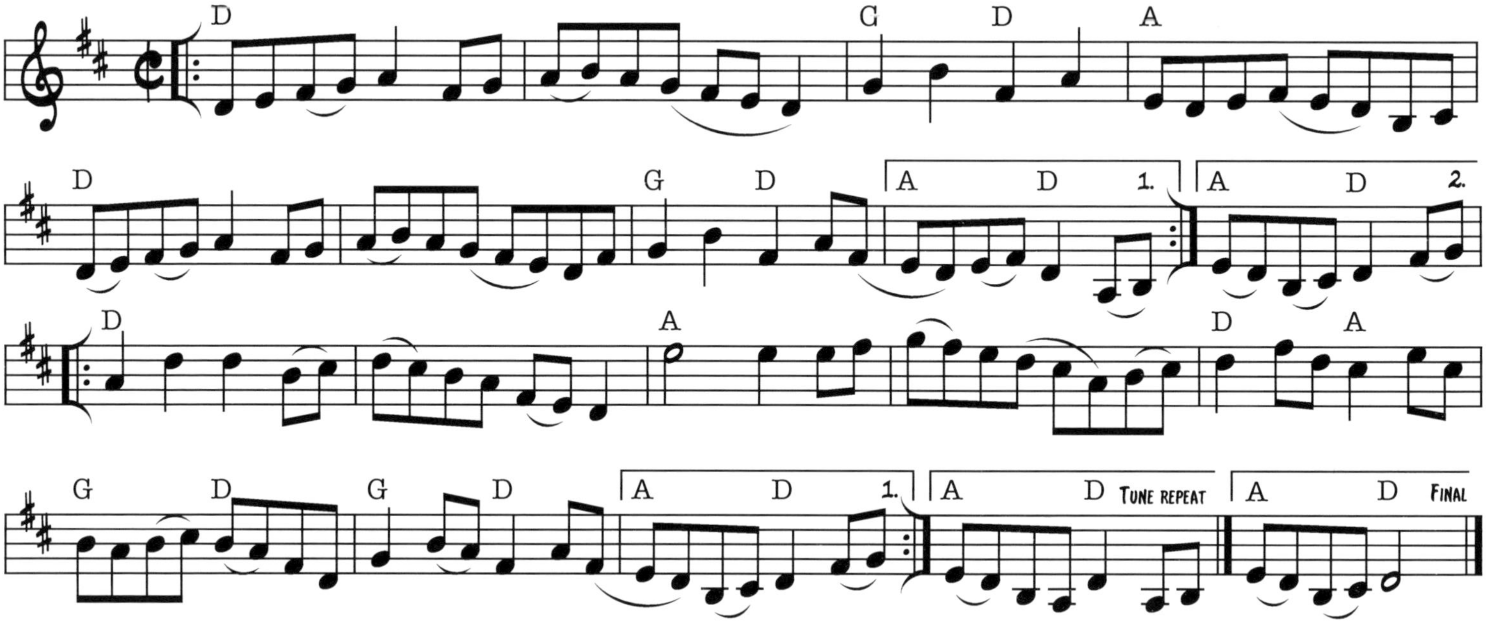

Whitesburg

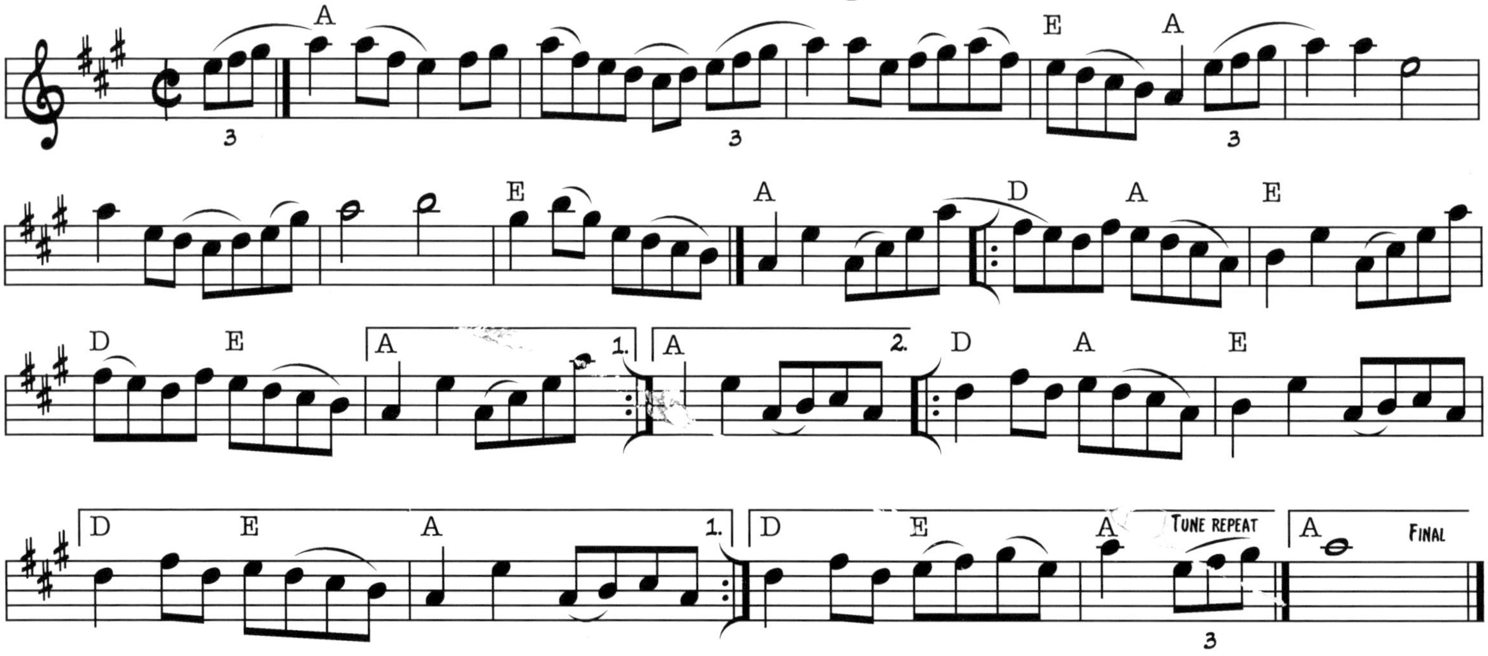

Wild Hog in the Woods

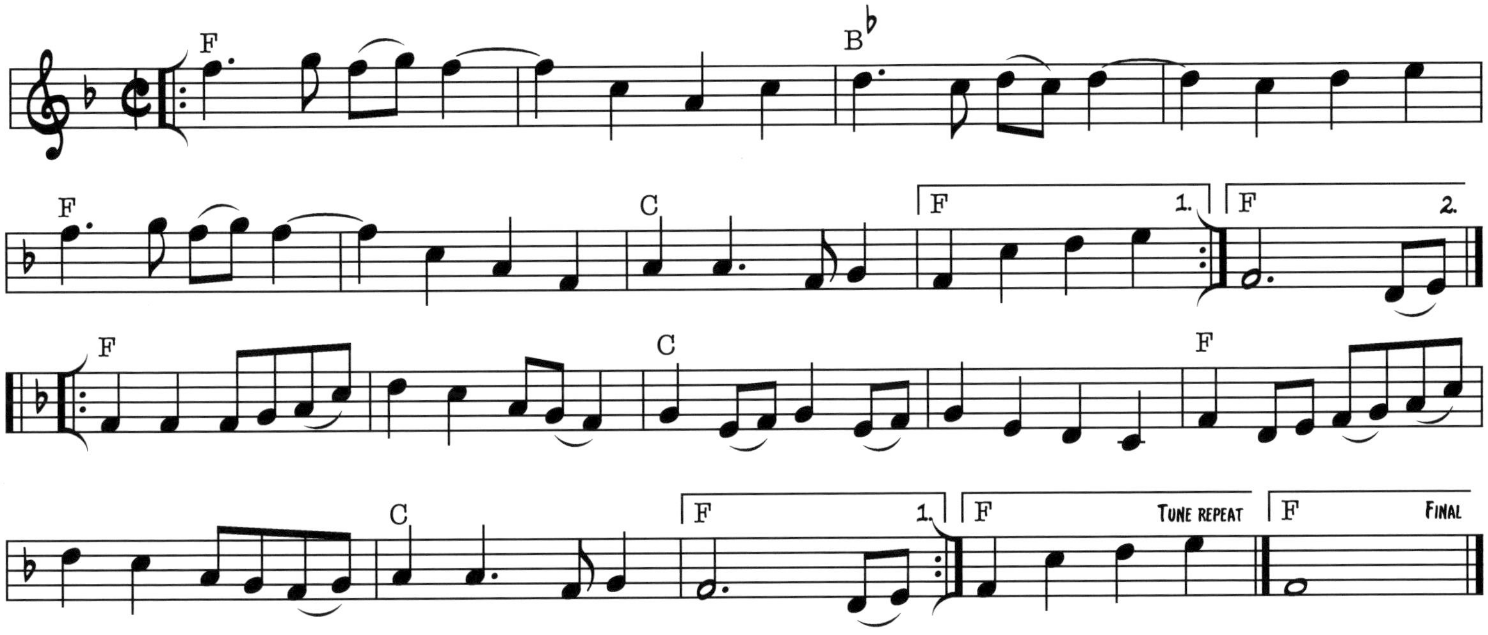

Wild Horses at Stony Point

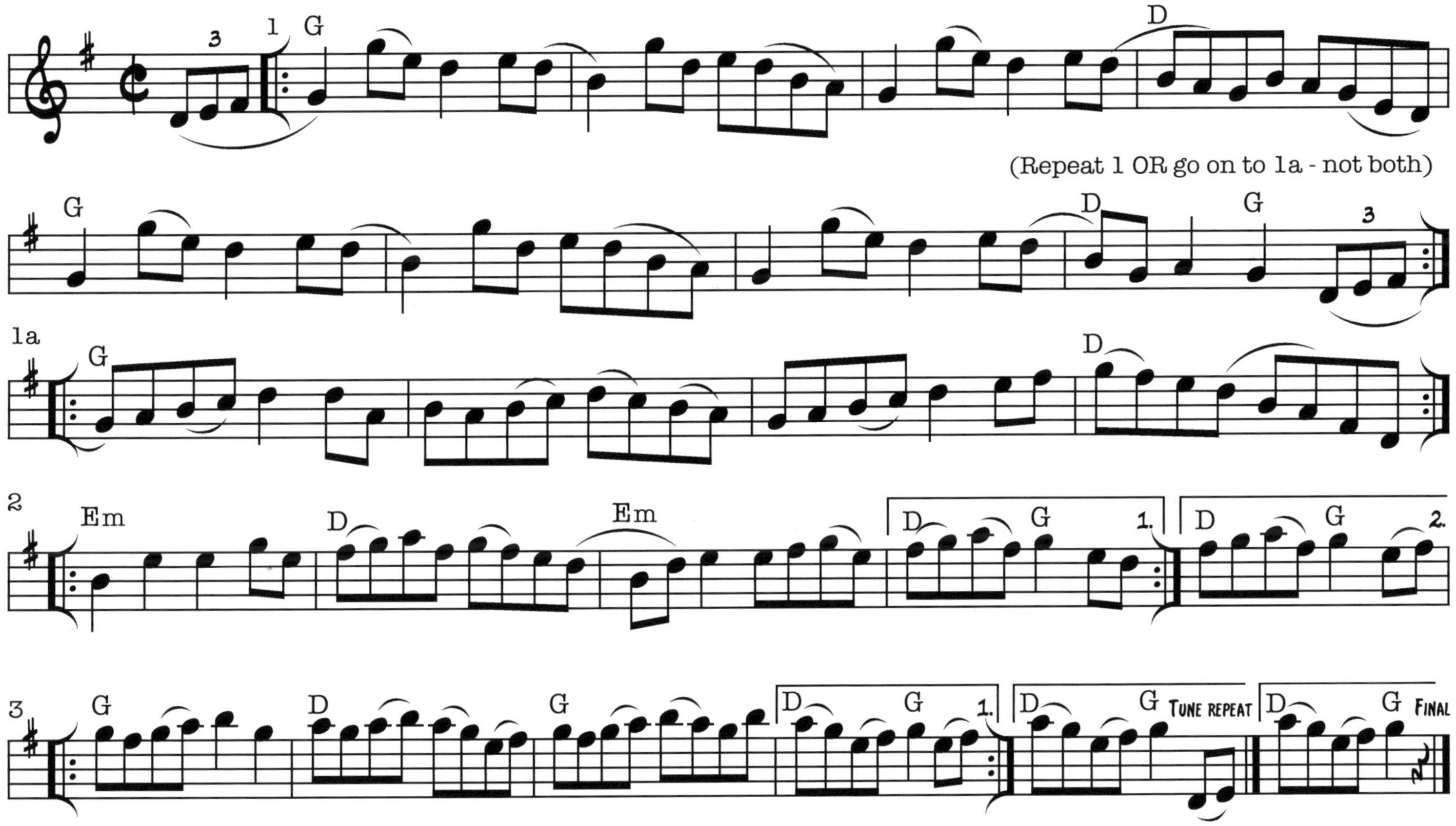

If you repeat part 1, you don't play 1a. The form is either 1, 1a, 2, 3 OR 1, 1, 2, 3. Mix it up if you like!

Woodchopper's Reel

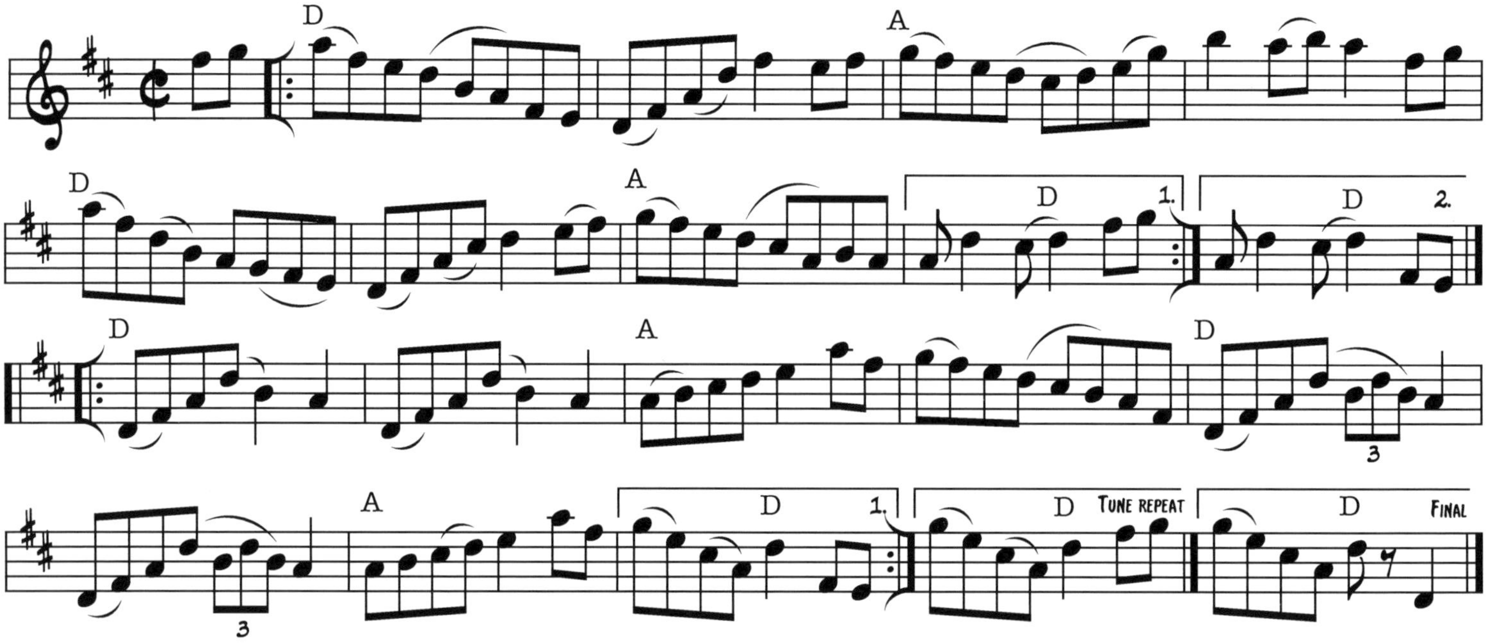

Year of Jubilo (aka Lincoln's Gunboats)

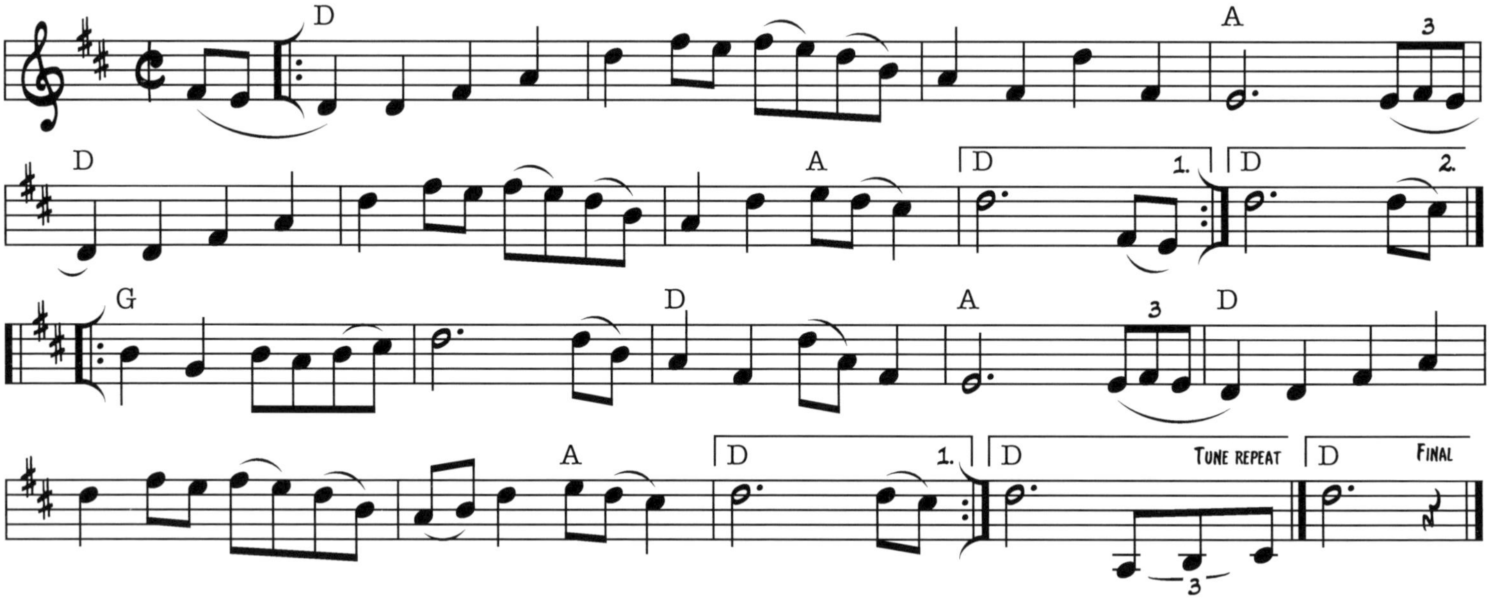

Yellow Barber

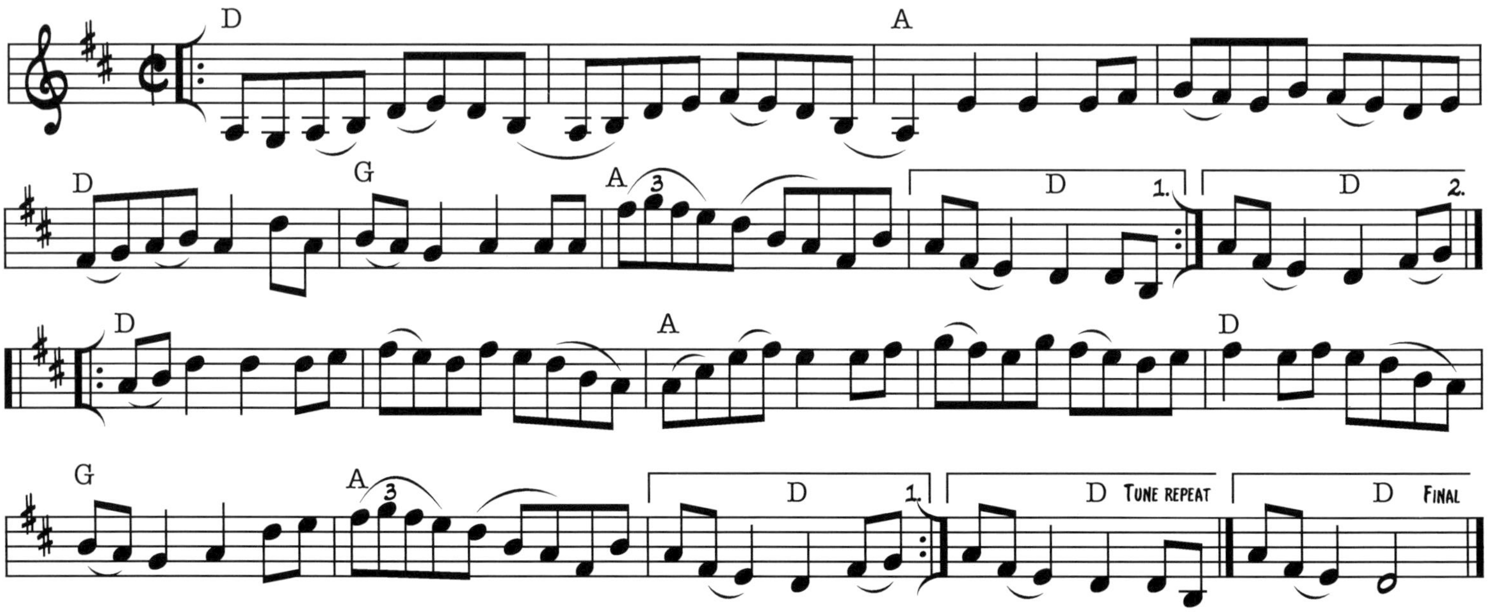

Y.Z. Hamilton's Special Breakdown

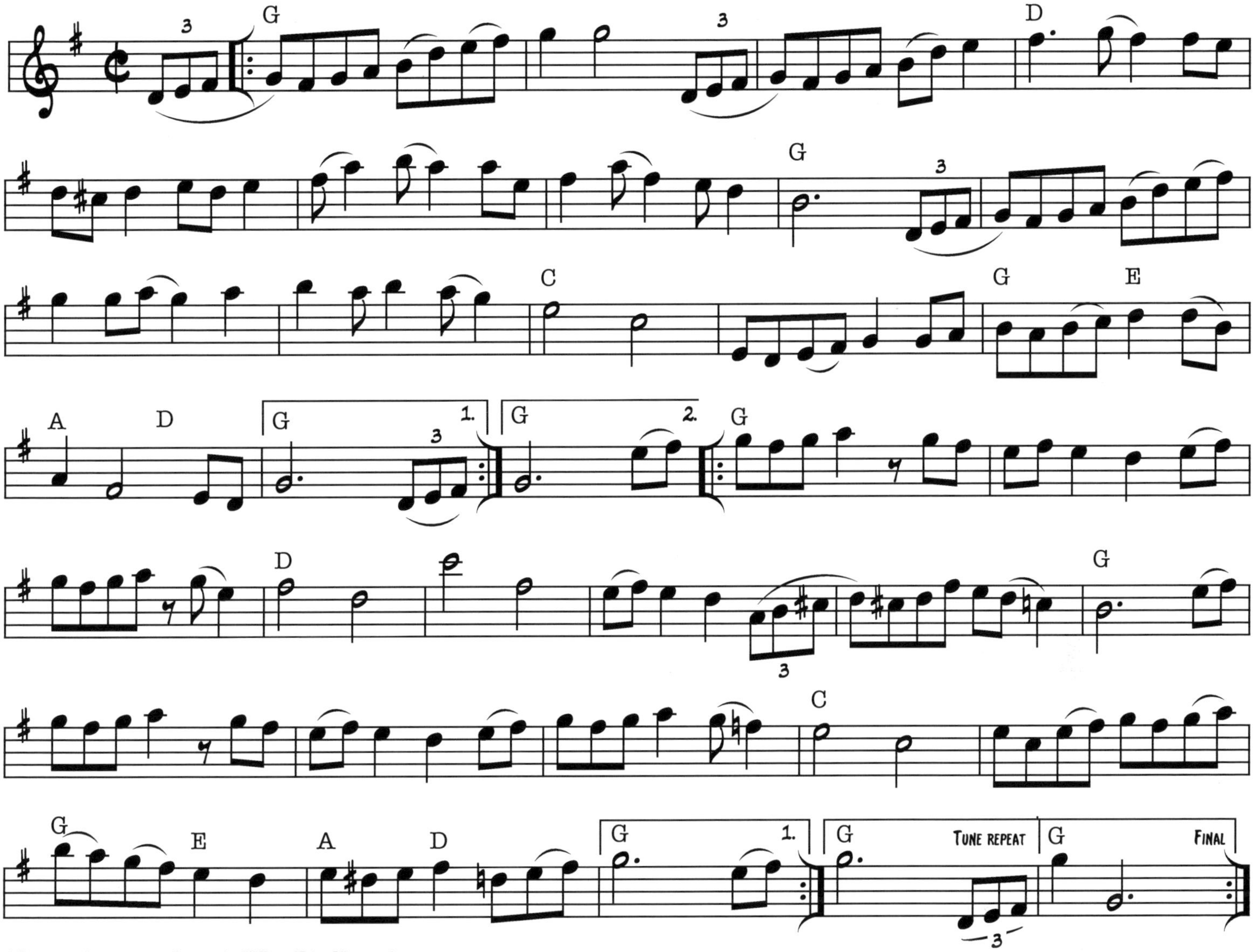

Alternate second part. "The Bird" part.

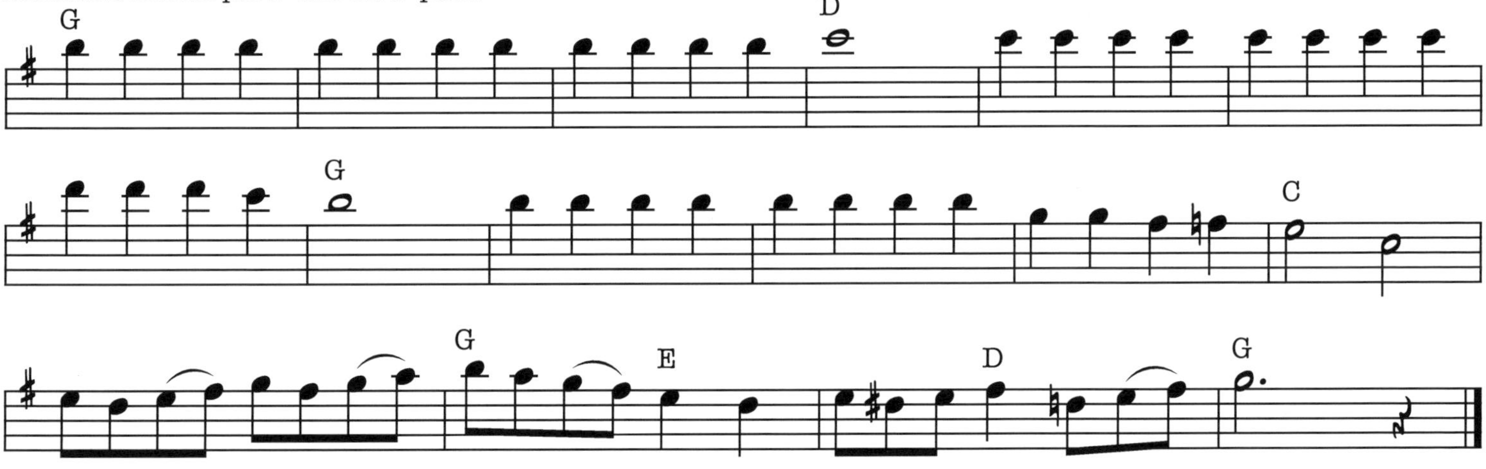

Yellow Gals

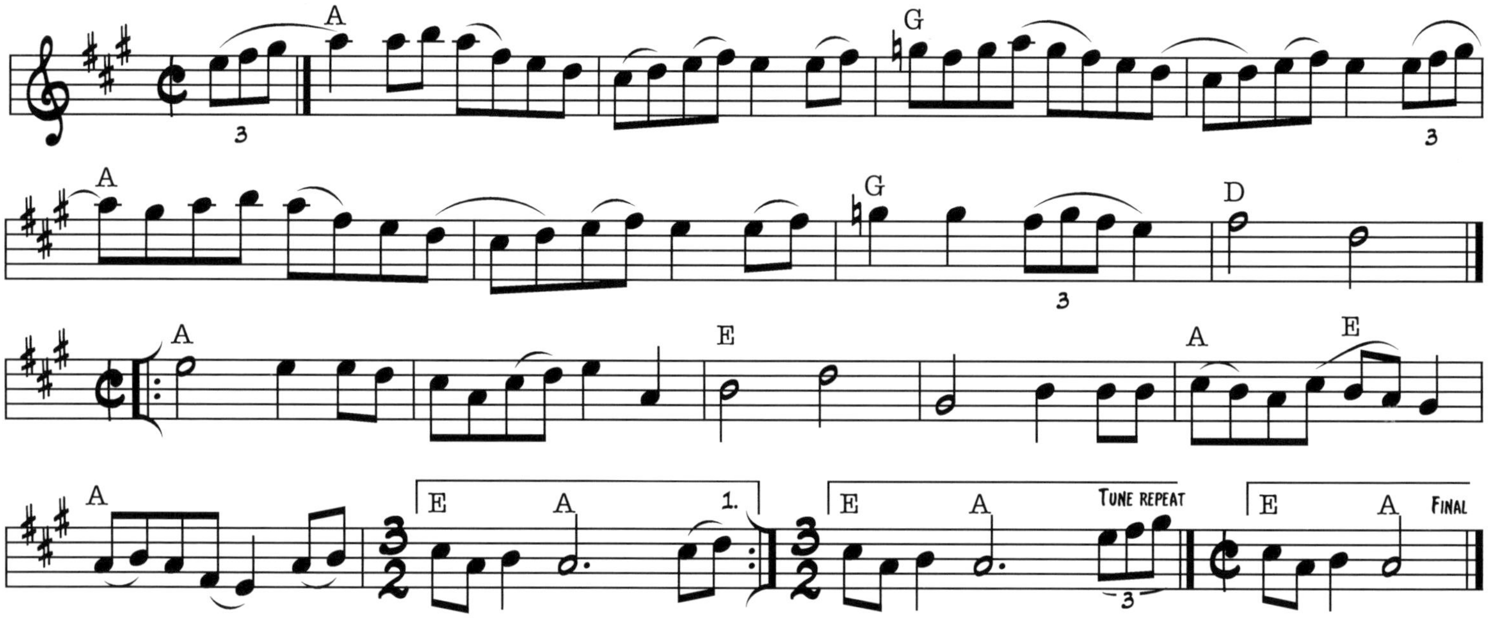

Yellow Rose of Texas

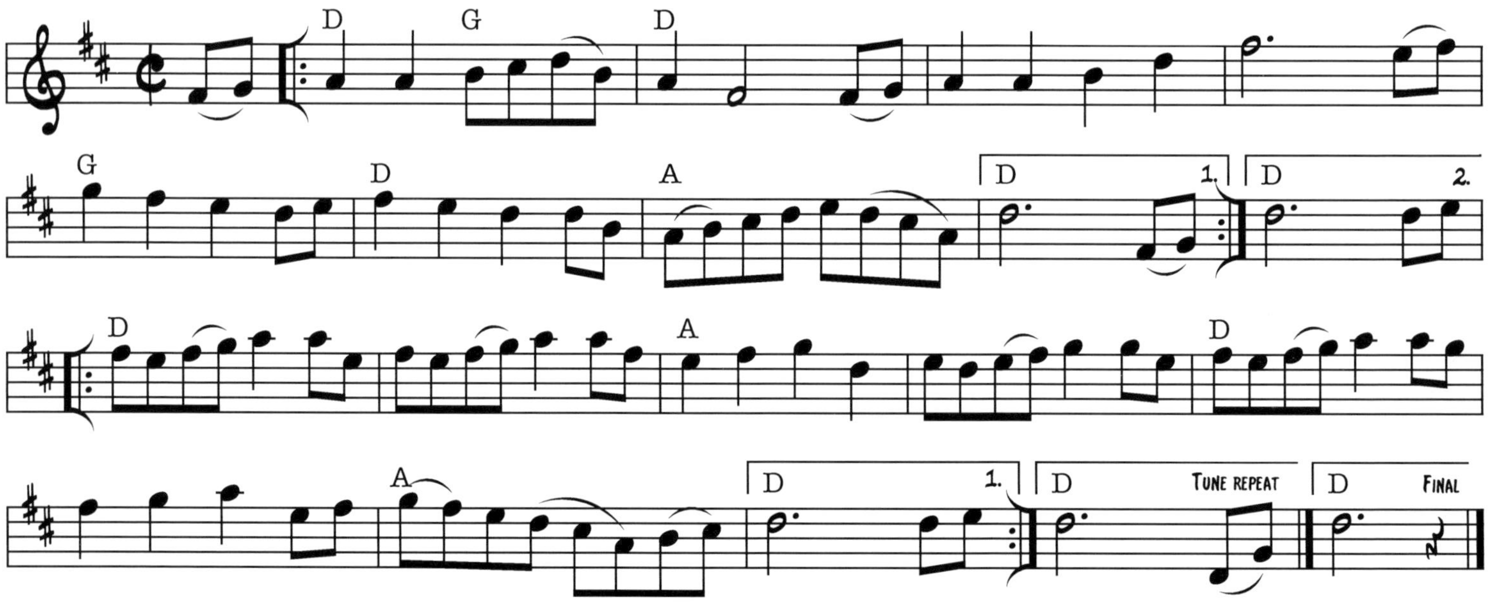

Book Tune List by Key

A tunes
Ain't Gonna Get No Supper Here Tonight - 9
Big Eyed Rabbit - 13
Big John McNeil - 13
Bill Cheatam - 14
Black Eyed Suzianna (aka Susiana) - 14
Black Hills Waltz - 15
Black Jack Grove - 15
Boatman - 16
Bob Tailed Mule - 16
Booth Shot Lincoln - 17
Breaking Up Christmas - 17
Buckin' Dun - 20
Buffalo Gals (in A) - 19
Bull at the Wagon - 20
Camp Chase - 21
Candy Girl - 21
Cherokee Shuffle (in A) - 23
Chinquapin Hunting (in A) - 25
Cluck Old Hen - 26
Cookhouse Joe - 26
Crow Creek - 27
Crow Little Rooster - 26
Cuckoo's Nest 2 in A (aka Richmond) - 28
Dinah - 29
Double File - 30
Drunken Hiccups - 31
Ducks in the Pond - 32
Elzic's Farewell - 36
George Booker - 39
Georgia Railroad - 39
Give the Fiddler a Dram
Glory Medley - 41
Goodbye Girls, I'm Going to Boston - 41
Greasy Coat (Hammons) - 43
Greasy String (Tommy Jarrell) - 44
Great Big Taters in a Sandy Land - 44
Grey Eagle - 45
Grub Springs - 45
Half Past Four - 47
Hangman's Reel - 46
Happy Hollow - 46
Henry Reed's Breakdown - 47
Hey Little Girl Do What You Want - 48
Hunt the Buffalo - 50
Icy Mountain - 50
Jeff Sturgeon - 53
Jenny on the Railroad - 54
Jimmy Shank - 54
John Brown's Dream - 55
John Henry - 55
John Sharp's Reel - 56
John Stenson's #2 - 56
Johnny Cope - 57
Jump in the Well My Pretty Little Miss - 59
Kansas City Reel - 61
Kash Kersey - 59
Little Billy Wilson - 64
Little Dutch Girl - 64
Little Girl with Her Hair Down Behind - 65
Lost Indian (Ed Haley) - 67
Meadow Prancer (Ryck Kaiser) - 68
Mike in the Wilderness - 69
Money Musk - 71
Money Musk (Wooliver's) - 71
Old Belle Cow (2 part) - 75
Old Belle Cow (3 part) - 75
Old Bunch of Keys - 76
Old Horse and Buggy - 76
Old Joe Clark - 76
Old Mother Flannigan - 77
Old Savannah (Beverly Smith) - 78
Policeman - 81
(The) Rattlesnake - 85
Red Bird - 86
Red Haired Boy - 87
Salty River Reel - 95
Sandy Boys - 95
Sugar in the Gourd - 103
Sugarbaby - 104
Tater Patch - 103
Texas - 104
Three Thin Dimes - 107
Three Way Hornpipe - 107
Tom and Jerry - 108
Tomahawk – 108
Train on the Island - 110
Trouble on My Mind - 111
Wake Up Susan (1) - 111
Wake Up Susan (2) - 111
Walk Along John to Kansas - 113
Waterbound - 114
Ways of the World - 115
Whitesburg - 116
Yellow Gals - 120

C tunes
Altamont - 9
Billy in the Low Ground - 14
Black Cat in a Briar Patch (C to G) - 15
Fun's All Over - 38
Get Off Your Money – 40
Goodbye My Little Darling - 42
High Yellow - 48
I Don't Love Nobody - 50
Monkey on a Dogcart - 70

New Money - 73
Oklahoma Rooster (aka Ten Strike) - 75
Old Melinda - 77
Pikes Peak - 80
Rattlesnake Bit the Baby - 85
Rocky Pallet - 90
Saturday Night Breakdown - 96
Texas Gals - 105
That's My Rabbit, My Dog Caught It - 106 Trot
Along My Honey - 110

D tunes
Angelina Baker - 9
Antelope Gap - 10
Arkansas Traveler - 10
Avalon Quickstep - 10
Banjo Tramp - 12
Blackbird Says to the Crow - 16
Bowl-a-rama - 17
Briar Picker Brown - 18
Buck Mountain - 18
Camp Meeting 4th of July - 21
Chase the Squirrel - 22
Cherokee Shuffle (in D) - 23
Chinese Breakdown - 24
Chinquapin Hunting (in D – Stamper) - 25
Coast Is Clear - 25
Crook Brothers Breakdown - 27
Cuckoo's Nest in D - 28
Doctor, Doctor - 29
Dogs in the Dishes - 30
Dry and Dusty - 30
Dubuque - 32
Duck River - 32
Ducks on the Mill Pond - 31
Durang's Hornpipe - 34
Dusty Miller - 34
(Mr.) Fishar's Hornpipe - 33
Five Miles From Town - 36
Fly Around My Pretty Little Miss (in D) - 35
Folding Down the Sheets - 37
Forked Deer - 37
Fortune - 38
Gaston - 38
Gilsaw - 39
Going Up Town - 42
Grand Picnic - 43
Grasshopper Sitting on a Sweet Potato Vine – 43
Grey Cat on a Tennessee Farm - 42
Green Willis (aka The Raw Recruit) - 45
Home With the Girls in the Morning - 49
I'm Going to Get My Mustache Blacked - 51
Indian Ate the Woodchuck - 51
Jackie Wilson - 51
Jaybird - 52
John Lover's Gone - 56
Johnny Don't Get Drunk - 57
Johnson Boys - 57
Jonah in the Windstorm - 58
Juliann Johnson - 58
Jump Jim Crow - 59
Just From the Fountain - 60
Lady of the Lake 1 - 61
Lady of the Lake 2 - 61
Liberty - 62
Little Betty Brown - 63
Little Burnt Potato - 63
Little Sadie - 65
Log Chain - 65
Logan County Blues - 66
Love Somebody - 66
Maggots in the Sheep Hide - 67
Martha Campbell - 68
Merry Blacksmith - 69
Mississippi Sawyer - 70
Mole in the Ground - 70
Moses Hoe the Corn - 72
Muddy Roads - 72
Needlecase (aka Latch Key) - 73
New Five Cents - 73
Nixon's Farewell - 74
Old Molly Hare - 77
Opera Reel (aka The Celebrated Opera Reel) - 79
Over the Waterfall - 80
Pig Ankle Rag - 81
Polly Put the Kettle On - 80
Porter's Reel - 83
Possum in the Well - 82
Quince Dillon's High D - 83
Ragtime Annie - 84
Railroad Through the Rocky Mountains (aka Marmaduke's Hornpipe) - 84
Red Fox Waltz - 86
Richmond Cotillion - 87
Rickett's Hornpipe - 87
Rochester Schottische - 89
Rock That Cradle Lucy - 88
Rock the Cradle Joe (1) - 88
Rock the Cradle Joe (2) - 88
Rocky Mountain Goat - 89
Rocky Mountain Hornpipe - 90
Rocky Road to Jordan - 91
Rolling River - 91
Run Down Boot - 92
Rye Straw (aka Joke on the Puppy) - 92
Saint Anne's Reel - 93
Sally Anne Johnson - 94
Sal's Got Mud Between Her Toes - 94

Sarah Armstrong (collected as Old Reel) - 96
Shepherd's Walk - 97
Shoo Fly - 97
Shuckin' the Brush - 99
Shuffle About - 99
Sleepy Eyed John - 100
Snake River Reel (Peter Lippincott) - 100
Snowbird - 101
Soldier's Joy - 101
Spotted Pony - 101
Star of Bethlehem - 102
Staten Island Hornpipe - 102
Step Around Johnny - 102
Sugar Hill - 103
Texas Quick Step (aka Rachael) - 105
Too Young to Marry (1) - 109
Too Young to Marry (2) - 109
Triangle Blues (misnamed Under the Parasol) - 109
Valley Forge - 112
Waiting for the Boatsman - 112
Walk Old Shoe (With a Heel Come a Draggin') - 113
Washington's March - 114
West Fork Gals - 116
Whiskey Before Breakfast - 116
Woodchopper's Reel - 118
Year of Jubilo (aka Lincoln's Gunboats) - 118
Yellow Barber - 118
Yellow Rose of Texas - 120

E tunes
Sleepy Eyed Joe - 100

A tunes
Wild Hog in the Woods – 117

G tunes
And the Cat Came Back – 11
Barlow Knife (John Salyer) – 11
Barlow Knife (Song) - 11
Been to the East - 12
Big Scioto - 13
Broken Down Gambler - 18
Buffalo Gals (KY version in G) - 19
Buffalo Gals (Common version in G) - 19
Chattanooga - 22
Cincinnati Hornpipe - 22
Climbing the Golden Stairs - 24
Colored Aristocracy - 26
Cuffy - 27
Dance All Night with a Bottle in My Hand - 28
Devil Eat the Groundhog - 29
Duke of Kent's Waltz - 33
Ebenezer - 34
Fly Around (Frank Blevins Tar Heel Rattlers 1929) - 35
Flying Clouds (aka Flying Cloud Cotillion) - 35
Flying Indian - 37
Girl I Left Behind - 41
Greasy String (Melvin Wine) - 44
Hollow Poplar - 48
Hooker's Hornpipe - 49
Hop Light Ladies - 49
Indian Corn - 52
I've Got No Honey Babe Now - 52
Jaybird Died of the Whooping Cough - 53
Jeff City - 53
Jimmy in the Swamp - 54
John Brown's March - 55
Johnson Gals - 58
Katy Hill - 60
Ladies on the Steamboat - 62
Leather Britches - 62
Lonesome Train - 66
Magpie - 68
McMichen's Reel (aka Hog Trough Reel) - 69
Natchez Under the Hill - 72
North Carolina Breakdown - 74
Oh My Little Darling - 74
Old Yellow Dog Come Trotting... - 78
Ora Lee - 78
Orvetta Waltz - 79
Possum on a Rail - 82
Rainy Day - 85
Roaring River - 89
Roscoe - 91
Run Rabbit Run - 92
Saddle Up the Gray - 93
Sandy River Belle - 95
Seneca Square Dance - 96
Shoes and Stockings - 97
Shortening Bread (Doc Roberts') - 98
Shove That Pig's Foot a Little Further Into the Fire - 98
Silly Bill - 99
Temperance Reel - 104
Thread the Needle - 106
Three Forks Of Reedy - 106
Tombigbee Waltz - 108
Waldorf Reel - 113
Walking in My Sleep - 114
Whistling Rufus (aka Way Down South) - 115
Wild Horses at Stony Point - 117
Y.Z. Hamilton's Special Breakdown - 119

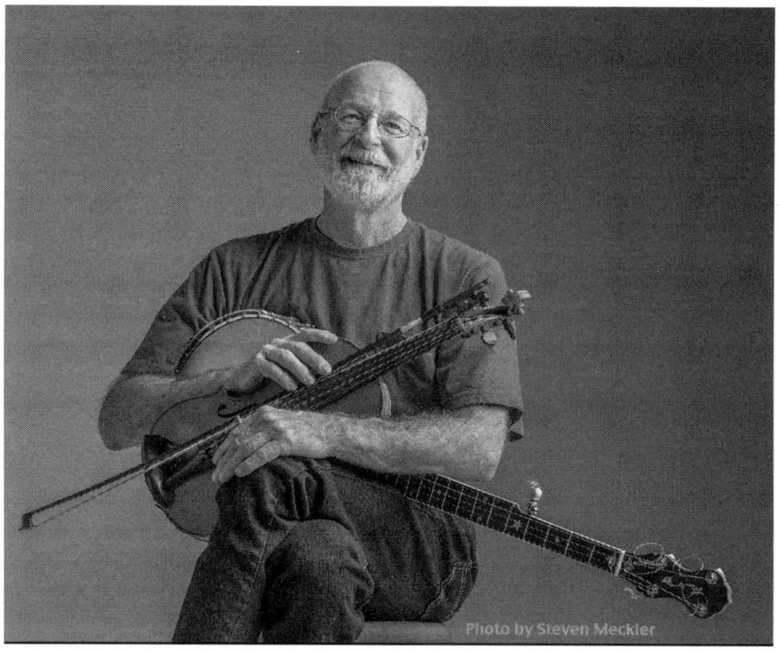

Dan Levenson is an Appalachian native who grew up with the music of that region. Today, he is considered a respected master teacher and performer of both the clawhammer banjo and Appalachian-style fiddle. *The Banjo Newsletter's* R.D. Lunceford describes Dan as "an interpreter, rather than a music re-creator". Fiddler Magazine's Bob Buckingham described him as "an accomplished fiddler and ...one of the best clawhammer banjo players in the country," and Ken Perlman has called him "The Johnny Appleseed of the Banjo".

Dan performs and teaches regularly throughout the world including in England, Ireland, Israel and Brazil. He has taught at many music schools and camps including the John C. Campbell Folk School, Blue Ridge Old-Time Music Week at Mars Hill University, the Maryland Banjo Academy, The Ozark Folk Center at Mountain View, Arkansas, Banjo Camp North, The Rolland Fiddle Camp, and his own Clawcamp and Old-Time Music instructional weekends held at various locations throughout the country.

Dan has won awards on both clawhammer banjo and old-time fiddle, including two Master Artist Awards from Arizona's Southwest Folklife Alliance (2017 and 2021), first place at the 2005 Ohio State Clawhammer Banjo Championship, and Grand Champion at the 2010 Ajo, Arizonia Old-Time Fiddler's Contest.

Dan has eight recordings of his own and is one of the most prolific authors of instructional and tune books for clawhammer banjo and fiddle. He is the author of many Mel Bay publications, including: *Clawhammer Banjo from Scratch; Old Time Fiddle from Scratch* and *the Clawhammer Banjo Masters* series with co-author Bob Carlin (Kyle Creed, Wade Ward and Fred Cockerham & Tommy Jarrell volumes available). He was also a writer and editor for *The Banjo Newsletter's* "Old-Time Way".

For more information about Dan, his books and recordings please visit:
www.Clawdan.com